DEMOCRATIC EQUALITY

Democratic Equality

James Lindley Wilson

PRINCETON UNIVERSITY PRESS
PRINCETON & OXFORD

Copyright © 2019 by Princeton University Press

Published by Princeton University Press
41 William Street, Princeton, New Jersey 08540
6 Oxford Street, Woodstock, Oxfordshire OX20 1TR

press.princeton.edu

All Rights Reserved

Library of Congress Control Number: 2019937951
ISBN 978-0-691-19091-4
ISBN (e-book) 978-0-691-19414-1

British Library Cataloging-in-Publication Data is available

Editorial: Rob Tempio and Matt Rohal
Production Editorial: Jenny Wolkowicki
Jacket design: Pamela L. Schnitter
Production: Merli Guerra
Publicity: Alyssa Sanford and Julia Hall
Copyeditor: Maia Vaswani

This book has been composed in Miller

Printed on acid-free paper. ∞

Printed in the United States of America

10 9 8 7 6 5 4 3 2 1

For Sarah

CONTENTS

Acknowledgments · ix

INTRODUCTION   1

PART I   FOUNDATIONS   15
CHAPTER 1   Equality as a Social Ideal   17
CHAPTER 2   Political Equality   48

PART II   CONCEPTION   73
CHAPTER 3   Against Equal Power   75
CHAPTER 4   Democratic Authority and Appropriate
              Consideration   96
CHAPTER 5   Elections and Fair Representation   116
CHAPTER 6   Democratic Deliberation   143

PART III   INSTITUTIONS   173
CHAPTER 7   Unequal Voting: The US Senate
              and Electoral College   175
CHAPTER 8   Proportional Representation   193
CHAPTER 9   Racial Vote Dilution and Gerrymandering   216
CHAPTER 10   Oligarchic Threats   241

CHAPTER 11   Judicial Review   268

CONCLUSION   283

Bibliography · 287
Index · 299

ACKNOWLEDGMENTS

I BENEFITED FROM a great deal of generous assistance and support during the years I was writing this book. For insightful and constructive feedback on earlier versions of the manuscript or its parts, I thank Chiara Cordelli, Emma Saunders-Hastings, Shmulik Nili, Alexander Prescott-Couch, Ben Laurence, Abe Singer, Adam Etinson, Adom Getachew, Demetra Kasimis, John McCormick, Sankar Muthu, Jennifer Pitts, Lisa Wedeen, and Linda Zerilli. Two anonymous reviewers commissioned by Princeton University Press provided remarkably perceptive and helpful advice on how to improve the manuscript. I thank my editors at Princeton University Press, Rob Tempio and Matt Rohal, for their hard work, support, and encouragement. Maia Vaswani provided excellent copyediting. This book grew out of my PhD dissertation. For outstanding advice then and since, I thank Charles Beitz and Philip Pettit. For essential help with that dissertation, I thank Sam Arnold, Ryan Davis, Jessica Flanigan, and Julie Rose.

I could not have finished this book without the kindness and companionship of my family, especially my mother, Rowan Lindley, my sister, Manda Wilson, and my brother-in-law, Jonathan Monten. My wife, Sarah Cobey, has been a partner in all things, of which this process of authorship has been only a small part, but one that nevertheless gave her occasion to show sympathy, generosity, and love in greater measure than I can adequately thank.

Introduction

But the fine old season meant well; and if he has not learnt the secret how to bless men impartially, it is because his father Time, with ever unrelenting purpose, still hides that secret in his own mighty, slow-beating heart.
—GEORGE ELIOT, *THE MILL ON THE FLOSS*

DEMOCRACY TODAY commands great allegiance. Billions of people live under regimes that reasonably consider themselves democratic, and, in much of the world, democracy in one form or another is virtually unchallenged among both citizens and political philosophers as the best form of government. The spread of democracy in theory and practice is remarkable for a form of government that spent much of the history of European politics and philosophy as a possibility quickly to be dismissed.

This widely shared foundational commitment to the rule of the people coexists with substantial disagreement about how, exactly, the people should rule. Disagreement suffuses not only familiar political questions about the proper scope of individual rights, economic regulation, taxation, and so on—disagreement about what decisions the people deciding democratically should make—but also the proper organization of democratic decision making itself. A broad commitment to rule by the people does not self-evidently determine how exactly to organize the complicated electoral and law-making apparatuses that in large modern states translate citizen judgments into political outcomes. The commitment does not spell itself out in rules for designing the structure of democratic regimes. So we witness among citizens, activists, policy makers, and philosophers— all sincerely committed to democracy—vigorous disagreement about, for example, the design of electoral districts; the structures of legislatures; the appropriate powers of and legal relationships between legislatures, executives, and courts; and so on. While the basic question of whether to have democratic regimes is settled in many states, the question remains what the democratic answer entails about political institutions.

These questions of democratic institutional design appear relatively fine-grained in contrast to the grand question of which regime is best that occupied political theorists from Plato onward. Disputes over representative apportionment, for example, may not always have the drama or the almost revolutionary promise of the great expansions of suffrage that have punctuated the history of democracies since the eighteenth century. But if these are not the broadest questions of political morality, they are hardly trivial. Citizens committed to democracy must decide how to manifest that commitment in the design of institutions that, in large states, affect the lives of many millions of people. Contemporary political scientists show us with elegant precision what constitutional designers have probably always understood, more or less clearly: relatively subtle differences in institutional design can have significant effects on the outcomes of political processes. So even if we doubt that good constitutional organization can guarantee good results in a nation of devils, different choices of electoral and law-making institutions can have substantially different effects on the lives of citizens. While the variation in these effects is limited by citizens' basic commitment to democracy, the rule of law, individual rights, and so on, in questions of constitutional design the moral stakes are high.

The moral seriousness of constitutional design trades partly on the effects of institutional choices on political outcomes. But this is not the sole reason for concern about those choices. Democracy draws much of its political and philosophical support from its claim to be the form of government in which citizens rule equally. Democracy has long been associated, however imperfectly and incompletely, with political equality of citizens. The greatest and most profound advances of democracy have been rejections of the most profound political inequalities: the demand that the "common born," the propertyless, and the poor; racial minorities; and women were among those with whom citizens were obliged to share in rule equally.[1] Democracy's claim to moral superiority as a regime draws from its claim to be the political reflection and expression of this equality among citizens.

---

1. I do not mean to suggest that history has shown a consistent or irreversible movement toward greater democracy or equality. Even within broadly democratic countries, antidemocratic retrenchment has not been uncommon. For discussion in the context of US history, see Keyssar, *Right to Vote*.

This close connection between democracy and political equality renders democracy's high standing especially remarkable in a world of great inequalities. Great economic inequalities, racial injustice, gender-based subordination, and other forms of inequality characterize not only the oligarchies and autocracies of the world, but some avowed democracies as well. The coexistence of political equality (or at least a conscious, sincere, commitment to political equality) with social inequalities raises questions about the purpose and value of democracy. Is political equality meaningless, or at any rate impotent, in the face of these inequalities? Does it justify inequalities in other domains? Or might it offer the promise of ameliorating or rejecting them? Confusion about these questions—about, in the most fundamental sense, the relationship between democracy and equality—fuels doubt not only about how to organize democratic institutions, but also about democracy itself. Even as democracy waxes in its official jurisdictional reach, its promise may wane as democratic revolutionary movements fail and as oligarchs consolidate control, whether by publicly rejecting democracy or by using democratic forms increasingly devoid of democratic substance. To worry about empty democratic forms is, however implicitly, to reach toward some idea of what democratic substance really is—what democratic forms are at their fullest. But this is just our confusion.

The democratic rejections of profound, explicit political inequality are achievements of great, continuing historical and philosophical importance. But they do not complete the democratic project of establishing egalitarian political institutions, or the philosophical project of understanding what those might be. Like the basic commitment to democracy, the near-universal extension of suffrage does not settle every important question about democratic institutions. Ostensibly democratic regimes have witnessed enough abuses to prove that basic suffrage rights are not sufficient to guarantee equality in rule; electoral and law-making systems may affront political equality without recourse to outright disenfranchisement. We need to choose among a wide variety of institutional arrangements consistent with near-universal suffrage, and some arrangements are more egalitarian than others.[2] A full account of political equality should, therefore, help us choose the institutions consistent with the democratic

---

2. I say "near-universal" suffrage to acknowledge persisting limits on the voting rights of some citizens. I do not assume the validity of any such limits, but neither do I wish to rule out the possibility that some limits could be consistent with the most attractive ideal of political equality. Limits on young children's voting rights may be one.

aspiration symbolized by the extension of suffrage. An account of political equality explains what this aspiration is, and why it matters—that is, why we are obligated to treat our fellow citizens as political equals. It shows why this obligation is a serious one, and why it should attract us. It reveals the great goods that people would experience in a democratic society of equal citizens. Such an account should also guide us in realizing such a society, by explaining how to evaluate institutions and practices in light of the political egalitarian ideal, and how to direct the shape of democratic reform.

This work aims to provide such an account of political equality: an account that can help guide our choices between electoral and law-making institutions and practices. I do not argue that political equality is the only criterion morally relevant to the choice of political institutions. The political outcomes that institutions may be expected to promote are also relevant in most (perhaps all) cases. I will argue that the requirement of political equality itself requires some institutional sensitivity to especially urgent claims of justice, which means that the requirements of political equality and of good outcomes will conflict with each another less than a narrower view of democracy might suggest.[3] I also argue that democracy, properly understood, involves and promotes meaningful social equality.[4] To the extent that such equality is a part of "good outcomes," then, again, there may be little tension between democracy and the best outcomes. Nevertheless, we can imagine situations in which these goals are in real tension—where political equality and good outcomes (or, speaking very roughly, democracy and justice) demand different institutional schemes. I will not provide a complete account of how morally to evaluate all cases of such tension. (Such an account would require a complete theory of justice, an undertaking beyond my abilities.) I take on the more limited task of understanding what political equality itself requires, and why it matters. While this understanding may not give us final answers to all questions of institutional design, a firmer grasp on the normative force behind political equality, as well as a more detailed understanding of its requirements, will give us a better sense of how and when to choose between competing values if we are forced to make such a choice. It also, I believe, will give us good reason to think that justice requires democracy, or at least that the most just societies would be democratic. Political equality matters enough to give us reason to support democracy absent extreme circumstances. Such, I will try to show, is the value of a society of political equals.

3. See ch. 6, § III.B.
4. See chs. 1 and 2.

I. Three Claims about Political Equality

At the most abstract level, in providing an account of political equality I will make three central claims. The first is that political equality fundamentally requires electoral and law-making institutions that are consistent with the equal political status of citizens. Institutions must reflect and express a public recognition of citizens' equal standing as members entitled to bring their judgment to bear on political matters and to share responsibility for organizing common life. I strive to explain how to determine which institutional regimes do in fact recognize citizens' equal standing. As we will see, any democratic regime will involve many kinds of institutional inequality. But not all of these inequalities are antidemocratic or politically inegalitarian. An account of political equality must therefore provide an explanation of how to distinguish inequalities that are in fact objectionable from those that are consistent with equal citizen status. I will show why we owe it to each other to grant one another this status, and thereby to relate to our fellow citizens on equal political terms. This task, in turn, requires reflection on how to argue for any kind of equality between persons—social, economic, or whatever—and demonstrates, I argue, how closely connected democracy is to these other egalitarian aspirations.

The second central claim I will make is that the norm of political equality regulates institutions that constitute democratic rule over time. In aspiration, these institutions mean to constitute democratic rule over the course of citizens' entire lives, and over the course of many generations of citizens. An account of political equality must be responsive to the temporal aspirations both of the institutions that it regulates and of the ideal it expresses, and so must be a plausible account of political equality over time. Political equality requires the maintenance of equal rule over time, rather than merely equal sharing in rule at individual moments, such as election day. By contrast, a standard approach to political equality, both in public democratic discourse and in legal and philosophical writing, identifies some decision procedure that involves an equal distribution of power with respect to that decision, and argues that institutions should use or mimic that decision procedure as much as possible. Such an approach—focusing as it does on narrow distributions of power moment by moment, and decision by decision—does not respond properly to citizens' interest in equal status persisting over time, which, perhaps counterintuitively, is not the same thing as equality in power moment by moment. Equal status obviously depends in part on one's present political entitlements and how they compare to those of other citizens, but it also depends on certain facts about the past and certain expectations about the future. Democratic institutions thus require some sensitivity to the past and preparation for the future. In the course of this work, I will attempt to explain in more detail the nature of this temporal sensitivity.

The third central claim of this work is that in order to understand what political equality requires, we must change how we identify the form of authority democratic citizens ought to have over political decisions. Departing from the tradition of interpreting this authority as a right of voters to issue commands to the state, I argue it is a wider entitlement to various forms of "consideration"—that is, powers to shape common deliberation and decision making. Rather than distributing to each citizen a certain amount of power or influence, democracy requires that we grant each citizen entitlements to consideration that include, but go beyond, the exercise of power or influence. With this new conception of authority in hand, we can better understand what democratic fairness requires of systems of judgment aggregation (such as elections) and systems of democratic deliberation.

These three claims are connected. Having equal political standing amounts to being in ongoing relationships of equality with other citizens. Just as the character of ordinary interpersonal relationships depends not only on the immediately present assets and characteristics of the people involved, but also certain facts about the history of the relationship and certain expectations about its future course, so too does the egalitarian character of political relationships depend in part on their past and expected future. The equal or unequal character of these relationships depends not only on the present distribution of power, but also on the history of the relationships and the reasonable, publicly backed expectations about their future. The relevant histories and expectations, moreover, involve not only mutual exercises of power, but also a range of interactions, responses, and dispositions, that together may constitute reliable expressions of mutual respect and shared authority. To put this another way, the demand for equal-status recognition itself incorporates certain demands for the security of that status over time, and this security requires confidence in one's rights to various forms of consideration. Keeping in mind the basic requirements of equality over time, understood as a requirement for ongoing democratic consideration, will therefore help us to make good judgments about which institutional equalities are in fact prerequisites of equal political status, and, by the same token, which institutional inequalities are compatible with, or even necessary for, democratic equality.

II. The Argument: Political Equality as Ideal and in Application

The best way to vindicate these abstract claims about equal political status over time is to begin developing the account of political equality that the claims mean to support, and then to show how this account can help guide relatively concrete judgments about electoral and law-making institutions. I begin in chapter 1 by articulating how the ideal of equal status connects to democratic aspirations, and why we should take that ideal seriously. Just what it means to enjoy equal status, or to participate in egalitarian relations, is something of a mystery, and I explain how we might clarify these ideals. In chapter 2, I argue that equal status demands respect for each citizen's authority over common life—not, as some other democratic egalitarians argue, neutralizing all power inequalities. When a regime guarantees respect for each citizen's authority, it instantiates egalitarian relationships between citizens. This gives us strong reason to organize our common life democratically, even when this might not produce the best policy outcomes.

An account of political equality should explain how the ideal of equal status regulates the design of collective decision-making institutions. In chapter 3, I consider what is probably the most common and most influential view of political equality: the view that political equality requires institutions that guarantee citizens equality of power over common decisions. This view implies that rule according to majority vote of all citizens (perhaps along with some basic free speech requirements) is necessary and sufficient to satisfy the demands of political equality. I argue that this position focuses too narrowly on one moment of the decision-making process: the moment of translating citizens' judgments into legislative outcomes. As a result, it neglects the need for fair processes both preceding legislative votes—processes of agenda setting, deliberation, and representation, for instance—and succeeding those votes; for instance, in administrative procedure. It also fails to respond to the need to secure political equality over multiple iterations of collective decision making. Instead of the equal-power view, then, we need a conception of political equality that reflects the democratic demand for equal political status over time.

I present and defend such a temporally sensitive conception of political equality in chapters 4, 5, and 6. I argue that political equality requires institutions and practices of collective decision making to guarantee all citizens appropriate consideration of their political judgments. There are a number of ways in which one can give consideration to another's judgment, and political equality requires that the regime grant consideration to each citizen's judgment in a number of respects over the course of the decision-making process. Reliably securing these various components of consideration grants citizens authority, or what I call "practical consequence," in the formation of common decisions. In chapter 4, I develop this conception of citizen authority as entitlement to appropriate consideration, and argue that it better captures democratic aspirations for political equality than do alternative conceptions of authority that emphasize citizens' equal rights to issue commands to the state. In chapter 5, I describe what appropriate consideration requires in terms of what are often called "aggregative" procedures—procedures for aggregating citizens' judgments into common decisions, such as the selection of representatives. I present requirements of basic, minimal consideration that apply to any aggregative scheme. Among other things, these requirements entail a shift in how we think about the responsibilities of representatives. Democratic representation requires an egalitarian synthesis of citizens' judgments, which is complicated by the fact that citizens render judgments at different levels of specificity. Citizens themselves differ as to how much discretion their representatives ought to have, and this disagreement should be reflected in representation. I explain how to determine whether institutional inequalities are objectionable when they do not violate these requirements of minimal consideration. I also argue that aggregative procedures must satisfy an "antidegradation" requirement that precludes rules and procedures that express or reflect a judgment that some citizen or citizens occupy an inferior political status. This is a kind of antidiscrimination rule for political decision-making institutions.

In chapter 6, I explain how the requirement of appropriate consideration regulates institutions and practices of political deliberation. These institutions and practices do not directly determine what the political community will do, as legislation does, but they shape the character of these decisions. Accordingly, they determine in significant part whether the regime is truly democratic. I first critique a family of views that claim fair deliberation requires equality of influence among citizens. These views, which share the equal-power view's emphasis on causal power over decisions, suffer from a number of difficulties that emerge when we closely analyze the concept of influence. The most basic problem with these views, however, is their narrow conception of citizens' interests in fair deliberation. This narrowness leads the views to largely ignore a variety of affective, unconscious, arbitrary, and discriminatory ways in which citizens respond to efforts at influence. I argue that, by contrast, the appropriate-consideration conception of political equality properly responds to the plurality of citizens' deliberative interests—which go well beyond the interest in overcoming obstacles to preformed views by exercising influence. I go on to suggest what appropriate consideration requires of common deliberation, and how we should vary the scope and character of the consideration granted to different citizen judgments under different circumstances. (For instance, the regime may be required to make special efforts to consider the judgments of those in small minority groups, or those with especially urgent claims of justice.) These requirements attend both to individual's claims for direct hearings for their views, and to broader concerns about a fair structure for synthesizing the various and conflicting judgments rendered by different citizens.

The theoretical issues I discuss in the first six chapters have interest in their own right, but a conception of political equality will have little practical relevance if it cannot help organize and resolve controversies about the proper design of democratic institutions. These applications, moreover, are important tests of the theoretical claims themselves—tests of whether the theory really does advance an attractive ideal of political equality. In chapter 7, I argue that while systems of moderately unequal voting power may be justified in order to protect vulnerable minorities, the inequalities involved in elections of the US president and senators do not pass this test. In chapter 8, I consider and reject claims, common outside the United States and among some democratic reformers and writers in the United States, that political equality categorically requires systems of proportional legislative representation. In chapter 9, I consider one important controversy bedeviling nonproportional, territorial-districting systems such as those that exist in the United States: the problem of racial minority vote dilution. I argue, contrary to influential skeptics, that vote dilution is indeed a serious political injustice, and that the appropriate consideration conception shows us why. In some circumstances, districting schemes diluting minority votes reflect and promote broader deliberative neglect of certain minority groups—that is, they reflect and promote failures of consideration. Recognizing these injustices does not, as skeptics often fear, commit one to supporting the proportional representation of groups in the legislature. The discussions of proportional representation and vote dilution together reveal that the fair representation of groups requires a variety of forms of consideration, and that there are few institutional means that will universally guarantee those forms of consideration in all political societies. These analyses also explain what is objectionable about partisan gerrymandering—that is, efforts to draw districts to favor a particular political party. Such efforts deny various forms of consideration to supporters of other parties.

Following that discussion of intersecting political and racial inequalities, chapter 10 turns to the intersection of political and economic inequalities. I explain how the influence of wealth in political processes undermines democracy, despite formal equality in voting rights, by promoting the deliberative neglect of poorer citizens. This conflict between the disproportionate influence of the rich and the appropriate consideration of the poor and economically middling results from general conditions of deliberative scarcity. In these conditions, which we almost always face, more speech for some—or, more precisely, more consideration for some, provoked by certain kinds of speech—really does come at the expense of consideration for others. Political equality requires a fair division of responsibility among advocates and listeners for ensuring this consideration is granted. Wealth inequality threatens such fairness. I defend a reformist response to this oligarchic threat in the form of policy solutions aimed at limiting the use of wealth for political power. The difficulty of truly severing economic and political power, however, suggests that political equality may as a practical matter be incompatible with great economic inequality, whatever the formal nature of democratic institutions. When we view democracy as primarily about the distribution of formal political power we ignore this practical incompatibility, at our peril.

In chapter 11, I ask whether judicial review of legislation is compatible with political equality. Judicial review typically involves the right of some group of judges—often with very distant, if any, electoral authorization—to overturn acts of elected legislative authorities. In empowering the unelected over the elected, many lawyers, philosophers, and ordinary citizens believe that such review is undemocratic. I argue that a well-designed system of judicial review could be compatible with political equality, despite the institutional inequalities it involves, if such review reliably promotes the consideration of citizens' judgments that would otherwise be neglected by the legislative process. Notably, this is not an argument that judicial review is justified because it protects individual rights (or other goods) from democratic abuse. It is an argument that judicial review is justified (if it is) because it contributes to a regime that as a whole better instantiates political equality than would a regime without such review. I argue, however, that the systems of judicial review in place in the United States and elsewhere likely require reform if they are to meet this standard.

These applications of this account of political equality hardly answer all the questions we have about how best to manifest a real democracy. One of the lessons of the appropriate-consideration conception is that political equality places demands on a wide variety of democratic institutions—or, to put it a bit more optimistically, that there is a wide variety of forms of consideration, and many ways of granting citizens the practical consequence that befits their equal status. I hope to do enough in what follows to establish that conceiving of political equality as a demand for equal status, which in turn requires the appropriate consideration of each citizen, is a promising way of addressing these and other problems of democratic institutional design. I believe, moreover, that political equality is itself a requirement of justice, though certainly not the only one. While political equality may sometimes conflict with other requirements of justice—because, for instance, democratic procedures may issue in unjust laws and policies—there is nevertheless a way in which a genuine commitment to political equality bends one toward a broader commitment to justice. This is at least true if justice requires, as I suspect it does, a society constituted by equality of status, and thus, in a sense that is not too metaphorically loose, democracy in its fullest manifestation.

III. Why Have a Theory of Political Equality?

Implicit in books like this one is some idea that the arguments in them matter. Do they? The subject, I do not doubt, is important. Political equality is a great good; it involves a meaningful regard that we owe to one another. But democracy may be important without democratic theory being important. It is a serious injustice to deny some people control over their lives on equal terms with others, but this does not mean that arguments about the nature of this injustice are necessary or even useful responses to that injustice.

Writing can respond powerfully to wrongdoing. It can articulate for readers interests in ending injustice they may not have known they had; it can strengthen their sense of justice, make them aware of others who share that sense, and generate feelings of solidarity that move people to act in common. Writers can outline strategies for resisting injustice, and coordinate plans for overcoming it. Writers in general need have no anxiety about the purpose and meaning of their efforts—or, at least, no more than anyone who takes on the risks of acting to improve the world.

Are writers of normative political philosophy entitled to such self-confidence? What good is done by arguing—sometimes painstakingly—that this or that practice is unjust, for this or that exact reason? Those who are already convinced of the seriousness of injustice, and its basic shape, may believe that whatever increased precision in understanding injustice comes from philosophical argument matters little in comparison to efforts, whatever they may be, to act against it. Those who support the practices, whatever their beliefs about their justice, may not be very likely to change their minds and their ways in response to elaborate argument—if, indeed, they ever choose to read the argument in the first place. Ending injustice, the thought goes, demands the development and exertion of power, rather than efforts at persuasion. Or if it requires persuasion, we best persuade through drama, comedy, irony, testimony, appeals to sympathy, sloganeering, or any of a number of other communicative approaches more effective than philosophical argument. It can be difficult to avoid the suspicion that normative philosophical writing is solely for the benefit of the writer himself, or at most a small group of fellow professionals and students who are engaged in a communicative practice that may have meaning (and sometimes deliver a paycheck) for them, but has no greater political or moral point. For all the weight and social significance of its subject matter, political philosophy may be depressingly self-absorbed.

Self-directed activity is not always useless. It can be the greatest, most valuable activity available to us at times, since we can more easily, or at least more profoundly, affect ourselves than others. Activity on oneself also grounds and shapes our relations with others. Sustained philosophical activity may primarily benefit the philosopher herself, but there need be no shame in that. Perhaps there can even be some satisfaction, or at least a Platonic relief that one is not obviously doing something worse. The discipline of philosophical argument itself could make a person engaged for so long in such argument more moderate, humble, charitable, and resilient. Reflection on democracy through long writing should make us, the writers, better able to relate to others in our lives on equal terms, to share authority over our lives, and thereby to enjoy, as much as is in our power, relationships of fraternity and sorority, of mutual respect and dignity—of a kind of conscious common freedom. To accomplish as much through philosophical writing would be, to borrow from one of Socrates's interlocutors in the *Republic*, to accomplish "not the least of things."[5]

"But not the greatest," replies Socrates. Should we not expect more from philosophy—especially political philosophy? Those who spend time thinking about politics typically do so (I imagine) because we care about politics itself, or about what political activity should or does achieve—justice, equality, freedom, happiness; injustice, inequality, domination, misery;

5. Plato, *Republic*, 497a.

and so on. We think about politics because we care about the people who experience goods and sorrows, not simply because such thinking is a useful tool for self-development. We should not discount the relevance for other human beings, at small or large scale, of self-development. But still, we may reasonably ask whether political philosophy has any meaningful connection to the wider political values that lead some of us to engage in sustained philosophical argument. Politics matters; philosophy matters, in its small way; but does philosophy matter for politics?

I do not know the answer to this question. The answer depends on how societies change—for instance, whether changes in people's normative beliefs cause significant change, and whether persuasion of a broadly philosophical type causes noteworthy changes in people's normative beliefs. Changes in normative beliefs certainly could lead to meaningful social change—if enough people changed their beliefs in similar ways, and acted accordingly, there would be little to stop the change—but this does not mean that producing such widespread change in beliefs is a promising strategic aim for writers (philosophical or otherwise) or activists. Which aims are strategic depends on much more detailed facts about the relevant situation and how actors could likely change such a situation for the better. I do not know enough such facts—nor do I have enough confidence in my judgment in responding to those facts—to provide a convincing defense that democratic political philosophy is a strategic response to the injustices of political inequality.

I write this book, then, with uncertainty about the extent to which it matters. I write philosophically (or what I hope is philosophically) about *political equality* because I believe political equality matters. I *write philosophically* about political equality because so much is written in defense of what seems to me to be political inequality. We are not in the happy position in which we all know what is unjust, and are tasked solely with acting to change it for the better. We—that is, people in general—disagree heartily on what is just and unjust, equal or unequal. Defenses of political inequality do not always identify themselves as antidemocratic; typically they do not. They defend what I believe to be inequality in the name of democracy. These attempted justifications of injustice call out for response and rebuttal. Defenders of the conclusions I support here often fail to appreciate, meanwhile, how difficult these conclusions are to defend, and thus may not respond adequately to challenges to those conclusions. I do not know if my response—or, better, the responses of a community of writers to which I contribute a very small share—is of any use. But it seems wrong to me to let arguments for injustice go unanswered, when we might answer them. It would be a great shame if some people found that they could put some answers to use for the cause of justice, only to discover that there were no such answers available and adequate to their need. So I deliver these few drops to the great river of argument about democracy and equality, so that those who aim to make political equality real may—if they ever feel the need to sustain themselves with its waters, or carry themselves along for a while on its current—never find it dry.

PART I

Foundations

CHAPTER ONE

Equality as a Social Ideal

DEMOCRACIES GRANT THEIR CITIZENS a status denied to some persons in other regimes. In democracies, citizens have entitlements to participate in collective decision-making processes, which enable citizens to take an active part in the regulation of their common life. These entitlements secure for citizens a standing in society they could not otherwise have—the standing of a ruler, if only one ruler among others. This status is valuable: it renders one a coauthor, with others, of one's life and world, rather than the subject of control by others who claim superior authority. But what exactly should these entitlements to participate be? What kind of standing can and should we all share? We often disagree about how best to realize democratic ideals. We disagree about what those ideals are—some even doubting that we should be democrats at all. This disagreement reflects confusion about what the status of a democratic citizen is, and the related question of why it matters that all people enjoy that status.

One of the most morally meaningful aspects of democracy is its promise to secure the equal political status of all citizens. Democracy constitutes a society of political equals. Keeping this ideal in mind is essential for determining how exactly democratic institutions can realize such a society.

Understanding the democratic ideal requires a more general argument about what is meaningful and valuable about equality between people. Such social equality is a broader ideal than the democratic ideal, but the two are closely connected. Arguments for general social equality provide illustrative parallels for those more focused on equality in political status. But the connection between democracy and equality is closer than that. A theory of political equality requires reference to, and support from, an account of what social equality is and why it matters. Only with such an account can we understand what it means to relate as political equals, and why we should guide our thought and action according to the democratic ideal of a society of equal citizens.

In this chapter, I present the idea of equal status that I see as the fundamental concern of a theory of political equality—that is, a theory that explains what it means for citizens to relate as political equals, why they should relate that way, and how to realize such relationships in political institutions and practices. I explain how an ideal of equal status, and the related ideal of a society of political equals, can help us understand what political equality is and why it matters. The rest of the chapter takes up the question of how we can use these very general ideals of equal citizens relating in an equal society to determine how we ought to treat one another and how we ought to organize our social and political institutions. There are many reasons to treat others as equals—and to avoid treating them as inferiors or superiors. Developing an ideal of a society of equals, and corresponding objections to inequality, involves organizing these diverse reasons into a coherent whole that can guide our thought and action. Having a sketch of such an ideal, including objections to inequality, in place, will equip us well for the discussion of specifically political equality that follows in the rest of this book. We will better understand and support democracy when we better understand and support social equality.

I. Democratic Status and Equal Political Relations

The word "democracy" refers, in a general way, to the rule of the people. What institutional arrangements would constitute the rule of the people? This is not a matter of determining what the word or concept "democracy" really means, in ordinary language or the history of philosophy, but a matter of judging which institutions most closely satisfy the moral and political aspirations suggested by the idea that the people should rule. In this section, I articulate what I see as the core democratic aspiration of political equality.

One way to think about the moral vision behind democracy is to try to analyze the idea of a "people," and then to work out how it might be that it (or they) might rule. This can be a useful strategy to answer some important political questions, but it is an approach that risks ignoring the concern for political equality that historically and morally lies at the heart of democratic theory and practice. Many historically influential analyses of a "people" as an entity capable of ruling describe one whose rule is compatible with a wide variety of institutional arrangements, many of which admit stark political inequality. Most infamously, Thomas Hobbes insisted that, once properly authorized, absolute monarchy amounted to the rule of the people just as much as did direct democracy.[1] Both constitutional orders, thought Hobbes, represented "the commonwealth" or "the people," which had no existence apart from the constitutional order itself and its scheme of representation. There may be views of "peoplehood" that are not as institutionally agnostic as Hobbes's. But accounts of democracy that begin by asking how a people could rule run the risk of Hobbesian, antidemocratic permissiveness. Virtually any government that does not present itself as an alien authority—in James Madison's words, as a "will in the community independent of . . . the society itself"[2]—will have some claim to manifest the rule of the people in some sense. This requirement of nonalien rule may be an important prerequisite of democracy: it may properly rule out as nondemocratic certain forms of colonial or imperial rule. But it barely begins to capture democracy's demand for political equality.

A better way to think about the moral aspiration behind the "rule of the people" is to focus not on the demand for rule of "the people" as an entity, but rather on the demand for rule of (nearly) *all* the people, rather than some. (For brevity's sake I will from now on leave out the qualifier, though we should keep in mind that even a commitment to the rule of all adult, more or less permanent residents in a society excludes some, such as young children and transients, from rule.) This demand for the rule of all, rather than some, opposes democracy not to alien occupation but to monarchy and aristocracy or oligarchy, all of which are based on the claims of some few (or one) to have special entitlement to rule. Democrats insist that every citizen is entitled to engage in political rule. They insist not only on universal inclusion, but inclusion on equal terms. The full rejection of oligarchy requires rejecting distinctions in political status between citizens: the rejection of any exclusive political rank or class, and thus the rejection of any lower class of limited, second-tier citizenship. Democracy grants every citizen the same, single rank and political standing.

The role of a theory of political equality is to provide criteria by which we can judge whether political institutions and practices fully manifest this rejection of oligarchy and this affirmation of equal political standing for all citizens, and to explain why they should.[3] There may be many reasons to support democratic forms of government: such forms may best keep the peace, satisfy individuals' desires, or otherwise promote the best

---

1. Hobbes, *Leviathan*, ch. 16, para. 13, and ch. 18, paras. 1–3.
2. Madison, "Federalist, No. 51," 351.
3. Beitz, *Political Equality*, 17; Dworkin, *Freedom's Law*, 17.

outcomes by the lights of some theory of good political outcomes. A theory of political equality need not deny the validity of such reasons to support democracy, but it aims to isolate and focus on the principle of equal political status, and the related ideal of a society of political equals, as an essential guiding principle by which to regulate the design of democratic institutions.

What, then, is the moral significance of the rejection of oligarchy? What does it mean to have a certain political status, and to have a status equal to that of other citizens? Following Colin Bird, I will say that a person's status is defined by a set of expectations regarding how one ought to be treated by others.[4] For a given status in a given social milieu, these expectations, and any sense of obligation to meet them—any sense that the status is directive or authoritative—may lack any moral backing. (Think of the status of "untouchable" or "slave," or of "commoner" in an aristocratic regime: these statuses are constituted by expectations of unjust treatment, or by a lack of authoritative expectations against such treatment.) In such cases, of course, people may nevertheless treat the expectations as authoritative, even if they are not morally warranted, and in that sense a person may have the status defined by those expectations. In other cases we may be morally obligated to recognize that individuals have a certain status, and thus to treat their status as authoritative in regulating our conduct toward them. Recognizing the status consists in regulating conduct according to the directives attached to the status. This attentiveness to the authoritative status of another in one's deliberations about one's conduct, and in a range of other practical dispositions (including, for instance, willingness to be held accountable by another for insufficient attentiveness to the other's status), constitutes a form of respect that Stephen Darwall calls "recognition respect."[5] In order to describe a certain status, one needs some idea of what its attendant recognition respect entails.[6] Understanding the status

---

4. Bird, "Status, Identity, and Respect," 222.

5. Darwall, *Second-Person Standpoint*, 120. Darwall distinguishes "recognition respect," which concerns "how our relations to [something] are to be regulated or governed" (123), from "appraisal respect," which is "an assessment of someone's conduct or character or of something that somehow involves these" (122).

6. It may seem inappropriate, or perverse, to speak of "recognition respect" for low statuses like "slave" or "untouchable." As Bird points out ("Status, Identity, and Respect," 213), the idea of "respect" usually implies that the object of respect commands an especially weighty place in one's deliberations. It also usually implies that there be some positive valence to the way the status shapes one's deliberations. But there is a sense in which the status is indeed being respected in such cases, precisely because the deliberator grants the status authority in her deliberations, however wrongly.

requires, for instance, knowing what the relevant expectations are that attend that status, to whom these expectations apply (that is, who is subject to their putative authority), and an explanation of the normative force of the expectations—for instance, whether they are purely conventional, or whether they have some convention-independent moral weight.

In actual social interaction, the expectations attending some status might not be met. This can be true even when the status and the expectations that constitute it are entirely conventional. Individuals might disobey the convention, or the convention itself might begin to break down. When the failure to meet the expectations, or to recognize the status, becomes sufficiently widespread, individuals no longer hold that status. In the case of entitlements to statuses that are not entirely convention dependent, however, we may want to resist the idea that someone loses her status in virtue of others (wrongly) failing to recognize that status. This is due to an ambiguity in the idea of "having" a certain status, or "being" someone of a certain status. When someone claims that she is a free person, for instance, she might mean to describe the social fact that others generally recognize that status (she is a free person: she is actually treated as free), or she might mean that she is entitled to be treated according to the expectations of that status (she is a free person: she ought to be treated as free). Lack of recognition will undermine the first kind of claim to have a status, but not the second. Similarly, the eighteenth-century abolitionist icon of a chained African man asking, "Am I not a man and a brother?" is an assertion of a status and its entitlements—say, entitlements to natural rights of man, and to treatment according to a Christian ethic of brotherliness—and a rebuke that this status was not being granted the recognition it was due. A claim to a status can be both descriptive and aspirational.

The democratic rejection of oligarchy claims an equal political status for all citizens in this aspirational sense. In insisting that all citizens share in the regime on equal terms, democrats demand institutions and practices that appropriately respect each individual's political status. A theory of political equality articulates what expectations properly attach to this status. It does so in part by explaining why we ought to treat one another as political equals.

The idea that democracy is valuable because it manifests a kind of equality is an old one. Aristotle notices (though does not endorse) the idea, and Rousseau vigorously defends it.[7] Alexis de Tocqueville puts the point

---

7. See Aristotle, *Politics*, bk. 3, ch. 9, 97–98 (1280a7–24); Rousseau, *Of the Social Contract*, bk. 2, ch. 4.

perceptively when he explains democracy as the political expression of a general historical movement toward "equality of conditions," an equality that would manifest not only in wealth distributions, but also in the disappearance of social status hierarchies: "each man having some rights and being sure of the enjoyment of those rights, there would be established between all classes a manly confidence and a sort of reciprocal courtesy, as far removed from pride as from servility."[8] This old democratic idea is enjoying a recent renaissance, through sophisticated works arguing that democracy is a partial (and perhaps necessary) constituent of valuable equal relations among citizens.[9]

The arguments in this book are squarely within this egalitarian democratic tradition. There are two main challenges to the tradition that the arguments address. First, democrats owe an explanation of why the kind of equality that political democracy involves is valuable and important enough to determine how we ought to organize our institutions and practices, in view of all the other important values at stake in political life. This is an especially urgent matter in the light of antidemocratic political movements and philosophical skepticism about the value of political equality.[10]

Second, if an egalitarian democratic ideal is to usefully inform deliberation about what to do, we must be able to explain in some detail how the ideal applies to decision-making institutions and practices. It is not enough to argue on behalf of "democracy" as a general regime type. In service of the aim of responding to these two challenges, this book develops an account of political equality, its value, and its application that departs from many existing accounts of democratic egalitarianism, though it owes much to those accounts and aims to remain true to its guiding ideals.

Responding to these two challenges—what exactly political equality requires, and why it matters—requires a general account of how to understand the value and implications of equality as a social ideal. Substantively, as I will argue in the next chapter, political equality draws much of its value from a more general ideal of social equality, so we must know what

---

8. Tocqueville, introduction to *Democracy in America*, 1, pp. 9, 14.

9. Kolodny, "Rule over None II"; Viehoff, "Democratic Equality"; Anderson, "Democracy"; Christiano, *Constitution of Equality*.

10. For skepticism, see Arneson, "Democracy"; Brennan, *Against Democracy*. Anderson, "Democracy," and Christiano, *Constitution of Equality*, make progress on this front. Kolodny and Viehoff do much to articulate the ideal of democratic equality but say less about its weight.

that ideal is. Methodologically, understanding how to argue for a social ideal of equality will inform a parallel argument for the value and implications of a specifically politically egalitarian ideal.

Recent philosophical efforts have made clear that arguments must connect claims about the proper distribution of goods—whether material goods, institutional entitlements, or political power—to the basic moral concerns to which the demand for equality responds.[11] At the root of these concerns is the imperative to respect the status of persons as free and equal, and the complementary ideal of relations between persons being conducted on equal terms, or having an egalitarian character.[12]

A demand for equal citizen status amounts to a demand for an egalitarian character of relations among citizens in at least two respects. First, to the extent that the status itself has an egalitarian character, the expectations that attach to the status will tend to require nonhierarchical modes of relating. Second, to the extent that every citizen is recognized to have a given status, each is entitled to a similar range of expectations in interactions with others. Recognition of equal citizen status, then, constitutes egalitarian relationships, and vice versa. John Rawls puts the point nicely when he says that in an egalitarian society:

> citizens are equal at the highest level and in the most fundamental respects. Equality is present at the highest level in that citizens recognize and view one another as equals. Their being what they are—citizens—includes their being related as equals; and their being related as equals is part both of what they are and of what they are recognized as being by others.[13]

Equality of status thus constitutes, and is constituted by, relations of an egalitarian kind. When people mutually recognize one another's equal status, they put themselves in an egalitarian relation. But there are further connections between status equality and egalitarian relations, in that the recognition of equal status in various respects helps promote relationships among citizens free of hierarchy, domination, servility, and the like. These further connections are contingent, depending upon truths of empirical

---

11. Scheffler, "What Is Egalitarianism?" 8; Anderson, "Point of Equality."

12. Along with the sources cited in the previous note, see Scanlon, *Why Does Inequality Matter?*; O'Neill, "Constructing a Contractualist Egalitarianism"; Schemmel, "Distributive and Relational Equality"; O'Neill, "What Should Egalitarians Believe?"; Scheffler, "Choice"; Hinton, "Must Egalitarians Choose"; Miller, "Equality and Justice"; Norman, "Social Basis of Equality."

13. Rawls, *Justice as Fairness*, § 39, p. 132.

sociology and psychology—about how, in fact, humans tend to respond to certain social conditions, like material or political inequality. For example, such empirical truths might include the fact that substantial material inequalities tend to promote interpersonal relations characterized by domination, superciliousness, shame, and other inegalitarian features. To describe the connections as contingent, however, is not to disparage them or to suggest that they are weak; on the contrary, such connections may rest on what Martin O'Neill calls a "deep social fact" about the way equalities or inequalities in various practices or institutional arrangements shape human relationships.[14]

A similar structure holds for the ideal of political equality. The shared status of "democratic citizen" is constituted by a range of expectations that regulate institutions and individual practices. We properly recognize that status when our institutions and practices meet those expectations. When citizens mutually recognize one another's status, they thereby engage in, and promote, valuable egalitarian political relations.

Historically, the concept of status has often played a role in justifying hierarchy, domination, and exclusion. In these cases, some privileged few claim a high status that, while perhaps entailing equal treatment of those with similar status, is defined in contrast to lower statuses that most people are said to occupy. Those with high status enjoy a general social precedence over those with low status—or who, at the limit, could be said to have virtually no status at all, like slaves. Drawing from historical examples of this pattern, some egalitarians infer that the concept of social status necessarily involves pernicious inequality, because it necessarily implies some complementary notion of those with low or no status.[15]

We should not infer, however, from the history of oligarchic claims to status that the concept of status cannot ground an egalitarian ideal. First, in the case of political status, some exclusions from the status probably are permissible, and compatible with the fullest democratic ideals. Most will agree that young children should not enjoy the full status of equal citizen. If one considers these exclusions compatible with political equality, then one could accept that a conception of status does define a complementary category of individuals without the status, but deny that this renders the conception inappropriate for a society of equals.

---

14. O'Neill, "What Should Egalitarians Believe?" 131.
15. John McCormick urged me to see the force of this point. Historically exclusionary conceptions of status are noted in Waldron, *Dignity, Rank, and Rights*; Ober, "Democracy's Dignity," 829–30.

Second, such conceptions need not imply any claims regarding the permissibility of exclusions. It may be that a conception of status necessarily implies a complementary conception of entities without such status. This does not mean that it implies a normative claim that any actual people should lack the status. A conception of equal citizen may define a complementary conception of entities without such status, whether humans, nonhuman animals, or objects. But it need not involve any claim that any humans are not entitled to that status. The conception of status may draw much of its force from our ability to conceive what it would be to lack the status, either through imagination or through attention to history. Precisely for this reason, the conception would illustrate why we should not deny people that status, rather than implicitly commit us to such injustice. An ideal of *equal* status, moreover, is one that explicitly incorporates normative principles that prohibit unjust exclusions and inequalities.

Derek Parfit suggests a related objection to the use of a conception of status to articulate our obligations. He claims that "for the idea of moral status to be theoretically useful, it must draw some distinction, by singling out, among the members of some wider group, those who meet some further condition."[16] Parfit argues that the claim that all people have a status that entitles them to be treated in certain ways adds nothing to the claim that all people ought to be treated in those ways. Such an egalitarian conception of status, he writes, need not be pernicious, but it is useless.

Parfit may be right that once we know what our obligations are, we could pass over talk of a status that involves certain entitlements, and simply discuss our obligations to respect certain entitlements, without any loss of meaning. But a conception of status may nevertheless be useful in helping us develop our understanding of our obligations in the first place. A conception of equal status may be a valuable heuristic—for instance, in emphasizing that everyone is entitled to high regard, even if that regard is no higher than the regard to which others are entitled. (It is higher, however, than the regard to which objects and some nonhuman animals are entitled, as well as higher than the regard with which many people have in fact been treated.) A conception of status, moreover, involves a corresponding relational ideal. As I will argue later in this chapter, this ideal

---

16. Parfit, *On What Matters*, 244. Parfit illustrates his point with the political examples of ancient Rome, in which only some people had full legal status, and contemporary democracies, in which children, among others, do not have the full status of citizens.

should shape our understanding of how we should treat others. Finally, a conception of status can be motivational, helping us to see why we ought to treat people this way, and why we ought to be satisfied with being treated this way—that is, because satisfaction of all the various norms of treatment together constitutes an attractive social standing, embedded in attractive relationships. In these ways, a conception of status can play a role in helping us understand our obligations, and a role in motivating us to meet our obligations, even if Parfit ultimately proves correct that a full statement of our obligations and their sources could be provided without reference to a conception of status.

Thus far I have been outlining a framework for understanding and arguing about the demands of equality—a framework structured around the concept of equal status and a corresponding ideal of egalitarian relations. We must now develop that framework, and use it.

II. Arguing for Equality

The proposition that the practical requirements of social equality are rooted in an ideal of equal relations or equal status is shared ground among a number of egalitarian theorists, variously called "social," "relational," or "democratic" egalitarians.[17] The purpose of the rest of this chapter is to develop this social egalitarianism so as to address the two challenges I mentioned above: to identify what exactly political equality requires, and to explain the extent of priority it should enjoy relative to other values. Existing work in social egalitarianism often more or less assumes that political democracy is an essential part of equal social relations. Indeed, authors often reference political equality as a central part of the social egalitarian ideal, sometimes as a challenge to egalitarians supposedly too narrowly focused on the distribution of material goods.[18] (Hence the occasional "democratic egalitarianism" name for this approach.) In claiming democracy for social egalitarianism against other forms of egalitarian thought, however, social egalitarians have not needed to say much in detail about just why political equality has such pride of place, nor what exactly political

---

17. See, e.g., Anderson, "Point of Equality"; Hinton, "Must Egalitarians Choose"; Miller, "Equality and Justice"; Norman, "Social Basis of Equality"; O'Neill, "Constructing a Contractualist Egalitarianism," and "What Should Egalitarians Believe?"; Scanlon, *Why Does Inequality Matter?*; Scheffler, "Choice," and "What Is Egalitarianism?"; Schemmel, "Distributive and Relational Equality."

18. E.g., Scheffler, "What Is Egalitarianism?" 22. How much this is a fair criticism is an interesting question, but cannot detain us here.

equality entails if it is meant to constitute equal citizen relations.[19] Similarly, important arguments about the foundations of egalitarianism have occluded questions about just how to identify suitably equal relations, and what they require. We must, therefore, return to the foundations of social egalitarian method in order to provide the necessary arguments. These efforts will address the two challenges facing egalitarian arguments for democracy by elaborating how an equal status or relational ideal guides choices of institutions and practices, and how we can establish that such status or such relations morally matter. Explaining the implications of the egalitarian ideal will also address skeptical challenges that social egalitarianism is too vague to distinguish good or permissible inequalities from bad or impermissible ones.[20]

What, then, are the expectations that, if authoritative, would constitute the status of an equal citizen? What does treating someone as an equal cocitizen require? We can answer these questions using two complementary approaches. First, we identify a vision of equal political relations between citizens—a positive vision of a society of political equals. Identifying this vision provides us a description of what it would be to live in such a society and to engage in such relations. It also helps us articulate reasons why such a society and such relations are desirable, and perhaps obligatory. Second, we take a more negative approach, identifying the most objectionable features of oligarchy—that is, societies constituted by public, manifest political inequality. By considering what is so bad about such societies—the "vices of oligarchy"—we identify the kinds of relations and status inequalities that a society of political equals must avoid. Pursuing both of these approaches allows us to draw lessons in a coherent way from both micro-level interpersonal relationships and macro-level social phenomena. Integrating these approaches gives us an account of what equality requires and why it matters.

II.A. A SOCIETY OF EQUALS

To begin with the more positive approach, it will help to distinguish between general equality among people, or what I will call *social* equality, and the distinct ideal of *political* equality. Political equality is a narrower

---

19. Elizabeth Anderson's landmark paper, for instance ("Point of Equality"), uses the ideal of democratic community as a model for economic and civil equality, but does not explain why relating as democratic citizens is especially valuable. In later work, she addresses this issue more directly: see "Democracy."

20. Arneson, "Democratic Equality."

ideal than social equality, because it involves equality in one specific, if important, domain of social life. To anticipate, I will argue that we ought to understand political equality as the ideal that all citizens are equally authoritative over matters of common life. Roughly speaking, all citizens are equally in charge of such matters.[21] Social equality, on the other hand, as I have defined it, involves more general equality in all domains of social life, or at least those consequential domains in which an ideal of equality applies. What the relationship is between social and political equality is a pressing, substantive question of political philosophy. (The theory of political equality presented in this book should help answer this question.) It is conceivable, however, that a society could enjoy political equality without social equality, or vice versa. Citizens could be equally in charge but enact policies that create or sustain social inequalities. Alternatively, some politically unequal society could conceivably create and sustain social equality, perhaps through the principled rule of some elite committed to egalitarianism. These may be unlikely scenarios; indeed, I will argue that the latter is substantively impossible. The point is simply that political equality is conceptually distinct from full social equality.

The focus of this book is political equality, rather than full social equality. But in pursuing our question of what expectations constitute the status of equal citizen, I will first discuss social equality, by sketching a vision of a society of equals in the general (not narrowly political) sense. This will clarify the elusive moral ideal of equality.

II.A.1. The Framework

A society characterized by social equality is one in which members relate on equal terms. The regular conduct of interpersonal relations on such terms constitutes the society as equal. Members enjoy such equality in familiar, ongoing relationships, and enjoy confidence that strangers and passing acquaintances will also treat them as equals, as will public institutional bodies. The value of relations with an egalitarian character is what

---

21. This is a narrow, somewhat artificial, conception of what is "political." In an ordinary sense, there are pressing issues that do not directly or primarily concern citizens' authority over common life, but which nevertheless are importantly "political" in the (different) sense that all citizens ought collectively to attend to such issues. How to respond to global climate change is a pressing issue to which citizens ought to attend, individually and collectively, and which touches on matters of equality and inequality. But it does not directly relate to who has authority over matters of common concern; it is more a question of how people should use what authority they have. We need some way to identify the democratic concern with equal authority, and "political equality" has come to be the term that identifies this concern.

gives us reason to move toward an egalitarian society, to sustain whatever social and political equality we have in place, and to treat people as equals. Relating to persons in such an egalitarian way—treating them in accordance with the standards that define relationships among people of equal status—expresses an egalitarian form of respect for those persons. This respect is more than just a belief about someone's worthiness or a positive attitude toward him. Respecting someone as equal involves expressing or manifesting respect through actions, and maintaining dispositions, also manifested where appropriate, to act reliably in the future in a way befitting an equal. We disrespect someone—or, at least, we fail to respect her as an equal—when we do not satisfy such norms in our treatment of her; for instance, by acting in ways that express contempt or disregard. A society of equals, comprising people in egalitarian relationships with one another, is a good to be promoted. An ideal of such a society articulates how people should be respected—that is, how we ought to respond to them, and to treat them.

It may be possible to respect someone in a nonegalitarian way; that is, as a superior or an inferior. Consider patriarchal forms of courtesy toward women, which manifest a kind of solicitousness of women by men, but in the context of judgments of women's inferiority, limited opportunities, narrowly constraining gender roles, and so on. A commitment to equality privileges respecting others as equals, rather than as superiors or inferiors. This does not mean that no hierarchical relationships of any kind could exist in a society of equals. There might still be religious and parental authorities, teachers, bosses or managers at work, and so on. The point is that the requirements of equality are morally fundamental, and take precedence over the requirements of more hierarchical ideals. Hierarchical relationships must be compatible with the ideal of equality, and the preservation of egalitarian relationships.[22] This may condition the nature of the hierarchy in certain respects—for instance, by limiting its domain. It may be a complex interpretive matter to distinguish expressions of equal respect from "respectful" inegalitarian attitudes, dispositions, and valuations. An account of social equality should guide such interpretations, and explain which local hierarchies are consistent with fundamental equality.

The claims in the preceding paragraphs, if justified, would show that several major moral theories would provide strong support for egalitarianism. If equal relationships are very valuable, consequentialist theories would require us to promote equality in the absence of some very serious

---

22. Kolodny helpfully discusses this matter in "Rule over None II," 303–7.

countervailing concern. If equal relationships promote and sustain the flourishing of individuals within them, virtue-based theories would require us to promote such relationships, and to become the kind of people who engage in such relationships. If inequality gave people strong reasons to reject principles that permitted such inequality, contractualist theories would likely reject inequality. If equality is an important part of respecting individuals' personhood and autonomous agency, other deontological theories would require such respect. Such matters of foundational moral philosophy are beyond the scope of this book. But these reflections give us reason to think that a concern for equality is not particular to any one approach, but could (and should) fit into many important theories of justice.

II.A.2. Basic Equality and Equal Relationships

To return to the idea of a society of equals: most fundamentally, egalitarian relationships are constituted by mutual recognition of the equal worth or value of all persons in the relationship. That is, each participant in the relationship recognizes all the others as equally valuable, and, accordingly, entitled to equal concern. People in relations among equals are confident of this recognition, and secure in their belief that it will continue to influence the attitudes and behaviors of others. This relatively simple or basic ideal of equality as equal worth, however, is as stated too simple to guide behavior, as it leaves too much unsaid about what the recognition of equal worth requires. There may be many ways of treating people that involve a norm of equality in some formal sense without meaningfully creating and sustaining a relationship among equals.[23] The ideal of equal relationships involves something more than this.

To understand what more this ideal requires, we might contrast two kinds of egalitarianism: *merely basic* egalitarianism and *substantive* egalitarianism. Merely basic egalitarianism recognizes the equality of persons in some fundamental sense—for instance, their equal value, or their equal status as holders of certain rights. What makes such egalitarianism "merely basic" is that it is compatible with many ways of satisfying such basic norms of equality, even if the result is substantial inequalities in people's life prospects, or in how people relate. Utilitarianism, for example, is basically egalitarian in that it insists that the happiness of each person is equally valuable, because each person is equally valuable. It is *merely* basically egalitarian in that, in principle at least, utilitarianism is open to the possibility that the greatest total utility might be promoted by societies

---

23. Sen, "Status of Equality."

with great social, economic, racial, sex-based, or other inequality.[24] Libertarianism is basically egalitarian in that it affirms that certain rights, such as rights against coercion, belong equally to all individuals. It is *merely* basically egalitarian because libertarianism implies that even societies extremely unequal in, say, economic or racial terms, would be just as long as those rights are not violated.[25] Merely basic egalitarian views reject what Nietzsche called the "privilege of the few"—the idea that some elites fundamentally matter more than other, more ordinary people. But they do not go so far as to endorse what Nietzsche believed was at the heart of the "privilege of the many": a substantive vision of equality that operated not just as a formal condition on justification but also as a principle or set of principles actively regulating social life.[26]

Substantive egalitarianism endorses some such of vision of social equality. Equality, according to such a vision, manifests itself regularly and visibly in relationships between people who conceive of themselves as equal in their social standing as well as in some fundamental moral sense. The vision of a society of equals is used to develop substantially egalitarian views by identifying what makes relationships meaningfully equal. In merely basic egalitarian views, any such conception of equal status would be derivative. According to such views, one's status is whatever status one has in societies that meet the requirements of basic equality—equal counting in the utilitarian calculus, equal libertarian rights, or whatever. Substantially egalitarian views are distinguished in part by the fact that the ideal of equal status is not merely derivative in this way, but actually generates the content of the requirements of equality, through its connection to the ideal of relationships among equals.[27]

II.A.3. Face-to-Face Norms and Friendship

Egalitarian relationships must satisfy several substantive—rather than merely logical or formal—criteria in order to be truly or fully egalitarian. They are complex because the value of equality is complex. Equality as a social value encompasses several related ideals, including fairness,

---

24. In practice, because severe inequalities often decrease total utility, utilitarian philosophers have often advocated for great decreases in social and economic inequality, and thereby have to some extent supported substantive egalitarianism.

25. See Nozick, *Anarchy, State, and Utopia*, chs. 7–8.

26. Nietzsche, *Genealogy of Morality*, I.16, p. 32. Nietzsche did not call this the "privilege of all," because he believed its egalitarianism was so substantive as to inhibit the flourishing of the great.

27. Scheffler, "Choice," 17; Hinton, "Must Egalitarians Choose," 80–81.

impartiality, fraternity and sorority, freedom from domination, and others.[28] These ideals shape the norms that constitute egalitarian relationships, and thus the expectations that persons of equal status should recognize as authoritative in their treatment of one another.

Participants express this recognition in many informal and quotidian ways when they directly encounter one another (whether face to face or otherwise). Tocqueville, as I noted earlier, described this egalitarian conduct as a manner of "reciprocal courtesy." In the passage in which he uses the phrase, Tocqueville does not say much about what that courtesy requires, or how we can tell if it is truly reciprocal. *Democracy in America* is a study of how a society enjoying "equality of conditions" among its white population practices such reciprocal courtesy, or at least approaches that ideal in some respects, and how various "mores" or customs, as well as social institutions, sustain such practices (or threaten them). Tocqueville's lack of immediate elaboration on the ideal of reciprocal courtesy may, however, reflect that he thinks the concept is intuitive and relatively easy to grasp, based on our own experiences of being treated with such reciprocal courtesy—and without it. If that is true, we ought to be able to elaborate this egalitarian ideal on the basis of this familiar understanding.

Exactly how to manifest such courtesy may be a matter of convention—for example, whether it requires formal address using titles such as "Mr." or "Ms."—but whatever the conventions may be, they express equal regard or concern in a suitably clear way.[29] Equal regard also requires responding appropriately—that is, without contempt and in a spirit of accommodation—to those who may be unfamiliar with these conventions, or who have objections (plausibly compatible with equal concern) to some convention.[30] Whatever the precise contours, treating someone as an equal involves some sensitivity to the needs and interests of others, and at least some minimal benevolence in accommodating and attending to those interests if it is not too costly to oneself. It involves accepting that one has

---

28. This is one of the major conclusions of recent work on equality. See Scanlon, *Why Does Inequality Matter?*; Schemmel, "Luck Egalitarianism"; Hausman and Waldren, "Egalitarianism Reconsidered"; O'Neill, "What Should Egalitarians Believe?"; Anderson, "Point of Equality"; Wolff, "Fairness"; Young, *Justice*, ch. 2.

29. On the importance of manners—that is, conventional displays of courtesy—in expressing respect, see Buss, "Appearing Respectful"; Anderson, *Value in Ethics*, ch. 2; Walzer, *Spheres of Justice*, ch. 11. See also Kolodny's discussion of equal "consideration" in "Rule over None II," 296–98.

30. On changing norms of courtesy in the light of moral argument, see Anderson, *Value in Ethics*, § 5.3; Dworkin, *Law's Empire*, ch. 2. On the importance of various forms of accommodation to equality, see Shiffrin, "Egalitarianism."

no general social precedence over others, whether that precedence is a matter of entitlement to customary forms of deference, priority in claiming material goods, authority over common decision making, or anything else.[31] Perhaps most clearly, it involves renouncing claims of hierarchy and superiority of status, claims typically manifest through contempt, superciliousness, condescension, and related attitudes—on which more shortly (see section II.B). Treating someone as an equal also involves rejecting any obligation to act as an inferior—for instance, through servility or excessive humility. Equals deny that they or others have any need to reassure others, as Dickens's Uriah Heep constantly does, that they are "'umble."

Relationships among equals need not be especially warm or close, or even entirely positive. They have room for anger, criticism, sarcasm, resentment, and so on, though these negative interactions themselves ought to be guided by egalitarian norms. (Anger directed at a recognized equal is very different from anger directed at someone regarded as inferior.) Friendship may be a helpful model: we typically (perhaps necessarily) consider friends our equals.[32] The norms that partially constitute the relationship—the common understanding between the friends of what it means to treat each other like friends—are egalitarian. I would not consider my friend someone who regularly expressed through speech and actions her belief that she was more valuable than me and generally deserved greater consideration and concern than I did—even if she were usually kind to me. We might have a good relationship of some kind, but it would not be friendship, except perhaps by a strained analogy.[33]

---

31. Relations among equals may sometimes involve special forms of precedence. What makes such forms of precedence special is that they are due to specific actions (like promising) or, perhaps, to particular kinds of relationships (like close family ties), rather than to a more general claim for precedence. Special forms of precedence may be compatible with a more general equality—for instance, if they are limited in scope. The distinction between special and general precedence may not always be clear: consider an agreement to serve as a slave in perpetuity. The precedence of the master would be special in the sense that it is rooted in one specific action, but very general in its scope and in the intensity of the precedence.

32. Aristotle claims "the friend is someone similar and equal": *Politics*, 115 (1287b32–24). His conception of friendship requires substantial reciprocity, though whether it requires substantial equality is less clear. See Cooper, "Aristotle"; Allen, *Talking to Strangers*, ch. 9. Friendship is at least in part constituted by moral norms: Scanlon, *What We Owe*, ch. 4. I claim that norms of substantial equality are among the moral norms that partially constitute friendship.

33. Some might think that there can be friendships worthy of the name between superiors and inferiors—say, between teachers and students, managers and workers, rulers and ruled, and so on. (Parents and children are a special case, because while parents typically enjoy some unshared authority over their children, parents should exercise that authority

Equality does not mean that we cannot be angry with our friends, or demand redress for wrongs, and so on. In a flourishing friendship, however, the friends manage such conflicts and grievances in a way consistent with their recognition of each other as equally valuable, and equal in standing in the relationship.

Friendships can exist among people who differ greatly in terms of wealth, beauty, talent, and other dimensions. Friends can even differ in how much they feel affection for one another.[34] Such inequalities, however, may be compatible with the equality of consideration and concern that I argue characterizes friendship. They also are compatible with the equal authority over the terms and conduct of the relationship that I will argue is central to friendship—and to relations of equality—in chapter 2. Indeed, equality of authority in decision making becomes all the more important as one partner in a relationship gains more power through wealth or talent or social regard than another. Such equality ensures that the friends together as equals, rather than the more powerful friend alone, are determining the course of the relationship. Commitment to such equality in decision making about what to do together is also an especially clear way of manifesting equal courtesy and consideration. Thus, the possibility of friends who are unequal in some dimensions does not establish that equality is unnecessary for friendship. On the contrary, it shows that equality in the bedrock of a relation—its norms of authority and consideration—is a precondition for true friendship. It also shows that wider social inequality may make friendship among people with different resources or attributes more difficult, as in the context of great inequalities of power and status it may be difficult for an advantaged potential friend credibly to grant equal authority in the relationship to disadvantaged others, and for the disadvantaged to show credibly that they value the advantaged friend for himself and not for the advantages of friendship with the privileged.

---

so as to help the children develop into persons entitled to equality with their parents and other adults.) I acknowledge that these relationships can be characterized by reciprocal good will, beneficence, and other characteristics shared by friendship. These are at most only partial or limited friendships, however, so long as the inequality plays a meaningful role in the relationship. I believe it only makes sense to call these relationships friendships if the special precedence of one person exists within a more general context of social equality (or if the ostensibly superior friend renounces that superiority as much as is possible, either explicitly or implicitly through conduct in the relationship). In any case, if these are forms of friendship, they are peculiar forms. The core conception of friendship incorporates norms of equality.

34. Arneson, "Democratic Equality," 41–44.

Just as a relationship among equals need not always and only involve warm, positive affect or feelings, neither does it require closeness, in the sense of a dense, regular pattern of interaction between specific individuals. We can treat as equals those whom we barely know, or only encounter once. We can even treat as equals those whom we never meet, but with whom we interact indirectly, through social institutions and networks of economic interactions. Equality can characterize such relationships in several ways: dispositions to treat others as equals, even in brief or episodic encounters; commitments to ensure that social institutions support egalitarian relationships (including of this brief and episodic kind), as well as reflect and express equal respect and concern themselves; and common knowledge that others reliably have such dispositions and undertake such commitments. Here, too, friendship may be a model, though less in the familiar sense of intimate relation and more in the classical sense of civic friendship—a kind of reciprocity, attentiveness, and mutual goodwill even in the absence of particular emotional connection.

Our familiarity with egalitarian relationships in ordinary interpersonal interactions, or reciprocally courteous meetings with acquaintances and strangers, shows that, as Tocqueville suggests, the idea of such a relationship is not empty, nor too abstract to be meaningful. Many of us understand when we are being treated as an equal, and we can identify when we are being treated as an inferior. (Some of us may be all too capable of identifying the slightest expressions of inequality; but if there is pusillanimity in objecting to every such slight, this does not mean our perception is inaccurate.) We should not assume our intuitive understandings of egalitarian relationships are infallible, nor give those understandings too much authority over our moral and political judgments. Individuals, groups, and societies at large may mistakenly believe certain dispositions and actions express equality when they do not. The privileged may be especially prone to such mistakes (if they are not avowed antiegalitarians who happily endorse a hierarchy in which they are at or near the top), not recognizing condescension, invidious discrimination, or differential neglect for what they are. Social and, especially, political equality themselves serve important epistemic purposes in correcting such biases, or at least preventing them from exerting much influence on social institutions and practices. But even in the absence of a thoroughly egalitarian society and its epistemic benefits, we should not allow the recognition of fallibility to imply that our informal understanding of equality is too corrupt or unreliable to guide us. Typically, even antiegalitarians have some conception of equal relationships (for instance, among the powerful or the virtuous).[35] They understand what the norms of equal relationships are, and how they may be followed or violated. They know what it is to be treated as a peer. When disagreements arise about whether some relationship is truly equal or not, we thus will have some common reference point for judging that question, for all our disagreement about how widely the norms of equality apply, or just how they apply outside the context of close, face-to-face relationships.

II.A.4. Beyond Face-to-Face Relationships

Knowing roughly what it is to relate as equals, a conception of egalitarian relations informs our ideal of a society of equals. We extend the egalitarian ideal beyond familiar interpersonal relationships to more complex relationships and social structures, with respect to which our immediate intuitions may be unreliable, uncertain, or simply absent. Institutions and social practices are consistent with the demands of equality if and only if they support egalitarian relationships of this familiar kind among members of society, and themselves express the egalitarian attitudes and dispositions that make up such relations among equals.[36]

The positive ideal of a society of equals shapes our development of various other abstract egalitarian ideals, such as equal concern, fairness, impartiality, and fraternity and sorority. We may derive from these abstract ideals principles for regulating society. The ideal of a society of equals conditions these derivations, by requiring that these egalitarian principles recognizably promote and express egalitarian ways of relating—and thereby reflect and support the equal status of persons in the society or societies to which the principles apply.[37] Similarly, in the light of some arguments on the basis of abstract ideals, we might realize that our conception of egalitarian relationships was in part mistaken, because it does not meet the requirements of some compelling principle. A reflective equilibrium ought to exist between abstract egalitarian principles and their implications on the one hand, and our substantive vision of equal relations on the other.

---

35. See Nietzsche, *Genealogy of Morality*, II.8; Aristotle, *Nicomachean Ethics*, 219–21 (1156b6–35).

36. Viehoff notes the importance not just of promoting equal relationships, but of manifesting them politically—"Democratic Equality," 362–63—but he says little about what it is to manifest equal relations in an anonymous or institutional context.

37. Kolodny suggests such synthesizing of different egalitarian ideals: "Rule over None II," 294, n. 5. G. A. Cohen implements one synthesis in combining "socialist equality of opportunity" (a distributive rule) with a principle of "community" (a relational ideal) in *Why Not Socialism?*

This method of achieving reflective equilibrium, in contrast to a method of deriving egalitarian principles strictly from one or a few abstract principles, is especially necessary given the complexity and plurality of ideals of moral and social equality.

II.B. THE VICES OF INEQUALITY

This complexity of egalitarian ideals requires consideration of the objectionable features of nonegalitarian relations. I will refer to such objectionable features of social inequality as the "vices of inequality."[38] (I will refer to the objectionable features of *political* inequality as "vices of oligarchy.") Consider some of the features of unequal societies that writers have described as objectionable and unjust: unfairness; domination; oppression; marginalization and exclusion from valuable opportunities, institutions, and practices; exploitation; stigmatization; cultural imperialism; contempt; envy; servility; arrogance; humiliation; infantilization; and resentment.[39] These features relate to unequal social relations in different (sometimes overlapping) ways. Inequality may reliably cause these features to arise; inequality may partially constitute the features, in that for the features to be present is, in part, for some inequalities to exist; the features may be ways that people express or respond to inequality; or the features may partially constitute inequality, in that what it is for relations to be unequal is, in part, to exhibit some of these features. These close connections to inequality make these features vices of *inequality*, and therefore relevant to inquiries about the meaning and value of equality. These features are *vices* in my sense in that they are objectionable: we have reason to eliminate such features of social life, and prevent them from arising, to the extent possible. These reasons may be diverse, deriving, for example, from our ideas about what best promotes the flourishing of individuals, or from some more direct requirement that respecting others or justifying the terms of our interaction with them is incompatible with maintaining or enabling relations with these features.

Each of these vices needs to be analyzed. Such analysis would lead us to know just what it is to be dominated, exploited, demeaned, stigmatized, and so on; what it is to avoid these vices; and how the vices are connected

---

38. "Vice" here is meant loosely, to refer to some bad or objectionable property. There is no special reference to virtue or character-based theories of morality.

39. Hausman and Waldren, "Egalitarianism Reconsidered"; Ober, "Democracy's Dignity"; "O'Neill, "What Should Egalitarians Believe?"; Scheffler, "Choice"; Anderson, "Point of Equality"; Young, *Justice*, ch. 2; Tawney, *Equality*.

to forms of inequality. Such analysis should also explain why these are vices—that is, features of relationships that make those relationships bad, and ones that we ought to avoid. Together, these analyses of the various vices of inequality would provide us an understanding of what the ideal of social equality is, and why it matters, by showing us what that ideal rejects, and why that rejection matters.

I will not say much about the vices of inequality here, because I believe their use in political argument is more familiar than the ideal of a society of equals. (I will say more about the vices of oligarchy in particular in chapter 2.) The challenge for egalitarians is less to identify the vices of inequality, as these have been the focus of much work, as to explain how particular analyses should be integrated into a global account of social equality.

One might object that this method of developing the moral content that determines the expectations attaching to the status of an equal person involves an argumentative circle. The apparent circle is as follows. We are trying to discover this moral content in part by reflecting on what the vices of inequality are. But if these features of inequality only count as vices—that is, as something objectionable—because they involve some kind of inequality, reflection on these vices cannot help explain the moral content of equality. Instead, the identification of the features as vices would depend on this very moral content that we are trying to discover. (A parallel objection could be made about the supposedly good features of a society of equals.) If, for instance, we concluded that oppression was bad because it instantiated some inequality, we could not rely on the badness of oppression to support an explanation of why inequality is objectionable. That, so the objection goes, would use the conclusion as a premise to establish itself.

This objection is mistaken. A theory of social equality explains and justifies principles that regulate equal relationships and thus define the status of equal persons. These principles derive from the goods of equality (as elaborated in the ideal of a society of equals) and the vices of inequality. The claims that the goods really are goods, and the vices really vices, require justification. Those justifications cannot simply refer to the principles regulating equal relationships for support. So, to continue the example, we cannot argue that egalitarian principles prohibit oppression, and then attempt to justify the claim that oppression is objectionable by noting that oppression runs afoul of egalitarian principles. That would indeed be circular. But justifications need not proceed that way. Instead, the claims require argument about why some feature of an equal relationship is good or why some particular feature of inequality is objectionable. There may be many diverse kinds of reasons supporting such arguments, involving the particular features—the particular manifestations of equality or inequality—under consideration. The social egalitarian principles that regulate relationships draw support and definition from all of these reasons to desire equality and reject inequality.[40] They do not reduce to a dogmatic assertion of the importance of social equality.

The circularity objection equivocates with respect to its use of "equality" (or "inequality"). Principles of equality draw justificatory support from our claims about the goods of equality. These claims, argues the objector, are justified by some claim that equality is good—that is, a claim that we might call a principle of equality. But there is equivocation here between the first principles of equality mentioned, which refer to global principles together defining and regulating social institutions and interpersonal relationships of an egalitarian character, and the second principle of equality mentioned, which refers to some local, more specific argument that some particular kind of equality—say, impartiality in distributing certain goods, or a particular kind of solidaristic relation—is desirable or morally required. The global egalitarian principles depend on the local egalitarian arguments, but the latter do not depend on the former, except in some general and noncircular sense that the principles are mutually reinforcing within a reflective equilibrium.

This structure of argument may make it seem as though the global principles of social equality are so derivative as to be uninteresting or unnecessary. It is true that these global principles, which together constitute a unified understanding of the meaning and value of equality, are not fundamental, in the sense of being the most basic, irreducible argumentative foundations of an argument for an egalitarian society.[41] What are fundamental are the arguments, presumably drawn from foundational moral theories, which support the local arguments for features of equality and against features of inequality.[42] But global egalitarian principles

---

40. On the plurality of egalitarian concerns, see Scanlon, *Why Does Inequality Matter?*; Schemmel, "Luck Egalitarianism"; Hausman and Waldren, "Egalitarianism Reconsidered"; O'Neill, "What Should Egalitarians Believe?"; Anderson, "Point of Equality"; Wolff, "Fairness"; Young, *Justice*, ch. 2.

41. Thus I could accept Arneson's claim that welfare (weighted in "prioritarian" fashion) is morally fundamental, not equal relations: "Democratic Equality," 27. My claim is that we ought to maintain relations of equality, understood in the way I articulate. (This may count as what Arneson approvingly refers to as "mid-level theorizing" [44].) Different claims about what is morally fundamental should, I argue, converge on this view.

42. Reference to foundational moral theories does not preclude the application of principles of public reason that restrict the content of public justifications to principles that all citizens could reasonably accept. (See Rawls, *Political Liberalism*.) If one believes

nevertheless can play an important role in our moral reasoning. They unify the various fundamental arguments for equality and against inequality, organize them coherently, and help us understand the relative importance of different features of equality. They also guide our responses to inequality, by defining an aim of our efforts, and by showing what are the most objectionable, and thus morally urgent, features of inequality that we should work to remove. The general principles help us understand just what equality requires, in a more global, and more usefully action-guiding sense. They strengthen our understanding of the local arguments for equality and against inequality. Reflection on the global ideal is also necessary to check that the ideal is appropriately stable in Rawls's sense: that is, that citizens living in a society guided by that ideal could reasonably be expected to come to endorse that ideal.[43] This question is not easily addressed unless the ideal is described with some completeness and coherence. So the global principles have practical and theoretical significance even if they are not the most fundamental parts of our reasoning about equality in the sense that they appear in a particular primary location in some argumentative chain.

These remarks should explain why we should give the ideal of social equality an important place in our political thought and deliberation, even though the value of some aspects of equality is derivative or instrumental. The core claim of part I of this book is that we have strong reason to establish and maintain egalitarian political procedures, and to aim consciously at establishing and maintaining such procedures. That is, we should aim to achieve politically equal procedures because they are politically equal. (I will say more about what "having strong reason" means in chapter 2.) It would be a mistake to attempt to decompose equality into its various supporting values and reasons, and to pursue those, without regard for a coherent, global ideal of equal status or relations.[44] First, reflection on the ideal of a society of equals and the vices of inequality suggests that equal

---

principles of public reason restrict the use of foundational moral theories in certain public justifications, then what is fundamental when it comes to those public justifications is, in Rawls's phrase, the "political conception of justice" (11). From the perspective of any individual citizen, though, what are fundamental are the parts of her comprehensive doctrine that justify the public political conception of justice. I refer to those parts as "foundational moral theories." How my distinction between principles of equality and foundational moral theories maps onto a distinction between the political conception of justice and comprehensive doctrines depends on the principles of public reason. I do not pursue the question here.

43. See, e.g., Rawls, *Political Liberalism*, IV.2; *Theory of Justice*, §§ 76, 86.
44. This seems to be Arneson's suggestion, in "Democratic Equality."

relations, and the enjoyment of equal status, are valuable for their own sake. This, I believe, is the implication of the friendship parallel, and likely many claims about vices of inequality that are bad in themselves.[45]

Second, a global account of social equality explains that equal relations have many positive features, some valuable in themselves, and some contingently—but robustly—connected to other goods. The contingency does not justify ignoring the relations in the pursuit of individual constituent goods, however. The robustness of the connection, and the public understanding of the robustness, makes public commitment to the equal relations a way of committing to the goods, and to the people who will enjoy the goods. This commitment is valuable as a way of manifesting equal respect, partly constitutes a valuable relationship, and is instrumentally valuable in achieving the goods that come with general confidence that one is robustly respected and socially secure.

II.C. CONNECTING THE ARGUMENTS

One might wonder why it is necessary, in developing such global egalitarian principles, to focus on the vices of inequality as well as on the ideal of a society of equals. There may be a simple, obvious complementarity between these vices and the social ideal: it may be clear that some vices of hierarchy are objectionable because, and only because, they prevent the realization of good, respectful egalitarian relationships. Similarly, some aspects of egalitarian relationships might be good because, and only because, they prevent the realization of vices of hierarchy that we independently consider objectionable. (Consider, for instance, that a good-making feature of friendship is security against violence or humiliation by the friend.) Call these cases of value complementarity. In these cases, the positive and negative egalitarian strategies might seem redundant. Even if all goods of equality and vices of inequality were cases of value complementarity, however, it would be necessary to pursue both strategies, in order to identify both the goods to be pursued and the vices to be avoided. Focusing on the goods alone, for instance, might leave us ignorant of important objections to inequality (because certain vices might be easier to identify than their complementary goods), and thus leave the ideal of equality impoverished.

In noncomplementary cases, the importance of pursuing both strategies is clearer. In these cases, for instance, it is not true that what is objectionable about some inequality can be fully comprehended or explained

---

45. O'Neill, "What Should Egalitarians Believe?" 130. See also § II.D below.

solely with reference to some good aspect of equal relations that is lacking. Instead, the inequality may be importantly characterized as something bad and objectionable in a way that is not fully evident when reflecting on the lack of some good. For example, reflection on the good of relations between people who are equally free may meaningfully inform our positive ideal of an equal society. But we may not fully appreciate this good—that is, what exactly constitutes equal freedom, what is necessary to support it, and why and how much we should value it—without substantial reflection on the most meaningful, objectionable features of inequality of freedom—features such as domination. Even if we ultimately concluded that freedom was best understood as the absence of domination, this would not be value complementarity of the kind I discussed above. Though "relations of equal freedom" and "relations of domination" might be complements, in the sense that the presence of one implies the absence of the other, the former could not be fully comprehended without reflection on the latter, and vice versa. That is because claims such as "freedom is nondomination" should not be understood as tautological, analytic truths, but as substantive moral claims backed by political-philosophical argument.[46] Perhaps once such claims became widely accepted and internalized, the meaning and value of "equal freedom" might be recognized as including everything important that one should understand about the meaning and value of domination. But the value complementarity imagined in such a scenario would be the result of argument that incorporated both the positive and negative strategies for understanding the meaning and value of one aspect of equality—argument that established a complementarity that was not evident before the argument's success. In the absence of such successful arguments about all of the relevant goods of equality and vices of hierarchy, both strategies ought to be pursued.

II.D. THE STOIC EQUALITY OBJECTION

Some might object that this dual approach to describing egalitarian concerns fails to aim at the proper target. If the moral and political concern is with a certain character of relations, so the objection goes, why not just focus our criticism on the relations themselves, or on people or the

---

46. See Pettit, *Republicanism*. Pettit does more than just argue that freedom has a certain definitional meaning—he argues that the values that we do (or should) associate with freedom are essentially connected to the objections we have (or should have) to domination.

character traits that produce relations of a certain undesirable kind? For instance, if our fundamental objection is to relations characterized by attitudes of superiority and inferiority, contempt and servility, why not just say that people ought not to treat one another with superiority or contempt, and so on, leaving aside claims about the arrangements of social or political institutions? Is it not possible to engage one another socially as equals despite material inequalities? To push the point further, why should our arrangement of such institutions be held hostage to people who (wrongly) take their greater store of economic or political goods to warrant superiority over others—or, for that matter, to people who inappropriately feel inferior or act in a servile way because of their economic or political poverty? Why not allow allocations of goods to be determined by some other ideal, and demand that people maintain fraternal relations whatever their store of goods? At most, the objector could continue, relational ideals, and concerns about the vices of inequality, give us reason to object to the particular abuses or vices of particular people; they do not give us reason to prophylactically regulate people's entitlements in order to prevent abuses by people who may never commit them. These reasons do not have much relevance for how we ought to structure social and political institutions. Call this the *stoic egalitarian* objection, since it claims that relational values only give us reasons stoically to preserve certain relations, whatever the distribution of wealth, political power, or other goods.

One might interpret this objection in two different ways. One way is to treat this line of thought as a *reductio ad absurdum* of the claim that status and relational equality is at the heart of the egalitarian ideal. It is a bad interpretation of equality, this version of the objection suggests, because it ultimately fails to provide any reason to limit inequalities in the distribution of goods, and more generally fails to provide determinate principles for what counts as a just distribution.[47] So egalitarians should look elsewhere for moral foundations. A second version wholeheartedly endorses the criticisms behind the line of questions: status equality may be the right interpretation of equality, but this just goes to show that equality ought not to determine the distribution of goods, whether economic or political. Perhaps we have obligations to treat one another according to norms of civic friendship and reciprocal courtesy and so on, but we do not have the right to alter people's entitlements in order to make them more likely to satisfy these obligations.

---

47. See Kymlicka, "Left-Liberalism Revisited"; Arneson, "Democratic Equality."

On either reading, the objection is unwarranted. Concern for equal status and egalitarian relationships among citizens provides powerful reasons to object to inequalities in the distribution of economic and political goods. First, certain inequalities constitute objectionably hierarchical relationships irrespective of people's attitudes about those relationships. Failures to respect individuals' status—for example, by refusing the authority of their interests or of their political judgments—may itself constitute an oligarchic manner of relating, however stoically the deprived individual avoids servile behavior, and however generously the powerful otherwise avoid overtly domineering behavior. Similarly, relationships of domination may be constituted by vulnerabilities created by inequality, whatever the attitudes or intentions of the persons involved.[48] A concern for egalitarian relationships imposes direct limits on economic or political inequalities.

The second way in which concern for equal status can provide reasons to oppose distributive inequalities is by reference to the contingent but robust links between distributive inequalities and status inequalities. If O'Neill is correct to describe these connections as "deep social facts" about how humans respond to distributions, then it is unreasonable to accept serious distributive inequalities on the grounds that people ought stoically to resist attaching social significance to these inequalities.[49] It is probably true that a more just society would encourage citizens to limit the wider social significance attached to particular distributive inequalities, including inequalities of political power that exist, say, between ordinary citizens and government officials.[50] But that is compatible with the egalitarian belief that it is unreasonable to expect the seriously deprived to refrain from developing attitudes of inferiority or behaviors of servility, or to place them at the substantial risk that the wealthy and powerful will fail to view their own place at the top of the distributive hierarchy with detached social indifference.

These constitutive and contingent connections between material distributions and egalitarian relations show that the relational ideal does not support antiegalitarian conclusions about our distributive obligations. For the same reason, there is no *reductio ad absurdum* from an egalitarian perspective: the focus on a society of equals and the vices of inequality does not imply any quietism about the distribution of economic and political goods. Relational ideals may not fully determine our judgments about

---

48. Pettit, *Republicanism*, ch. 2.
49. See also B. Williams, "Idea of Equality," 113.
50. Rawls, *Theory of Justice*, § 82, 477.

all possible distributions. There may be a space of possible distributions within which egalitarian concerns lead us to be indifferent between distributions. Citizens would be secure in their equal status whichever of these distributions manifested. But this lack of completeness is no problem. As long as citizens can understand that the social institutions and practices within which the distributions arise are justified by their role in establishing and maintaining a society of equals, there should be no resentment at the distributions that arise, nor any sense of objectionable arbitrariness. Moreover, the fact that egalitarian principles do not completely determine our judgments does not mean that citizens would have no reason at all to prefer some distributions over others. They could, for instance, refer to other, nonegalitarian values, such as aggregate welfare or respect for property rights, within the constraints set by the egalitarian norms. Or, alternatively, they could take a "pure procedural" approach, and judge that any distribution that results from egalitarian institutions and practices is justified, and to that extent nonarbitrary, even if such a distribution is in part determined by chance or other factors that are not morally salient. The strategy for articulating and justifying egalitarian principles here provides substantial structure for our judgments about material distributions. This structure ensures that citizens can recognize distributions satisfying egalitarian principles as fair and nonarbitrary.

II.E. THE VICES OF EQUALITY?

An objector might ask why we should generate the moral content of our political philosophy by reflecting on the ideal of a society of equals, and the vices of hierarchy, but not by reflecting on other, non- or antiegalitarian ideals, and on identifiable vices of equality—uniformity, mediocrity, pusillanimity, envy, or whatever they might be. If we ignore such alternative ideals and vices, how could we provide any convincing conclusions about how we ought to relate to one another?

Responding to arguments against social equality is, of course, essential to defending egalitarian principles. This important concern is addressed by what I have called the local arguments for equality and against inequality. These arguments aim to provide convincing reasons why some inequality is objectionable, even if (say) it makes easier certain kinds of greatness or promotes aggregate welfare. They must similarly provide convincing reasons why some features of egalitarian relationships are desirable or obligatory, in part, say, because they do not require stifling uniformity or envious pusillanimity. Convincing local arguments such as these must directly address claims on behalf of what some might call vices of equality or antiegalitarian ideals. The global egalitarian principles that draw from these local arguments, moreover, show that an egalitarian ideal is coherent, and that this ideal is indeed desirable (and stable) when understood properly and fully. To that extent the global principles support the local arguments against antiegalitarian objections.

A theory of equality of the kind I am discussing, encompassing this structure of global principles and local arguments, is not, however, a complete theory of justice—that is, a complete theory of how we ought to organize society and our relations with one another.[51] Such a theory of justice would have to consider a range of social values and ideals besides equality, and a range of vices and objectionable social conditions besides those associated with inequality. It would have to explain what, all these things considered, we ought to do together. Even a complete theory of equality would likely not be so systematic. But a theory of social equality would make substantial contributions to the development of a comprehensive theory of justice, by providing a proper understanding of what equality is, what it involves, and what is good about it. These contributions alone would involve wide-ranging and important insights into a great deal of the perils and possibilities of social life, even if they did not systematically address all of our concerns.

This work is primarily concerned with political equality. Because I cannot provide a comprehensive theory of justice, this book cannot provide a complete justification of democracy, or a complete accounting of the place of politically egalitarian institutions and practices in a fully just society. The arguments of this book are incomplete to the extent that they do not address, as a theory of justice would, every major concern, and how that might shape our social and political obligations. Like even an ambitious theory of social equality, a theory of political equality is limited. But in the course of this work, I will address many substantial objections to democracy—that is, to the egalitarian organization of political authority. I will not simply assume political equality is obligatory, as the objector we are considering believes (wrongly) that social egalitarians simply assume that more general equality is obligatory. Thus, while much of the book is aimed at explaining what political equality requires of institutions and practices—a matter of pressing concern for those who are convinced that

---

51. Some internecine debates among egalitarians—e.g., between social egalitarians and "luck egalitarians"—may be due to lack of clarity as to whether the various conceptions of equality in play are meant to serve as comprehensive accounts of political morality.

societies, or at least their own society, ought to be democratic—I will also argue that we have good reason to believe that justice does, in fact, require political equality. I begin that task in the next chapter, using the structure of arguments for equality we have considered here to show why we ought to treat one another as political equals.

CHAPTER TWO

Political Equality

DEMOCRACY, IN ITS BEST, aspirational sense, is a political regime in which all citizens recognize one another as equals in political status. In the last chapter, I explained what it is to have a social status in general: it is to have others take as authoritative in their deliberations certain (status-defining) expectations of how to treat one. These expectations define corresponding norms for relations between people who occupy various statuses. Equality of status involves securing the same status for all those who enjoy the equality, and defining that shared status with reference to specifically egalitarian expectations and relations. We can determine what these egalitarian expectations and relations are by reflecting on an ideal of a society of equals, and on the vices that attend various forms of inequality. We thereby develop and confirm norms that define an egalitarian status—norms that, if widely followed, would achieve the goods of a society of equals and avoid the vices of inequality.

In this chapter, I use this general egalitarian framework to argue for political equality in particular. I identify what it means to enjoy specifically political equality. I argue that we have reason to pursue and support politically egalitarian relationships—to respect the equal political status of citizens. I first consider instrumental reasons to support political equality. Then I argue that we have reason to pursue and support political equality even if it does not better contribute to good ends than other political arrangements. In making that argument, I first detail a vision of a society constituted by politically egalitarian relations, and then I outline objections to political inequality—that is, oligarchy. The result is a strong case for democracy.

I. Equal Political Status and Respect for Political Judgment

To affirm equal political status is to recognize each citizen as equally entitled to render authoritative judgments as to how to organize and regulate all citizens' common life. Citizens have equal political status when common institutions and practices reflect and express the idea that they each have the capacity to judge matters of justice and political morality, and the entitlement to exercise that capacity by rendering judgments that have public authority on equal terms with others. Citizens have this authority when they have the power to obligate others to attend to their own judgments, and to give weight to those judgments, in the course of their deliberations about what we ought to do. Such an obligation makes it impermissible for other citizens to ignore one's views, or to treat consideration of those views as merely optional or discretionary.

Admitting citizens into the common project of political rule—to a share in the regime—respects them, by granting authority to their political judgment. To borrow from John Locke, political equality consists in the recognition of citizen equality "in respect of jurisdiction or dominion one over another."[1] Locke's emphasis on each citizen's "jurisdiction" brings together both the idea of judgment and that of recognized authority: if institutions are to respect citizens' equality of jurisdiction, they must respect each citizen's capacity to judge political matters and her equal entitlement to have her judgment acknowledged as authoritative in determining how common life will be politically organized.

A politically egalitarian society, then, regulates matters of common concern through decision-making processes that respect equally each citizen's authority, or jurisdiction. A theory of political equality has two main aims. First, it explains why we have reasons to create or maintain a politically egalitarian society. A theory of political equality need not establish that these reasons to support political equality are always decisive. Perhaps sometimes other considerations of justice cancel or outweigh our reasons to support politically egalitarian institutions and practices. But political equality would hold little interest if it did not generate reasons of considerable strength and broad applicability. A theory of political

---

1. Locke, *Second Treatise of Government*, § 54, 304. Locke describes this equality of authority as the core sense in which people are naturally equal.

equality must show why political equality matters. That is the task of this first part of the book.

A second aim of a theory of political equality is to explain how collective decision-making procedures can satisfy the requirements of political equality. This involves, first, showing that it is possible to have a decision-making procedure that respects equally the authority of all citizens. We must show that this is possible even when, as is virtually always the case, citizens disagree about what to do. In this, a theory of political equality faces, in a democratic form, the general problem of social contract theory: how common decision making could be consistent with the equality of all citizens. The problem is democratic because a theory of political equality involves a more demanding and particular conception of equality than do some versions of traditional contract theory.

A theory of political equality also aims to explain which institutions and practices, in which circumstances, do or do not satisfy the requirements of political equality, and why. If the theory can provide such guidance, it will help us address controversies about the design of political decision-making systems. This is the aim of the second and third parts of this book.

These two aims—justifying demands for political equality, and explaining what political equality requires—might be pursued independently of each other. I will argue, however, that we must pursue the aims together. There would be no point to arguing about which decision-making procedures are fair, in the sense of being egalitarian, if that fairness did not matter. And we cannot understand properly what fairness consists in if we do not understand why fairness matters. Without understanding why we should pursue and support political equality, we cannot understand what it requires of us.

I dedicate the rest of this chapter to arguing that political equality matters. We have strong reasons to pursue and support politically egalitarian arrangements. The reasons are strong in the sense that they apply in virtually all circumstances, and that they can only be outweighed or defeated by reasons of considerable urgency. I will argue, if not decisively prove, that these countervailing reasons not to respect the demands of political equality are rare, or at least not a standard feature of social life. Generally speaking, we ought to live together democratically.

II. The Instrumental Value of Political Equality

I argued in chapter 1 that we have strong reasons to support substantively equal social relations, to the extent that the ideal of a society of equals is an attractive one, and to the extent that we should object to various forms of inequality. This way of thinking about the value of general social equality illuminates two ways of arguing for political equality.

Political equality contributes to, or promotes, equal social relations in two senses. The two ideals are causally connected and constitutively connected.[2] Political equality causally contributes to the existence of egalitarian relations, understanding the latter as something distinct from political equality itself. We have an ideal of relations among equals. Citizens who enjoy political equality, the causal argument goes, generally also develop and maintain relations that better approximate that egalitarian ideal than do politically unequal citizens. The experience of interacting as equal authorities over matters of common concern leads citizens to view one another as social equals in general—people entitled to equal respect, concern, and treatment in all facets of social life.

This causal claim is subject to empirical falsification. Perhaps political equality does not, in fact, meaningfully promote egalitarian relationships beyond the political domain. Convincing data would be hard to gather, since these claims are about what would follow from highly ideal political systems, with which we have little experience. Our credence in the causal argument should be limited by the fact that the connection between political and social equality is somewhat speculative. Still, we may be able to infer some relevant conclusions from studies of less ideal systems.

A strong version of this causal claim states that political equality is causally necessary for social equality—that is, social equality, while conceptually distinct from democracy, is impossible without it. People cannot, or will not, sustain lasting, reliable relationships as equals if they do not respect one another as equal authorities. Thus, the argument goes, it is impossible to sustain a society in which some few egalitarian aristocrats monopolize political authority, but people in general enjoy equal relationships characterized by fairness, fraternity and sorority, and so on—even when they interact with the aristocrats. A weaker version of the argument holds that, while social equality is possible without political equality, political equality makes social equality much more likely to arise and easier to sustain. Even this weaker argument would, if sound, give us strong reason to support political equality, if we have strong reasons to support social equality.

The second sense in which political equality contributes to, or promotes, social equality is constitutively. Social equality involves people

---

2. On causal and constitutive relations, see Pettit, *Republicanism*, ch. 3, and *Robust Demands*, 144–45.

reliably treating one another in accord with the norms of egalitarian relationships. Part of what it is to treat people in such a way—that is, as people of equal status—is to treat them as equal authorities, at least with respect to certain common matters. Sharing authority equally is an essential part of respecting and expressing their equal standing. We respect that equality not just through fair treatment (in the distribution of benefits and burdens, for instance), conventional expressions of courtesy, and so on, but also, and importantly, by acknowledging others' equal entitlement to shape what we do together. Equality requires renouncing any claim to general precedence in authority, as well as precedence in entitlements to certain forms of treatment by others. Political equality, then, partially constitutes relationships of social equality. A strong version of this claim states that political equality is a necessary constituent of social equality—that is, fully egalitarian relations are never present unless those relations involve equal sharing of authority in the relevant domain. A weaker version states that some kinds of valuable egalitarian relations are partially constituted by political equality, though it leaves open the possibility that there may be different kinds of egalitarian relations, some of which do not involve political equality.[3] Whether the strong or the weak form of constitutive connection holds, political equality is valuable because it manifests, however partially, a valuable and perhaps obligatory way of relating to one another.

I argue in the next section that we have strong reasons to support political equality because it partially constitutes a valuable form of social equality. In the rest of this section, I focus on the claim that we should support political equality because it causally promotes valuable social equality.

Political equality helps promote egalitarian relationships by publicly manifesting a commitment to equal authority, which likely has some influence over other social norms and practices, and by raising some political barriers to the accumulation of wealth and power by a few. Even if democratic institutions are not sufficient to secure wider social equality, they likely play an important part in securing such equality when it is secure, and in preventing some of the worst kinds of inequality. I will not here attempt to marshal and evaluate all the available evidence about the connection between political and social equality. I simply note that the

---

3. This leaves open the possibility that in some cases political equality would not promote social equality. If a society enjoyed social equality without political equality, it is conceivable that introducing political equality could (causally) undermine the egalitarian relations in that society. In that case, political equality would not promote social equality. The arguments for political equality I make in this chapter, however, show that this possibility is remote.

connection is plausible and worth further investigation. The arguments I make in the rest of this chapter about the ways in which political equality helps constitute wider equality also give reason to think that political equality helps to cause distinct forms of equality.

Institutions and practices satisfying the demands of political equality may promote many goods, such as stability, peace, respect for individual rights, aggregate wealth, and so on. To the extent that they do, we have reasons to support those institutions and practices. Why focus on the causal connection to equality?

There may be many strong instrumental reasons to support institutions and practices compatible with political equality. I focus on the causal connection to social equality because those other, not-equality-related ends rarely give us reason to value or pursue political equality *as political equality*. They do not give us reason to strive consciously to arrange our institutions and practices in an egalitarian or fair way. They do, by hypothesis, give us reason to strive consciously to arrange our institutions and practices in ways that happen to accord with the demands of political equality, because of the good outcomes that will result. But they do not provide any direct reason to care about political equality per se.[4] For all that these instrumental arguments show, if there were other, politically inegalitarian ways to pursue the good ends, we should pursue them that way. At any rate, we would not, on the strength of these reasons alone, have cause to worry about whether our institutions or practices were fair or equal ones. If we were faced with a choice between various institutional arrangements, it would be a distraction, from the perspective of these reasons alone, to ask which of the arrangements were most fair. The real question would be about which arrangements produced the good ends. As a result, there would be no need for a theory of political equality that explained which decision-making institutions and practices were, in fact, egalitarian.

This result does not hold for the claim that political equality causally produces social equality. If political equality produces social equality, I suggest that is largely because political and social equality are homologous: they share a similar structure. Politically egalitarian institutions and

---

4. We might have indirect reason, if we find political equality a useful heuristic to use when aiming at non-equality-related good ends. There may also be another kind of indirect reason, if citizens generally happen to value political equality (perhaps without good reason), and providing citizens the kinds of institutions they value helps promote the good ends (such as stability, civil peace, and resulting wealth production). But in neither case is there a reason to pursue political equality because political equality itself produces the good ends.

practices causally promote relations of social equality, because those institutions and practices are egalitarian. This is one example of the general, long-recognized truth that some causal relationships obtain at least partly in virtue of a homology between cause and effect. Where such homology exists, an analysis of this homologous structure, and its manifestation in both cause and effect, is useful in guiding practical reasoning about how to produce the desired consequences. Consider Platonic arguments about harmony in music and in the soul, or justice in the soul and the city. In both cases, Plato suggests that different entities can exhibit a similar structure (both souls and musical pieces or chords can be harmonious; both souls and cities can be just). Moreover, partly in virtue of this shared structure, entities exhibiting that structure can help produce that structure in other entities—exposure to musical harmony can help produce harmonious souls, and just cities can help produce just souls (and possibly vice versa). When this is true, we have reason to understand and aim for the right structure in the causal entity, in order to produce the desired structure in the affected entity. We have reason to understand musical harmony in order to produce harmonious souls (apart from whatever intrinsic reasons there are to value musical harmony). There is no need to endorse any metaphysical conception of Platonic forms to believe that some entities exhibiting a certain structure can help induce a similar structure in other entities, in significant part because of that structure. So, for example, relationships exhibiting political equality can induce wider social equality in relationships, in significant part because of the initial, political equality.

The experience of living in a politically egalitarian society, and participating in collective decision making on equal terms with other citizens, leads people to act in ways that support and constitute other forms of social equality. This is a standard view of democratic theorists of various kinds, including critics of democracy; a version of this view is held by Plato, Aristotle, Rousseau, Tocqueville, and J. S. Mill.[5] It is not merely coincidence, according to all versions of this view, that democratic decision-making institutions tend to promote other forms of social equality (including by promoting hostility to various forms of inequality): it is specifically the egalitarianism of the political constitution and the practices that accompany it that promote social egalitarianism. Political democracy contributes to democracy in a wider social sense.

---

5. Plato, *Republic*, bk. 8; Aristotle, *Politics*, bk. 6; Rousseau, *Of the Social Contract*, bk. 2, ch. 4; Toqueville, introduction to *Democracy in America*; Mill, *Considerations on Representative Government*, ch. 3, and *Subjection of Women*, pt. 2.

If democratic institutions and practices promote social equality in virtue of their egalitarianism, then we have reason to care about just how egalitarian those institutions and practices are, and we have reason to aim directly for political equality. Accordingly, this instrumental argument, if successful, would establish the need for a theory of political equality that identifies what makes institutions and practices truly egalitarian.

III. The Intrinsic Value of Political Equality

Our reasons to support and pursue political equality are not limited to instrumental ones. Political equality is valuable for its own sake. The concept of intrinsic value is philosophically vexed, but I do not believe the current argument depends on any controversial stand on the nature of value. By intrinsically valuable, I mean just that there are reasons to value political equality whether or not it causally produces other good ends or outcomes.[6] We have reason to be democrats whatever outcomes we expect democratic institutions and practices to produce.

At the beginning of the last section I outlined one reason why political equality is intrinsically valuable—namely, that relations of political equality partly constitute relations of social equality among citizens. Part of what social equality involves is political equality. Equality involves and is partly made up by democracy.

The core argument of this section is that political equality is valuable in its own right, even if, for some reason, it is not a constituent of some more encompassing value of social equality. For instance, if social equality were possible without political equality (meaning that only the weaker form of constitutive connection described in the last section applied), we would nevertheless have reason to pursue and support political equality in particular. Similarly, we should value political equality even in societies that are otherwise socially unequal—in which case the political equality would not partly constitute some wider equality. Even in such an unequal society, equality in collective decision-making procedures would have considerable value.

As I mentioned in chapter 1, this argument that democracy is valuable because it manifests equality is both old and enjoying recent philosophical

---

6. This thin conception of intrinsic value allows me to remain agnostic among the claims that we have reason to pursue and manifest political equality because it is good in itself, that it is derivatively good because it is partly constituted by other goods, and that we have reason to pursue and manifest political equality because of some obligation that does not depend on any obligation to produce goodness or value.

elaboration.[7] There, I mentioned two remaining challenges to this idea: explaining systematically why the kind of equality constituted by political equality is valuable, and explaining what exactly it entails. In this chapter, I address this first challenge. Following the structure developed in chapter 1, I first develop a positive vision of the reasons to value relationships in which authority is shared on equal terms. Then I argue negatively, explaining why we have reasons to object to political inequality—that is, oligarchy.

III.A. CIVIC FRIENDSHIP AND THE POLITICALLY EGALITARIAN IDEAL

To see the positive attraction of political equality, consider, as we did in the last chapter, friendship. Friendly relations are constituted in part by several norms that the friends recognize (if sometimes only implicitly). Friends treat each other with sensitivity and attention, benevolence and goodwill, and forms of courtesy. Friendship involves mutual recognition of equality—for instance, by each friend renouncing any general precedence over the other. Friendship need not involve close intimacy or warmth at all times. Friends can sometimes be upset or angry with one another without ceasing to be friends, or to treat each other as friends. If someone started to claim a general precedence over another, however—by demanding favors without ever reciprocating, always claiming a greater share of goods available to the friends, requiring forms of courtesy without extending that courtesy, and so on—that person would not be a good friend, and perhaps would not count as a (true) friend at all. From this observation that true or good friendship requires equality, we can extrapolate, I suggested in the last chapter, that citizens in general have reason to pursue and support equal social relations.

Here I add that friendship involves, as a constitutive norm, equal sharing of authority over matters common to the friends. Friends exhibit equality in their relationships not only by reciprocating benevolent actions and sharing goods, but also by sharing equally the authority to decide what they will do together.[8] Friends are in this sense political equals. Calling friends "political" equals may seem overstated or silly if one thinks of "political" as primarily referring to matters common to the polis at large,

---

7. See Kolodny, "Rule over None II"; Viehoff, "Democratic Equality"; Anderson, "Democracy"; Christiano, *Constitution of Equality*; Tocqueville, introduction to *Democracy in America*; Rousseau, *Of the Social Contract*, bk. 2, ch. 4; Aristotle, *Politics*, bk. 3, ch. 9, 97–98 (1280a7–24); and ch. 1, § I.

8. See Scheffler, "Practice of Equality," 27.

which matters may not come up much in a relationship of two friends. But if we understand "political" as referring to authority relations—very roughly, who has the right or power to determine who does what—then identifying friends as political equals reveals an important truth about friendship. While friends obviously do not share authority over everything each friend does, when it comes to matters that are relevantly common to the friends, or part of the friendship, good or true friends determine what they will do together on equal terms.

I confess I find this claim about the centrality of political equality, or equality of authority, to friendship to be intuitive and fairly obvious. It strikes me as at least as obvious as the claim that one is not a good friend if one always takes the cake and leaves the crumbs for one's supposed friend, or that one is not a good friend if one demands deference and humility from one's supposed friend while treating her with arrogance and condescension. I find this claim somewhat difficult to argue for in a way that would be persuasive to a reader who does not share these intuitions. One way to clarify the point (if not, perhaps, to provide further argument) is to consider what it would mean for a supposed friend to reject this sort of equality. Someone who always dictated to his companion what they would be doing together, and never gave meaningful deliberative attention or deference to her judgments about what to do, would, I judge, be an obnoxious companion and no friend. (He might be less obnoxious if he did not presume to be a friend, but instead properly occupied some role that involved inequality of authority, such as a parent of a young child. I will discuss shortly whether we should consider it proper for citizens generally to relate on such hierarchical terms. For now, I emphasize that such a relationship is no real friendship, and that such behavior in a supposed friend would warrant resentment.) His companionship would be unfriendly even if the autocratic "friend" made his decisions in ways that otherwise promoted equally the interests of both companions (deciding on activities that the two equally enjoyed over the long run, and sharing goods equally, say), and even if he otherwise exhibited friendly courtesy.[9] Patriarchal marriage ideals sometimes recommended this sort of relationship between a benevolent and courteous but autocratic husband and a deferential but well-cared-for wife. Feminists are right to criticize such ideals (and such marriages), in part because the political inequality

---

9. For a similar claim about loving relationships (though focusing more on respecting the beloved's right to set her own ends than on respecting authority over matters common to the relationship), see Ebels-Duggan, "Against Beneficence."

involved makes it impossible for spouses to enjoy friendship, the goods of which necessarily involve equal authority.[10]

Political equality between friends need not be formal or explicit. There need not be avowed, regular procedures for deciding what to do together. The equality could even be "virtual" in the sense that one friend generally defers to the other's suggestions about what to do or how to share goods. This could still count as a relationship in which authority were equally shared, so long as the deferential friend could refuse to defer, that the refusal would be respected, and that there is suitably common knowledge between the friends about these facts. The fact that friendship requires political equality does not mean that people who have particular desires and a need to plan cannot be friends with people who are usually happy to just go along. It does mean, however, that no friend should be expected to go along just because the other says so.

Equality of authority among friends is valuable, and is an important constituent of friendship, even if in some cases one friend rarely gets her way, in the sense that the other friend or friends rarely do what she judges they should. For example, one person might often be in a minority among a group of friends when it comes to her preferences or judgments about what to do. She might be the only one who likes going to a certain kind of restaurant, say, or the only one who likes going to the symphony. So it might be that the group rarely goes to such restaurants, or to the symphony, in favor of other group activities chosen by the other friends. But this need not involve any unfriendly inequality of authority. If the friends sincerely and recognizably attend to the judgments of their idiosyncratic comrade, the friends may genuinely share authority, and may be genuine friends. Equality, and friendship, may require making special efforts to be sure that the friend who is usually in the minority is properly heard, her authority within the friendship properly respected, and that her acquiescence in the decisions of others is not taken for granted. (The friends also must take care that they do not neglect the interests of the idiosyncratic friend—for instance, by causing her to get much less pleasure from the relationship than others do. This is an egalitarian concern, though not directly a concern about equality of authority.) This may mean agreeing to go to the symphony together every once in a while, even if most of the

---

10. There are, of course, many other reasons to criticize such patriarchal ideals, paralleled to some extent by the objections to oligarchy I discuss below. As I mentioned in ch. 1, § II.A.3, equality of authority is an essential part of the explanation of how friendships (and good marriages) can exist among people who are unequal in resources or talents.

other friends would otherwise prefer not. But there are also ways to respect her authority short of doing what she judges they ought to do, from taking care to talk seriously about her suggestions to deferring to her more fine-grained suggestions about how to execute a common plan (going to a baseball game) the broad contours of which she did not initially endorse. These are relatively familiar features of friendships, though most of us probably do not explicitly think of them. We know how to respect the authority of our friends, we often know when our supposed friends are not respecting our authority within the relationship, and we worry when we think they might not be. We can distinguish a relationship in which we are respected, though we do not often get our way, from a relationship in which we do not get our way because the others do not care what we think or want—or one in which we get our way despite others not caring about what we think or want, because we happen to share their judgments about what we ought to do. If I am right about this, then we know, roughly, that friendship requires equal authority, and that equal authority is distinct from equal success in actually determining what the participants in the relationship do.

These reflections suggest that it is a mistake to think, as Niko Kolodny and Daniel Viehoff have both suggested, that the absence of authority can be sufficient for (and, for Viehoff, perhaps characteristic of) valuable, equal relations.[11] Certainly many vices of oligarchy can be avoided through the total (and thus equal) absence of authority. But if my account of friendship is correct, good relations involving sustained interaction and coordination require not merely the absence of unequal power or authority, but also the presence of mutual respect for equal authority in decision making about what to do together. Libertarian friendship—just happening to coordinate to the extent that preferences coincide, with no deference to what one's supposed friend judges the friends ought to do—involves a kind of equality, but it is a thin, noncommittal friendship, not worthy of the name.[12]

---

11. Kolodny, "Rule over None II," 313–14; Viehoff, "Democratic Equality," 340, 351, 371.

12. I believe that Kolodny and Viehoff reject equal, positive authority as a necessary constituent of good, equal relations because they (understandably) have in mind standard conceptions of authority as command. I explain in ch. 4 why these conceptions are not helpful for explaining the nature and value of political equality. For present purposes it is enough to notice that my account of friends sharing authority does not require obedience to one another's commands. This also means that, contrary to Kolodny ("Rule over None II," 295) and Viehoff ("Democratic Equality," 352), equality of power (as distinct from authority) has a complicated and ambivalent place in an account of equal relations, since the requirements of equal power and of equal, positive authority are sometimes in tension, as I explain in pt. II of this book.

Friendships are valuable relationships that are partly constituted by equality, including equal sharing of authority in matters relevant to the relationship. A similar valuable relationship exists when people generally interact on equal terms, including on terms of political equality. We have reason to treat one another as citizens in a full, democratic sense, as people with whom we share authority on equal terms in matters of common concern. By granting one another shared authority on equal terms, we manifest civic friendship. Like ordinary friendship, civic friendship is partly constituted by general norms of social equality: reciprocal goodwill and benevolence, the rejection of general precedence, and so on. Also like ordinary friendship, civic friendship requires specifically political equality—in the civic case, "political" not only in the sense of sharing authority, but also in that the domain of shared authority comprises matters of concern to the polity as a whole. Treating someone as a civic friend—as a democratic citizen—requires acknowledging her right to share equally in determining what the citizens will do together. Civic friendship does not require constant intimacy or warmth. It is consistent with some emotional distance, as long as that distance is compatible with motivation to observe the norms of the relationship, and with occasional anger or resentment, as long as there is some mutual commitment to repair.

Many of the attractions of ordinary friendship should attract us to civic friendship. Relationships with fellow citizens, even in small states, inevitably lack the intimacy of close, or even casual, friendships. They lack some of the goods that come with intimately relating to others on friendly terms. But the goods of civic friendship are nevertheless substantial. As I noted in the last chapter, Tocqueville claims that democratic rights ground confidence and "reciprocal courtesy" in our general interactions with others. Political equality constitutes (and causes) good relations with others, even if we interact with them only episodically. These relations exhibit good features even when they involve conflict or dislike, if the conflict and dislike are limited and regulated by commitment to the egalitarian norms of the relationship. Civic friendship involves mutual respect and restraint that sets parameters that cabin conflict and dislike, as well as setting foundations for cooperation and goodwill. So civic friendship may be good because it promotes the development of ordinary friendships among citizens. Good (that is, democratic) citizens make good friends. But we have reason to enjoy civic friendship even if it does not promote ordinary friendship. It is itself a valuable social relationship.

The reciprocal courtesy and respect entailed by political equality are themselves good ways of relating. Tocqueville also emphasizes the confidence of citizens in a flourishing democracy, and here he once again identifies a valuable aspect of politically egalitarian relations. Respecting the equal political status of citizens supports the self-respect of those citizens. Politically egalitarian decision-making practices respect each citizen's authority. (In doing so, they respect each citizen's autonomy, as I shall argue in the next section. That is one reason why this is an important, generally obligatory, form of respect.) Granting citizens this authority over common matters publicly affirms their capacity for practical judgment, and their entitlement to exercise that capacity. This supports their self-respect, understood here as their belief that they have the capacity and the entitlement to decide upon and execute their own life plan (consistently with their obligations to others).[13] Authority over oneself and shared authority over others are both part of one's jurisdiction, to return to Locke's term, and involve similar (often the same) practical capacities. Publicly affirming one's jurisdiction over shared matters thus supports one's confidence in one's authority over one's own life—an important constituent of self-respect.

Politically egalitarian institutions and practices therefore may cause citizens to enjoy self-respect—that is, cause them to believe in their capacity and entitlement to decide upon and execute their life plans. Political equality may be instrumentally valuable for that reason. But this connection to individual self-respect also reveals another aspect of political equality's intrinsic value. If it is good for citizens to enjoy self-respect, that is partly because it is good for them to enjoy the status of persons who have the relevant authority over their own lives. (When they have self-respect, they effectively believe that they have that status, and are motivated to act accordingly. It is good for them to have these beliefs and motivations because it is good for them to have this status.) This is not just good in the sense that it might improve the person's welfare to enjoy this status—say, because his life will go better if he has general authority over much of it. It is good in the sense that it is fitting or apt for him to enjoy the status: he is the kind of being who is entitled to that status. (I am more or less assuming this is true, in line with a wide variety of broadly liberal views.)[14] If it is good and fitting for someone to enjoy some status,

---

13. Here I follow John Rawls, though I focus on the way in which political equality in particular, rather than just social relations in general, supports self-respect. See *Theory of Justice*, § 29, 155–58.

14. I emphasize the broadness of the sense of liberalism here. Many views that their proponents would label conservative or socialist or communitarian, say, and thus in important respects antiliberal, would share support for the claim that it is fitting for individuals

it is generally good and fitting for others to respect that status, unless that somehow requires them to fail to respect the morally authoritative status of others. Since it is good and fitting for people to respect themselves as authors of their own lives, and because, assuming something approximating equal freedom is possible, this does not require denying anyone else's authoritative status, it is good and fitting to respect that status. Political equality is good in part because it does just that: it fittingly treats people as one should expect authors of their own lives to be treated when it comes to matters of common concern.

If this argument is sound, politically egalitarian relations are good even if they do not cause all citizens actually to enjoy self-respect (because some suffer depression, for instance, or because there are other features of the social world—unjust public policies, say—that undermine self-respect), because they fittingly treat citizens as persons worthy of self-respect. We have reason to treat people this way even if it does not cause them to enjoy that self-respect, and even if failing to treat them this way would not cause them to lose their self-respect (perhaps because they were especially resilient).[15] To return to Tocqueville's terms, we have reason to treat our fellow citizens as persons entitled to confidence. Granting them democratic authority is one part of doing just that.

Together, these goods of politically egalitarian relationships constitute a positive vision of a society of political equals, and thus support the argument that we have strong reason to support and maintain democratic institutions and practices. One might object, however, that even if politically egalitarian relationships do have these good features, some forms of politically hierarchical relationships may have as good or better features. Can we not say as much or more on behalf of an oligarchic ideal as we can about a democratic one?

The primary justifications for oligarchy—the rule of the few—come in two broad forms: first, that oligarchy produces better outcomes, and, second, that oligarchy is itself intrinsically good. These arguments can be compatible, as in Plato's argument in the *Republic* that rule by

---

to have a great extent of authority over their own lives. Some views are illiberal even with respect to this thin conception of liberalism. My argument for the value of political equality on the grounds that it supports self-respect would therefore not appeal to those who endorse such illiberal views.

15. Thus, arguments that political equality is not necessary for self-respect (or for developing certain capacities as an agent) do not undermine the argument for political equality. Cf. Wall, "Rawls"; Brennan, *Against Democracy*, ch. 4.

philosophers both produces just outcomes and itself constitutes a just (and therefore good) relation between citizens.

The instrumental argument for oligarchy (presented, in this guise, as aristocracy, in the sense of the rule of those who produce good results)[16] is probably the most influential argument. This supposedly good feature of oligarchic organization does not refute the intrinsic goodness of political equality. The typical argument asserts that, whether political equality is good or not, oligarchy produces sufficiently better results to outweigh the intrinsic and instrumental goods of equality. My aim is to show that we have strong reasons to support political equality, meaning that we generally have such reasons, and they can only be outweighed or canceled by reasons of considerable urgency. If the oligarchic argument is only that there are sometimes reasons of such great urgency that do in fact outweigh the claims of political equality, my aim would still be achieved.

The oligarchic argument is usually more ambitious than this. It is that some form of oligarchy (for instance, rule by the most virtuous or most judicious) is generally preferable to political equality. Thorough evaluation of this claim requires a theory of justice and a good deal of evidence. But there are good reasons to doubt the claim without undertaking such a comprehensive inquiry. For one thing, the instrumental attitude itself tends to undermine some of the goods of political equality. If the quality of relations is determined in part by participants' firm commitment to the norms of the relationship, a contingent, instrumental attitude precludes full enjoyment of egalitarian relations.[17] Moreover, we often have reason to object to inequalities even if those inequalities promote better results, by some metric, than equality. We often bristle when others presume to give us orders even when there is good reason to think that following the orders would make things go better for us than making decisions on our own. I will argue in the next section that this resentment is often warranted: however much good others might do us by directing our wills, denying our authority often objectionably fails to respect our autonomy. This can be true both when others deny our entitlements to authority over our own lives, and when they deny our entitlements to share authority equally over common matters. This should be familiar from interpersonal friendships: a supposed friend who presumed to order another around

---

16. This is distinct from aristocracy in the sense of the rule of those who are themselves good. Aristotle notices the distinction. *Politics*, bk. 3, ch. 7.

17. I pursue this argument further in "Against Instrumentalism about Democracy." On the importance of robustness to relational quality, see Pettit, *Robust Demands*.

would not be treating the latter as a friend even if her orders would be for the best for both of them. Often, this is enough to make it wrong to claim such unequal authority.

To argue that we ought to decide matters democratically is not to argue that any outcome a democratic process produces is just. Democratic citizens have obligations of justice beyond their obligations to respect the political equality of their fellow citizens. They often fail to meet these obligations. At best for the oligarch, this means that in some circumstances the goods of political equality should be sacrificed for other ends. But this would be a considerable sacrifice. Political equality has intrinsic superiority to oligarchy. We should pursue just ends through just procedures—that is, if my arguments succeed, through democratic procedures. Even if instrumental oligarchs are correct that in some cases the obligation to pursue just ends outweighs or cancels our obligation to pursue our ends through just procedures, it would be still better to satisfy both obligations simultaneously.[18] Oligarchy is always nonideal. It always leaves moral traces of its compromise, in the form of obligations for democratic reform and obligations of repair to those denied equal authority.

One final point about oligarchic instrumentalism: quite apart from philosophical questions about the weight of different values, we face practical problems of institutional design. Good "constitutional engineering" in large part involves overcoming moral dilemmas by designing institutions and developing practices that avoid them—for instance, egalitarian procedures that reliably lead to good outcomes. This can only be done well, however, by attending to both horns of the potential moral dilemma. So an account of political equality is desirable even for those sensitive to weighty goods that could in principle be achieved by oligarchic institutions.

What of the claim that oligarchy is intrinsically good? There are many possible varieties of this argument; I will consider one representative version. The basic idea is that some hierarchical social arrangements are good for all involved, in part because they involve suitable (if different and unequal) forms of respect appropriate to all persons given their roles or positions in the social order. Those higher in the order—those with more power, authority, or wealth, for instance—may expect certain forms of deference, but this is appropriate, as long as they reciprocate according to norms of care and courtesy to those below them. If the superiors observe these appropriate forms of noblesse oblige and condescension, everyone in the society is respected in a way fitting to their social role. What constitute

---

18. Elizabeth Anderson notices this point: "Democracy," 225.

the appropriate norms of conduct depends on the particular argument for hierarchy at issue: the precise norms could differ between a perfectionist vision of the rational ruling the less rational and an argument for a divinely ordained hierarchical chain of being, for instance. But the basic idea is available to all versions of the argument: what matters is not respect of everyone's equal status, but respect of everyone's appropriate status, combined with some claim that social statuses are appropriately arranged in some hierarchical form.[19]

As a small aside, I doubt hierarchical societies ever exhibit universal (or even near-universal) adherence to the norms regulating the treatment of the inferior by the superior. Instead, hierarchical ordering makes it easy for such norms to be flouted, and for superiors to dominate and oppress inferiors, even if this is not countenanced by the hierarchical vision. Perhaps it is not fair to hold this against hierarchical ideals. Any ideal can be abused, and this fact does not necessarily mean we do not have reason to achieve the ideal. Near-universal observation of egalitarian norms is also rare. Still, there is an asymmetry between egalitarian and hierarchical social relations. People in the lower ranks of hierarchal societies (which, typically, is a substantial majority of them) are much more vulnerable to such violations than are people in egalitarian societies. They are more vulnerable in two senses: violations of norms defining respect for lower-status individuals are more likely, because those individuals have less capacity to hold norm violators to account, and violations are more consequential, because of the power imbalance between social superiors and inferiors, and the generally more precarious position of those with few resources and low social standing.

This vulnerability to violations of respect norms in hierarchical societies is itself an objectionable feature of hierarchical relations. There are separate and important questions about what to do when we know there will not be compliance to some norms—questions of so-called "nonideal theory"—but we can set these aside for the benefit of the hierarchical position. The asymmetry of vulnerability to noncompliance between hierarchical and egalitarian societies is a consideration against the former, however, even if the noncompliance—that is, the disrespectful treatment—does not manifest. The fact that inferiors in a hierarchical society are vulnerable to such violations, that they have such little protection beyond the goodwill

---

19. A weaker version of the argument holds only that respecting everyone's status matters, and remains agnostic on whether people should enjoy equal or unequal status. (It may just be a matter of convention, for instance.)

and conscientiousness of their superiors, gives those inferiors reason to reject the hierarchical ordering.[20] People who might be superiors in a hierarchical society, but who find themselves in an egalitarian one, have no reason of comparable strength. In the egalitarian society, they are granted various forms of consideration and respect. These forms do not include the deference and material rewards to which they might be entitled in a hierarchical society, but this deficit provides a much weaker reason to reject the egalitarian ordering than does the vulnerability of the inferior provide the latter to reject the hierarchical ordering.[21] The loyal vassal has stronger reason to reject even the most ideal feudal society, despite the compassion and grace of his liege, than does the person of great rationality or holiness or martial skill have to reject the chafing limits of an egalitarian order. In this sense, a hierarchical society is less intrinsically valuable than an egalitarian one. We have reason to pursue the latter rather than the former.[22]

I acknowledge that these considerations cannot decisively reject claims for the greater intrinsic value of hierarchical relationships. Any particular hierarchical ideal could bring with it particular reasons for the hierarchical ordering it endorses. It is at least possible that those reasons would be even stronger than the reasons the putatively inferior have to object to the proposed hierarchy. What we can say on behalf of egalitarian relationships,

---

20. I am influenced here by Philip Pettit's work on domination, as I mention in my discussion of objections to inequality in the last chapter and this one.

21. Niko Kolodny also notes what he considers an asymmetry between the objections of the inferior to a hierarchical ordering—even if it is a "chivalric paradise"—and the objections of putative superiors to an egalitarian ordering. See "Rule over None II," 301–3. I have tried to provide some reasons to support that claim of asymmetry.

22. If a society has a well-established hierarchical ordering, and generally the norms of status-respect are observed, then there may be reasons to preserve the social order, if attempts to reform in an egalitarian direction are likely to fail, or create very harmful forms of disorder or strife. But this would not deny the point that the egalitarian order is superior, and that members of the hierarchical society had reasons (reasons not canceled by the prudential considerations) to become more egalitarian. On surviving reasons to reform, I am influenced by Julius, *Reconstruction*. Kolodny makes a similar point about hierarchical societies having reasons not to reform, though my position may be stronger than his in insisting that there are persisting reasons to reform. See "Rule over None II," 302–3. I am also less convinced than Kolodny seems to be of the relevance of the fact that members of a hierarchical society have reasons of partiality to prefer the hierarchical relationships they already enjoy. I doubt such reasons are strong enough to counter the reasons members of inferior classes have to reject those relationships. Tocqueville was right that the disruption of some aristocratic relationships (between masters and servants, say) involved the loss of some valuable relationships. But he was also right that the democratic argument for the well-being of the majority represented a stronger claim. See *Democracy in America*, 245.

however, is that there are strong reasons to support and pursue them, and that there are considerable reasons to reject hierarchical alternatives. I have discussed our positive reasons to support politically egalitarian relations of civic friendship. Let us now turn to the objections to oligarchy.

III.B. THE VICES OF OLIGARCHY

One simple way to think about the problem of unequal political status—to get a sense of its seriousness and some of the identifying features of lower political rank—is to consider what a straightforward denial of equality of jurisdiction might mean. Since the worst abuses of the Jim Crow South ended, the United States rarely sees debates about political institutions in which any partisans publicly and explicitly embrace any claim for general inequality of political status.[23] Such inequalities as persist are—depending on how charitably we interpret their proponents—inadvertent, negligent, or masked by appeals to some account of political equality that attempts to justify the inequalities. As a result, in the United States—and similarly in other long-standing democracies—we rarely confront full-throated appeals to inequality of political authority (though such appeals are not so historically distant). Still, it may be helpful to consider the nature of the disrespect expressed by such appeals, so we have a better sense of what political inequality amounts to, and so we can better identify it in its more subtle contemporary guises.

The most direct way to establish political inequality would be to deny some citizens political authority altogether. This would create a political underclass of citizens. The precise meaning of this inequality—the precise nature of the disrespect it entailed—could vary by the context (for instance, it might vary according to the publicly avowed reasons for the inequality). But the inequality would certainly amount to a degrading public judgment of the unworthiness or unfitness of those excluded as judges of political matters.[24] The denial of a citizen's jurisdiction indicates her untrustworthiness as a responsible authority over common life. Demotion to a lower political class also reflects and expresses a stigma that those excluded are outcasts with whom it is not appropriate for those in higher

---

23. Perhaps the closest examples involve laws permanently disenfranchising felons. The disenfranchisement of children and noncitizens are also interesting cases.

24. Sometimes disfavored citizens in these cases might deny that there is anything degrading about such a judgment. I do not believe this changes the fact that the judgment is degrading. I discuss this issue, with reference to the exclusion of women from the suffrage in the United States, in ch. 5.

political castes to share the activities and responsibilities of rule. (Such demotion might well create such a stigma if it did not already exist.) The denial of jurisdiction might also indicate that the outcast citizens were not worthy of equal concern: given the reasonable view that a person's own judgments are at least helpful in indicating their interests, a refusal to consider their judgments may indicate not only disrespect for the judgments but also lack of concern for the citizens themselves.

John Stuart Mill famously doubted that political inequality necessarily involved any objectionable disrespect: "Every one has a right to feel insulted by being made a nobody, and stamped as of no account at all. No one but a fool, and only a fool of a peculiar description, feels offended by the acknowledgement that there are others whose opinion, and even whose wish, is entitled to a greater amount of consideration than his." That we should accord greater weight to the opinions of the wise is a proposition we are rightly, says Mill, "accustomed to acquiesce in."[25] Set aside the difficulty of holding both that total exclusion (even on meritocratic grounds) is objectionably insulting, while inclusion with inequality is not. There are several reasons to reject Mill's argument.

First, political equality is consistent with Millian "acquiescence" in one sense. Equally authoritative citizens may decide that others are wise or knowledgeable or just, and exercise their authority on behalf of those judged to be their superiors—for instance, by deferring to the latter's judgments or voting as the latter prefer. Egalitarian democracy is entirely compatible with the core commonsense intuition behind Mill's argument. Thus, the intuition that some people really do know or act better is insufficient to support political inequality. We need an argument that some citizens are entitled to require such acquiescence of others, presumably on an ongoing basis, in conditions where they refuse to acquiesce voluntarily. The fact that we often freely defer to others does not provide such an argument.[26]

Second, systematically depriving people of the goods of equality, and subjecting them to (other) vices of oligarchy, is disrespectful treatment. This is the obverse of the argument that good, egalitarian relations constitutively require commonly known commitments from members in the relationship to relational norms that reliably produce the goods produced by

---

25. Mill, *Considerations on Representative Government*, 335.

26. Similarly, it is a mistake to infer from the fact that nobody has a moral permission to exercise authority unjustly to the claim that we are entitled to strip authority from those who exercise authority unjustly. Cf. Arneson, "Democracy," 40.

the relationship. The absence of such commitments constitutes disregard for others' social standing, and thus a straightforward form of disrespect.

The degrading nature of political exclusion is clearest when we distinguish respect for a person's judgment (or capacity for judgment) from respect for the person himself. The former often connotes what Darwall calls "appraisal respect," or an evaluation of the quality of the judgment or capacity at issue. When that form of respect is at issue, it is often appropriate to make hierarchical distinctions.[27] Respecting persons, however, is a form of Darwall's "recognition respect," which is not a matter of appraisal, but a matter of responding properly to another's status. I have been arguing that each citizen is entitled to a status that includes equal political authority. There is no foolishness in seeing denial of that status as a substantial form of (recognition) disrespect.

Such public establishment of lower-class citizenship requires the disempowered persons to live in a society that has literally degraded them. The society must appear to them as increasingly alien, in that its basic organizing principles are established without any authoritative input from them. Even in the most egalitarian systems, political decisions are regularly beyond our individual control. But lower-class citizens face not just the limited responsiveness inevitable in a society full of other people with other judgments, but an institutionalized unresponsiveness in which the higher-class citizens actively embrace (or culpably support) keeping the political system wholly alien from some of those subject to it. Political inequality establishes a kind of heteronomy for some citizens that affronts even modest views of political self-rule.

Political inequality denies citizen autonomy in the following specific sense. Let us distinguish "first-order" autonomy claims to determine one's actions without direct interference from "second-order" autonomy claims to determine the set of actions one may undertake. If not a logical inconsistency, there is an untenable tension between demanding respect on grounds of self-direction in the first-order case but denying the need for such respect in the second. When the actions of others substantially determine the array of options open to us, these actions *direct* our wills in the sense that they put pressure—often by giving us good reasons—to act in some ways rather than others. These actions also *implicate* our wills in the sense that they shape how we are responsible for our actions and our agency. (For instance, others' actions may make it difficult for us to avoid

---

27. Darwall, *Second-Person Standpoint*, 122–23; Arneson, "Democracy," 52; Viehoff, "Democratic Equality," 348.

contributing to the maintenance of certain social systems.) The direction and implication of our wills are not necessarily wrong; they are inevitable parts of sustained social interaction. The direction and implication have substantial effects on the exercise of our agency and our first-order autonomy, however. Respecting and honoring others' autonomy, therefore, arguably requires granting them authority over the terms according to which the direction and implication take place—in this sense, respecting their second-order autonomy. If everyone in some scheme of social interaction has equal claim to autonomy, and is equally subject to direction and implication of the will by others in the scheme, this requires equal sharing of authority over the terms of that scheme. Political inequality denies disadvantaged citizens this autonomy claim.[28]

The public degradation of lower-class citizens, and the imposition of alien rule, constitutes a substantial assault on those citizens' self-respect.[29] Such citizens may nevertheless maintain their self-respect, whether through sustenance from family or other nonpolitical associations, or through strong inner conviction. But this self-respect would persist in spite of public assaults, and its robustness among some citizens would hardly vindicate those assaults. It is unreasonable to place on some citizens the substantial burden of maintaining their self-respect under such unfavorable conditions, and unreasonable to expose them to the risk that others will develop domineering, supercilious, or other objectionably hierarchical manners of relating to them as a result of the distributive inequalities.[30]

The public degradation implied by unequal political status would poison relations between citizens. Public declarations of inequality in authority on basic political matters involve assertions of superiority and inferiority between citizens as to an important constituent of one's identity as a judging, deciding, and acting agent. In any political order, ordinary disagreements may involve assertions of superiority of judgment in the limited sense that partisans claim to be right or accurate in a way that their opponents are not. Inequalities of political status involve more substantial and profound assertions of superiority and inferiority in entitlement to authority, that span all of the citizens' particular judgments on specific questions, and the assertions are presumably of indefinite duration. This blanket assertion of inequality of jurisdiction expresses and entrenches

---

28. I pursue this argument in detail in Wilson, "Autonomy-Based Argument."
29. See Rawls, *Theory of Justice*, § 37, 205; J. Cohen, "For a Democratic Society."
30. See the argument against "stoical equality" in ch. 1, § II.D.

inequality far beyond the minimal, provisional, and occasional inequality implied by simple disagreement. The establishment of such inequality in political institutions can hardly fail to sanction and promote hierarchical relationships between citizens, however much lower-class citizens maintain, against the grain of public political culture, their own sense of self-respect.

A society of unequal political status might maintain sufficiently egalitarian relations between citizens if the laws and policies of the regime (apart from those regulating entitlements to exercise political authority) promoted social equality—perhaps by limiting the unequal distribution of wealth and other resources. Such a regime is conceivable, if historically unlikely. But even if the upper-political-class citizens were scrupulous about promoting equal treatment of all citizens, such regimes would find it difficult to cabin the disrespectful nature of the regime's political inequality. The regime we are imagining manages in fact to be equally responsive to all citizens' interests. But by institutionalizing its unresponsiveness to those citizens' judgments, the regime fails to provide any safeguards, apart from the wills and judgments of upper-class citizens, to ensure that this equal treatment will continue. A refusal to respond to citizens' judgments indicates a public willingness to leave them especially vulnerable to unequal treatment. Present equality of treatment cannot erase this vulnerability, nor can it erase the hierarchical social relationships inevitably encouraged by the creation of this vulnerability of some citizens to the judgments of their political superiors.[31]

Political inequality, then, displays and engenders disrespect toward lower-class citizens in a number of ways. Institutions establishing inequality of political status publicly deliver degrading judgments as to the incapacity of some citizens as agents, they reflect and promote social stigma, they establish over some citizens an alien rule that denies autonomy to a degree far beyond ordinary political or legal restrictions, they assault citizen self-respect, and they expose some citizens to a vulnerability in a way that expresses disrespect even if those citizens are in fact treated equally. Equality of political status, by contrast, embodies a commitment to publicly respect all citizens' capacities as political agents, underwrites all citizens' self-respect, and provides support for citizens to conduct their relationships on equal terms. Equal political status also allows citizens to see the government as their own, at least in the limited sense that each is

---

31. Arguably such systematic vulnerability just *is* subjection to domination, and *eo ipso* deeply inegalitarian. See Pettit, *Republicanism*, 90–92.

an equal participant in the common activity of political rule. While not guaranteeing fully equal treatment of all citizens, equal political status at least expresses a public commitment to securing citizens against predictable vulnerabilities to serious inequality in treatment.

IV. Conclusion

We have strong reasons to pursue and support collective decision-making practices and institutions that constitute relations of political equality among citizens. These reasons apply generally and can only be canceled or outweighed by reasons of considerable urgency. There are instrumental reasons to concern ourselves directly with the egalitarian character of our decision-making processes, as the very egalitarianism of the processes causally contributes to valuable relations of social equality. Political equality is also intrinsically valuable: we have reason to treat one another as political equals even if alternative, unequal institutions and practices might produce better laws and policies. Political equality constitutes a valuable relationship of civic friendship, and supports the self-respect of citizens, who are entitled to authority over their own lives. Oligarchy, by contrast, is objectionable for a number of reasons, degrading citizens, undermining their self-respect, and denying one aspect of their autonomy.

These reasons to realize and support politically egalitarian practices and institutions require us to develop a conception of political equality that identifies which practices and institutions are properly egalitarian in this sense. This conception will guide us in our efforts to resolve disputes about which democratic institutions and practices are truly consistent with the requirements of political equality. This book provides such a conception, grounded in the values of political equality canvassed in this chapter.

PART II

Conception

CHAPTER THREE

Against Equal Power

IN THIS CHAPTER, I examine one tempting way of trying to articulate what political equality requires. This approach holds that political equality requires strict equality of political power among all citizens, often in the form of equally weighted votes in some decision procedure. This commitment has substantial consequences for one's view of political institutions: among other things, the ideal of equal distribution of political power lies behind many arguments for majoritarian, as against "countermajoritarian," decision-making procedures. This equal-distribution approach has obvious appeal, for its apparent simplicity and for its formidable dialectical position: any opposition to the view seems to carry with it a faint whiff of oligarchy.

We should not be too quick, however, to accept that the ideal of political equality requires strict equality in the distribution of some political good. Equal status does not necessarily imply equal distribution, nor does equal distribution imply equal status. As it turns out, equal power distribution is often incompatible with respecting the equal authority of citizens.

Equal-distribution principles struggle to articulate what would constitute an equal distribution of political power over time. Many of our intuitions, and even our most thorough philosophical reflections, about the importance of equal political distributions refer to distributions of power over discrete acts or decisions, narrowly localized to one moment in time. We think about equally divvying votes in a single election or legislative vote—about the moment of translating votes into outcomes. But a collective decision involves a political process that takes place over an extended period of time, encompassing formal and informal public agenda setting, coalition building, and so on, as well as formal voting (and all with expectations of future execution and enforcement). Proper respect for the equal standing of citizens requires that equality inhere in that entire extended process. Equal-power requirements on discrete decisions are often compatible with inequality over time; sometimes, indeed, efforts to equalize power at such moments introduce inequality of citizen authority overall. These conclusions support the claim in chapter 2 that equal authority, rather than equal power, is central to equal political status. I elaborate the conception of equal authority in subsequent chapters.

In what follows, I demonstrate the influence of distributive ideals on thinking about democratic procedures. I then discuss some difficulties the equal-distribution approach has in accounting for the temporally extended nature of political decision making—in particular, its failures to account appropriately for the importance of good representation and good deliberation to political equality. I then further widen the temporal lens, and ask how an equal-distribution approach might explain what is required for citizens to be politically equal over the course of many common decisions throughout their lives. I argue that none of the contending accounts of equal distribution over time satisfy the demands of political equality and the need to sustain relationships among citizens of equal political status.

I. Democracy as Equal Power

Many arguments about ideal democratic procedures draw their persuasiveness from an ideal of equal distribution of power. Something like distributional language accompanies demands for universal suffrage, and for equal district size in territorially based systems of representation: "one person, one vote" was a slogan consciously intended to evoke the idea of distributive fairness.[1] John Stuart Mill's plural voting scheme (more votes for better qualified voters) represents a nonegalitarian distributive ideal,[2] and the general disfavor in which democrats hold that scheme today reflects a different vision of the just distribution of the suffrage. More recently, Robert Dahl suggested that political equality requires that in governmental decisions, "the preference of each member [of society] is assigned an equal

---

1. The US Supreme Court compared unequal district sizing to plural voting in the original reapportionment case, *Reynolds v. Sims*, and argued that "the resulting discrimination against those individual voters living in disfavored areas is easily demonstrable mathematically." 377 U.S. 533, 563 (1964).

2. Mill, *Considerations on Representative Government*, ch. 8.

value."[3] Many political scientists have dedicated themselves to specifying this idea of equally valued votes, partly in the service of electoral reform litigation.[4] Work in formal social choice theory often recognizes equality as a feature of social choice functions to the extent that the functions give each individual's input equal significance in determining the outcome.[5] So we have some familiarity with the idea that procedural fairness involves the just (usually equal) distribution of votes, and of voting weight or strength. Often we talk about the conditions necessary to make procedures (like a vote) fair or equal without explicit reference to any distributive ideal, so it may be worth taking a moment to explain how many ideals of procedural fairness in fact trade on distributive ideals.

Votes are abstract measures of citizens' judgments, made to be counted, and so we find it rather natural to apply distributive requirements to the extension of voting rights and to the counting process. As the reapportionment cases, rotten-borough problems, and many other historical examples have shown, however, the equal distribution of votes fails to prevent many objectionable procedural inequalities, in which some ostensibly equal votes appear more equal than others. We can specify conditions on the voting process or context in such a way as to ensure that these objectionable inequalities do not arise—in such a way, that is, as to achieve the moral ideal behind the demand for equal votes. These conditions can often be redescribed as requirements for the equal distribution of various metrics of voting power or influence.

Many familiar conditions on procedures amount to demands for equal distributions of voting power. Calls for equally sized districts in territorially based representative schemes—calls for "one person, one vote"—reflect a demand for equally weighted or "undiluted" votes.[6] Holding the number of votes for each alternative constant, differing distributions of

---

3. Dahl, *Preface to Democratic Theory*, 37.

4. For an early discussion of this development, and a useful, if now dated, bibliography, see Still, "Political Equality." For an early Supreme Court case in which the Court explicitly considered (and rejected) the merits of a political scientist's account of equal voting power, see *Whitcomb v. Chavis*, 403 U.S. 124 (1971).

5. See Mueller, *Public Choice III*, 134–35. Public choice theorists do not uncritically accept this equality of input as normatively significant; for discussion, see ibid., 135, and generally chs. 4–6.

6. Jonathan Still describes the equal district size rule as satisfying a requirement he calls "equal probabilities," according to which "each voter has the same statistical probability of casting a vote which decides the election (under certain assumptions)": "Political Equality," 380.

voters among equally sized districts can produce different outcomes.[7] In response, some have suggested that fair procedures would include a requirement that the outcome of the procedure remains the same under all possible distributions of voters within the positions (e.g., their geographic location) in the electoral system.[8] This "anonymity" condition ensures that the impact of a citizen's vote will not vary with what may seem like arbitrary facts about her position in the electoral system; the condition thus renders the equal weighting of her vote more robust across different possibilities—or, to put it a different way, equalizes a more demanding measure of "weight," or voting power.

Majority rule combines the robust equal weighting of the anonymity condition with a condition of symmetry or neutrality between outcomes—effectively ruling out supermajority requirements, which favor one outcome (usually the status quo) over others.[9] Majority rule—or, as it is sometimes called, "majority decision," in order to specify its role as a specific procedure for collective decision making, as opposed to a general principle of popular sovereignty—often receives support as a uniquely fair or egalitarian way of making decisions.[10] This claim for the unique procedural equality of majority decision turns heavily on the idea that it distributes to voters robustly equally weighted votes, guaranteeing a kind of equal power wherever a voter is located in the electoral system and whatever the alternatives at issue may be.[11] In most serious treatments, majority

---

7. If this point is not familiar, consider this example: suppose there are five districts in the state, each with ten voters, and each district follows first-past-the-post voting rules. Voters vote either Whig or Tory, and all vote. There are 30 Whig voters and 20 Tory voters in the state as a whole. If the districts are gerrymandered so that the districts have, respectively, 6, 6, 6, 1, and 1 Tory voters, the Tories will win three of the five seats despite winning only 40% of the vote overall.

8. See May, "Necessary and Sufficient Conditions."

9. See ibid. For some refinements of the claim about supermajority rules, see Goodin and List, "Special Majorities Rationalized." See also ch. 11.

10. See Waldron, *Law and Disagreement*, and *Dignity of Legislation*, ch. 6; Christiano, *Rule of the Many*. (Christiano's views of majority rule are more nuanced in *Constitution of Equality*. Even there, however, he continues to think that majority rule has unique claims to egalitarianism absent special circumstances; see 290–91.) John Rawls does not argue that majoritarian political procedures are the most just, but claims that majority rule provides the greatest extent of equal political liberties. See *Theory of Justice*, § 36, 197. The well-known anxieties among constitutional scholars about the "counter-majoritarian difficulty" presented by judicial review similarly rest on views privileging majority rule. More venerable claims for something like the unique egalitarianism of majority rule can be found in John Locke, Thomas Hobbes, and (more critically) Aristotle. For some healthy skepticism, see Beitz, *Political Equality*, 60–66.

11. Christiano, *Rule of the Many*, 70, 82; Waldron, *Dignity of Legislation*, ch. 6, especially 160.

rule or equal power is not defended as sufficient for political equality; most believe that some kind of free speech is also necessary for procedural fairness, and perhaps much more. Equal voting power does, however, have considerable support as a necessary condition of political equality.

In what follows, I cast doubt on the distributive approach as the centerpiece of an account of political equality. I will conclude this section with two brief observations about this general distributive approach.

The first point is straightforward. The fact that different possible conceptions of power to be equalized present themselves means that a theory of political equality cannot simply be a presentation of a procedure that involves the equalization of some political good. There will, in other words, have to be some background theory of equality that tells us what we ought to distribute, and how.[12]

The second point about the distributive approach is that one standard version involves power with respect to significant decisions at individual moments. The approach exhibits concern for equality in the more or less instantaneous translation of citizen judgments into collective decisions: the typical approach considers one decision, like a single election of representatives or a single referendum, with respect to which citizens all have fixed views, and asks what procedure would secure an equal distribution of voting strength across a certain range of circumstances. This equality, however, is temporally narrow; in the rest of the chapter, I will try to suggest that this equality is morally narrow as well.[13] (An influential alternative conception, which requires a kind of equal power across extended processes of deliberation and voting, deserves separate treatment; I discuss it in chapter 6.)

II. The Extended Political Process: Representation and Deliberation

Even a single political decision—say, a vote on some proposed legislation—involves a process extending over a long period of time, and over many separate, discrete acts. A proposition only makes it onto the legislative

---

12. Mathias Risse makes what I take to be a similar point when he argues that Waldron's arguments in favor of majority decision are "too amorphous" to provide the "fine-grained discernments" between candidate decision-making procedures: "Arguing for Majority Rule," 54. See also Beitz, *Political Equality*, 11.

13. Jed Rubenfeld recognizes something like this point in *Freedom and Time*. Rubenfeld emphasizes (and criticizes) the majoritarian aspiration to be free, in the present, of the constitutional constraints of the past. I am emphasizing (and criticizing) the limited aspiration of majoritarianism to be equal in a certain respect at moments of decision.

"ballot" after agenda setting, deliberation, coalition building, and so on. These activities take place within official bodies and among the public at large. Over the course of these activities, many citizens' judgments are effectively dismissed (if only provisionally), as part of the process of winnowing down the wide range of diverse judgments into a single decision. Such dismissals do not only occur according to the consent of those whose views are dismissed, nor according to formal votes subject to rules of equal power distribution. The basic concern of political equality—the concern that each citizen is publicly recognized and respected as an equally authoritative coruler—extends throughout this process. The equal respect should be manifest constantly, not only episodically at moments of final formal decision. One might claim that the momentary equality of the final voting stage is sufficient to secure this extended equality throughout the process; the fact that someone has a vote gives him an importance and a standing that surely influences the foregoing process, so equal voting may give that process an egalitarian cast. Nevertheless, equal voting at the end of a process does not guarantee equality throughout that process. In particular, momentary equal power in voting on legislation does not suffice to secure full political equality in representation and deliberation.

Representation involves straightforward and stark inequalities in voting power. Whenever the US Congress votes on legislation, for example, all but 535 citizens are disenfranchised with respect to that specific vote. This is about as dramatic an example of momentary inequality in voting power as there could be; an equal-power theory of democracy must therefore either reject representation as antidemocratic, or explain how such severe inequality in voting power is compatible with political equality understood as equality of power. I consider these possible approaches in turn, and show that neither approach can rescue the view that political equality simply is (or necessarily involves) equality of voting power. Thinking about the virtues of representation, as well as the need for representation to be properly democratic, reveals the shortcomings of equal-power views, and suggests something about the shape of a more promising alternative conception of political equality.

II.A. EQUAL POWER AS THE REJECTION OF REPRESENTATION

A proponent of an equal-power view might reject representation altogether. According to this response, only direct democracy, a system in which all citizens have equal voting power on all decisions, satisfies the demands of political equality. Ubiquitous practices of representation do not show that there are features of democracies that the equal-power view cannot capture, this line of thought continues, but only that the states we call democratic do not live up to the name.

There are few contemporary proponents of exclusively direct democracy.[14] If the equal-power view requires direct democracy, many readers might consider this reason to reject the view. But we ought to make sure that this rejection of direct democracy is warranted, and not simply the result of oligarchic prejudices. Moreover, if we do conclude that the rejection is warranted, it is important to be clear about just why direct democracy is objectionable, and what this tells us about political equality.

The most common complaint about direct democracy is that it is infeasible or unworkable—not just in the sense that it produces bad decisions (though this is also a common complaint), but that it is more fundamentally impossible, or extremely costly, to realize. In states of any significant size, it is impossible for citizens to all gather together to vote on anything, and expecting them to vote on every collective decision would be exorbitantly costly even if it were possible (and even if they made all the right decisions). Advances in communication technologies may make repeated mass voting possible without robbing the citizens of all their time and resources. But administrative problems seem to doom direct democracy before any wider concerns about the quality of decision making under such a system enter into our evaluation.

These administrative problems are serious ones. But can we say that these are *democratic* concerns? If we reject direct democracy on the grounds that it presents insuperable administrative problems, are we rejecting it in favor of a more democratic (or at least equally democratic) alternative? Or are we just rejecting democracy in favor of an administratively smooth oligarchy and the power attainable by large states?[15] If our considered rejection of direct democracy depends exclusively on nondemocratic reasons, such as the importance of state power, then the rejection of direct democracy would not show that the equal-power view

---

14. I have not been able to identify an example of a supporter of exclusively direct democracy in relatively recent political philosophy literature. Bernard Manin, a prominent recent critic of contemporary practices of representation, clarifies early on in his work that his criticisms should not be taken to support direct democracy. (His preferred alternative to election is lottery selection, which maintains inequalities of political power.) Manin, *Principles of Representative Government*, 41.

15. See Wolin, "Democracy: Electoral and Athenian"; Rousseau, *Of the Social Contract*, bk. 3, ch. 15.

is a poor interpretation of political equality. Instead, it might show that political equality is an unappealing, or perhaps even chimerical, ideal, one which we tend to repudiate as soon as we know what exactly equality requires.[16]

The rejection of direct democracy does not require such oligarchic bullet biting, however. Direct democracy is not necessary to establish a regime of political equality: I will argue in subsequent chapters that representative systems can satisfy the requirements of political equality. Nor is directly democratic voting on laws sufficient to establish political equality. Moreover, if a regime incorporating such voting did satisfy the requirements of political equality, that would not be simply because it satisfied some requirement of equal power. This is because, as I will begin to argue in this chapter, political equality requires more than equal voting power over the laws. Directly democratic voting, for instance, is compatible with significant inequality in the conduct of common deliberation and agenda setting. Thus, if the equal-power view does commit its supporters to direct democracy—as the most straightforward reading of the view would suggest, and as I will argue in the next section—then this would be a serious problem for the view for at least two reasons. First, the view fails to register the potential democratic gains from certain practices of political representation—the potential superiority of representative over direct democracy, understood even when we measure "superiority" in exclusively politically egalitarian terms. Second, the form of direct democracy the view endorses—a form concerned exclusively with the equal distribution of political power—is an impoverished one that does not well reflect the moral aspirations of political equality.

Directly democratic regimes may, for all I have argued, be politically egalitarian.[17] But the equal-power conception of political equality does

---

16. Could we not instead accept political equality, and accept its requirements that we radically shrink contemporary polities? Absent extreme social and economic changes, the smaller polities would be mutually dependent (and probably vulnerable), raising questions about the organization of interstate and transnational connections. For our purposes, questions would arise about how these substantial policy questions could be resolved on terms of political equality. On the equal-power view, something like the direct-democracy problem would reemerge. (Rousseau recognized this problem, deferring it to a never-written work on international "confederations": *Of the Social Contract*, bk. 3, ch. 15.)

17. There are two major challenges to direct democracy on politically egalitarian grounds. The first is the concern about transnational politics I mentioned in the previous note. The second involves concerns raised by James Madison, who suggested that the formally democratic features of direct democracy would not be able to guarantee meaningful democracy in the actual operation of government. For example, it might not be possible to

not provide the correct standards to judge whether that is so. Instead, it requires a directly democratic system that is too permissive in allowing unfairness outside the voting context, while being too strict in denying democratic gains through representational structure. Because the equal-power conception is wrongly (if unwittingly) committed to such a system, we should reject the conception.

It may be easier to appreciate the reasons for these claims after we examine the failures of the equal-power view in more familiar representative settings. As we will see, the equal-power view fails properly to explain how representation can be democratic, but its failures are not specific to practices of representation. Instead, they apply generally to any temporally extended political process—which is to say, any political process. Nothing about the absence of representation would save the equal-power view from its inability to secure equality over the extended course of political deliberation, decision making, and collective action.

II.B. THE FAILURES OF FAIR AUTHORIZATION

Typically, supporters of the equal-power conception of political equality do not intend to endorse direct democracy. Accordingly, they need to explain how the view can accommodate the stark inequalities in voting power that attend legislative representation. The natural response is to refer to some features of the foregoing process that legally and morally authorize the representatives to wield exclusive voting power—features such as their election through some sufficiently fair and egalitarian process. I believe that something like this response does explain the compatibility of representation and democracy, but it raises immediate complications for a distributive approach to political equality, because it suggests that extreme distributive inequalities at certain moments may be justified by certain historical features of a political process.

One might argue that equal distribution remains a necessary component of individual decisions, like election or legislative vote, and that the equality of the entire process depends on the equal distribution of power

---

preserve meaningful equality for all in the decisions the government would constantly have to make. The administration of such procedures could be extremely difficult, and exemplify in the extreme Madison's principle that as assemblies grow in size, "the countenance of the government may become more democratic; but the soul that animates it will be more oligarchic." Madison, "Federalist, No. 58," 396. This is a problem for any democratic system, but it is possible that good representative institutions would better enable democratic control over administration.

[84] CHAPTER THREE

within the enfranchised group at every stage of decision making within the process.[18] According to this logic, for example, fair votes within a legislature composed of fairly elected legislators (where fairness amounts to the equal distribution of voting power) would suffice to constitute an egalitarian process (perhaps together with some basic free speech rights). We might call this the "fair-authorization" view, because it admits inequalities only if they were authorized by a fair process—that is, a decision in which all citizens had equal voting power. The strategy has a slightly Rousseauvian flavor, in that it suggests that all political acts must ultimately derive their authority from an act of a kind of democratic sovereign, to which strict rules of procedural equality apply.[19]

The fair-authorization view faces a number of crippling problems. First, despite its insistence on equal distributions of power at key stages in the political process, it departs substantially from the ideal that each citizen have equal power over political decisions. Equality in the initial authorization stage (e.g., election of representatives) is not equivalent to equal power over the final decision, even if decision makers in later stages are subject to their own requirements of equal distribution. The point of the fair-authorization view, of course, is to justify inequalities later in the process, but the power inequality at the final decision stage is real, and so the view cannot claim in its support whatever intuitive appeal attaches to the idea of equal power of everyone over final decisions. Initially equal election of representatives in no way guarantees that ordinary citizens will have equal power over final decisions. This should be familiar from age-old concerns about fidelity of representation.[20]

---

18. This line of reasoning is a bit obscure, as it depends on the idea that the political process can be neatly separated into discrete stages, to which equal-power norms apply. As will become clear, I have my doubts about the possibility of slicing up political time in this way.

19. Jeremy Waldron's considered view seems to be something like this. Despite occasional suggestions that majority decision is the only fair way to act politically, he supports a kind of legislative supremacy, in which acts involving some unequal power (including some modest judicial review) are acceptable as long as the majoritarian legislature, itself elected through majoritarian procedures, has the ultimate authority to reverse those acts. See Waldron, "Case against Judicial Review," and *Law and Disagreement*, 109–10. Alexander Bickel, the writer who coined the phrase "counter-majoritarian difficulty," expresses a similar view in *Least Dangerous Branch*, 19. *The Federalist* suggests something like a fair-authorization view of what counts as a "republic": "It is *sufficient* for such a government, that the persons administering it be appointed, directly or indirectly, by the people." Madison, "Federalist, No. 39," 251.

20. Even if representatives did reliably mimic directly democratic votes, this would not amount to equally distributing power to all citizens. It would simply amount to producing

A second, more important problem with the fair-authorization view is that it cannot distinguish the egalitarian credentials of very different electoral and representative schemes. Both Westminster-style legislative supremacy and Washington-style judicial review, for example, satisfy the requirements of fair authorization, given a few idealizing assumptions. US Supreme Court justices, like members of a parliament, can trace their authorization back to (roughly) majoritarian elections (in the justices' case, of the president and the Senate), and the decisions of the Court are themselves rendered according to majority decision.[21] So the fair-authorization view presumably must say that each system is equally permissible. Similarly, the view has no grounds to distinguish "Long Parliament"–style representative abuses, through which officials rarely stand for reelection, from an assembly in which members are elected at frequent intervals.. Given that the aim of theories of political equality—and actual democratic activism—is to arbitrate these kinds of institutional choices, a view that has little advice to offer fails to respond to important democratic concerns. It is no flaw in a view of political equality that it concludes that many different institutional schemes may satisfy its demands. But in failing to distinguish such major differences between regimes—indeed, in failing even to register why there might be contention over the democratic nature of such regimes—the fair-authorization view casts its indifference far too widely.

This view, by placing so much weight on initially equal distributions of voting power, tolerates radically inegalitarian delegations of power. It appears to be compatible with a Hobbesian account of unanimous (or even majoritarian) authorization of a single absolute monarch. The most egregious alienations of equal political power might be avoided if we insist that there be some opportunity for acts involving equal power—for example, the reconvening of the democratic sovereign assembly—at periodic intervals.[22] Even with this requirement, however, the view tolerates highly unequal distributions of political power during the interregnums between

---

outcomes that accorded with what such a process of equal empowerment would produce. This is a standard on outcomes, not a standard on the actual operation of political processes.

21. The primary majoritarian objection to the US system, according to this view, would be the inequalities of power involved in the Senate and the Electoral College. These may be troubling inequalities, but if these are the only "counter-majoritarian" features of judicial review that the fair-authorization view picks up on, something seems to be missing.

22. As plausible as such a requirement seems, it appears rather ad hoc from the perspective of the equal-power view. Why should we require periodic fair authorization? The natural response seems to be a concern that equality persist over time, rather than exhausting itself in initial founding moments. But this commitment to equality persisting over time leads one away from the equal-power view, as I will argue.

narrowly equal acts.[23] This is an example of the general problem Hannah Pitkin identified for formal-authorization views of representation, according to which representation is solely judged according to the way in which it was authorized: such views seem to have no way to account for the varying quality of the representation authorized.[24] In practice, such views gain plausibility from the fact that the equally empowered acts (such as popular elections) happen frequently enough to ensure a roughly egalitarian quality to the representation itself. But from the perspective of the view that conditions political equality only on the presence of narrowly egalitarian authorization, this benefit is a happy accident. To the extent that we think the structure of representation itself should be regulated by egalitarian concerns, we have to move beyond the fair-authorization view. Whereas the basic distributive approach places too much weight on equality at the moment of final decision making, the fair-authorization view places too much weight on equality at the earlier moment of representative election. Neither is sufficient to guarantee egalitarian representation throughout the collective decision-making process.

We should not be surprised by the conclusion that political equality in a representative system requires some kind of egalitarian quality to its practices of representation. Representative devices serve to winnow down the many, diverse (and often vague) citizen judgments on various issues into detailed collective decisions. These devices partly accomplish this winnowing through simple aggregative processes, as representatives secure election by more or less favoring the judgments of winning coalitions in fair elections (or leading enough electors to support the representative's judgments). But representatives do not merely advance electoral winners' judgments and slough off those of electoral losers.[25] In significant part because it is not obvious what "winners' judgments" are, given their relative incompleteness and their diversity even within a winning coalition, we expect representatives (and the representative system as a whole) to forge judgments that are not simply transmitted from voters. Once we recognize that representatives play this role of winnowing citizen judgments in a manner not entirely determined by elections, we ought to be concerned that this winnowing, like that accomplished by elections, is

---

23. For an example of this problem in a contemporary context, see ch. 11, § III.

24. Pitkin, *Concept of Representation*, chs. 1–2.

25. To think the opposite would be to embrace a radical, majoritarian version of a delegate theory of representation, according to which representatives not only refuse to exercise independent judgment, but refuse to advance the judgments of those outside their electoral coalition.

consistent with the equal respect for citizens' judgments that constitutes equal political status.

In order to articulate how individual representatives, and the representative system as whole, can integrate the judgments of citizens in a manner consistent with political equality, a plausible theory of egalitarian judgment integration will include some qualitative element that is resistant to simple quantification and patterned distribution. Elections leave representatives with discretion, and our representatives ought to exercise that discretion in a manner that respects political equality. A constitutional order, moreover, ought reliably to encourage representatives to exercise their discretion in such a democratic way. The equal-power view, and its fair-authorization variant, fail to appreciate these requirements, and so we should reject those views. I develop my own views on fair representation in chapter 5.

How ought we to think about the proper, egalitarian way to exercise discretion in judgment formation and decision making? This is a question suitable for ordinary citizens as well as representatives: there is always some point at which a citizen does not have fixed views on a political matter, and political equality, as I argued in chapter 2, demands that citizens grant some authority to the judgments of other citizens in coming to their own conclusions. This question about the process of judgment formation in common with other citizens leads us to what at the beginning of this section I described as the second basic element of the democratic political process that resists distributive logic: deliberation. Deliberation—the process of forming judgments about what to do, a process that can occur individually or in common with others—is one part of the practice of representation: politically egalitarian representatives must be politically egalitarian deliberators. But nonofficial citizens also engage in democratic deliberation, and this important part of the collective decision-making process poses problems for a distributive theory quite apart from the structure of the representative system.[26]

II.C. DELIBERATION AND FAIRNESS BEYOND POWER

Deliberation among citizens is an important part of the political process—important not only, as many recent defenders of deliberative democracy

---

26. Because this basic problem of judgment winnowing through deliberation does not depend on the existence of representation (nor do other forms of winnowing apart from voting, such as agenda setting), direct democracy based on equal voting power would not avoid the problem.

argue, as an occasion to show respect to one's interlocutors, but also in determining which judgments actually prevail in the decision-making process. The character and structure of public deliberations—how people are heard—play an important role in determining what issues emerge on the formal political agenda, as well as how public opinion develops about the issues on that agenda. Like representation, deliberation is part of a winnowing process that moves from diverse citizen judgments to final (if provisional) collective decisions. In the course of this process, various citizen judgments are effectively dismissed, in the sense that most people no longer actively engage with those judgments as salient candidates for formal decision. This disengagement occurs without any formal vote. This process of dismissing some judgments in favor of others must be consistent with equal respect for citizens' authority.

Because this deliberative process is largely informal, equal voting rules are not sufficient to guarantee appropriately egalitarian deliberation. Deliberation can of course be influenced by power, and so egalitarian deliberation may require that certain power inequalities be minimized or neutralized, but this is not the same thing as granting each citizen some equal measure of power or influence. Instead of focusing on equal power, then, we must recognize a plurality of citizens' deliberative interests that together shape our understanding of what it means for those citizens to be equally authoritative in common deliberation. These interests include, for instance, a deliberative context in which each citizen has the opportunity to form judgments in an informed manner, and has a "fair say" or receives a "fair hearing" for her views.[27] An account of democratic deliberation can identify the individual ethos and the institutional structures necessary to respond to citizens' deliberative interests, and thereby to recognize them as authorities throughout deliberative processes. Votes are a significant component of a citizen's right to be heard, both because of the impact of the vote itself and because of the standing and relevance the franchise gives to the citizen's views throughout the decision-making process. But a vote will not always suffice to secure a fair hearing or other interests, and so a theory of political equality requires more than a theory of fair voting.

The basic point that fair-aggregation rules ought to be supplemented by good deliberation is probably familiar. I am not suggesting, however, merely that a theory of political equality should consist in a theory of fair aggregation on the one hand, and a theory of fair deliberation on the other. Instead, what constitutes fair aggregation itself—what counts as a

---

27. I say much more about this in ch. 6.

fair process of winnowing diverse judgments into collective decisions—depends on the character of the deliberation and representation that accompany formal aggregative rules. Different aggregative rules—different practices of districting, structures of representation, distributions of power between branches of government, and so on—in different contexts can promote representative and deliberative practices of varying quality, and so we cannot necessarily determine what constitutes a fair aggregative rule apart from considering such implications. Abstract features of an aggregative rule, such as the way it distributes voting power at a certain moment in time, will be relevant to our judgment about whether a system including the rule accords with the demands of political equality, but that judgment will ultimately have to be a holistic one, considering the entire temporally extended political process. It is telling that many thought experiments meant to evoke intuitions in support of majority decision or other momentary distributive rules involve small groups in which discussion could be virtually unlimited and there is no formal representation.[28] In such cases, momentary equal distribution of political power and universal fair hearings are largely compatible. But in large democracies, this may not always be so. Equal distributions of power in aggregation do not guarantee fair deliberation—equal power is not sufficient for political equality. Moreover, in some cases, typically involving neglected minorities, equal power may undermine fair deliberation, meaning equal power is not necessary for political equality. Because the extended political process inevitably involves practices to which our egalitarian concern applies, but which tend to resist quantification, our holistic judgments cannot primarily rest on facts about distributions of power. We must be prepared to make more qualitative assessments of whether institutional regimes respect citizens' equal political status.

III. The Iterated Political Process

In the last section, we discussed what it means for citizens to enjoy equality as corulers in the course of making what we can loosely describe as one collective decision. As we have seen, "one decision" encompasses a number of acts over an extended period of time, so the demands of

---

28. Consider, for example, Waldron's "Hobbesian" account of the fairness of majority rule, involving five people, in *Law and Disagreement*, 148–50; Peter Singer's model of democracy patterned after decision making in "a common-room association of a university college," in *Democracy and Disobedience*, 13–17; and Brian Barry's discussion of five passengers in a train car deciding whether to permit smoking, in "Is Democracy Special?" 30.

political equality must be similarly extended. Even viewing the political process so expansively, however, amounts to a narrow temporal view of a constitutional order, which aims to develop, regulate, and sustain political institutions over the entire lives of citizens, and indefinitely across generations.

This temporal concern raises challenges for the equal-power view. If political equality requires equal power, we must ask over what time period citizens' power should be equalized. A parallel question arises when thinking about distributive justice more generally: we can ask whether a mandate for equal distribution (of welfare or resources, say) requires equality at each moment, say, or equal sums of the relevant goods (or perhaps equal expectations) over the course of citizens' entire lives.[29] Writers in such discussions often assume, or at least very quickly establish, that the central moral concern is equality over lives.[30] The centrality of the lifelong perspective is usually derived from the possibility of intrapersonal compensation—the possibility of compensating a person for a disadvantage at one time with an advantage at another time. Might similar logic apply to the equal distribution of political power? Can shortfalls in political power at certain moments for certain citizens be compensated for by disproportionately greater power at some other time?

The question is not so far-fetched. The ancient democratic principles of lot and rotation aimed at something like the equal distribution of political power (or the expectation of political power) among citizens over the course of their lives.[31] At any given time, citizens selected for office by the lottery have more power with respect to collective decisions than citizens not selected; but so long as rotation among citizens is rigorous and rapid enough, citizens maintain the expectation that they will come into office at some point, and thus that over the course of their lives they will enjoy equal political power. The basic Aristotelian ideal of political rule among equals—to "rule and be ruled in turn"—is straightforwardly an ideal describing a certain distribution of power over time.[32] Adopting the equality-over-lives view need not require the adoption of an Athenian lottery-based system; we might make modest alterations in the electoral system that consciously admit certain inequalities at times if we have

---

29. McKerlie, "Equality and Time," and "Dimensions of Equality."
30. See, e.g., Rawls, *Theory of Justice*, § 15; Nagel, "Equality," 120; Dworkin, *Sovereign Virtue*, 83–84.
31. See Manin, *Principles of Representative Government*, especially ch. 1.
32. See, e.g., Aristotle, *Politics*, 56 (1261a28–b10).

confidence that those inequalities will be reversed through something like rotation over time.³³

The obvious problem with "complete lives" equality, however, is that it arguably tolerates what should be intolerable inequalities at any given time.³⁴ It is compatible with radical inequality, so long as the advantaged and disadvantaged parties trade places evenly. But such a system of rotating political lords and serfs runs strongly against the grain of our democratic intuitions. It is possible that our intuitions are not very reliable about this far-fetched scenario, in which, on the one hand, severe discrepancies in power exist at any time, but, on the other, the system publicly guarantees fair rotation into positions of mastery. (What makes the scenario far-fetched is that such stark inequalities of power are imagined to be compatible with reliable guarantees of fair rotation—that is, that any given set of lords will not use their supposedly temporary power to entrench their rule.³⁵) It could be that in such a world, the public guarantees of rotation would render any present inequalities of power compatible with a reasonable sense of equal status among citizens, and would encourage proper respect for the authority of all citizens, in the same way that we imagine the Athenian lottery and rotation system might have done. On the other hand, it might be that the sense of present mastery and servitude would be so extreme as to promote degrading social and political relations despite the guarantees of lifetime equality. Because it is hard to imagine the extreme case, it is hard to judge whether the example proves that complete-lives equality is an unacceptable principle. It is hard to know, that is, whether the example amounts to a *reductio ad absurdum* or a proof that a public guarantee of complete-lives equality is a robust guarantee of equal political status.

The ambiguity of the thought experiment shows that our commitment to complete-lives equality, if we have one, is derivative. We would abandon the commitment if we thought it were compatible with inequalities in power that undermined citizens' relations as persons of equal political

---

33. See, e.g., Cox, "Temporal Dimension."

34. The phrase "complete lives" equality and the basic objection are taken from McKerlie. See, e.g., "Equality and Time," 479.

35. This is not an objection to the complete-lives approach to distribution per se, since the problem discussed here is that large inequality at given times is contingently incompatible with equality over complete lives. It does suggest, however, that something like intrapersonal compensation over time for political inequalities may be difficult to achieve, and so the complete-lives approach might ultimately recommend minimizing inequality at any given time, and so collapse into the "simultaneous segments" view discussed below.

status, or otherwise failed to respond to the authoritative expectations of that status. As I argued in chapters 1 and 2, the fundamental commitment of political equality is to the preservation of those relationships through recognition of that status. The commitment to a distributional rule like complete-lives equality turns on whether the rule actually would guarantee such relationships and amount to such recognition.

We have good reason to think that some ways of implementing equal power over complete lives would fail this test. First, it is hard to believe that equality of formal power over the course of citizens' lives would properly guarantee meaningful equality of authority over common life. Issues of varying seriousness occur at different times; being out of power when very serious matters are at stake is not well compensated by being in power when only more mundane matters are on the common agenda. Second, the path dependence of practices and institutions may mean that people with greater power earlier may have more meaningful control over the course of a society (and the citizens' lives) than those who come to power later—even if there is no problem of explicit political entrenchment violating the equal-power principle.[36] Some power inequalities at given moments may well be compatible with equal status, and one reason may be that the inequalities will be (roughly) reversed later. But the complete-lives equal-distribution view in principle admits too much power inequality at given times, and this fails to respond adequately to citizens' continuous claim to equality.

A proponent of the equal-power view might respond by endorsing the primary alternative to a complete-lives approach to defining equal distributions over time: the view that equality over time requires equality at every discrete interval of time. This "simultaneous segments" view, as Dennis McKerlie calls it (because it requires equality over a given segment of time among a set of people living simultaneously through that time),[37] may seem to fit better with the intuitions behind the distributive approach to political equality, which tends to focus on equality of power at individual moments of decision. Equality at these moments is apparently thought to constitute equality over the "segments" of time leading up to the decisions. The case for simultaneous-segments political equality, however, is a dubious one.

---

36. Older people arguably always have this advantage over younger people, and to the extent that this is inevitable it is no injustice. But the complete-lives approach permits this kind of inequality when it is not inevitable, and it is to that extent objectionable.

37. McKerlie, "Equality and Time," 481.

One problem with a simultaneous-segments approach to distributive equality generally is that, in the absence of perfect equality in every temporal segment, the demand to minimize inequality in every segment is compatible with large and seemingly objectionable inequalities in lifetime totals of the relevant currency.[38] The strategy of minimizing inequality in every segment might leave the same person or group at the bottom of the distribution in each segment, and thus far worse off than others over the course of lifetimes. Whether this example actually constitutes an objection to the view depends on whether we think the permitted distributive inequality really would undermine citizens' status equality. A proponent of the simultaneous-segments approach to political equality, however, might sidestep this problem by arguing that, unlike the case of distributing resources or welfare, it is possible to guarantee the strictly equal distribution of power within each segment.[39] If that were true, then a system that guarantees such equality in each segment would also guarantee complete-lives equality. The proponent might justify this line of argument by pointing to familiar claims that certain decision procedures—such as majority decision, say—do indeed guarantee an equal distribution of power (understood in the relevant way), and thus that political institutions implementing such procedures could guarantee equality in every temporal segment.

The problem with this response from the proponent of simultaneous-segments political equality is that the moral significance of equality of power at moments of decision is limited. Moment-by-moment equality of power rules out representation; it cannot account properly for the democratic need for good representation and good deliberation in the fair winnowing of judgments; and, generally speaking, it does not provide a good account of equality over the course of the extended political process. The simultaneous-segments view thus faces a problem in defining the relevant "segment" within which equal distribution should be ensured. If the segment is narrowed down only to moments of decision, leaving aside as irrelevant other parts of decision-making processes, the normative basis of the view is thin. But if the segment is expanded to encompass the extended process of collective decision making, we have seen that equality of power does not appropriately encompass all of citizens' interests in equality

38. See ibid., 481–82.
39. This claim would be much harder to defend for proponents of "equal-influence" views, which I discuss in ch. 6. It is much more difficult to equalize strictly equal influence than it is to equalize formal power, and so this problem of compounded inequalities over time is a serious one for equal-influence views.

throughout the process. If segments are narrowed to vanishingly small moments, and all of them (including moments that do not include formal decision making) are meant to be equalized, the problems multiply.[40] So the equal-power view does not itself have the resources to explain which interval matters (suggesting some other principles must be at play, since the choice does not seem to be completely arbitrary), and the view fails for any given choice of interval. Like the complete-lives view, then, the appeal of a simultaneous-segments distributive approach to political equality depends on a conception of equal political status that, in turn, depends on nondistributive facts such as the guarantee of a fair political hearing for all citizens in the course of collective decision making. How ideally to distribute political power over the repeated decisions that constitute citizens' lives depends on what kinds of institutions can reflect and sustain relationships of equal political status. Political equality must be continuous, but this requirement is not well decomposed into discrete segments within which principles of power distribution apply.

IV. Conclusion

Our concern for political equality is one that persists throughout our lives, and beyond them into future generations. Moreover, at the more microcosmic level, we are creatures who deliberate and decide, individually and collectively, in a process that takes some time to unfold. Our concern for political equality demands an equality of status throughout that process. We should expect democratic institutions to respond appropriately to these concerns. My thesis in this chapter has primarily been a negative one: we cannot respond to these democratic concerns properly by focusing on the distribution of political power, whether at a given moment or over time. In the course of this negative argument, however, some conclusions have emerged that may help us develop a positive theory of political equality. A theory of political equality must include an account of political authority that would help us test whether the authority various citizens enjoyed under certain political institutions and practices was compatible

---

40. It may be hard to understand what power is within vanishingly small time periods. Or, if we can identify what it is (on the grounds, say, that exercises of power over normal, human-scaled intervals like days must encompass exercises of power over every smaller interval within the larger), it may be hard to see why equalization over such small intervals is morally significant. Finally, McKerlie's problem of compounded inequalities over lives returns with a vengeance. For further criticisms of this idea of ubiquitous majority rule, see Rubenfeld, *Freedom and Time*, ch. 4.

with broader equality of status. With this conception of authority—and properly equal authority—in hand, the conception of political equality will also include accounts of egalitarian representation and egalitarian deliberation in the service of explaining what is required to give citizens their fair say over the course of political processes. The basic goal would not be to secure any particular distribution of power or influence, whether at given moments or over lives, but rather to identify institutions that secure citizens' equal status at each moment of their lives. A democratic constitution ought to reflect the ambition for permanent, rather than episodic, political equality.

CHAPTER FOUR

Democratic Authority and Appropriate Consideration

EQUALITY OF POWER does not adequately respond to citizens' demand for sustained political-status equality over time. In the next few chapters, I propose and defend an alternative conception of political equality, which better responds to this democratic demand. I argue that political equality requires that the institutions and practices of collective decision making guarantee all citizens *appropriate consideration* of their political judgments. A regime or constitutional order ought, in the course of generating its laws and policies, to give, as a matter of right, recognition and attention to the views of all of its citizens suitable to their status as equal authorities over their lives together. This recognition is constituted in part by reliably connecting the outcome of collective decisions to citizens' judgments. As I argued in the last chapter, however, a quantum of power or influence over decision outcomes does not exhaust the consideration that is properly due to citizens. Instead, citizens may demand that their views be taken into account in a number of ways over the course of decision making (and, indeed, afterward). By giving all of its citizens due consideration in these ways, a polity respects each of those citizens as authoritative, and it constitutes and supports relations appropriate to political equals.

In part I, I argued that political equality requires respecting each citizen's equal authority over the common life of a society. In this chapter, I begin by explaining what it is to have authority in general, and why authority claims are the relevant subject matter of a theory of political equality. This requires a different conception of authority from that often used by political philosophers when discussing a different species of authority—that is, the authority of a state or government over its citizens.

The conception of authority must recognize diverse ways in which one can obligate others to deliberate and act in response to one's own judgments about what to do. I introduce claims to consideration as constituting a form of authority of this flexible kind, and explain the different forms consideration can take. I then explain why we should see a demand for consideration as an appropriate expression of citizens' authority, or, to use the language of chapter 2, as a form of respect for citizens' political jurisdiction. I address concerns that, by shifting the focus away from authority as command, the consideration conception unduly waters down citizen authority. I argue to the contrary that restricting ourselves to a command conception of authority prevents us from appreciating the diverse and extensive claims of democratic citizens. The consideration conception, by contrast, does not require any abandonment of citizens' claims to direct a democratic regime and its laws and policies continuously.

I. Authority as the Subject Matter of Political Equality

The status of equal citizen is constituted by expectations of treatment that others should take as authoritative. In particular, valuable egalitarian relationships are partially constituted by granting each participant in the relationship equal authority over matters common to the relationship. So political equality consists in an equal sharing of authority. What exactly is supposed to be shared?

In political philosophy, discussions of authority often involve what is called "political obligation"—the obligation (if any) of citizens to obey the laws, or the decrees of officials.[1] Our question is different: instead of asking whether, and under what conditions, citizens should obey the dictates of their regime, we are asking what it means for citizens to determine the dictates of their regime—and, in particular, what it means for them to do so on equal terms. These issues may be related substantively: one influential hypothesis is that the authority of the law depends in part on the extent to which the law is determined on egalitarian terms.[2] The issues both involve some agents purportedly creating obligations for other agents to act in certain ways—either the state (purportedly) obligating citizens to

---

1. See, e.g., Estlund, *Democratic Authority*, 2: "By *authority* I will mean the moral power of one agent (emphasizing the state) to morally require or forbid actions by others through commands."

2. Kolodny, "Rule over None II"; Viehoff, "Democratic Equality"; Christiano, *Constitution of Equality*. Earlier versions of this hypothesis are present in Locke and Rousseau.

obey its laws, or citizens collectively (purportedly) obligating the regime to act according to the results of some egalitarian process.[3] Both issues involve authority. These contexts, however, and the substantive concerns the contexts involve, are sufficiently different that we should not assume that the relevant conception of authority is the same.

We must also distinguish the two ways in which I have already used the idea of authority in this book. In chapter 1 (and earlier in this section), I referred to expectations of certain treatment as being "authoritative." Others should take such expectations as determining what they ought to do in relevant contexts. So, for instance, a vassal takes a lord's expectations of deference as authoritative if, for instance, the vassal doffs his hat and bows when in the lord's presence, because the vassal thinks he ought to follow the norms of deference defining those expectations. The vassal need not explicitly think of his action in those terms. But taking expectations as authoritative does involve giving the expectations considerable weight in one's deliberations about what to do. The example also shows that we can take as authoritative expectations that are not authoritative in a moral sense. (Vassals in unjust but stable feudal systems might be prudent to act according to their superiors' expectations of deference, but the expectations are not morally authoritative, in that, given the injustice of the hierarchy, the vassal does not owe such treatment to the lord. A prudent vassal does not treat the expectation as authoritative if he acts in accordance with it only out of a desire to avoid punishment or retaliation.)

For present purposes, the point is that we can, and sometimes ought to, take expectations of treatment as authoritative independently of any choice or declaration of the person we are treating. Lords and vassals deeply immersed in the prevailing ideology might both believe that inferiors in the great chain of being owe deference to superiors irrespective of any claims or choices made by those superiors. We generally ought to treat as authoritative others' expectations that we do not cause them pain, irrespective of any claim or choice made by those others. Certainly the explicit claims and choices of others are relevant to how we treat others—a point that implicates the second sense of authority, which I will address shortly—so, for instance, a patient's decision determines whether it is permissible for a surgeon to cut her in certain ways. But nevertheless

---

3. Citizens generally aim to determine the regime's actions in the hopes that the regime's acting in some way will have desirable consequences for society at large, usually by shaping people's behavior. Strictly speaking, this shaping need not involve any claims to authority by the regime in a technical sense. A regime may be able to affect behavior, and even change people's reasons for acting, without exercising any authority.

there are expectations we ought to take as authoritative that do not depend on a choice or explicit claim of the person we are treating with our behavior.[4]

Contrast this authority of expectations with what we might call the authority of persons. A person is authoritative in a broad sense when her decisions about what others ought to do create obligations for those others to deliberate or act in ways that take positive account of her decisions. By taking "positive" account I mean deliberating or acting in accord with that decision (rather than, say, taking it into account negatively by working to reverse or reject it). The most familiar example involves commands: a person has authority over another in some context if, in that context, when she issues a command to that other, she thereby obligates that other to obey the command. The authoritative person's command is authoritative in much the same way that expectations can be authoritative: the person who is subject to authority takes the command as determining what he ought to do in that context. The difference is that, when persons are authoritative, it is their decisions about what others ought to do that have this directive role, rather than standards or expectations that are partially or fully independent of a person's decision.

Many matters of political and moral philosophy involve expectations of treatment that others ought to take as authoritative largely independently of any decision of the people treated by given institutions or practices. We might owe one another a basic social structure that satisfies certain principles, say, not because of any authoritative pronouncement of any of us, but because we each have pronouncement-independent claims to such a structure. Political equality, however, requires equal authority in the sense of authority of persons. One has authority over common life when one's decisions about what others (often including oneself) ought to do create obligations on the part of others to adjust their deliberations and actions in ways that take positive account of those decisions. Political equality requires some way of arranging common life—what we do together—so that each citizen's decision about what we ought to do in that domain has equal authority over what, in fact, we do. This was the conclusion of chapter 2.

One consequence of this emphasis on authority of persons is that political equality requires that decision-making procedures grant authority to citizens' judgments about what to do, rather than granting authority to

---

4. It may be that the moral authority of any such expectation is ultimately derived from the authority of persons—the second sense of authority that I am about to discuss. This is roughly the thesis of Darwall, *Second-Person Standpoint*.

their interests. A person's judgment about what to do can endorse action that does not advance, and may even set back, her interests. I can judge that we ought to have a much more progressive income tax, even though that might set back my interests (even taking into account my interest in relations of fraternity and sorority with citizens benefited by the tax receipts). How to take my *interest* properly as authoritative depends on one's view of justice, and need not depend in any direct way on my judgment about what to do; taking *me* as authoritative in this case requires treating as authoritative my judgment that we ought to raise income taxes for people like me. The authoritative citizen requires that we, to adapt David Estlund's helpful phrase, "do as she says, not as she wants."[5] This raises the possibility that treating citizens as equally authoritative will often require the regime to do something different than treating their interests as equally authoritative would require. Respecting political equality is not the same as providing equal treatment.[6]

A democratic citizen's authority requires treating as authoritative the citizen's judgment about what to do. I emphasize the breadth of the category "judgments of what to do." Such judgments might be put in very general terms: "treat people equally"; "respect people's property rights, according to the best conception of those rights"; "act compatibly with the requirements of the true religion"; and so on. Or they might be very specific: "appoint this person as my congressional representative"; "pass this bill." Or they can be put in some intermediate level of generality: "we should establish a national health-care system fitting the following criteria." In my view, to treat someone as authoritative requires treating his practical judgments—his judgments about what to do—as authoritative, at whatever level of generality he communicates the judgments.[7] Part of having the authority is having the discretion to decide the level of generality of one's judgments.

Some democratic theorists disagree that citizens may claim authority for judgments at any level of generality. Thomas Christiano, for instance, thinks that citizens have the right to determine political aims, while

---

5. Estlund, *Democratic Authority*, 76.

6. Cf. Charles Beitz, who considers equitable treatment one of the three regulative interests that determine whether some procedure satisfies the requirements of political equality: *Political Equality*, 110–14.

7. I do assume there is an obligation generally to rule by (general) laws rather than by (particular) decrees, or bills of attainder. There are reasons of substantive justice to be wary of the latter, and I believe that authority over general norms regulating interaction responds adequately to the equality and autonomy claims canvassed in pt. I.

representatives have the discretion to pursue means to those aims.[8] Eric Beerbohm argues that citizens have authority over general principles of justice, but more specific matters, such as how to implement those principles, are left to representatives.[9] There may be good reasons to establish a division of labor between citizens and representatives roughly along these lines. If representatives are our agents, who implement our directives about important matters (aims, principles), while deploying expertise about policy means, this may produce better outcomes than a system in which citizens make particular decisions about policies and actions. And this may be a way of rendering a system of representation consistent with social and political equality, as the representatives are not superior to their electors if the latter really set the agendas and constrain the officials.[10] So I have no quarrel with the suggestion that we organize representative systems with such a division of labor in mind.

I do reject, however, the claim that we respect the authority of citizens when we restrict their authority to judgments about general aims or principles. A citizen may often have good reason to restrict her authoritative statements or actions (whether in deliberation, voting, or whatever other function) to those that communicate such general matters. But if she chooses to emphasize some more particular practical judgment, we treat her as an authority only when we respect that judgment. (I am leaving aside for now how we could be sure what a citizen is communicating within any given institutional scheme; I focus on the question of what judgments we should, in principle, treat as authoritative when we can identify them.) To reject her authority claim over what we should do in some more particular sense substantially restricts her authority as person.

Proponents of authority only over generalities (e.g., aims or principles) might respond that, while they do limit citizens' authority, they do it on equal terms: everyone is equally restricted. Representatives, they could say, get authority over particulars (as well as the general authority they have as ordinary citizens), but this is because, and only to the extent that, they are appointed according to an egalitarian process. On its own, this response is insufficient. Equal but minimal authority does not correspond to the reasons we have to support political equality. Egalitarian relationships, as I argued in chapter 2, require equally sharing authority over what

---

8. Christiano, *Rule of the Many*, 165–204.

9. Beerbohm, *In Our Name*, 197, and ch. 8 generally.

10. Kolodny makes this point about the egalitarian features of a principal-agent model of representation, though he does not claim that this model requires representation exclusively of aims or ends: "Rule over None II," 317–20.

we do. Sharing authority over some small sliver that partially determines what we ought to do falls well short of this standard.[11] This mutual acknowledgment is too thin to constitute or support recognition of equal political status.

The proponent of authority over general principles or aims might respond that such authority is not minimal. After all, principles and aims constrain the selection of means and particular actions. If there is a kind of logical hierarchy of aims or principles over means and actions, then authority over the former largely amounts to, or includes, a kind of authority over the latter—just as authority over a middle manager largely amounts to authority over the middle manager's subordinates (even if one does not have authority over the subordinates directly). So, the argument goes, authority only over generalities is substantial, and maybe even effectively complete authority over what we do.

This response rests on a mistaken view of deliberation and action. I grant that, in principle, general principles of justice and/or aims regulate and constrain more specific principles, means, and particular actions. Let us accept the (controversial) thesis that, for any choice between actions, there is some general principle or aim that determines which choice to make, or at least defines an acceptable set of choices.[12] But this does not mean that, for any given deliberation about what to do, the constraining or regulating function of some identified principle or aim is more important than some particular judgment directly about an intermediate principle or choice of means or action. Let me explain.

Sometimes I am more confident in my judgment about some particular action, or some intermediate principle, than in any of my judgments about principles or aims that might determine whether or not to choose that action. I am more confident, for instance, that race-based slavery is wrong than I am in any principle of justice that explains that wrongness. Or I might be more confident that killing *that* person under *these* circumstances is wrong than I am confident in any particular account of the ethics of killing, including any account of what aims might justify killing. In cases like this, my judgments about intermediate principles or particular actions are more important to me than my judgments about

---

11. I pursue this claim that political equality is incompatible with "leveling down" equality in ch. 5.

12. This stipulation aids my objectors. If principles or aims do not always fully determine choices, then authority over only principles or aims leaves a significant gap in citizens' authority.

general principles or aims.[13] It is not just that they are subjectively more important, in that I care more about them, though that will often be true. It is that I judge them as truly or objectively or really more important.[14] In such a case I would believe that our acting according to my more particular judgment is more urgent than acting on whatever judgments I have about principles of justice or about aims.[15] One could gerrymander one's principles to issue the desired particular judgments, but this may have unintended implications—which is precisely why one might be more confident in the particular judgment than in any principle. Moreover, it seems perverse to insist that citizens engage in such gerrymandering of their judgments in order to claim authority.

Prioritizing more particular judgments is compatible with believing that there are principles of justice or statements of aims that explain the more particular judgments. The point is that I do not necessarily know what those principles or aims are, or how best to articulate them. (Or, at least, I am less certain about the validity of those general matters, or how the general judgments apply to the more particular matters.) In that condition of relative uncertainty, I prioritize my relatively particular judgments.

In such familiar positions as these, respecting only citizens' authority over general matters is not fully respecting their authority. It denies their authority over what practically matters, as they themselves understand it. The fact that a citizen conceivably could come up with principles of justice or statements of aims that would determine the more particular matters does not mean that, in the world that is, with the citizen as he is, denying his authority over the more particular matters is trivial. The judgments on particular matters are precisely his contribution, as he understands it, to the common deliberation about what we ought to do. To deny the authority of that contribution is to deny his authority, not to respect it.

13. Beerbohm endorses Rawlsian reflective equilibrium as a method of justification, and acknowledges that this method involves treating judgments at different levels of generality as equally probative. In light of that equality of significance when it comes to justification, it is odd to treat only the most general principles as the object of citizen authority. *In Our Name*, 202.

14. I do not rest my argument on any particular metaethical view. The point is just that in these cases I believe the more particular judgments are more important for reasons independent of my caring about the judgments more. The argument proceeds even if it is a mistake to believe that things matter independently of how much we care about them.

15. Henry Richardson makes a similar point about the relationship between means and ends in deliberation; it is not always the case that one determines ends, which in turn determine means. See Richardson, *Democratic Autonomy*.

Such denial is not just a matter of respecting citizens' authority equally but minimally. If citizens do not have authority over intermediate principles, others—likely representatives—are exercising that authority. That would be consistent with political equality either if citizens always made judgments about principles or aims that determined more particular matters, and took those judgments to be more meaningful than their judgments about how those principles or aims bore on the particular matters, or if the citizens clearly and freely authorized the representatives to make all determinations about more particular matters. Perhaps under some circumstances these conditions are met. But there is no basis for believing in general that citizens' authority claims are adequately respected when we treat as authoritative only their judgments about general matters.

I will make one last remark about citizen authority as the general subject matter of political equality. Often a claim to authority carries with it a claim to decision-making discretion. The person with authority, it seems, can act for any reason, or for none, and those subject to authority remain subject. In the light of this traditional connection between authority and discretion, it may seem objectionable to ground any defense of political procedures on claims to citizen authority. If we must act for good reasons when it comes to political matters, and if, further, we often owe others an account of our reasons for supporting certain laws or policies, is it not objectionable to license all citizens with discretion? Is this not permission for arbitrary rule?

It is objectionable to act without good reason in most political contexts. But this is not a reason to deny citizens authority over what we collectively do together. Authority claims do involve a kind of discretion, in that the authority of some practical judgment means it creates obligations for others in the others' deliberations and actions independent of any other reasons for or against that judgment. (I will say more about this below.) So one properly subject to authority must treat the authoritative person as if she had discretion to make the judgment she did—because the reasons for the judgment do not bear on the obligations of the person subject to authority.

None of this, however, means that any citizen has, or is given, moral discretion when it comes to political matters. The moral obligations we have to act on reasons, and to give an account of our reasons to others, apply to us even when we have claims to authority. (They may apply more urgently when we have authority over others, and the greater responsibility that entails.) A claim to authority does mean that, absent extreme circumstances, one does not forfeit the power to create obligations for others' deliberations and actions when one violates one's relevant moral obligations.[16] For instance, this authority claim means my wrongly voting for a candidate who will enact unjust policies does not cause me to forfeit the authority involved in my right to vote. By this I mean that I have not forfeited my claim that, if I vote, others should treat that vote as authoritative (despite my morally poor track record of voting) according to the norms of the politically egalitarian electoral system. This is consistent with acknowledging that in a sense I have lost my moral "right" to vote, in the sense that I ought not to vote if doing so would entail or promote injustice. The fact that citizens do not typically forfeit authority when they violate (many) moral norms does not mean that they are free from the demands of political morality. In that sense, citizen authority does not amount to discretion or a license to arbitrariness. Authority is consistent with obligation—it is just inconsistent with some ways others might enforce those obligations.

II. Claims to Consideration as a Form of Authority

Political equality requires that citizens equally share authority over common life. This equal sharing of authority, I claim, requires that institutions and practices reliably and publicly secure what I call *appropriate consideration* of all citizens' views in the course of collective decision-making processes. The reliability requirement ensures that consideration of citizens' views is not accidental, nor, say, the result of official whimsy, but rather a robust and persistent feature of political society. The publicity requirement ensures that this assurance of appropriate consideration for all is, or reasonably could be, recognized and known by all citizens. The public declaration of the guarantee of consideration, and citizens' common knowledge of that declaration (their knowledge of the declaration and their knowledge that others know of it), constitutes and supports recognition of citizens' equal political status.[17] Reliability and publicity

---

16. Extreme circumstances could include risks that wide enfranchisement would cause some kind of disaster the avoidance of which is more urgent than the claims of political equality. Or it could include some egregious actions that warrant individual forfeiture of authority claims—perhaps violent crimes, or political crimes such as treason or election fraud. Even in many of these cases, however, it may be wrong to deny the citizens' authority indefinitely.

17. Thomas Christiano similarly insists that political equality requires the publicity of that equality: *Rule of the Many*, 67. John Rawls argues that a society's commitment to justice must be publicly accessible if the society is to properly respect citizens' equal status: *Theory of Justice*, § 23, 115. For the parallel point regarding the status of free person, see Pettit, *Republicanism*, 60-61, 70-73.

are basic, and possibly familiar, requirements on social institutions. What about appropriate consideration?

By *consideration* I refer to certain ways of granting others authority. A person has authority just when her decisions about what others ought to do create obligations for those others to deliberate or act in ways that take positive account of her decisions. This is a broad conception of authority. In much recent political philosophy, authority is understood more narrowly in terms of what we might call *command authority*. According to this conception, a person has authority over another in some context if and only if, in that context, when she issues a command to that other, she thereby obligates that other to obey that command.[18] As I understand authority, command authority is one important species of the wider genus of authority. To keep the terms clear, call this broader conception of authority *practical consequence*. A claim to consideration from some other person is a claim to practical consequence with respect to that other. It is important to keep the possibilities of practical consequence and consideration in mind, because, as I will argue shortly, command authority alone is inadequate for understanding the forms of authority democratic citizens have a right to claim over their regime.

How exactly is practical consequence a form of authority? Practical consequence involves the power to create obligations for others to respond to the consequential person's judgment about what to do. In the case of command authority, the authoritative person creates obligations to obey the command—that is, to do what the authority commands, because he commands it. But there are other obligations one might create for another, that bear on that other's deliberation about what to do, that do not involve obligations to obey.[19] For example, for a given judgment in favor of some course of action, a person might have the power to obligate another to consciously deliberate about whether to act in accordance with that judgment (rather than ignore the possibility altogether); to discuss explicitly the judgment with the person who formed it (perhaps with certain requirements on the conduct of that discussion); to give a certain weight in that other's deliberations to the mere fact that the person endorses the action; to give an account to the person of the other's decision and action; and so on. (This is not an exhaustive list.) These are obligations to grant various forms of consideration to a person's judgment.

---

18. Cf., e.g., Raz, *Authority of Law*, 3–27; Estlund, *Democratic Authority*, 2.

19. Arthur Applbaum makes a parallel point in discussing the state's legitimacy vis-à-vis its citizens in "Legitimacy."

None of these forms of consideration involve obedience. Nevertheless, practical consequence involves having a special standing in another's deliberations about what to do: the other is not entitled to just take or leave a consequential person's judgments as the other sees fit. One way to appreciate this standing is in terms of what Joseph Raz calls "exclusionary reasons."[20] One provides another exclusionary reasons for an action just when one gives that other not only a reason that weighs in favor of some action, but also a reason to exclude the consideration of other reasons that would otherwise bear on the choice of action. In the case of command authority, the obligation to obey excludes consideration of other reasons for or against the commanded action. Contrast my telling you that a bear has been recently sighted near your usual walking route to work. I have provided you a good reason to take another route to work. But, absent unusual circumstances, this is not an exclusionary reason. I have not created any obligation for you not to consider all the standing reasons bearing on your choice of route, including distance, convenience, the possibility for good wildlife photographs, and so on. Even if the reason I have given you is overriding, in the sense that you should act as the reason directs no matter all the countervailing reasons, the reason is not exclusionary because you nevertheless have no reason to give those countervailing reasons due weight in your deliberations about what to do.

Since forms of practical consequence short of command authority do not create obligations to obey, they do not exclude all other reasons bearing on some deliberation and action. As such, they may appear to be what Hobbes called mere "counsel"—that is, merely calling attention to reasons that another may consider or not at his discretion.[21] For Hobbes, counsel is something close to a complement to command: if reason giving is not in the form of a command, it is mere counsel, and vice versa. According to a Hobbesian model, then, practical consequence short of command has dubious claim to being considered a form of authority.

In this sense the Hobbesian model is mistaken: there are meaningful forms of authority short of command. Forms of practical consequence do indeed provide exclusionary reasons to those subject to the consequence. For instance, assume that in communicating my judgment to you that we ought to do A, I cause you to be obligated to think seriously about doing A, to discuss A and its alternatives with me, and to give me an account of your decision whether to do A or not. It is true, for all this, that in deciding

---

20. See, e.g., Raz, *Morality of Freedom*, 46.
21. Hobbes, *Leviathan*, ch. 25, 166, para. 3.

what to do, you do not have obligations to exclude all other reasons bearing on whether to do *A*. But you do, I submit, have reason to exclude other reasons bearing on how to structure your deliberation and your accounting of your action after the fact. Your stipulated obligation to discuss your decision with me before making it, for example, excludes consideration of other reasons bearing on how to spend your time or to organize your discussions about what to do. And the same is true for the other deliberative obligations listed. That is, in communicating my judgment about *A*, while I do not give you exclusionary reasons when it comes to the reasons to do *A* or not, I do give you exclusionary reasons when it comes to structuring your deliberations about *A*. This is authority of a kind, and grants me a special standing in your deliberations.

Practical consequence short of command authority thus involves authority, and exclusionary reasons, bearing on the deliberative process of others. It can also, as I have suggested, involve a kind of authority bearing directly on the actions considered in the deliberative process. Practical consequence can involve a claim that one's judgment in favor of some action *A* be granted a certain weight in another's deliberations, independently of the weight of the reasons for or against *A*.[22] At some extreme level of weight, this just becomes command authority: all other reasons are rendered effectively irrelevant in the light of the consequential person's judgment in favor of *A*. But there are lower levels of weight that have deliberative significance short of amounting to command authority. Some high levels of weight might amount to an overriding reason to do what the authority says, but without creating all-encompassing exclusionary reasons that foreclose the consideration of other reasons. Lower levels of weight would not amount to overriding reasons, and so might only determine another's choice if other reasons are relatively balanced. Spouses, I submit, have considerable practical consequence for each other—though, in most cases, this is short of command authority. If a wife tells her spouse that she thinks they should go to the park, this may not on its own obligate the spouse to go to the park. But it may well determine that the spouse should go to the park if other reasons for and against going to the park are relatively balanced.[23] This, again, involves considerable standing in

---

22. For helpful discussion of the metaphor of "giving weight" to reasons in deliberation, see Pettit, *Robust Demands*, 54–59.

23. These other, balanced, reasons include, for instance, the reasons to satisfy the wife's stated desire, the reasons to maintain satisfaction with the marriage, and so on. Those are all reasons that bear on the spouse's decision independently of the wife's communication of

the spouse's deliberations, without involving the power robustly to create obligations to obey.[24]

I am not sure if, in the cases of claims to creating obligations to give one's judgment deliberative weight, it makes sense to say that one has given another exclusionary reasons. One gives the other a reason to exclude reasons against granting that weight, but that seems to stretch the concept more than is warranted. Other reasons are in a sense given less relative weight than they would otherwise have, but this does not amount to exclusion. Whether or not exclusionary reasons are involved, however, the claim to create deliberative weight captures one important dimension of authority: the claim to consideration of one's judgment beyond consideration of the reasons independently bearing on that judgment. And so this form of practical consequence captures one morally significant feature of authority.

The significance of these forms of practical consequence shows that Hobbes is misleading in suggesting that command and counsel exhaust the relevant possibilities when it comes to the extent of authority one's judgments may have over others. As an aside, analysis of practical consequence shows how rare "pure" counsel may be—how unusual it is for someone's communication of a judgment to create no obligations whatsoever bearing on another's deliberations. Generally, we—the counseled—have some obligations of minimal courtesy or politeness to pay attention to the counselor, and to acknowledge the counselor's point.[25] Typically, you would be very surprised if you starting telling someone what you thought you should do together, and he just walked away without listening. The exception may be when you have no preexisting relationship with the person: then, launching into unsolicited advice would usually be odd—perhaps objectionably presumptuous—and the person may have no obligation to listen to you. The obligations of politeness, when they do exist, may be trivial in the context of the counseled person's deliberations. But

---

her practical judgment. The practical consequence manifests in the extra weight given to the fact that the wife has communicated this judgment about what to do.

24. In the imagined case, the wife's judgment does create an obligation, in the sense that it results in the spouse having an obligation to go to the park where it didn't previously exist. But the power to create that obligation is not robust, in that, by hypothesis, the wife's judgment would not have resulted in that obligation had the independent reasons been less balanced—if the spouse had urgent work obligations, for instance, that overrode any reasons to go to the park.

25. Hobbes might well resist this claim. In particular, he could resist the claim that the sovereign would have any such obligations to its counselors, which is the main context of Hobbes's discussion of counsel and command in *Leviathan*.

the counselor nevertheless has obligation-creating power. Just how trivial these obligations are may well depend on the context of deliberation. In a sense, then, what constitutes "mere counsel," in the sense of only trivially obliging another's deliberations, may be context dependent, rather than grounded in the counselor's total absence of practical consequence. By the same token, merely having some practical consequence—claims to another's consideration—may not be very significant. It matters just what forms of consideration one can claim. And this, of course, is a central concern in political contexts.

III. Political Equality as Appropriate Consideration

Political equality, I have claimed, requires that each citizen's judgments about what to do be granted appropriate consideration. In general, what constitutes "appropriate" consideration of another's judgment varies considerably by context. The relevant norms of propriety—what makes it the case that a certain kind or extent of consideration is warranted—may also have different sources. If I have a duty to care for someone, such as an infirm relative, I may in some circumstances be obliged to give substantial consideration to his views about what is best for him, but I may also be obliged to consider the matter myself and not defer to him completely. Promissory duties may require me to defer completely to a promisee's judgment about some relevant matter; promissory rights may permit me to ignore that judgment completely, or to give it only minimal consideration. In the political context, the democratic ideal of equal political status supplies these propriety norms when it comes to the consideration due to citizens in collective decision-making processes.

Put in these general terms, one might consider virtually any attempt to specify how to organize collective decision making to be an account of what consideration is due citizens. We can understand a simple equal-power theory to claim that the consideration due to citizens is exactly that specified by the conception of voting power. We can roughly describe the consideration norm supplied by such a view, for example, as the requirement that a citizen's judgment, as expressed in her vote, must be taken as fully authoritative if she and others who voted in the same way constitute a plurality of those who voted on the question. The view suggests that the citizen's judgment need be given no consideration beyond that constituted by counting the vote.

So, again, almost any view of political equality could be seen as an "appropriate-consideration" view in a broad sense. By describing my view as an "appropriate-consideration" conception of political equality, however, I emphasize the variety of ways in which one may give consideration to others in the course of even a single decision, and suggest that citizens ought to be guaranteed a number of these constituent forms of consideration. What is appropriate consideration in the political decision-making context is determined by norms of political equality, but I do not call this equal consideration. These very norms may require different institutional forms of consideration for different citizens. (This is obviously a matter of substantive argument, which I take up in later chapters. But notice this differentiation is present in all representative democracies.) Because a call for equal consideration might misleadingly imply a call for identical consideration, instead I say we are entitled to appropriate consideration suitable for political equals.[26]

The conception of political equality as a demand for appropriate consideration suitable to citizens of equal status has several advantages over conceptions that view authority as command. First, as I argued in the last chapter, citizens have diverse interests and claims at different stages of political decision-making processes. We are concerned about fairness in the context in which we develop our individual views, in individual and collective agenda setting, in coalition formation, in deliberation, in voting, and so on. Different forms of authority are relevant for these different contexts. Conceiving political equality as involving claims to diverse forms of consideration responds to this diversity of ways citizens command respect throughout decision-making processes.

Second, and relatedly, the appropriate-consideration conception better explains how citizens can enjoy equal authority, and thus equal political status, continuously, as opposed to episodically. Satisfying different claims to consideration relevant to different stages of the political process treats citizens as equals over time. By contrast, equalizing command authority (over laws and policies, or over representative selection) does not, as we saw in the last chapter, constitute or support sustained equality.

It may be difficult to give up the sense that the appropriate-consideration conception of political equality waters down citizens' democratic rights by de-emphasizing the right to issue obligation-creating commands to the state or regime. Such a concern misconstrues the relevant conceptions of citizen authority, however. Let me explain.

---

26. Here I follow Charles Beitz in distinguishing equality as a moral principle regulating procedures and equality at the level of specific institutional entitlements. Beitz, *Political Equality*, 17–19.

Command authority is not sufficient to explain the authority of citizens in a politically egalitarian decision-making process. What would it mean for citizens to only have command authority? One natural interpretation is that citizens would share direct-democratic control over the laws, through majority-decision procedures. Jeremy Waldron connects the command view of citizen authority and the restricted conception of political equality when he tries to articulate the respectful nature of majority rule. Waldron suggests, drawing from Hobbes, that we think of opposing votes as cancelling each other out—as equal and opposing forces of consent or authority. On this view, any votes that are left uncanceled after all votes are tallied remain as uncontroverted authoritative acts, which become law.[27] The arguments from chapter 3 show how this equal-power conception of political equality is inadequate, given its inability to explain citizen authority in deliberation and representation.

These deficiencies cannot be remedied by expanding command authority beyond equal voting power. What, after all, would it mean to have command authority in the context of deliberation preceding final votes on the laws? A deliberative context in which citizens could command others to vote for particular laws hardly makes sense. As I will argue in chapter 6, citizens have entitlements that create obligations in deliberation: obligations to attend to one's views in certain ways. But this is not command authority.

Appreciating forms of authority beyond command can substantially increase an agent's meaningful standing in the deliberations of others. One can have command authority over another while at the same time having no control over one's access to information, and thus, in an important sense, one's own deliberative agenda. One can have command authority while also being subject to manipulation and coercion. Recognizing someone's claims to consideration beyond command can give that person protection from such ways of undermining her standing in the deliberations of others—that is, her effective authority. Practical consequence can require more than giving weight to someone's final judgment, by including also collateral requirements to engage with that person's deliberative process only in certain permitted ways. This potential for practical consequence to be stronger than command authority gives further reason to think that command authority alone is not sufficient to explain citizens' entitlements in an egalitarian political system.

27. Waldron, *Dignity of Legislation*, 137–48; Hobbes, *Leviathan*, ch. 16, para. 15.

Might command authority be a necessary part of any bundle of claims to consideration that satisfies the demands of political equality? This is a more difficult matter. Consider, for example, the claim that the kind of command authority involved in electing representatives is one valid way of manifesting the purportedly necessary command authority of citizens.[28] As discussed in chapter 3, a great deal turns in representative systems on how the interactions of representatives themselves, and the interactions of elected representatives and their constituents, determine actual laws and policies (what I called there the process of winnowing). So, as we have just seen, the command authority of elections needs to be supplemented with other claims to consideration to properly respect citizen authority. This "command-authority-plus" model can recognize that citizens have authority claims that bear on these winnowing processes among representatives. The significance of the "plus," however—the claims to consideration beyond voting, including with respect to nonrepresentative deliberation—make it difficult to determine a priori whether claims to command authority are strictly necessary to respect citizen authority. What if some system that involves no command authority in representative selection nevertheless incorporates so many other forms of citizen practical consequence that the result is better and more egalitarian consideration of citizen's judgments? (Proponents of lottery systems may believe this is the case, at least in some circumstances; it is an advantage of the appropriate-consideration conception that it can give coherent grounding to this traditional democratic defense of lottery representation.)[29] If that is so, then why shouldn't we sacrifice the command authority (indirect as it is, anyway, in the representative system) for the more robust practical consequence overall with respect to the laws themselves?

I accept that the idea of directly causing certain outcomes exerts a strong pull. (Here I accept for purposes of argument the success of some arguments such as those made by Richard Tuck and Jeremy Waldron to the effect that voting can be understood as causing outcomes in some

---

28. There are reasons to doubt that we should think of representative selection as a close parallel to the exercise of command authority. First, the process of representative selection is tightly constrained by structural features of the electoral system, which narrowly constrain the ways in which citizens might exercise their command authority. Second, there is the question of whether command authority over representative selection is an appropriate stand-in for command authority over the laws themselves.

29. See Aristotle, *Politics*, 131 (1294b8–9); Manin, *Principles of Representative Government*; Stone, "Logic of Random Selection"; Guerrero, "Against Elections."

important sense.)[30] And exerting command authority may be, or may be more easily seen to be, causing the outcome, compared with exerting other forms of practical consequence. In the latter cases, too, there is some causation, in that the exercise of consequence, if effective, shapes deliberative processes. But I acknowledge it is less clear whether this counts as causing the resulting laws or policies. Such causation has to operate in part through the egalitarian public culture's influence on other citizens, and on elected and unelected officials. The connection of any citizen's practical consequence to that causal effect may be very murky, and the causation might easily be lost—at least as an epistemic matter of being able to observe and identify it, and maybe even as a matter of metaphysical fact. (This connection is murky in any representative system, since causing the election of a representative is not the same as causing a law to be passed.)[31] So I do not say that the argument of the previous paragraph (asking whether we might prefer more of the consideration "plus," even at the expense of the "command") is decisive. It does raise doubts about the claim that granting citizens command authority is necessary to respecting citizens' authority in the required sense. But the essential claim of this chapter is not this challenge to the necessity of command authority, but the challenge to its sufficiency. Political equality requires consideration beyond command.

IV. Conclusion

Political equality requires the reliable and public guarantee of appropriate consideration for each citizen over the course of collective decision-making processes. An entitlement to consideration is an entitlement to some practical consequence; the character of that consequence can take many different forms. While not necessarily involving the power to create obligations to obey, this practical consequence is nevertheless a form of authority in the broad sense, securing a special standing in the deliberations of others. Appropriate consideration can include traditional forms of command authority, but it is not limited to those forms. Political equality requires that each citizen receive due consideration, but it does not foundationally require any particular distribution of command authority or

---

30. For Tuck's argument, see *Free Riding*, 30–62; for Waldron, see *Dignity of Legislation*, ch. 5.

31. I discuss authority and citizens' causal power further in ch. 6.

power. Instead, citizens have diverse claims to consideration, suitable to the diversity in the stages of political decision making.

What consideration is appropriate is determined by the regulative ideals of equal political status and corresponding egalitarian political relations. In the next two chapters, I discuss how to determine just what consideration we owe to one another as equal citizens.

CHAPTER FIVE

Elections and Fair Representation

CITIZENS OWE ONE ANOTHER appropriate consideration of their judgments about what to do when it comes to matters of common concern. In this chapter I will focus on what this general requirement entails in terms of principles of "fair aggregation." Processes of election, representation, and voting on laws are relatively formal processes that aggregate many citizens' judgments into one common decision. In the next chapter I will focus on fairness in more informal processes of deliberation. This division is more a matter of convenience, however, than any expression of deep substantive differences in the subject matter. As I briefly suggested in chapter 3, and go on to argue, the divide in moral significance between formal aggregative procedures and process of deliberation is less stark than the common separation of political procedures into these two categories sometimes suggests. Instead, respect for citizens' equal jurisdiction requires attentiveness to their judgments in a number of respects, which are not subject to any obvious order of precedence. Some forms of consideration may be facilitated or encouraged by both deliberative and aggregative processes, in part because the character of deliberative processes may influence the character of aggregative processes, and vice versa. Nevertheless, as we shall see, citizens do have claims to consideration bearing directly on how their judgments are synthesized with others to produce common action.

    For any collective decision-making process involving a significant number of people, aggregation is complex, and includes many different components, both formal and informal. It includes the varied processes that determine what questions are put to a vote, the votes themselves (including both selections of officials and votes on laws or policies), and at least some aspects of the execution and enforcement of the decisions reached through voting. Deliberation, on the part of both citizens and officials, can be aggregative to the extent that it is part of the process of winnowing citizens' judgments into a single decision. Much of the discussion in this chapter will be general, and apply to these different features of aggregation. But I will focus more on elections, legislation, and legislative representation than on other aspects of aggregation. These familiar political processes serve helpful illustrative purposes. Moreover, a virtue of the equal-power conception of political equality is that it places clear and firm constraints on these central, formal aggregative processes, and so it is important to show that the appropriate-consideration conception can support adequate egalitarian constraints on these processes.

I first argue that appropriate consideration requires a kind of "sufficiency"—a guaranteed minimum set of political entitlements for all citizens. These entitlements together are significant and put substantial egalitarian pressure on any aggregative processes. These support an ideal of representation centered on enacting equal citizen authority, in contrast to traditional conceptions of representation. I then discuss violations of political equality that do not involve stripping anyone of basic entitlements. I explain when inequalities in aggregative procedures constitute or cause wrongful deliberative neglect—and thereby explain when procedural inequalities may be justified. I argue that aggregative procedures must obey certain antidiscrimination requirements. Such processes must not express nor reflect the degradation or devaluation of citizens or their capacity to form political judgments. Together, these requirements have considerable egalitarian force.

I. Sufficiency of Consideration

There are virtually infinite possible sets of entitlements to forms of consideration. There are many different ways one agent may have practical consequence in shaping the choices and actions of another. For collective decisions and actions, there is also a wide range of institutional forms and practices that might implement these forms of consideration for many citizens. So we want guidance about which sets of entitlements, both abstractly and in terms of institutional form, are consistent with political equality. I first consider what I call the "sufficiency principle." I discuss the grounds of the principle, and then consider its implications for individual entitlements, electoral systems, and the obligations of representatives.

The sufficiency principle claims that a process of collective decision making is consistent with the requirements of political equality only if it publicly guarantees to each citizen a sufficient set of entitlements to consideration. Equality requires a basic minimum of political entitlements. So far as the sufficiency principle goes, some differences in citizens' entitlements (for example, measurable differences in voting power) may be permissible, but no scheme is permissible that denies any citizen his minimal entitlements to consideration.[1] The political sufficiency principle focuses not on relational questions of how some individual's set of entitlements compares to those of others, but rather on the nonrelational question of whether an individual's set is enough to potentially qualify as appropriate consideration of a democratic citizen's jurisdiction.

The demand for sufficient consideration precludes one baleful interpretation of political equality: the idea that equality is satisfied if all persons equally have virtually no entitlement to consideration. One general problem with distributive-equality principles is their susceptibility to such "equality of poverty" interpretations—which not only ratify objectionable institutions or states of affairs, but might demand that we move toward such institutions or states despite less equal alternatives that guarantee everyone more of the relevant good. Derek Parfit labeled this the "Leveling Down Objection" to distributive equality.[2] In the political case, equal-but-low consideration might require random selection of policies. If political equality condones or requires making everyone politically poor or irrelevant, we would have good reason to doubt that political equality was a worthy goal.

The sufficiency principle prevents leveling down below the minimum level of consideration required by the principle. One might wonder whether a conception of political equality is entitled to a basic minimum principle such as this, and the easy denial of the leveling-down objection that the principle supplies. Isn't equality just concerned with how the entitlements of some citizens compare to those of others? If so, isn't the call for a basic minimum less a requirement of equality than an ad hoc exception to the demands of equality?

We can answer this line of complaint handily if we keep the proper conception of political equality in mind. The leveling-down objection applies straightforwardly to distributive conceptions of equality, whether the

---

1. For a parallel argument in the case of economic goods, see, e.g., Frankfurt, "Equality."
2. Parfit, "Equality or Priority?" 98. For discussion partly focused on the political context, see Christiano, *Constitution of Equality*, 32–42.

subject is welfare or resources or political power. Such views arguably do require us to prefer, or to move toward, systems that equalize power at the expense of reducing everyone's meaningful input into collective decision making.[3] (The strict equal-power view's demand for direct democracy is a kind of leveling down, to the extent that radically direct democratic systems preclude meaningful consideration of citizens' judgments.) But when our focus is on maintaining equal political status, there is a natural way in which the commitment to equality precludes objectionable leveling down. This is because the status of citizen itself, according to the egalitarian ideal, involves the possession of *some* meaningful jurisdiction or authority—some nontrivial set of authoritative expectations that attaches to the status. Equal refusal to consider any citizen's political judgments would be equality of a kind, and it might even constitute or contribute to some forms of egalitarian relations. But such a system would not respect citizen status. Nor would the relations it supported bear much relation to the ideal of egalitarian relations we surveyed in chapters 1 and 2. Relations constituted by equality of status require that the relevant status be meaningful, or nontrivial—not just the denial of everyone's standing, but a social and political affirmation of the standing of each.[4] So political-status equality implies a minimal level of consideration; equality of indifference cannot satisfy the relevant moral demand.

In what follows, I identify the requirements of the sufficiency principle. Citizens must have adequate consideration at each stage of aggregative processes. There are limits to permissible "compensation" between stages—though this is compatible with institutional entitlements being focused on one stage, if that adequately guarantees consideration at other stages.

I.A. INDIVIDUAL ENTITLEMENTS

A commitment to minimal consideration of citizens' judgments supports familiar participatory rights for each individual citizen. In particular, such consideration requires universal extension of basic freedoms of political

---

3. David Estlund raises doubts about the requirement that citizens are entitled to equal influence, on the grounds that such a view involves leveling down, in "Political Quality."

4. Cf. Colin Bird: "Implicit in the idea that something is reckonable is the idea that it rates highly in some presupposed rank-order of considerations bearing upon deliberation." Bird, "Status, Identity, and Respect," 213. See also Anderson, "Point of Equality," 326. By contrast, Niko Kolodny and Daniel Viehoff both support equal-but-low power or authority as consistent with political equality: see ch. 2, § III.A, and Kolodny, "Rule over None II"; Viehoff, "Democratic Equality."

speech and assembly.⁵ Severe restrictions on such speech directly preclude consideration of citizens' judgments by denying them any place on the common deliberative agenda. Consideration of citizens' expressed judgments is also an importantly directed form of respect—it manifests deliberative accountability *to* the citizen or citizens better than an impersonal process of considering possible relevant judgments. Limitations on such speech furthermore express disrespect for citizens' judgments, either by denigrating the speakers as variously irrational, dangerous, or immoral, or by denigrating potential listeners as incapable of critically reflecting upon and appropriately responding to the speech. Restrictions on speech and assembly reflect or express political hierarchy in that they generally favor partisans of the status quo (or at least the current rulers) over critics, or they otherwise distribute free speech rights in a way that favors particular citizens or particular viewpoints. To say that free participation in processes of public communication is a morally significant part of citizens' development and expression of political judgment admittedly assumes that respect for political judgment requires more than opportunities for private reflection and for rendering formal inputs into decision-making processes. But this assumption reasonably reflects the fact that judgment formation and expression—both individual and collective—comprise an extended process of deliberative agenda setting, information gathering, reflection, and so on, and one that importantly involves interpersonal elements such as those involved in political speech. Equal respect for citizens' jurisdiction requires equality not only in the recognition given to citizens' verdicts—to their formal votes, say—but also basic equality in the deliberation through which they form those verdicts, set the common agenda, build coalitions, and establish the context in which they will formally render their verdicts. Universal freedom of speech serves as a basic component of equality in this extended political process.⁶

The requirement of minimal consideration of citizens' judgments in collective decision making may also ground other individual entitlements. Exactly what entitlements are necessary to publicly secure minimal

---

5. See Mill, *On Liberty*, ch. 2; Meiklejohn, *Free Speech*; Habermas, *Between Facts and Norms*, especially ch. 8; Post, *Citizens Divided*; Brettschneider, *When the State Speaks*. Many of the democratic virtues attributed to free speech implicitly trade on an idea of political equality, including, for example, the suggestions of Habermas, Post, and Brettschneider that certain structures of free communication are necessary for democratic legitimacy.

6. This basic defense of political speech rights leaves room for disagreement on the proper scope and demarcation of those rights. Recognizing this democratic ground for speech rights helps us specify that content.

consideration of citizens' judgments will vary with social and institutional context, because different contexts render different entitlements meaningful or useful in ensuring citizens various kinds of practical consequence. Meaningful consideration may require granting citizens individual entitlements to direct consideration of various kinds by official decision makers. Speech rights provide protections and support for more directed speech—speech directed at particular officials or institutions, say, and speech that might constitute a demand for consideration of some kind—but in certain institutional circumstances there may be need for more directed, formal guarantees of consideration of citizen judgments by officials.[7] These guarantees may be especially important in relation to sites of formal collective decision making, such as legislatures, courts, or administrative agencies. If administrative agencies are granted substantial rule-making power, for instance, minimal respect for citizens' judgments may require citizen entitlements to present objections to the rule-making bodies and to demand a reasoned response to those objections.[8] Rights of individuals to contest government action through agencies and courts not only protect individual liberties, but also can secure meaningful consideration of the judgments of citizens especially affected by that action.

In the abstract it is impossible to conclude that any particular right to direct consideration is demanded by the sufficiency principle. Some institutional schemes may be able to guarantee meaningful consideration of each citizen's judgments in a publicly visible way without such direct guarantees of citizen consideration. For instance, instead of granting citizens individual entitlements to demand consideration, or to hold officials accountable for withholding proper consideration, a system might try to achieve the same end through accountability relations between different parts of the government. If such intragovernmental checks do indeed visibly and reliably secure consideration of citizens' judgments (and not just other goals such as prudent, noncorrupt decision making), then perhaps individual entitlements to demand consideration would not be necessary. In the absence of such solutions, however, the individual entitlements become more pressing.

---

7. This connection between speech rights and rights to demand direct consideration from officials is implicit in the First Amendment's guarantee of the right "to petition the Government for a redress of grievances." U.S. Const. amend. I.

8. In the United States, citizens have such rights under the Administrative Procedure Act, codified at 5 U.S.C. § 551 et seq. (2006); see especially § 553 (establishing "notice-and-comment" requirements for agency rule making).

Given the variety of institutional measures of securing consideration, individual rights to direct consideration may therefore not be necessary at every important formal decision point. Whether necessary or not, however, sets of such rights will likely not be sufficient to guarantee citizens proper consideration of their judgments. Direct consideration by officials of each individual citizen's judgment, serially one citizen at a time, is infeasible in states of any significant size. This is not just an efficiency problem. The impossibility of the thorough consideration of each would inevitably force a kind of triage or rationing by the relevant official or institution, and the result may be objectionably inegalitarian without some structure, formal or informal, imposed on that triage process.

One way to help address the inadequacy of individual claims to direct consideration is through the protection and promotion of group organization. When individual citizens' judgments on relevant matters are sufficiently similar, individuals may deem their judgments adequately considered to the extent that those judgments are articulated and publicly presented by others, and are in turn given due consideration in the course of decision-making processes. In such cases, individual claims to fair hearings are subsumed into group hearings. Formal representation is, of course, one version of such a process, as officials present and advocate for the shared views of many of their constituents. But less formal representative structures and possibilities also may be needed, including, for instance, assembly rights, and the freedom to form political parties.[9] This minimal commitment to adequate representation of groups is not itself a commitment to any kind of proportional representation, nor to any other formal representative principle. Nor does this commitment yet tell us much about which groups have a valid claim to representation of any kind.[10] It does at least prohibit, however, representation structured in such a way that it effectively precludes adequate consideration of judgments through group organization, if such organization is necessary to secure the consideration of individual judgments. This requirement is likely to have consequences for legislative representation if direct consideration of judgments in the legislature is a critical component of consideration in the regime as a whole.

---

9. These entitlements to group formation and representation are reducible to, and derived from, the claims of individuals—that is, claims to consideration that are facilitated by coalition building and reliable guarantees of adequate hearings for the judgments shared and expressed by the group.

10. I discuss the fair legislative representation of groups in chapters 8 and 9.

I.B. ELECTIONS AND REPRESENTATIVE SYSTEMS

The basic foundation of regime accountability to individuals will often be citizen votes, whether directly on laws and policies, or on representative selection. Similarly, one important aspect of group organization in any representative democracy involves formal representation, including in the legislature. The question arises, then, whether the commitment to minimal consideration implies anything about individual entitlements to vote or to restrictions on the distribution of voting power.

As I noted in chapter 4, appropriate consideration may not require voting, whether direct or in representative selection. It is at least conceptually possible that appropriate consideration could be publicly and reliably guaranteed through institutional structures that do not involve voting. Systems based on representation by lottery seem most likely to realize that possibility, if any system can.[11] I will not pursue here this specific inquiry into whether nonelectoral systems, such as lottery systems, may in fact secure appropriate consideration. The question from the perspective of the sufficiency principle would be whether a lottery-based system could secure at least minimal consideration of each citizen's judgments in a variety of ways—for example, in the course of legislative decision making, in constituent casework, in public deliberative accountability, and so on. The question seems open to me. The possibility that such a system might secure consideration as well or better than electoral systems supports the view that a conception of political equality should not be foundationally

---

11. What about a system based on the benevolent rule of an absolute monarch dedicated to appropriately considering each citizen's judgments according to the dictates of political equality? We probably all agree such a system would be very unlikely to materialize in practice, but might worry that if the view *would* endorse such a system when it did materialize, the view is inadequately democratic. In response, I believe the view would condemn such a system, because appropriate consideration in such an autocratic system would be insufficiently robust (it is not robust against changes in the monarch's intentions), or, if it is in fact robust (because the monarch's democratic psychology is unalterable, say), that robustness would not be publicly recognizable (how could we know that fact about the monarch's psychology?). If one wants to insist on a hypothetical case where the absolute monarch's political egalitarianism is robust and public, then I might concede that the view may endorse that monarchy, but I am not sure this is a damaging concession—for the hypothetical has effectively transformed the monarch into an ideal representative system, which happens to be embodied in a human being, but which maintains the transparency usually precluded by embodiment. In more realistic cases, the appropriate-consideration view rules out government by benevolent monarchs or aristocrats, or well-meaning but unaccountable "consultation hierarchies." (On this last, see Rawls, *Law of Peoples*, § 9.)

committed to electoral systems—though of course it may turn out that electoral systems are the most reliably egalitarian.

What if we determine that elections are in practice required to ensure political equality? What then does minimal consideration demand of the design of the electoral system? The answer requires reference to the diverse aims of such systems. Elections do not just grant citizens a share of authority over representative selection or lawmaking. They are part of an institutional scheme designed to secure citizens a variety of forms of consideration. The electoral system encourages candidates for election, including representatives in office seeking reelection, to provide these forms of consideration as part of the process of courting votes. The possession of a vote helps empower citizens to set the agendas of campaigns, of the representative while in office, and perhaps of the regime more generally. The vote encourages candidates and representatives in office to attend to the enfranchised, and may lead officials to engage in various forms of constituent casework.[12] The ability to remove representatives through election gives citizens the potential to sanction officials for failing to provide due consideration, a form of accountability that itself reflects recognition of citizen authority. The right to vote also serves a symbolic function, publicly reaffirming the right of the enfranchised to these forms of consideration and others, thereby putting further deliberative pressure on officials and fellow citizens to attend to one another's political judgments.

Elections thus ideally serve to secure many different forms of consideration, and to some extent the necessary distribution of votes and voting power, and more generally the structure of the electoral system, ought to be guided by the extent to which those distributions and that system successfully secure such consideration. The need for basic consideration of each citizen requires universal or near-universal suffrage, as well as prohibitions on inequalities of voting power so severe as to render some individuals' votes trivial or virtually meaningless. There is also a more direct, intrinsic reason that each citizen is entitled to suffrage and to some minimum of voting power—or, to put it another way, to limited inequalities in the distribution of voting power. Large formal inequalities are symbolically degrading for those on the short end of the inequality, a feature that not only directly undermines equal status and egalitarian relations, but also supports and

---

12. Votes might also be consequential in that a representative's margin of victory might in certain circumstances change how it is permissible or obligatory for a representative to act (roughly, by determining the scope of the representative's "mandate" from the voters). A vote may thus contribute to the character of representation despite not being decisive. For discussion, see Guerrero, "Paradox of Voting."

magnifies the system's unequal effects on the consideration granted to different citizens.[13] As I discuss in section II of this chapter, some inequalities (including in voting power) may be justified on the grounds that they are necessary to secure proper consideration for citizens who might otherwise be neglected.[14] But it is difficult to imagine scenarios where a remedy like plural voting would not be an overcompensation that created a new disfavored class. Moreover, the ostensibly compensatory nature of the large inequality would be difficult to establish in a reasonably public, recognizable way, in stark contrast to the very public signal of degradation sent by the large inequality itself. These factors may leave open the slight possibility that large differences in voting power, including possibly even plural voting, might be adequately egalitarian if the system visibly and reliably assured the proper consideration of each, but the prospect appears unlikely, and proponents of such a system would have to overcome strong prima facie reasons to reject the system given its symbolic character and its likely consequences for other forms of consideration.

This view of the relationship between political equality and the distribution of voting power has extensions that many will find appealing. It provides a way of identifying malapportionment in territorial districting, or the presence of "rotten boroughs," as a serious defect in a democratic system. It does so, moreover, without committing to strict equality in district size as an unbending universal requirement—a rigoristic view questioned by election-law scholars in the United States.[15] But the emphasis on consideration instead of on the distribution of voting power itself may appear to have more disturbing implications as well. In particular, one might worry that the appropriate-consideration view improperly permits exclusionary forms of representation under some theory of "virtual representation."

The intuitive idea behind virtual representation is that a representative system can adequately and fairly represent citizens without those

---

13. See Beitz, *Political Equality*, 35–40.

14. Mill's case for plural voting takes something like this suggested shape: he argues that plural voting is necessary to counter the neglect of elite views that Mill believed would accompany universal suffrage: *Considerations on Representative Government*, 326–45. But his case underplays plural voting's symbolic affront to the disadvantaged, and it relies on what proved to be vastly overblown concerns about the undue consideration that would be given to working-class voters at the expense of elites.

15. See McConnell, "Redistricting Cases." Scholars such as McConnell worry, for example, that focus on equal district size (and, implicitly, equal voting power) diverts attention from more subtle ways that districting schemes can undermine political fairness—and ways in which some systems might be more fair despite minor differences in district sizes.

citizens having formal entitlements to representation. Exactly which entitlements define the distinction between virtual and "actual" representation varies with the conception of representation at issue: one may claim that actual representation requires actual presence (and a vote) in whatever assembly directly votes on laws and policies, or it may only require having someone suitably similar to oneself (in terms of interest, or social class, or whatever) with a vote in the assembly, or it may only require having the right to vote in legislative elections. Proponents of virtual representation suggest that fair representation does not require the actual representation of every citizen. This view has a bad name, especially in the United States, because it is associated with the claim that Britain was not obliged to grant American colonists representatives in the Westminster parliament because they were virtually represented by the existing parliament despite the absence of any member elected by the colonists themselves.[16] Theories of virtual representation were also used to defend the denial of women's suffrage in the United States: the view in that case was that women were virtually represented at the polls by male family members whose interests were assumed to align with those of their female relatives, and who would vote accordingly.[17] Most of us today think it a prerequisite of any plausible theory of political equality that it reject systems like the disenfranchisement of the American colonists or the disenfranchisement of women.[18] The appropriate-consideration view might appear to endorse these kinds of virtual-representation schemes, because it denies the fundamental significance of equal voting power, which power is, according to this line of criticism, what makes representation sufficiently "actual." Wouldn't the view, then, imply that a system might secure proper consideration without full extension of the suffrage, and thereby imply the possible validity of the arguments of British imperialists and male supremacists?

The appropriate-consideration conception does not require these conclusions. The response to the criticism takes two stages. First, the wholesale criticism of virtual representation trades on implausible ideals of universal actual representation. If actual representation requires actual

---

16. Wood, *American Republic*, 173–81.
17. See Siegel, "She the People."
18. The American colonial case is complicated by questions about whether the Americans should have been under British rule at all. But the debates about representation often occurred under the assumption that the colonies were British. Accepting this assumption for the sake of argument, it is still clear enough that the Americans were not fairly represented in Westminster without their own representatives.

presence (and a right to vote) in the deliberative chamber that decides the laws, universal actual representation—that is, direct democracy—is probably infeasible, and would likely introduce a number of defects into the democratic process.[19] If actual representation requires the presence in the deliberative chamber of representatives sufficiently like oneself, this, again, is virtually impossible to satisfy for every citizen, short of implementing direct democracy. Attempts to remedy this by specifying more permissive criteria for likeness (for instance, one is actually represented if there exists a legislator from the same sector of the economy as oneself, or of the same race or ethnicity) introduce virtual elements into the representation—the hope that those with actual power will adequately represent people like them who do not have power. Similarly, we have reasons to doubt that voting power alone can define a meaningful distinction between actual and virtual representation. Voting is significant in large part because it is an important and effective way of securing various forms of consideration of citizens' judgments. But this consideration is, effectively, a form of virtual representation, if that means granting practical consequence to citizens who do not themselves directly legislate. So the primary ways of distinguishing actual from virtual representation cannot establish that universal actual representation is a plausible or meaningful democratic ideal. If virtual representation involves representation of others, it is inevitable. If, instead, the core of actual rule is authority, rather than consideration by grace of the representatives, then the appropriate-consideration conception does require actual rule.

This brings us to the second stage of the response to the concern about oligarchic forms of virtual representation. If virtual representation of some kind is inevitable—if no democratic system can fairly grant every citizen direct authority over the laws—then the important question for a theory of political equality is *which* structures and practices of virtual representation are fair, and which are not. We must be convinced that structures of virtual representation reliably and publicly secure the appropriate consideration of each. When it comes to the two cases at hand, the appropriate-consideration view would likely condemn the pre-Revolutionary system of representation in Westminster, and would certainly condemn the exclusion of women from the suffrage. In both cases, the arguments for the fairness of the virtual representation entailed by the policies were very weak. To briefly illustrate in the women's suffrage case, the exclusion policy in the United States was often defended in explicitly degrading terms right

---

19. See ch. 3, § II.A.

up to the end (that is, the passage of the Nineteenth Amendment in 1920), and the evidence was quite clear that representatives—and male voters—consistently failed to grant appropriate consideration to women's judgments.[20] Therefore both intrinsic and instrumental reasons for extension of the suffrage applied. Moreover, the lack of any opportunity for formal recourse by women in response to failures of consideration undermined the publicity and reliability of any consideration the system did provide in the form of conscientious male voters and representatives, free speech rights for women, and so on. These few sentences are hardly enough to make the case on their own, but assuming that the argument could be filled out along these lines, the appropriate-consideration standard would rightly condemn the denial of women's suffrage. It is true that the condemnation is not entirely a priori: it relies on evidence about what we can expect from actual representative schemes and practices, and on judgments of symbolic degradation that are probably at least in part empirical rather than a priori. This does not constitute a troubling lack of rigorism in the view; instead, it is a way of ensuring that we condemn the condemnable for the right reasons.[21] The example further shows that the ideal of appropriate consideration puts strong pressure on electoral systems to grant universal or near-universal suffrage, and in particular to avoid exclusions from the suffrage that would reflect or exacerbate other patterns of social inequality.

20. Siegel, "She the People," 987–93.
21. Is the refusal to declare the judgment of symbolic degradation necessary and a priori a symptom of only half-hearted egalitarianism? It is important that certain extensions of a theory (such as the impermissibility of sex-based disenfranchisement) be sufficiently robust. The judgment of degradation is partly empirical because it depends on claims about social and psychological tendencies of voters and representatives, and on claims about diversity of citizen judgments and interests, all of which seem to me to be empirical rather than a priori. (Perfect rational beings might be reliably and transparently capable of granting appropriate consideration to others even in the absence of any formal constraints.) That the claims are empirical, of course, does not mean that their validity is not extremely well entrenched; they may even be metaphysically necessary in the sense that the claims would be valid about human beings in every possible world. So the claim that a judgment is a posteriori is compatible with a very robust commitment to that judgment—as is the case with the judgment that sex-based disenfranchisement is objectionably inegalitarian. Finally, if the sufficiency principle rules out disenfranchisement, then this an easy case, with sex-based disenfranchisement ruled out categorically. I do not emphasize this last response because I assume the general objection questions whether the appropriate-consideration conception is entitled to that conclusion. This extended response helps show that it is.

I.C. REPRESENTATIVE OBLIGATIONS

I argued in chapter 3 that in a representative system, political equality requires not only an egalitarian system of representative selection, but also an egalitarian character to the representation itself. We can now put this point in terms of consideration: citizens have claims to consideration from representatives not just during the selection process, or in the selection itself, but also during the representative's time in office.

In the course of coming to voting decisions, representatives are engaged in deliberation, internally and interpersonally, about what we should do. They are, thus, subject to norms of appropriate consideration in deliberation, which I will detail in the next chapter. Representatives obviously need to attend especially to one another, both because of the need to form coalitions and assess possibilities for action, and because granting consideration to other representatives to some extent amounts to granting consideration to those representatives' constituents. But these deliberative obligations are owed to ordinary citizens as well, as those citizens have continuous claims to respect for their authority.[22]

The discussion of consideration in chapter 4 illustrates how representatives can grant consideration to their constituents (and to other citizens).[23] Representatives have obligations to grant citizens some control of their deliberative agenda—what it is the representatives spend time thinking about, working on, getting staff to research, and so on. They have obligations of accountability—that is, of giving an explicit account of their reasons for acting the way they do, in the light of citizens' claims one way or another. And they have obligations to grant some weight to citizens' judgments in their own deliberations—that is, they should grant weight to the fact that the citizens hold those judgments, beyond whatever weight attaches to reasons for or against the citizens' favored actions, or principles, or whatever. This weight need not amount to granting command authority to the citizens (equally apportioned, say): the representative need not treat majority positions among his constituents as mandates.

---

22. Here I am in broad accord with Eric Beerbohm, who provides an excellent, detailed discussion of representative obligations: Beerbohm, *In Our Name*.

23. Assuming the representative system overall meets the requirements of political equality, the representative probably has reasons to prioritize consideration of her constituents. But there may be remainder obligations to attend to citizens outside her constituency (beyond attending to their official representatives). On this "surrogate representation," see ch. 9, § III.

Representative discretion in deciding what, ultimately, to do is consistent with granting citizens considerable consideration.

This task of granting consideration to many citizens raises challenging questions about proper egalitarian synthesis. Many citizens' judgments are notoriously inchoate, when it comes to both particular actions and general principles.[24] Even when clear, citizens' judgments operate at different levels of generality. And it is not reasonable to expect great precision in assigning exact weights to each citizen's judgments in a representative's deliberation, even if there were some specific, defensible function that could translate a set of judgments into a suitably egalitarian practical conclusion. While exactness cannot be expected, however (from philosophers articulating principles of fairness or from representatives aiming to deliberate fairly), egalitarian norms provide some guidance. Representatives must integrate citizens' judgments at different levels of generality where possible, and, absent special considerations, should grant more weight to a given judgment the more citizens there are who endorse it.[25] Together with obligations with respect to deliberative agenda and accountability, these obligations to grant weight amount to considerable requirements on representatives, even if they allow representatives some discretion.

Why does political equality require so much of representatives who (let us assume) are fairly selected? One might claim that in voting, a citizen authorizes the elected representative to engage in deliberation and decision making, in the precise sense that the citizen (along with her fellow constituents) transmits whatever authority claims she has to the representative. If the vote constitutes such a temporary alienation of authority, then citizens would waive any powers to create deliberative obligations for representatives while the latter are in office.

This interpretation of voting as alienating all authority is mistaken.[26] First, we cannot infer from a citizen's vote (or opportunity to vote) any consensual alienation of all claims to consideration. Some citizens may intend their vote as a sign of consensual alienation of this kind; some may not. There is nothing in the act of voting itself that constitutes a tacit signal of such consent. We should doubt any such inference of tacit authorization, given how much the electoral system as a whole structures the citizen's opportunity to vote. If the citizen wishes to claim the consideration

---

24. See Achen and Bartels, *Democracy for Realists*, ch. 2.
25. Guerrero, "Paradox of Voting"; see also ch. 6, § III.B.
26. Citizens alienate *some* authority in voting, in that—if the system is justified—winning the election entitles the representative to authority in decision making that citizens do not have (but perhaps would have, absent the representative system).

constituted by influencing representative selection, but does not wish to alienate other claims to consideration, there is no way, in standard electoral systems, for her to communicate that through voting. So we have no reason to attribute to voters actual alienation of all authority.

Might we say that, though voters do not consensually alienate authority, they are obligated to alienate such authority, and so we are permitted to treat them as if they did? The obligation, the argument goes, applies when the election system satisfies obligations of political equality (and, perhaps, other requirements of justice). Under those conditions, is it not fair to say that representatives are entitled to deliberate and act unburdened by obligations of consideration to citizens who have already had the opportunity to participate in a fair selection process?[27]

This argument fails to explain why we should treat votes as waivers of claims to consideration. I have argued that citizens have continuous claims to consideration throughout the political decision-making process. If that argument is successful, the position that representatives have no obligations of consideration to citizens depends on actual waiver by the citizens. If citizens actually waived claims, then a system in which representatives were free of such claims might be compatible with the position that citizens do in fact have those claims (absent waiver). But the argument in the last paragraph depends on denying that citizens have those claims in the first place. It asserts that they are obligated to give up such claims, which amounts to not having the claims at all. It is not an argument about waiver in the relevant sense at all, and so is incompatible with the view that political equality requires continuous authority.

There is a second problem with the claim that voters authorize representatives in a way that frees them to deliberate unburdened by claims to consideration. Citizens do not have the right to deliberate about matters of common life free from the claims of others to consideration. They cannot alienate to representatives a right they do not have.[28] Citizens do not have this right because they have obligations to grant consideration to other citizens in democratic deliberation, as I will argue in the next chapter. Instead, a citizen alienates to the representative part of the citizen's right to engage in an egalitarian synthesis of her own views and those of others

---

27. The proposed objection draws from David Estlund's conception of "normative consent": the idea that it can sometimes be fair to act as if someone consented, even if he did not, because that person is obligated to consent. See *Democratic Authority*, ch. 7.

28. Cf. Locke's argument that persons cannot alienate absolute authority to a sovereign, because no person has that authority in the first place: *Second Treatise of Government*, § 135.

who are due consideration. Citizens select, in an egalitarian way, someone to engage in that synthesis more directly—not by standing in for any given citizen alone (or the winning coalition), but by engaging in fair representation. (Of course, the citizens may aim to select representatives who will try to advance certain substantive agendas, consistent with this commitment to egalitarian deliberation.) Even this alienation of authority is limited. The institutional system, including representation itself, helps relieve citizens of the full burdens of egalitarian deliberation, but it does not absolve them completely from the rights and responsibilities of deliberating about matters of common concern—which, in turn, shapes how the citizens relate to their representatives.[29] Accordingly, the obligations of egalitarian consideration are an essential part of the role of representatives.

The result is an ideal of representation that emphasizes neither the promotion nor the fair adjudication of citizens' interests, but rather the fair integration of citizens' authority claims.[30] This ideal offers an alternative to the common distinction between "delegate" representation, according to which representatives are tasked with advancing the positions preferred by their constituents, with "trustee" representation, according to which representatives are meant to best advance constituents' interests (or perhaps justice generally), irrespective of constituents' policy preferences.[31] The appropriate-consideration conception is delegate-like in requiring representatives to treat constituents' judgments as authoritative. But this obligation leaves representatives considerable room for independent judgment. This is partly because, as explained in chapter 4, citizens exercise authority at various levels of generality, some of which allow for representative discretion in implementing general principles or pursuing aims. It is also because fairly integrating different citizens' authoritative judgments involves a difficult task of interpretation, creativity, and innovation. Democratic representation involves exercising judgment in the course of constituting a process that respects the equal authority of citizens.

---

29. Eric Beerbohm similarly emphasizes the value of systems in relieving ordinary citizens of some of their deliberative obligations, and holds that citizens retain some responsibility for their own and their officials' actions. Beerbohm, *In Our Name*.

30. That representatives ought primarily to advance citizens' interests (or fairly adjudicate between them) is profoundly influential, present in the works of, for instance, Madison, Burke, James and J. S. Mill, democratic Marxists, pluralists, and public choice theorists.

31. For perceptive criticism of the delegate-trustee binary (though one that retains focus on the relationship between representatives and constituent interests), see Mansbridge, "Clarifying the Concept," 627–28.

The commitment to the minimal consideration of each citizen's judgments has substantial consequences for how we should design decision-making institutions. This still leaves us, however, with the question of whether satisfying the demand for minimal consideration of each is enough to secure political equality. Some institutional means for securing components of consideration appear amenable to straightforward equal distribution—such as speech rights, or rights to contest laws or agency rules judicially. But this is not the same as ensuring equality of the components of consideration themselves (for example, actual consideration by officials or the system more generally of the judgments expressed by citizens invoking speech or contestatory rights). This gap between the institutional means of securing consideration and the consideration itself also explains why in some cases inequalities of institutional means—most notably, voting power—might be consistent with equality in the sense of appropriate consideration for each citizen. There is also the possibility of violations of political equality that do not involve severe deprivations in violation of the sufficiency principle. I focus on such inequalities in the next part of this chapter.

II. Inequalities in Aggregation

Some features of political procedures are objectionable despite everyone's being secure in their guarantee of basic, minimal consideration, so far as formal aggregative rules are concerned. Some distinctions and inequalities are obnoxiously hierarchical without leaving disfavored citizens politically voiceless.[32] Some historical instances of what to many today appear to be paradigmatic political injustice involve such inequalities over the political poverty line. The infamous "Tuskegee gerrymander," for example, involved an attempt during the Jim Crow era to redraw the city of Tuskegee's boundary lines so as to exclude virtually all black voters from the newly defined city, while not removing any white voters.[33] The policy did not (officially, at least) deny black residents the right to vote outside the newly drawn city limits of Tuskegee, but most of us would probably retain our judgment that the policy was flagrantly antidemocratic even if

---

32. Thomas Christiano makes the parallel point about equality generally, in *Constitution of Equality*, 27–30.

33. The US Supreme Court found the boundary redefinition to violate the Equal Protection Clause of the Fourteenth Amendment in *Gomillion v. Lightfoot*, 364 U.S. 339 (1960).

we had some confidence that blacks would be permitted to exercise their suffrage in the new "suburbs." (Equal voting in this new region would not involve meaningful control over important city policies and services—a problem not easily captured by formal features of the election system.) To cite another Jim Crow example, "whites-only" political primaries, which were meant to allow white supremacists to determine the electoral slate by agreeing on which white-supremacist candidate to support in Democratic primary elections, did not formally prevent nonwhite citizens from voting in general elections, nor, in some variations, in the final party primaries occurring after the white primaries.[34] Nevertheless, those primaries denied political equality in clear terms, a fact which suggests that serious violations of political equality can occur without directly stripping citizens of their most basic political entitlements. Sometimes, the objectionable institutional schemes may involve what are easily seen to be inequalities in some institutional metric, such as voting power. In other cases, there may not be inequalities in any obvious metric; instead, citizens occupy different positions within some formally equal institutional scheme, and the question arises whether the differences in position are objectionable. In this section, I propose two principles for judging whether such inequalities or differences violate the requirements of political equality: a prohibition on deliberative neglect, and a prohibition on discriminatory procedures.

II.A. INSTITUTIONAL INEQUALITIES AND DELIBERATIVE NEGLECT

Deliberative neglect is present in any failure of appropriate consideration. When one fails to grant another the practical consequence that other is due, one neglects that other's legitimate claims to shape one's deliberations. Political decision-making systems, or constituent parts of those systems—call these "procedural features"—violate the requirements of political equality when they either cause or constitute deliberative neglect.

Sometimes procedural features are not objectionable in themselves, considered abstractly, despite whatever inequalities or differences in institutional position they may entail. They do not constitute neglect. But they may nevertheless cause neglect in particular contexts. Some feature of an aggregation procedure may cause failures of consideration by contributing to, or enabling, the violation of some claims to consideration in deliberative processes. It is also possible that it might cause (but not constitute)

---

34. See Issacharoff et al., *Law of Democracy*, 90–129.

failure of consideration in aggregation in unusual cases in which small inequalities in one stage of aggregation lead to large inequalities in the process overall. Claims of racial vote dilution, for instance, often involve assertions that a territorial-districting system differentially positions citizens in racially patterned ways that cause failures of consideration in both deliberation and aggregation, despite equality in voting power.

What does it mean for a procedural feature to constitute deliberative neglect apart from causing other recognizable failures of consideration elsewhere in the decision-making process? Institutions and practices that violate the sufficiency principle constitute neglect in especially stark ways. Procedural features could constitute neglect without violating the sufficiency principle by reflecting or expressing demeaning judgments about some citizens—a matter I will treat in the next section. Inequalities also constitute neglect when they are arbitrary—by which I mean that they are nontrivial inequalities that are not justified by some need to prevent the deliberative neglect of those who are favored by the inequality. An inequality is nontrivial when it could reasonably be expected either to affect outcomes or to cause meaningful differences in the forms of consideration granted to different citizens.[35] Some such inequalities might be justified as means of preventing deliberative neglect; if there is no such justification on offer, however, a procedural feature, by introducing pointless but consequential inequalities in consideration, constitutes deliberative neglect. This is one reason to object to moderate discrepancies in the population of territorial districts for electing representatives, if those discrepancies are not justified by the need to prevent the deliberative neglect of those in less populated districts. The appropriate-consideration conception therefore does not mandate equality at the level of institutional entitlements, but it does require that departures from inequality be justified with reference to the requirements of appropriate consideration themselves.

These forms of deliberative neglect may be unintentional. Neither the people who designed and chose the procedural feature, nor the people who act according to the rules partially constituted by the feature, need

---

35. The border between substantial and trivial inequalities in voting power is admittedly vague. The US Supreme Court has struggled with this issue in confronting the question whether the "one person, one vote" doctrine permits any deviation from strict equality of population between electoral districts. See, e.g., Karcher v. Daggett, 462 U.S. 725 (1983) (requiring "absolute population equality" in apportionment of federal congressional districts), and Mahan v. Howell, 410 U.S. 315 (1973) (permitting a Virginia state redistricting plan that included a district 6.8% more populous, and a district 9.6% less populous, than the equal population distribution standard).

intend to neglect others in order for the feature to involve deliberative neglect. While some forms of deliberative neglect may be intentional (as is obvious in cases of disenfranchisement, for instance), it is also possible for neglect to be a matter of unintentional wrongdoing—that is, negligence.

II.B. POLITICAL ANTIDISCRIMINATION

Some procedural features are objectionable because they express or reflect a judgment that some citizen or citizens occupy an inferior political status. Procedural features must not visibly disrespect citizens in their political capacities. This principle often would be violated by some procedures that also violate the sufficiency principle: disenfranchisement or massive inequalities in voting power are likely to be degrading to the citizens such policies disfavor. But the principle also applies in cases where no citizen is obviously denied a basic minimum of political entitlements, if in such cases degrading distinctions are made between citizens. In short, political equality imposes antidiscrimination requirements on procedural features.

Just what constitutes wrongful discrimination by public bodies is a complicated matter, on which there is no general consensus. (Prohibitions on discrimination by private citizens raise different issues.) Here I focus on the wrong involved when political procedures reflect or express demeaning judgments about some citizens. Whether this antidegradation norm defines the wrong of discrimination, or describes only one of several wrongs potentially involved in discrimination, or is merely an implication of some deeper truth about discrimination, I cannot resolve here.[36] I take it to be a core truth that the state should not treat citizens differently in ways that stigmatize or degrade, or that tend to create or reinforce social caste hierarchies.[37]

The reasoning behind broader antidiscrimination principles, and their application, may help inform the defense and application of the political antidegradation principle. But there are some unique features of the political case that separate it from more standard cases where discrimination is at issue, such as those involving distributing rights or other goods. For instance, in contrast to discriminatory policies that burden some citizens' exercise of religion or ability to buy a home, political inequalities—particularly, those not violating the sufficiency

---

36. See Hellman and Moreau, *Philosophical Foundations*.
37. See, e.g., Hellman, *When Is Discrimination Wrong?*; Siegel, "Equality Talk"; Fiss, "Groups."

principle—tend not to directly burden citizens' activities or to deprive them of goods, but instead to constitute or encourage a kind of neglect.[38] This neglect likely facilitates the passage or perpetuation of other discriminatory policies, but the neglect itself is a different form of degradation. At any rate, even if it is true that, according to the best antidiscrimination theory, the political principle is just a straightforward example of broader prohibitions, some attention to the political case is necessary in order to work out what kinds of distinctions in political entitlements are in fact objectionable, and why.

Why is degradation prohibited by the appropriate-consideration conception? First, and most obviously, symbolic degradation denies and undermines political equality. Procedures that explicitly communicate the inferiority of some citizens, or that rely on public justifications involving the inferiority of some citizens, directly assault and deny the equal political status of those citizens. Degrading procedures constitutively fail to secure appropriate consideration because they provide different forms of consideration to citizens according to some vision of political hierarchy. Such a pattern of consideration is inappropriate according to the equality ideal that grounds the conception's norms of propriety.

A second, related reason is that degradation undermines our grounds for believing that decision-making procedures secure appropriate consideration for the degraded individuals or groups. That is, degradation gives us powerful reason to think that there will be failures of consideration over and above the impropriety constituted by the degrading distinction itself. The presence of degrading distinctions in procedures likely reflects a more general disposition to deny or diminish the consideration of disfavored citizens. John Hart Ely's discussion of the courts' role in identifying representational failures due to "prejudice" elaborates a similar point: some distinctions give overwhelming reason to suspect invidious failures of consideration, and prohibiting such distinctions is one important way

---

38. Thus it is not clear that Sophia Moreau's account of discrimination as that which burdens our "freedoms to have our decisions about how to live insulated from the effects of normatively extraneous features of us, such as our skin color or gender," applies to political degradation. Moreau, "What Is Discrimination?" 147. One might reply that political neglect "burdens" political activity (and that such activity relevantly involves "decisions about how to live") in the sense that it makes it more costly for disfavored citizens to secure consideration. That is not an unreasonable phrasing, but I believe it is still fair to say that different ways of "burdening" different activities raise different moral questions. This is arguably a consequence of Moreau's own view, as it requires case-by-case argument about why some feature should count as "normatively extraneous," and how the deliberative freedoms of different parties should be balanced.

of preventing and repairing such failures.[39] Enshrining degrading distinctions in public decision-making procedures signals public acceptance and approbation of such invidious denials of consideration—itself a degrading public judgment, and one which tends to facilitate further denials of consideration over time, as both the procedural feature and the public degradation persist. Degrading rules and procedures thereby pose an especially powerful and persistent threat to fair consideration of citizens' judgments, whether or not the rules and procedures themselves directly violate the sufficiency principle, and thus the appropriate-consideration conception supports the prohibition established by the antidegradation principle.

How do we identify rules and procedures as objectionably degrading? How, that is, should we distinguish inequalities in political entitlements that are trivial or that actually facilitate the appropriate consideration of each from those that express and reflect judgments of hierarchy and inferiority? One important piece of evidence might be how the targeted citizens themselves view the relevant rule or procedure. If the citizens find a rule (or its justification) degrading, one line of thought suggests, it thereby is; if the citizens do not find it so, it is not. As simplistic or crude as this approach sounds, it does have some appeal. Aren't the targeted citizens themselves best positioned to judge whether some policy fails to respect them? How can a policy be degrading if it is not perceived as such? The epistemic point is a strong one, and citizens' own perceptions probably count among the better pieces of evidence as to the degrading character of a rule or policy. But citizens are not infallible, and this undermines the claim that degradation exists only where it is perceived by those targeted.

The claim that perceptions of degradation infallibly track (or constitute?) actual, objectionable degradation faces the difficulty that, in many cases, the citizens disfavored by some rule or procedure will disagree about whether the rule or procedure is in fact degrading. This may be true even in cases in which we today see the degradation as obvious and incontrovertible.[40] Notoriously, there were many women in the United States in the early twentieth century who claimed not to see any degradation in the denial of women's suffrage; some even claimed to find the policy respectful of women's ostensible domestic sphere.[41] However preposterous we might

39. Ely, *Democracy and Distrust*, 152–70.
40. Citizens also could and do disagree as to policies most think obviously innocent of any degrading character; virtually any procedure could provoke an oversensitive soul, or a crank, or someone with errant judgment.
41. For divisions surrounding the women's suffrage question, see Siegel, "She the People"; Keyssar, *Right to Vote*, 139–78.

consider those views today, they apparently were sincerely held by some of the citizens whom we consider disadvantaged and degraded by the exclusion. Many other women, of course, disagreed, and found the exclusion objectionable. Given the disagreement, targeted citizens' actual perceptions of degradation fail to settle whether or not a policy is degrading. A principle suggesting that unanimous perception or judgment of degradation must hold for a policy to be degrading in fact seems unnecessarily strict, and to place too much weight on the views of a few dissenters; other principles specifying some proportion of citizens necessary to establish the fact of degradation appear ad hoc and unmotivated by any principle. Explaining away some citizens' perceptions on the grounds that inequalities or other injustices have improperly led those citizens to unwarranted but adaptive perceptions or judgments about the character of procedures is plausible (in some cases), but this moves us away from the claim that degradation is a matter of actual citizen views, and toward the idea that we need to judge independently whether citizens' views that a policy is degrading or not are warranted.

How to determine which policy distinctions are objectionably discriminatory is a complicated and controversial question within antidiscrimination theory: it can be difficult to identify precisely the kinds of distinctions that tend to support or promote subordination or caste hierarchy, and the individuals or groups liable to subordination if they are disfavored by some policy. There are easy cases, but firm general principles are more difficult to establish. A few remarks may help to guide particular inquiries into whether political decision-making rules and procedures are objectionably degrading.

The basic test, recall, is whether the rule or procedure at issue reflects or expresses a judgment of inferiority with respect to some citizens. Some policies will wear such hierarchical judgments on their sleeves, as it were, as was the case with the white primaries. Some may be facially neutral, but obviously a pretext for hierarchy, as in the case of the line drawing that, relying on geographic segregation, tried to render Tuskegee exclusively white. But absent some very explicit oligarchic content built into a procedure or its public rationale, the determination whether a policy reflects or expresses a judgment of inferiority will be a matter of interpretation. In most cases there will be a "best interpretation"—an interpretation that is more warranted than any other.[42] The warrants, however, will often be contextual,

---

42. On the idea of a best interpretation of a social or legal practice, see Dworkin, *Law's Empire*.

in the sense that they depend on the given society's history and patterns of hierarchy, and the way in which given institutional forms of decision making might perpetuate or even create such patterns. Partly for this reason, citizens' attitudes may also be relevant: not because beliefs that something is degrading necessarily make it so, but because degradation is in part an intersubjective phenomenon. That is, degradation is not only or primarily a matter of denying some people goods, but is also a certain way of relating. Whether given procedural features support or constitute an objectionably hierarchical way of relating will therefore not necessarily be evident from the abstract character of those features themselves, but will partly depend on what Justice Harlan famously described in dissent in *Plessy v. Ferguson* as the "real meaning" of those forms in the given society.[43] "Real" social meaning is hard to establish in any pleasingly deductive fashion, but this is not to say that meaning is just whatever the citizens make of it.[44]

The idea of appropriate consideration may be of some help in ordering interpretations of social meaning aimed at resolving whether some rule or procedure is objectionably degrading. One way to focus the interpretive task is to ask whether the distinctions established by the rule or procedure could reasonably be thought to reflect or express the idea that some identifiable group of citizens is entitled to lesser consideration or practical consequence. The extent to which the disfavored citizens are "identifiable" is significant. To borrow an idea from Jean-Jacques Rousseau, equality requires that political institutions express a will that can be described as general. This, in turn, requires more than that those institutions avoid

---

43. Plessy v. Ferguson, 163 U.S. 537, 560 (1896) (Harlan, J., dissenting). In *Plessy*, the Supreme Court upheld a law requiring racial segregation in train carriages. Harlan argued that the "real meaning" of the law was that "colored citizens are so inferior and degraded that they cannot be allowed to sit in public coaches occupied by white citizens": id. In effectively overruling *Plessy*, the Court in *Brown v. Board of Education* referred to the "feeling of inferiority" generated by segregation: 347 U.S. 483, 494 (1954). But to determine whether such "feelings" are warranted, we require inquiry into something like the "real meaning" of the policy.

44. The majority in *Plessy* expressed this kind of skepticism about "real meaning": "We consider the underlying fallacy of the plaintiff's argument to consist in the assumption that the enforced separation of the two races stamps the colored race with a badge of inferiority. If this be so, it is not by reason of anything found in the act, but solely because the colored race chooses to put that construction upon it." 163 U.S. 537, 551 (1896). The parallel to the case of social equality may help: just as the "stoic-equality" view (see § II.D of ch. 1) fails because it unreasonably expects citizens to maintain egalitarian relations in the face of severe material inequality, the *Plessy*-style view that citizens should just hold their heads high in the face of any public policy, and refuse to perceive any slights or degradation, unreasonably expects citizens to ignore basic realities of their social world.

"particular" willing, in the sense of targeting particular citizens. Generality, Rousseau says, also requires the absence of any particularity in the constitution of the will itself—the absence of decision-making procedures that target some relatively fixed, identifiable groups or individuals for lesser consideration in a way parallel to the way particular acts of willing target relatively fixed, identifiable groups or individuals for disfavor.[45] "Particularity" of this kind is especially likely to be degrading—to violate the ideal of equality that grounds the commitment to the general will—because, to the extent that the targeted population is relatively fixed and identifiable, the formal disfavor of *those* particular people will persist over time (rather than falling at various times on different people across the population), and because it is more clear that the public disfavor attaches to *them*, rather than constituting some burden generally shared by the population at large. The persistence of the disfavor and its attachment to identifiable individuals constitute and promote lesser consideration of those individuals.

It is notoriously difficult to provide a clear formal distinction between "particular" and "general" rules or policies.[46] Contextual practical wisdom will have to enter when deciding cases. The extent to which the inequalities or differential positions in the procedural system track other political hierarchies present (or recently present) in the society is relevant. So too is the extent to which particular individuals move between different positions within the system, such that they experience both benefits and burdens from the system over time. These factors are relevant because they address whether the scheme targets individuals in a way that sets them apart as publicly judged worthy of lesser political consideration. This, in turn, is central to establishing whether the scheme is degrading in violation of the commitment to political equality.

III. Conclusion

Granting citizens appropriate consideration requires guaranteeing them basic political entitlements, protecting them against deliberative neglect, and observing antidiscrimination norms in organizing political

---

45. Rousseau makes this distinction between generality in the "enacting will" and generality in the matter under consideration in *Of the Social Contract*, bk. 2, ch. 6.

46. As John Rawls puts it: "Unfortunately deep philosophical difficulties seem to bar the way to a satisfactory account of these matters." *Theory of Justice*, § 23, 113. Rawls goes on "to avoid the problem of defining general properties and relations and to be guided by what seems reasonable," and to "[understand] the notion [of generality] here in an intuitive fashion." Ibid.

procedures. I do not claim that these are the only principles one might derive from the more basic commitment to the appropriate consideration of each over time, but their connection to the basic commitment is relatively clear, and their consequences for democratic institutional design substantial. Moreover, discussion of these principles illustrates the way one can apply the appropriate-consideration conception of political equality, and use that conception to organize political argument, thereby forestalling worries that the conception suffers from the lack of a simple algorithm such as that offered by equal-power conceptions. So the principles seem worthy of focus and sustained investigation. That said, other principles may be warranted, if appropriate consideration, as interpreted in the light of the basic commitment to equal political status, demands it.

I have tried throughout to respond to worries that by admitting inequalities of political power, and by de-emphasizing command authority over the laws, the appropriate-consideration conception is too permissive, or insufficiently egalitarian. The equal-power conception careers between undue permissiveness—it is not clear that an equal-power principle itself is capable of ruling out institutions like white primaries or racial gerrymandering—and undue rigor—the views inflexibly condemn any deviations from equal district sizes, for example, and even when warranted do so without regard for many of the most relevant reasons. Both of these problems—undue permissiveness and undue rigor—stem from the views' refusal to recognize the variety of important forms of consideration, and the variety of reasons one might support or reject a representative scheme on grounds of compatibility with political equality.

The principles canvassed here put substantial limits on permissible procedural inequalities. They help explain a range of important democratic judgments, and they help to order debates about more difficult cases, some of which I will treat in part III. In the next chapter, I focus on fairness in political deliberation. Institutions and practices of deliberation are important venues for equality and inequality in their own right. Moreover, the discussion of fair deliberation will further elaborate what it means to secure the consideration of each in an egalitarian way, and, because of the continuity between aggregation and deliberation implied by the appropriate-consideration view, will thereby further elaborate what political equality requires of aggregative procedures.

CHAPTER SIX

Democratic Deliberation

POLITICAL EQUALITY requires deliberative processes that, along with the regime's aggregative processes, publicly and reliably secure the appropriate consideration of each citizen's judgments. Political deliberation involves the formation, through individual reflection and interpersonal interaction, of judgments about what the regime ought to do. Deliberative processes precede the formation of any clear policy agenda and continue through the narrowing and focusing of that agenda to any final votes on laws or policies. In representative democracies, deliberation plays an important role in aggregative processes, as the character of aggregation—how an elected representative responds to the votes and the expressed judgments of her constituents, for example—is shaped by the deliberations of officials with other citizens. In this chapter I explore what political equality requires of these processes.

The issue has considerable practical significance. Social inequalities may cause or constitute substantial political inequalities despite reasonably free and fair election systems. Great and increasing wealth inequalities appear to give the wealthy political advantages over poorer citizens.[1] Racial and gender-based inequalities prevent racial minorities and women from participating in public deliberation as political equals.[2] Understanding whether and how any of these problems constitute objectionable political inequalities requires understanding what political equality requires of public deliberation.

---

1. See ch. 10.
2. Karpowitz and Mendelberg, *Silent Sex*; Mendelberg and Oleske, "Race and Public Deliberation."

While there is not a great deal of philosophical attention to these matters, one influential conception of equality in deliberation involves a requirement that citizens enjoy equal opportunity for political influence—roughly, equal chance to causally affect policy outcomes.[3] I believe the equal-influence view is, however, mistaken. The view is plagued by ambiguity. It also has disturbing implications, primarily because it ratifies as equal processes characterized by considerable unfairness.

We cannot expect to resolve these problems with improved analyses of influence or equality of opportunity. This is because, as we will see, equal-influence views must isolate a citizen's opportunity for influence independently of how other citizens exercise their own judgment about what laws or policies (or representative selection) to pursue. Equal-influence views directly target inequalities in such opportunity, but (for good reason) do not target inequalities in actual influence that result from citizens' judgments. In making this separation, however, such views miss a critical category of factors shaping the uptake of efforts at influence: the ways citizens exercise their judgment that are not themselves determined by their judgments. There are a variety of affective, unconscious, arbitrary, and discriminatory ways in which citizens can exercise their judgment about the views and propositions of others, and these ways of exercising judgment are not always themselves grounded in the judging citizen's judgments. Equal-influence views sweep all these factors shaping the exercise of judgment into the category of judgment itself, and thus any inequalities resulting from these factors are treated as unobjectionable. I will argue, however, that many such inequalities cause or constitute deliberative unfairness.

Equal-influence views have little to say about the obligations of citizens as listeners (or readers): those who respond (or not) to efforts by advocates to influence them. The presence of listener obligations raises the question of what constitutes a fair division of responsibility between listeners and advocates for ensuring that influence occurs on egalitarian terms. This question cannot be answered with reference to a distributive principle for opportunities for influence. The remedy for the ambiguity and error of equal-influence views is a more general theory of fair deliberation.

Claims to appropriate consideration, regulated by an ideal of equal status, generate obligations on listeners to respond to advocacy, and to efforts at judgment formation, in ways that avoid the deliberative unfairness

---

3. Brighouse, "Egalitarianism and Equal Availability"; J. Cohen, "Money"; Kolodny, "Rule over None II."

untouched by the gaps in equal-influence accounts. An account of obligations to grant consideration defines a division of responsibility for eliminating unintentional and systemic forms of unfairness.

I begin by analyzing what it means for citizens to have equal opportunity for influence. I criticize the view that citizens' claims to egalitarian deliberation are adequately captured by some variant of equal opportunity for influence. Citizens' interests with respect to fair deliberation are not in overcoming obstacles to the prevalence of their views per se; the relevant interest is in participating in deliberation that secures appropriate consideration for each, an overarching interest that encompasses several more specific interests. I discuss implications of these criticisms, including the possibility that political equality is compatible with some inequalities of influence and resources. I conclude by arguing that the appropriate-consideration approach sidesteps concerns that deliberative democracy unfairly privileges social and economic elites.

I. What Is Equality of Influence?

Some citizens (and corporations) appear able to assert massively disproportionate influence on the outcomes of political decisions. If we see the evil as an inequality in the ability to get one's political way, it is natural enough to demand the equalization of that ability. Hence the idea that fairness requires equality of influence.

What does it mean to have influence over political decisions? Ronald Dworkin analyzes someone's political influence as "the difference he can make not just on his own [i.e., by voting] but also by leading or inducing others to believe or vote or choose as he does."[4] Dworkin elaborates the idea of the difference one can make in terms of subjective probabilities. First, one considers the probability one would assign a given outcome of a collective decision-making process if one knew nothing about anyone's views on the matter, nor anything about anyone's ability to affect outcomes.[5] Then, one considers the probability one would attach to a given outcome if one knew the citizen's preferred outcome, and knew that he would exert maximal effort to secure that outcome. The difference

---

4. Dworkin, *Sovereign Virtue*, 191. Dworkin does not endorse equality of influence, but his is an influential analysis.

5. Dworkin assumes that under these conditions one would be justified in assigning equal probabilities to any outcome. I am not so sure. See Rawls, *Theory of Justice*, § 28, 145–50.

between these probabilities gives that citizen's influence. Equality of influence requires equality in this probability differential for all citizens.[6]

Equality of influence does not require equality of *actual influence* for any decision. We might loosely think of actual influence as one's actual causal contribution to an outcome (however that might be quantified). For any given decision there will likely be many citizens who do not exert any influence, for reasons that do not suggest any political inequality. But the influence of those citizens as Dworkin measures it might still be positive, since it may still be true that each citizen makes a difference when she exerts effort. What matters, then, is opportunity for influence, not actual influence.

Equality of influence also requires more than equality in what we might call (opportunity for) *conditional influence*. Some citizens' support for some outcome may positively affect our probability judgments, not because they have any causal effect on outcomes, but only because we know they tend to support political winners.[7] These bellwether citizens may have high conditional influence—conditional on their support for an outcome, our estimate of the probability of the outcome increases substantially—but our influence measure presumably means to capture some kind of efficacy.

The natural response is to develop a conception of influence that measures the effects on outcomes that citizens *would have* if they exerted effort. We consider a possible world in which a citizen makes an effort on behalf of a given outcome, and consider the probability of that outcome in that world. Exactly how to define one's *counterfactual influence* depends on further details of the analysis. Equality requires that things be arranged so any citizen would have the same effect on outcomes if he exerted effort as would any other citizen.[8]

With this counterfactual conception in mind, we can now focus on the claim that political equality requires equal opportunity for influence. Proponents do not endorse merely formal equality of opportunity for influence—equal legal right to engage in efforts aimed at influencing the decisions of others. Instead, the aim is to guarantee equal opportunity in some more substantive sense—perhaps, again, in terms of guarantees of certain probabilities of success. Harry Brighouse defines the "amount

---

6. Dworkin, *Sovereign Virtue*, 191–92.
7. This is arguably true of many poor citizens in the United States: their views are just good predictors of the views of richer, more influential citizens. See, e.g., Gilens and Page, "Testing Theories," 571–72.
8. On political power or influence as a counterfactual notion, see, e.g., Beitz, *Political Equality*, 10.

of influence available to someone" as "the probability we would assign to their getting their way, if they and everyone else engaged in political activity, and we knew nothing of what any other citizens wanted."[9] In general, substantive (that is, not merely formal) conceptions of equality of opportunity require equalizing relevant starting conditions, or otherwise ensuring that only the proper criteria determine the outcomes at which opportunity holders aim. For instance, Rawlsian "fair equality of opportunity" requires that only effort and ability determine who achieves offices and positions to which social and economic inequalities are attached.[10]

The Rawlsian example reveals an ambiguity in requiring equal opportunity for influence. This may require equalizing certain starting conditions, or otherwise ensuring that only the proper factors (whatever those are) determine the actual influence of those who aim at influence. Distinguish this approach from one requiring opportunities for equal influence—that is, a guarantee that, given effort, one will have actual influence matching that of others who exert effort. Emphasizing equal opportunity for influence admits potentially great inequalities of actual influence among those trying, so long as these result from proper factors, whereas equal opportunity for equal influence does not. As we will see, both strands of the equal-opportunity ideal are present among proponents of equal opportunity for influence, though they are not always clearly distinguished.

II. Against Equality of Influence

Traditional ways of construing the ideal of equality of opportunity for influence fail to capture citizens' claims to fair, egalitarian deliberation. In this section, I survey some shortcomings of this family of views. These limits reveal the need to incorporate into our account of fair deliberation a range of claims to consideration, which are not reducible to claims on the distribution of causal influence.

II.A. EQUALITY AT WHAT LEVEL OF ACTIVITY?

The first problem with the equal-influence standard applies to conceptions, like those of Dworkin and Brighouse, that require equal influence conditional on political activity (across a range of counterfactual circumstances). It is not clear what it means to for people to be, as Brighouse puts

---

9. Brighouse, "Egalitarianism and Equal Availability," 119.
10. Rawls, *Theory of Justice*, § 12, 63.

it, "engaged in political activity."[11] Are we to assume, as per Dworkin, that everyone is making the maximal effort possible to ensure that his or her preferred view prevails? That everyone is engaged, but possibly at different levels? Or that everyone is engaged at some equally moderate level? A guarantee of equal influence given some distribution of levels of effort (all try hard) may be compatible with inequalities at other distributions (all try modestly). One can imagine a society in which engaged elites, for instance, might be neutralized by vigorous action by opposed non-elites, but casual elites may have much more influence than casual non-elites. Some specifications of equal influence may not capture the proper range of concerns.

One might suggest that equal effort levels should imply equal probabilities of success. (One might suggest that influence should be proportional to effort.) This view has its own problems. First, it ignores inequalities in the costs to different citizens in political engagement at certain effort levels. Some of these differential costs to entry might constitute serious political inequalities.[12] Second, equal effort alone should not guarantee equal actual influence. Exerting effort in the right way (whatever that is) should (or at least permissibly can) matter. This is the basic intuition of many equal-opportunity views: good exercise of one's opportunity may entitle one to better results. That intuition is not compatible with the views that insist on opportunity for equal influence.

Perhaps there is a right answer here. But what counts as the right answer will depend on a conception of the fair division of responsibility between citizens in their efforts to influence one another. That is, we need some account of how much effort it is appropriate to expect of citizens (in their different roles as advocates and as listeners) in order to be entitled to some prospect for influence. The relevant conception of opportunity depends on a prior theory of fair deliberation, including claims to consideration and corresponding duties.

II.B. DOES CONTENT DETERMINE INFLUENCE?

Brighouse says that equality of available political influence requires that we be able to assign an equal probability to each citizen's getting her way

---

11. Recall that Brighouse measures influence with reference to "the probability we would assign to their getting their way, if they and everyone else engaged in political activity, and we knew nothing of what any other citizens wanted": "Egalitarianism and Equal Availability," 119.

12. A citizen with higher costs for some effort level still has an opportunity for equal influence. Other analyses might deny that this counts as a suitably *equal* opportunity.

under the specified counterfactual circumstances.[13] This formulation leaves open the possibility that, when measuring the available influence of each citizen, we allow the content of the citizen's getting his way to vary with the identity of the citizen.[14] Consider two citizens, Brutus and Anthony. For Brutus, "getting his way" means reestablishing the republic. Imagining the specified counterfactual circumstances, we arrive at some probability of that outcome. For Anthony, "getting his way" means establishing a triumvirate. Imagining the specified counterfactual circumstances, we arrive at some probability of *that* outcome. Variation between these two probabilities could be explained either by the citizens' means for achieving outcomes, or by differences in the outcomes they prefer. We are not to know what any other citizen wants, so differences in the probability of different outcomes could not be explained by different support levels. But the probabilities could still differ for other reasons. Basic facts of history and sociology may incline one to give a higher probability to the breakdown of the republic.[15] Or one might know that citizens have non-judgment-based tendencies—tendencies not deriving from what they judge to be what they "want" (on which more shortly), and so not screened out by the measure of influence—to reject republics.

If the probabilities are being influenced by the content of the views, then this is not a measure of a *person's* available influence. If Anthony's probability is higher simply because we think a triumvirate more likely than a republic (independently of what other citizens prefer), this would not imply that Anthony has more influence in a meaningful sense than Brutus—but the official measure would claim that he does. Conversely, the probabilities might be equal, but this could mask deep inequalities between citizens in means and abilities. On this reading, the measure of available influence does not track the objects of our concern.

One could specify that, when comparing citizens' available influence, we hold fixed what it means for the citizen to get his way. So we would compare the probability that the republic would be reestablished with Brutus as its proponent to the probability that the republic would be reestablished with Anthony as its proponent. (We might require that these

---

13. Brighouse, "Egalitarianism and Equal Availability," 119.

14. Brighouse says that person A's influence is determined by probabilities judged in ignorance of what other citizens want, but does not say we judge the probabilities in ignorance of what A wants.

15. If we insisted on ignorance of any such general facts, assigning probabilities may become impossible. How are we to know meaningful facts about the possible avenues of influence of the citizen in absence of basic knowledge of the organization of the society?

probabilities be equal across all issues.) Now a new problem emerges. Consider a case in which, for any given promoter, the view that the rich ought to get substantial tax cuts has an equal, high probability of prevailing. Furthermore, for any given promoter, the view that the poor ought to receive important medical services at low cost has an equal, low probability of prevailing. (Nothing in what follows turns on the relative justice of the promoted views.) In both cases, we arrive at these probabilities in ignorance of what other citizens endorse (what they "want"), but we have good reason, based on our knowledge of the structure of the society and its communications, to think that pro-rich policies do better than pro-poor policies, owing to factors independent of citizens' political judgments.

Let me clarify how this is possible. Brighouse's measure of available influence focuses on the effects of activity aimed at causing one's preferred policy to prevail. In measuring those effects, it screens out the results of "what others want," because there is generally no unfairness in one citizen's influence being limited by the policy-relevant judgments of other citizens.[16] But political outcomes—including the effects of efforts at influence—are not entirely determined by conscious judgments or desires regarding what we ought to do (what we "want" in the relevant sense). Accordingly, we must ask whether unintentional or non-judgment-based factors—factors not reducible to policy-relevant beliefs or desires—might undermine the fairness of deliberative conditions. Differences in probability for certain outcomes may, for instance, be due to differences in citizens' receptivity to certain outcomes (or to advocacy for those outcomes). If this differential receptivity is traced to citizens' exercise of relatively autonomous (and otherwise procedurally acceptable) judgment formation, then there is no objectionable inequality.[17] But differential receptivity may be explained instead by (non-judgment-based) prejudice, patterns in what grabs people's attention, deliberative heuristics, or simple arbitrariness. People may dismiss certain positions or arguments out of hand, or may not attend to them with due seriousness, possibly without realizing they

---

16. See Kolodny, "Rule over None II," 333–36.

17. I distinguish here limits on influence due to others' own judgments, and those not reducible to their judgments, which thus might involve political inequality. The standard for what counts as a citizen's "own" judgment may be fairly relaxed, and not require anything like a neo-Platonic conception of rule by one's best self. Moreover, an inegalitarian limit on influence could stem from another citizen's "own" psychology—dispositions that are truly hers—but still constitute a failure of consideration. Respecting another citizen's equality sometimes requires overcoming one's own dispositions (for instance, regarding what to take seriously), though it does not require setting aside one's own judgments.

are being dismissive. It is not hard to imagine differentials in consideration that are not due to what policy outcomes citizens consciously judge they want, but instead are due to unconscious factors or ignorance, which in turn may be traceable to social and economic structures. In these cases, I posit, there are objectionable failures of consideration, but in our imagined circumstances, available influence would be judged equal. This is our first example of how equal-influence views do not address unfairness in how citizens come to make their judgments.[18]

We are assuming in these cases that the inequalities in influence do not attach to specific people. Anyone who challenges the patriarchy, say, will have an equally low probability of success. So this may seem like favoritism to positions, but not to people.[19] I believe this characterization is incorrect. There is unfairness to the people who, as a matter of fact, do support the positions that receive diminished consideration. These citizens suffer deliberative neglect—unfulfilled claims to consideration. The fact that they would not suffer such neglect if they had different views, or that other citizens would suffer such neglect if they held the same views, may make the neglect less severe. The neglect is less robust, and thus less particular to the disfavored citizens. But this does not mean it is unobjectionable.

We should therefore be concerned with certain content-based inequalities in influence—inequalities in receptivity to advocacy not traceable to citizens' autonomous judgments. This is a departure from a focus on individual influence, because it points us to patterns in receptivity to certain judgments independent of the identity of would-be influencers. This shows the importance of social and communicative structures that do not promote or enable differential consideration. Relatedly, it suggests the importance to deliberative fairness of citizens' processes of forming judgments, some aspects of which are reducible neither to others' influence nor to other judgments of one's own.

II.C. QUALITATIVE DIFFERENCES IN INFLUENCE

The third problem involves qualitatively different types of causal contribution to outcomes. Compare, for instance, influence due to uncoerced, idealized persuasion, and influence due to manipulation or other, more

---

18. The objection is not that good policy recommendations are being neglected. The objection is procedural: patterns in the way citizens form judgments in response to advocacy cause some citizens' advocacy to be unfairly neglected.

19. Cf. Kolodny's discussion of supermajority rules: "Rule over None II," 323–25.

maleficent practices. It is difficult, both in practice and theory, to distinguish persuasion from improper manipulation. But unless we skeptically deny any distinction between different forms of influence, we need a theory of equality in deliberation that acknowledges such differences.

A view that did not distinguish different types of influence would ratify as fair deliberative conditions that intuitively seem suspect. If, for instance, political society is characterized by a balance of power among relentlessly manipulative citizens, each with equal resources and skills with which they deploy their strategic efforts at getting their way, equality of available influence obtains. This is equality of a sort, and it may well be preferable to a society in which most are at the mercy of a manipulative few. But citizens in this society do not grant one another claims to consideration. There is little respect for another's authority if one treats that other only as an object to be manipulated (and defended against). Moreover, such consideration as there is in this balance-of-power politics is not robust, since, by hypothesis, cooperation is exclusively strategic, and so conditional on circumstances of one's strategic position.[20] Equal manipulative influence does not constitute egalitarian political relations.

A second questionable implication of not distinguishing different types of influence is that the resulting view rejects as unfair scenarios in which one citizen has greater influence because she is more persuasive—that is, better at adducing considerations that appeal to others in advocating for her preferred views. But this is not always objectionable—and, indeed, is often desirable. It is compatible with granting each citizen considerable consideration, since granting such consideration to another is compatible with retaining discretion to form one's own judgments, which may of course involve evaluating reasons that others have brought to one's attention.

Proponents of equal-influence views understand these problems, and so distinguish different types of influence. Brighouse distinguishes influence that stems from "the persuasive presentation of good evidence and argument," from influence that stems from "subliminal manipulation that bypassed the rational capacities of the voter."[21] Brighouse takes this position

---

20. Institutions manifest a kind of respect to the extent that they ensure equality in manipulative influence. But if the citizens grant no corresponding consideration within the institutional structure, they deny one another consideration. This follows from deliberative democratic theorists' critique of "purely aggregative" democracy: there are requirements on citizens' deliberative "ethos"—their dispositions and motivations—that cannot be entirely outsourced to aggregative institutions.

21. Brighouse, "Egalitarianism and Equal Availability," 125–26.

because, he says, when one adopts a view because one has been persuaded, the view becomes "genuinely" one's own view. By contrast, the view of one who has been manipulated into holding that view is not that citizen's "authentic view."[22] The suggestion is that when a view is genuinely one's own, then for purposes of political equality, we need not be concerned about its provenance. Any subsequent influence exerted by the persuaded citizen counts as her own; it does not add to the account of the original persuader, as it would if the subsequent influence were the result of manipulation.[23] The result is a requirement that manipulative influence be equal, along with permission for inequalities in influence due to persuasion.

This is not an implausible view. Still, there are reasons to be concerned about great inequalities in what I will call de facto persuasiveness. One's de facto persuasiveness is the extent to which one achieves success, without manipulation, in getting others to endorse what one wants them to. We can expect great inequalities in such success: some people are more politically savvy, more charismatic, more engaging writers, and so on. While some inequalities due to persuasive "talent" are unobjectionable, some are much more troubling. One may be unperturbed by inequalities in converting opportunities into persuasion when one imagines persuasive people as helping point everyone else to True Reasons for acting, which everyone then autonomously considers. But even if that is what the talented people sincerely aim to do, in practice these characteristics may also effectively aid partial or (unwittingly) biased agendas. This may be due to objectionable inequalities in what are judged to be talented attempts at influence: in what listeners count as good reasons (as in the discussion of differential receptivity to content in section II.B), or in whom they count as good advocates (such as those who possess what a patriarchal society tends to identify as an appealing rhetorical ethos, say).[24] In these cases, the distribution of what is perceived to be talent either tracks underlying social inequalities (as in the case of discriminatory uptake of advocacy), or it may cause or constitute political inequalities (as when patterns of arbitrary or otherwise benign differences in talent recognition, perhaps

---

22. Ibid., 125.

23. See ibid., 125–26; Brighouse, "Funding of Political Speech," 479–80.

24. Melissa S. Williams convincingly argues that perceptions of what count as a reason (or who is persuasive) tend to track group-based inequalities, and that a plausible conception of deliberative ethics must address this problem. M. Williams, "Uneasy Alliance." This parallels in practical reasoning and authority what Miranda Fricker calls the "testimonial injustice" of inequalities in who is granted or denied credibility as to matters of fact. Fricker, *Epistemic Injustice*.

traceable to structural features of a society, systematically disadvantage certain citizens). All of these strike me as clear failures to treat the relevantly disadvantaged citizens as authorities of equal status in deliberation.

Similar problems arise for some differences in de facto persuasiveness that arise from "true" or "natural" talent differences (as opposed to skewed social perceptions of talent). Such inequalities are not in themselves undemocratic. But it may be that those who, in a given context, happen to have the most natural talent as advocates tend to have similar political views, or similar priorities for the deliberative agenda. This, too, may be unobjectionable. If, however, the effect of greater receptivity to the advocacy of the naturally persuasive is premature dismissal or undue neglect of the advocacy of the less talented, this would amount, in my view, to an objectionable failure of consideration for the latter. The objection is not that the less talented lose the political contest. The free judgment of citizens will inevitably disadvantage advocates who cannot persuade. The problem instead is that the process may fail to ensure to the less talented a fair hearing for their views. Egalitarian deliberation requires that listeners grant such hearings to others in the course of their judgment formation. Once such hearings are granted, judgments of unequal persuasiveness are inevitable and desirable. But such desirable discrimination must not preclude a hearing for equal citizens who happen to have less individual persuasive talent. From the perspective of advocates, there are reasons to object to this denial of consideration. From the perspective of listeners, there are reasons to object to a system in which the information (including identification of relevant reasons) available for the formation of their own judgments will be skewed by the different capacities of others. Equal-influence requirements cannot account for these reasons.

One final aspect of an equal-influence view that distinguishes persuasive and manipulative influence is that it appears to imply that equality of manipulative influence is acceptable, no matter how high the levels of manipulation.[25] I have already raised doubts that equal manipulation satisfies the demands of political equality. It is more important to protect citizens from manipulation than to guarantee to them the capacity to manipulate in turn. One might counter that in common, nonideal circumstances in which manipulative efforts are widespread, some are bound to succeed,

---

25. If, following Brighouse, any influence exerted by a manipulated citizen accrues to the manipulator, then counter-manipulation by the manipulated citizen cannot even the influence score. But this is consistent with equality of *available* influence. There just would be a huge first-mover advantage, potentially equally available to all.

and, in that case, citizens are entitled to equality of manipulative influence. But this response mischaracterizes the relevant entitlements. The ability to counter-manipulate is not of much use if one is not protected from the manipulation of others. For a third party, the proper response is not countervailing manipulation, since such manipulation hardly respects the authority of the manipulated person. There may be claims to resources with which to counter manipulation through proper means (such as persuasion). But this is another point that moves us beyond an insistence on equal influence, even if that insistence includes a distinction between persuasion and manipulation.

II.D. EQUAL RESOURCES FOR CHANGING MINDS

Some equal-influence views abandon the aim of equalizing probabilities of success in favor of what I called more traditional equal-opportunity conceptions. These conceptions, recall, require equal starting conditions or other requirements that ensure relevant inequalities are determined only by the proper factors. In the context of political influence, equal starting conditions might involve equal distribution of those resources that can be used to influence others' political judgments and actions.[26]

Niko Kolodny makes a distinction in types of influence that could support something like this interpretation of equal opportunity for influence. (Kolodny's own view is more complicated, as we will see shortly.) He argues we should equalize judgment-independent influence such as, in his example, the influence that results from access to a printing press, but permit inequalities in judgment-dependent influence such as, for instance, influence that results from giving what are seen as good reasons.[27] Since inequalities in resources usable for influence (such as a printing press) constitute judgment-independent inequalities, Kolodny's distinction lends support for a requirement of equality of resources for influence.[28]

The equal-resources view is compatible with great inequalities once people take (or decline to take) their opportunities. If the view only requires equal resources for influence, this may involve considerable inequality in actual manipulative influence, since most resources for influence are "dual use" in that they may be used for either persuasive or

---

26. See Christiano, *Rule of the Many*, 90; Sanders, "Against Deliberation," 349; Dworkin, *Sovereign Virtue*, 203.
27. Kolodny, "Rule over None II," 334.
28. Ibid., 333.

manipulative influence. Consider again the printing press, or, more simply, wealth. Moreover, some people are better than others at translating resources into persuasive influence. Accordingly, equal-resource views face the problems involving inequalities in de facto persuasiveness discussed in section II.C.

A sophisticated equal-resources proponent might respond by accounting for citizens' "internal" resources—talents and capacities that aid in translating external resources (like money or printing presses) into influence. There are well-known difficulties with attempts to measure and equalize such a metric. For example, it may be hard to establish suitably public measurements of citizens' resources, and public judgments that one has few internal resources (one is unintelligent or uncharismatic, say) may be demeaning.[29] Perhaps some of these problems can be avoided. The need to avoid the problems, however—the need for a deliberative system not to be demeaning, for instance—adds another requirement beyond equal resources.[30] More importantly, these efforts to compensate for lack of actual influence miss the real target: deliberation in which all citizens are guaranteed appropriate consideration. Resource subsidies may be a suitable means to that end in some cases, but we should not mistake a useful practical maxim for a fundamental principle.

Kolodny moves beyond a simple equal-resources view by adding several extra conditions to the requirement of equal opportunity for judgment-independent influence. He argues that the opportunities must be for "informed" and "autonomous influence: influence knowingly in accord with judgments that are themselves reached by free reflection on what one takes to be relevant reasons."[31] This rider rightly rules out manipulation. (Once manipulated, a citizen no longer has an opportunity for autonomous influence). But it introduces some internal tension to the view, because resources may need to be distributed unequally in order to protect everyone adequately from manipulation. (Some may need more resources to achieve autonomous decision making, and thus autonomous influence of their own.) This unequal distribution, however, may violate equality of judgment-independent influence. If the resources are fungible, resources granted for autonomy protection might provide recipients

---

29. Anderson, "Point of Equality."
30. The dialectical pattern on display in this paragraph helps explain why several egalitarians converge on the view that social equality is a plural ideal that includes concerns about both fairness and respect. See ch. 1, § II.A.3.
31. Kolodny, "Rule over None II," 310.

greater opportunities for influence.[32] More generally, these riders make the defensibility of the equal-influence view depend on an account of autonomy-respecting deliberation. This seems correct to me, but it is another respect in which concerns about appropriate distributions and types of influence are subordinated and constrained by a wider conception of fair deliberation.

The more serious problem with Kolodny's refined equal-resources approach is that it does not adequately address the problems of unequal de facto persuasiveness that plague equal-opportunity views generally. Kolodny's distinction between impermissible, judgment-independent inequalities in opportunity for influence and permissible, judgment-dependent inequalities grants citizens total moral discretion in how they exercise their judgments, at least insofar as political equality is concerned. As a result, with regard to political equality, this view grants societies total discretion as to how their institutions and practices of deliberation shape patterns in the formation and exercise of judgment. Inequalities due to judgments shaped by arbitrariness or bias in deliberative attention or perception "result from the influenced person exercising his judgment" and therefore would be deemed unproblematic.[33] But these practices of judgment can cause or constitute serious political inequality.

Like other equal-influence views, the equal-resources view ignores citizens' obligations as listeners—that is, obligations to grant consideration to the views of other citizens about what to do together. Claims to consideration do not entail an equal-resources requirement (or any other measure of equal influence we have considered). Nor do equal resources guarantee satisfaction of such claims, precisely because having equal resources for influence does not imply that anyone is listening to anyone else in the required sense.

III. Fair Deliberation as Appropriate Consideration

What have we learned? I begin with some remarks about how we should understand citizens' claims to properly democratic deliberation, and address what constitutes a fair hearing for citizens' judgments, given those

---

32. This problem would be mitigated to the extent that autonomy-protection resources were granted in kind (e.g., through education), and so were less amenable for use in judgment-independent influence. The problem would also be mitigated if policies could limit the use of the otherwise-fungible resources for influence.

33. Ibid., 334.

claims. Finally, I discuss what this implies about the relationship between political equality and economic and social inequalities.

III.A. CONSIDERATION AND THE PLURALITY OF DELIBERATIVE INTERESTS

Equal-influence views identify citizens' interest in the prevalence of a view they have settled on before interpersonal deliberation as their central interest in this common process of judgment formation—or, at least, as the central interest relevant to political equality. But the idea that we best conceive citizens as battling for the supremacy of their pregiven preferences is one of the old canards that theories of deliberative democracy were developed to deny. On the contrary, common deliberation at its best can hardly be conceived as an exercise of power at all.[34] I do not claim that power does not operate in processes of common deliberation. Rather, if we conceive of power as a counterfactually defined probability of overcoming resistance to the advancement of one's ends, then citizens who respect one another as equals do not aim primarily to exercise power. They do not have a purely strategic orientation to fixed ends, because they are willing to alter their ends upon persuasion. None of this implies that citizens do not or should not engage in instrumental behavior—just that they should regulate their instrumental pursuits according to a suitable ethic of fair deliberation. Fairness in deliberation requires limits on power inequalities, so as to prevent abuses in a sufficiently robust way, but this does not mean fairness *consists in* equality of power. Because deliberation involves forming judgments, citizens aim to form and develop views that they do not already have at hand, to organize their views in a coherent way, and to discover which views on particular matters fit best into their broader structure of value judgments. Similarly, they are concerned that others respect their authority over common life, not that they can causally contribute to the changing of others' minds at the same level as others.

Citizens have a variety of interests in the deliberative process. Citizens have interests in an environment conducive to autonomous and informed judgment formation. This includes protections from manipulation, and communicative structures that do not skew citizens' receptivity to advocacy. These protections must be continuous, rather than satisfied in a starting-gate manner that leaves citizens vulnerable if they mismanage their entitlements. Citizens are entitled to have their judgments receive

---

34. See Beitz, *Political Equality*, 12–14.

appropriate consideration by others—that is, to have a fair hearing for their judgments. This is both a matter of an advocate's capacity to command attention, and a listener's granting the advocate consideration required for that fair hearing. (This entitlement, too, is continuous, and generally cannot be lost.[35]) When these interests and claims to consideration are satisfied, the result is not only fair hearings for any given citizen's judgments, but also a fair system of deliberative synthesis—responding to diverse judgments in a way that recognizes the equal authority of each citizen. (Fair deliberation thus has implications for structures and practices of representation, something not easily accounted for by equal-influence requirements.)[36] The exercise of authority and its recognition are intersubjective, constituting a relation between advocates and listeners. The norms regulating these relationships are not captured by norms regulating the distribution of advocates' influence. Instead, the norms derive from a conception of egalitarian political relations constituted by equal authority over common life.[37]

A claim to a fair hearing from others includes a claim to a chance at influencing those others, but the satisfaction of the claim is not measured by actual or available causal influence.[38] A claim to deliberative weight in the judgments of others (see chapter 4) is close to a claim to causal influence, but the actual causal effect of the weight depends considerably on the constellation of relevant reasons applying to those others. Similarly, citizens' deliberative interests have consequences for the distribution of resources, but there is little reason to think the proper distribution is strictly equal.[39] One consequence of rejecting the equal-influence view is that we

---

35. I leave open the possibility of forfeiture of claims in the case of serious crimes, including political crimes such as election fraud.

36. Kolodny endorses separate requirements of equal opportunity for formal influence (regulating electoral systems), equal opportunity for informal influence (regulating deliberation), and delegate-like representative practices in "Rule over None II." These requirements may be in tension, if equal opportunity for influence admits substantial political inequalities that could render (or require!) representation less in the mode of an (egalitarian) delegate. Ryan Pevnick notes limitations of equal-influence views in treating representation in "Egalitarian Rationale."

37. The ground for Kolodny's commitment to the equal-influence requirement is an intuitive claim that particular inequalities are compatible with overall social equality only if those particular inequalities were endorsed through a process in which each party had equal opportunity to influence the outcome. "Rule over None II," 305–6. This chapter proposes an alternative standard for what kind of process could render certain outcomes compatible with social equality.

38. See Dworkin, *Sovereign Virtue*, 203.

39. Cf. Knight and Johnson, "What Sort of Political Equality," 281.

can better understand which of various inequalities are in fact compatible with political equality.

III.B. FAIR HEARINGS I: PROPORTIONALITY

What would it mean to grant a fair hearing to a citizen's view or judgment?[40] There are a number of dimensions on which such hearings could vary, corresponding to the different dimensions of consideration canvassed in chapter 4. So, for instance, one might place a judgment higher on the common deliberative agenda, spend more time and effort attending to the judgment and the reasons in its favor, grant the judgment greater weight in deliberations, satisfy more stringent requirements of deliberative accountability, and so on. Institutional means for varying the consideration of different judgments in these ways may be limited, and in some cases incapable of the finest fine-tuning. But there is no doubt that the structure of democratic institutions and practices can shape the nature of public deliberation, and thus to some extent the scope of the consideration the regime secures for citizens' judgments. We return to the question, then, of what constitutes due consideration.

The egalitarian intuitions behind the equal-influence view suggest the straightforward idea that consideration should be equal in scope for each individual who claims a public hearing for his view. Further, perhaps the scope of consideration for a judgment should similarly expand in proportion to the number of its adherents or proponents (assuming problems of manipulative influence are set aside).[41] This "proportional-consideration" view aims to combine the distributive equality of the equal-influence view with the qualitative appreciation of citizens' claims to consideration.

The proportional-consideration view has a number of serious problems, however. Some judgments require consideration out of proportion with their numerical support. First, certain kinds of judgments, or judgments rendered by certain citizens, may be at especial risk of deliberative neglect or failures of consideration. Perhaps historical or present-day

---

40. Citizens' interests are fundamentally in the hearing their judgments get in the process as a whole—by the regime, as it were. Officials and citizens may have parallel obligations to vary their hearings according to the principles I discuss, but different obligations may attach to particular roles or positions in society consistently with granting a proper hearing in the process as a whole.

41. Lani Guinier indicates support for something like this view—what she calls "proportionate minority influence"—in *Tyranny of the Majority*, 92.

hostility to certain groups creates a risk that others, and thereby the regime as a whole, will systematically neglect the judgments of members of such groups. Even in the absence of hostility, some minority groups may be so small that a substantial and sustained risk of neglect would exist absent granting special attention or weight to their judgments.[42] Or there may be reason to suspect that, through intentional dismissal or otherwise, democratic deliberations tend to neglect judgments of certain content—for example, judgments demanding protections for unpopular speech, or rights for criminal defendants. The claim in this latter case is not that democracies tend to make decisions that undermine or fail to respect certain values. The claim is that judgments expressing those values regularly fail to garner proper consideration over the course of democratic deliberations, which failure constitutes a failure to respect the political status of the citizens who render those judgments. Failing to consider during deliberations and failing to value in decisions are likely to be correlated and even causally linked. But they are conceptually distinct, and the warrant for special consideration I am suggesting here stems from predictable failures of deliberative attention, rather than from supposed predictable failures to reach a decision properly accounting for all the relevant values.[43]

A second line of reasoning supporting special consideration for certain judgments refers to the content of those judgments. Some political judgments, that is, may warrant extended consideration because of the matters they address, or because of the positions they take. In general, what constitutes appropriate consideration does not depend on the content of the judgments; respect for citizens' jurisdiction implies that the

---

42. It may be that the small minorities require the same actual consideration, but that special institutions or formal rights are needed to guarantee that consideration. Or it may be that special consideration of some type (e.g., attention) itself is required, owing to the risk of neglect absent that consideration (e.g., because of tendencies not to recognize reasons given in the idiom common to the individuals at risk of neglect).

43. Jeremy Waldron objects to arguments along these lines that they express disrespect to citizens, by grounding decision-making procedures on an assumption that citizens will act wrongly. Waldron, *Law and Disagreement*. In response, first, the judgment that neglect is predictable is not objectionably particular in the sense discussed in ch. 5: it does not identify any particular individuals or groups as especially likely to engage in deliberative failures, but rather refers to deliberative blind spots we generally share as citizens. Second, the judgment that neglect is predictable need not impugn any individual (even in general terms): neglect at the regime level may emerge out of collective patterns of action and deliberation, without any individual engaging in culpable neglect. (See Pettit, "Responsibility Incorporated.") Finally, there is no disrespect in accurately identifying deliberative unfairness and remedying it. I have benefited here from Thomas Christiano's discussion in *Constitution of Equality*, 282–83.

mere fact that the citizen has rendered the judgment gives that judgment claim to consideration by the regime. But there may be some features of a judgment's content that warrant consideration of special scope. One such feature, I submit, is the urgency of the claims identified by a judgment. When a citizen judges that some matter fit for collective decision implicates especially urgent claims on the part of some persons, that judgment may warrant special consideration so as to protect against the possibility that those urgent claims go unsatisfied. Urgent claims, as I understand them, are claims that some prospective action or omission by the regime threatens great harm or great injustice. What standards a claim must satisfy in order to be "urgent" for these purposes, and when those standards are met, will inevitably be matters of democratic controversy and contention themselves. But the fact of controversy denies neither the presence of genuinely valid standards for urgency, nor the possibility that citizens will often manage to agree on at least some of these standards and their application. Judgments implicating urgent claims may warrant special consideration even if there is no reason to expect what would, apart from the special demands of the urgency principle, constitute deliberative neglect of those judgments.[44]

Some might worry that granting special consideration to certain judgments on the grounds that they feature urgent claims smuggles into the conception of political equality concerns about justice or general social equality. This might be a worry about properly identifying and categorizing the demands of different values. Or this might take the stronger form of a complaint that altering procedures according to some broader vision of justice or equality wrongly violates political equality.[45] Special consideration of urgent claims, however, need not unduly privilege any individual or group, nor denigrate any citizen's status as an equal citizen. On the contrary, such a commitment is a natural and fair component of a general strategy of deliberative triage. It does not require any constitutional commitment to tendentious principles of justice. Finally, the urgency principle states that urgent claims may merit special consideration, not that political equality itself requires the just and proper satisfaction of urgent claims. The demand, again, is for a fair process of considering

---

44. Formally instituting differential consideration according to urgency may be difficult in many cases, not least because it gives incentives for citizens to render all their judgments in the most urgent terms. So it may be that the requirements of urgency are best met by proper democratic ethos among citizens (including officials).

45. See Waldron, *Law and Disagreement*, especially 114–16.

diverse claims under conditions of scarcity, not for the most just decision in the light of those claims.[46]

Proportional consideration, then, risks deliberative neglect in cases where disproportionate consideration is required. Proportionality also involves giving greater consideration than is required in many cases. As Thomas Christiano points out, even in relatively simple, ordinary cases of adjudicating between a few judgments, in which there is little risk that any view will be neglected altogether, consideration of views in proportion to their support is inappropriate.[47] Christiano points out that the satisfaction of each citizen's deliberative interests often does not require adding extra consideration for a judgment for each additional proponent. To a great extent, each proponent is satisfied by a given, adequate level of deliberative attention. Moreover, to the extent that citizens have deliberative interests not only in the prevalence of the judgment they currently hold, but also the prevalence of the right judgment (or, at least, the one most appropriate by the lights of their basic value structure, given available information), citizens benefit from deliberative attention to other judgments and from a deliberative process that tends to synthesize judgments in a way responsive to information and citizens' values.[48] Because both values and the evaluation of information and evidence vary, citizens retain some interest in the prevalence of what they see as the right judgment given the right value structure and the right interpretation of evidence. But this divergence of grounds for evaluating judgments does not eliminate altogether some overlapping interests in deliberative procedures that all can appreciate as valuable. This overlap gives citizens reasons to be concerned with deliberative consideration of judgments apart from their own, and thereby undermines the proportionality principle.

III.C. FAIR HEARINGS II: EQUALITY

Christiano recommends replacing the proportionality principle with a principle requiring equal time (or, perhaps more broadly, equal deliberative attention or consideration) for each view.[49] Equal consideration of

---

46. This distinguishes my view from those that claim political equality requires in part that procedures tend to promote just or egalitarian outcomes—for instance, the views of Ronald Dworkin and Charles Beitz. See Dworkin, *Sovereign Virtue*, 185–90; Beitz, *Political Equality*, 110–14.
47. Christiano, *Rule of the Many*, 91.
48. Ibid., 91–93.
49. Ibid., 92.

all views arguably reflects the deliberative ideal of "universal access," and mirrors to some extent Jürgen Habermas's "ideal speech situation."[50] But this mirroring feature of the view is not an advantage in the actual world, characterized as it is by the scarcity of various deliberative resources such as time, attention, and the material resources needed to support communication.[51] Where scarcity is not severe, perhaps something like an equal-consideration standard ought to apply. So, for instance, in the public sphere at large, if communication were relatively cheap, and, across all citizens, there were an abundance of time and attention, the fair satisfaction of the deliberative interests of each might require something close to the equal consideration of views.[52] But in general such abundance of deliberative resources does not hold. For example, there are fairly severe limits on the deliberative resources of formal decision-making bodies, such as legislatures, executive agencies, and courts. There are also constraints on the time and attention of citizens and officials. This significant scarcity requires a kind of deliberative triage in the collective decision-making process.[53] There are a number of reasons to think that equal time or consideration for all views is not the ideal triage principle.

First, the intuitions behind the proportionality principle have some merit. There are reasons in many cases to grant greater consideration to certain judgments to the extent that many citizens share them. Citizens have nonoverlapping interests in the prevalence of their well-informed, reflective judgments (nonoverlapping because these judgments differ), and while this may not warrant proportionality, this provides a reason to give special attention to widely held views under conditions of deliberative scarcity. Popular support is a relevant factor in determining the scope of consideration, even if it is not the sole factor; this is one aspect of granting each citizen deliberative weight. Equal consideration of all views, because it fails to honor that factor (or suggests offloading it entirely onto aggregative processes), cannot serve as a principle for deliberative triage.

---

50. Habermas, "Discourse Ethics," 89. Habermas does not intend his description of the ideal speech situation to model actual deliberation; he expresses reservations about the phrase "ideal speech situation," and prefers to describe his principles as a set of counterfactual presuppositions inevitably made by anyone engaging in argument. See ibid., 88.

51. See Estlund, *Democratic Authority*, ch. 10.

52. I do not mean that there ought to be laws requiring the equal airing of views, or equal attention to all views; the equality principle might only require an egalitarian ethos requiring citizens and media sources to attend widely to a variety of views.

53. For more on deliberative scarcity in the public sphere, see ch. 10, § IV.A.

These reflections show that several factors determine the proper scope of hearings for each citizen's judgment. Given the scarcity of deliberative resources, particularly in more formal, central decision-making arenas, political equality requires principles of deliberative triage. Such triage should be guided by the commitment to secure for citizens appropriate consideration and practical consequence as is warranted in the light of their deliberative interests. This includes a ceiling of sufficient consideration for most views in order to protect against the deliberative neglect of citizens with other views. A regime implementing this deliberative ideal would respect individuals' claims to be heard, and thus their subsidiary claims for an opportunity to influence others. Such a regime would also attend to the need for fairness in the way that the regime synthesizes the consideration of each in the extended process of democratic deliberation.

III.D. JUSTIFIED INEQUALITIES

It is difficult to make general pronouncements about what autonomous judgment formation requires of institutions or resource distributions. Much depends on specific matters of context and political sociology. All citizens require access to the education necessary to develop relevant moral and intellectual virtues. They also require communicative structures that make relevant information widely available in unskewed fashion. While these may require considerably more egalitarian social organization than we enjoy today, none of these requirements entail the need for strict equality of resources. On the contrary, they suggest that, in conditions of secure autonomy protection, some economic inequalities may be compatible with political equality.

This conclusion might strike some as obvious. But some egalitarians worry that any significant economic inequality undermines political equality. These concerns manifest in a line of criticism (or critical reinterpretation) of John Rawls. Rawls's first principle of justice requires equal political liberties, and that citizens all enjoy the "fair value" of the political liberties.[54] The "fair value" proviso denies the justice of a system in which citizens have equal formal political liberties, but in which some have much greater substantive control than others. Rawls's concern was that the wealthy would use their riches to gain undue control of elections or representatives. He suggested that vigorous systems of campaign-finance regulation could protect the fair value of the political liberties despite

---

54. Rawls, *Theory of Justice*, § 36, 198.

the economic inequalities permitted by his second principle of justice.[55] Some critics have suggested, however, that Rawls was wrong about this: that the second principle on its own admits more wealth inequality than is compatible with political equality.[56] Rawls's theory can accommodate this problem, because the priority of the first principle means that economic inequalities that undermine the fair value of political liberty are unjust even if they would otherwise be permitted by the second principle. But we would face a major shift in the implications of Rawls's view if the difference principle, say, were rendered effectively irrelevant because of the economically egalitarian pressures of political equality.[57]

If my arguments here are correct, however, Rawls's "insulation strategy"—his belief that a fair political process could be insulated from any corrupting effects of *some* economic inequalities—appears more plausible.[58] Final verdicts depend on the facts of political sociology, as well as just how extensive the inequalities permitted by the second principle are. The more general point is that a commitment to democracy does not entirely determine one's distributive commitments. This is an encouraging result, to the extent that there are democracy-independent reasons (whether Rawlsian, consequentialist, grounded in economic freedom, or other) to permit some economic inequality. If democracy is compatible with some such inequalities, there is to that extent less of a conflict between democracy and distributive justice.

My arguments about fair deliberation do not just open up space for some economic inequalities. Rejecting an equal-influence requirement implies that some inequalities in the political process itself are permissible, and perhaps desirable. Consider David Estlund's argument for inequalities in political "inputs"—that is, citizens' "absolute quantity of political participation."[59] Estlund argues that inequalities in inputs would be justified if those inequalities were necessary to increase each citizen's input (for instance, through a tax-and-subsidy political donation voucher scheme), and if the result were better decisions in general. As Estlund notes, his position is probably incompatible with a requirement of equal opportunity for influence.[60] In my view, such a scheme might be justified,

---

55. Ibid., 198–99; Rawls, *Justice as Fairness*, § 45, 149–50.
56. Thomas, *Republic of Equals*, ch. 4; Daniels, "Equal Liberty."
57. Uncoincidentally, Brighouse endorses this revisionist reading of Rawls in "Political Equality in Justice."
58. The term comes from O'Neill, "Free (and Fair) Markets," 82.
59. Estlund, "Political Quality," 135.
60. Ibid., 127.

if it existed in a context of suitable autonomy protection and unskewed political culture, and if the input inequalities did not amount to oligarchic control of the political agenda by denying consideration to some citizens' judgments. These egalitarian criteria are not needed to satisfy Estlund's epistemic standards of improved outcomes. So the constraints I favor are in this respect stricter than his. But if the egalitarian criteria of appropriate consideration are met, then Estlund is right to say that the promise of epistemically superior deliberation could justify the inequality of inputs.

Relatedly, some inequalities of influence could be justified in suitably egalitarian contexts. My arguments do not amount to an "equal-influence-plus" view—a requirement of equal influence as well as other necessary conditions. Consider the following, admittedly highly idealized, scenario, to illustrate the point. Say a society meets the conditions of autonomy protection and unskewed culture, such that citizens resist manipulation and grant appropriate consideration to others in deliberation. In that society, some wealthier citizens are especially politically motivated, and use their abundant resources to fund unbiased research in hopes that the findings would support their preferred policies with what other citizens would see as genuinely good reasons. Assume that there is a sufficiently democratic culture such that these efforts by the wealthy would not amount to undue control of the political agenda—countervailing reasons and evidence would still be accessible and heard, perhaps through the efforts of groups or coalitions. In such a case, rich individuals might well have greater available influence than others, since their wealth gives them a higher probability of translating their preferences into outcomes via the good reasons their funded research uncovers, and which might not always be countered by good reasons brought to bear by countervailing coalitions. I do not see any inequality of authority in such a case. The inequality in influence is due to greater likelihood of bringing reasons to bear that are judged consequential by other, unmanipulated and equally authoritative, citizens, in the context of an unskewed culture and an open, accessible deliberative agenda. Such a case differs little, in my view, from the extra influence a person might have owing to "internal" resources such as intelligence or moral perceptiveness. Inequalities in such resources can be troubling if they track or constitute a skewed culture (say, when those who are perceived as intelligent have political biases or gain credence because of cultural skews such as white privilege). This is why we must be careful about inequalities in de facto persuasiveness. But such inequalities do not intrinsically constitute political inequality. They are compatible with political equality in the presence of suitable egalitarian constraints.

III.E. DELIBERATIVE OLIGARCHY

I have taken for granted that deliberation is amenable to regulation (whether legal or otherwise) according to principles of political equality. Some critics of deliberative democracy argue that this assumption is unwarranted: that deliberation (or deliberative democratic theory) involves an aristocratic exclusion of citizens who do not regularly communicate in the deliberative idioms said to be preferred by theorists.[61] The worry is that deliberative theories of democracy tend to be "logocentric" in their emphasis on explicit ratiocination and the reasoned justification of policy positions. Some citizens may not engage in advocacy in a way that fits this logocentric mold, so emphasis on a particular style of communication risks unduly discrediting the views of such citizens.

This is a serious concern, but it is a concern internal to political equality. If we are committed to fair deliberation, we demand that all citizens receive appropriate consideration of their views. The very concerns that motivate some deliberation skeptics—exclusion, disrespect, the disempowerment of historically mistreated groups, and unjust policy making—all tell in favor of requiring serious consideration of views that do not carry their explicit philosophical defense on their sleeves.[62] Something might fairly count as one's judgment, and thus ground one's claim to consideration, without one having a ready defense of that judgment in traditional philosophical terms. Policies must ultimately be publicly justified by reasons, so in the course of deliberative synthesis it would be important for citizens collectively to tease out the reasons behind judgments initially supported by emotional exhortation, narrative testimony, comedy, or whatever else. But that does not imply that deliberation—which here simply means the process of judgment formation, and does not prejudge the form of inputs into that process—requires that citizens detail explicitly these reasons as a condition of respecting their authority. A plausible account of fair deliberation demands much more easily negotiable conditions of entry.

Proponents of equal-influence views of fair deliberation would likely agree with these remarks. But the requirement of equal opportunity for

---

61. Sanders, "Against Deliberation"; Young, "Activist Challenges."

62. Sanders objects that deliberative democracy refuses to allow explicit consideration of one's identity—for instance, one's membership of certain groups—in the course of deliberation: "Against Deliberation," 353. But appropriate consideration under certain circumstances might require just that kind of attention—if identity were an indicator of likely deliberative neglect, for example.

influence may not capture the critics' concerns. I argued above that equal influence is compatible with a skewed culture in which certain judgments are neglected either because of their content or because of the manner or idiom in which they are presented (say, in a manner marked, consciously or not, as unmasculine, nonwhite, or unintellectual). The demand for equal opportunity for influence therefore cannot remedy these forms of political inequality. Of course, in racially unjust or patriarchal societies, racial minorities and women are likely also to suffer unequal influence. But this is not the entirety of the injustice.

One reason for this problem turns on yet another question about how to measure opportunity for influence. It may be that in a less-than-thoroughly racist society, persons of color could achieve influence equal to that of white compatriots if the former publicly comported themselves in a way traditionally marked as white (in terms of diction, clothing, accent, cultural references, and so on). If, however, they could not achieve such influence if they did not act in ways marked as white, this would constitute substantial political inequality. Citizens would be denied appropriate consideration on grounds that are at best irrelevant and at worst track and perhaps constitute social subordination. The version of equal opportunity for influence I am considering here cannot properly recognize such injustice.[63] Perhaps a Kolodny-style view could arrive at the correct result, by considering cultural whiteness to be a judgment-independent resource that is unequally distributed. This is not implausible, but difficulties arise in the case of nonwhite citizens who "have" the resource of cultural whiteness in the sense that they *could* comport themselves as white if they so chose. In my view, there is still an inequality if they are required so to comport themselves in order to achieve influence. This is another example of how equal-influence views do not adequately specify who has the responsibility for guaranteeing the relevant influence (or, in my preferred view, consideration). By focusing our attention on the obligations of listeners or readers—in this case, citizens who have obligations to attend to views expressed in conventionally nonwhite manners or idioms—the appropriate-consideration view ensures a fair division of deliberative responsibility suitable for political equals.

---

63. Measuring influence on the basis of the influence one is likely to achieve given the actual efforts one is likely to make, as opposed to the most effective efforts one could possibly make, comes close to requiring opportunity for equal actual influence, the shortcomings of which I outlined in § II.

IV. Conclusion

Complaints about deliberative exclusions share with equal-influence views the worthy motivation to end the oligarchic way in which some citizens and corporations in contemporary democracies wield massively disproportionate influence over collective decisions. Nevertheless, in challenging oligarchic institutions and practices, we need to get the competing vision of democracy right. This the equality-of-influence family of views cannot do, because they too narrowly construe citizens' interests in deliberation as interests in instrumental success. Criticisms of deliberative exclusion are limited to the extent that they fail to offer principles of fair deliberative inclusion, and misguided to the extent that they reject the idea of fair deliberation altogether. The rejection of oligarchy that lies at the heart of the demand for political equality therefore requires a richer conception of deliberative fairness than either of these critical stances offers. We must guarantee citizens neither a quantum of power, nor an indeterminate promise of inclusion, but rather a quality of consideration commensurate with their status as political equals.

By moving us away from a narrow focus on causal influence, the ideas about fair deliberation developed here may display, to borrow a term from G. A. Cohen, "unlovely heterogeneity."[64] There is, perhaps, a loss of theoretical elegance. But this heterogeneity in citizens' deliberative claims better reflects the moral reality. It also follows much contemporary egalitarian theory in identifying a plurality of values served by social and political equality. These values demand not equalizing a specified metric, but securing opportunities for influence—and other modes of deliberation—suitable for equals.

My view admits certain kinds of inequality to be compatible with democracy in its fullest sense. But this is no apology for the rule of the rich (or the white, or men), now or in the future. The critique of equal influence reveals the importance of cultural and structural critique; the importance of widespread access to education and information; protections for the autonomy of all citizens; and the obligations of each citizen to attend to others, including those with historically devalued forms of expression. "What is important," says the egalitarian historian and theorist R. H. Tawney, is not that all people "should receive the same pecuniary income. It is that the surplus resources of society should be so husbanded and applied

---

64. G. Cohen, "Currency of Egalitarian Justice," 921.

that it is a matter of minor significance whether they receive it or not."[65] The view outlined here is consistent with the spirit of Tawney's thought. While democratic ideals place constraints on the extent and manner of economic inequality, the arguments here suggest the possibility of democratic institutions and culture that empower all citizens, such that whatever inequalities in resources or influence are permitted by distributive justice have no bearing on their equal authority.

65. Tawney, *Equality*, 113.

PART III

Institutions

CHAPTER SEVEN

Unequal Voting

THE US SENATE AND ELECTORAL COLLEGE

A THEORY OF POLITICAL EQUALITY aims not only to explain the value and importance of democracy, but also to guide debates about what democratic ideals require of political decision-making processes. In this part of the book, I discuss how the principles of political equality developed in the last part should inform various controversial questions of democratic institutional design. In this chapter, I argue that the inequalities in voting power involved in the US Senate and in the Electoral College used to elect the president violate the requirements of political equality.

The Senate comprises two senators from each state.[1] States with large populations get the same number of votes in the Senate as do states with small populations. Because the states vary considerably in population, there are large inequalities in how many citizens are represented by a senate delegation. The 563,000 citizens of Wyoming elect the same number of senators as the 37,253,000 citizens of California.[2] In intuitive terms of voting power, the apparent malapportionment is equivalent to granting citizens of Wyoming about seventy-four votes compared to one for Californians when it comes to Senate elections, a plural voting scheme of a magnitude far beyond that imagined by John Stuart Mill.[3] Is this inequality in voting power justified?

---

1. U.S. Const. art. I., § 3, cl. 1.

2. State population figures are from the 2010 US Census, as reported in Mackun and Wilson, "Population Distribution and Change," 2.

3. Mill seems to have imagined giving those who benefited from his plural voting scheme only a few votes each: *Considerations on Representative Government*, ch. 8.

[175]

The answer to this question is simple for majoritarian ideals of democracy, such as those implied by the equal-power conceptions considered in chapter 3. The Senate is straightforwardly undemocratic by the lights of such conceptions. But the appropriate-consideration conception of political equality does not rule out all inequalities in voting power. As I argued in chapter 5, such inequalities may be justified if they are necessary to prevent the deliberative neglect of those favored by the inequalities. So the question arises whether the Senate can be justified along such lines—namely, that it protects citizens of small states from deliberative neglect that would, the argument goes, likely obtain if Senate representation were proportional to population. Treating this question elaborates and clarifies how to determine whether voting inequalities are compatible with citizens' claims to appropriate consideration.

I argue that this line of justification fails; the unequal representation of individuals in the Senate constitutes objectionable political inequality. There is no reason to think that citizens of small states require special deliberative solicitude in the federal legislature. Whatever claims to special consideration there may be among relevant groups, moreover, are not well satisfied by the Senate, and come at the expense of the substantial neglect of large-state citizens. States themselves may have some claim to political autonomy in a federal system, but whatever claims these are should not be secured by national political inequalities favoring small states. The Senate is thus unjustifiably undemocratic.

This conclusion has implications for the election of the US president, as the Electoral College process for such election tracks what I argue is the malapportionment of the Senate. This inequality, too, is objectionable, and it should be eliminated. The reasons for a more egalitarian election of the president are all the more urgent given that the inequalities in the Senate are much more constitutionally entrenched, and thus likely to remain. The election of the president should mitigate that inequality rather than exaggerate it.

I. Special Consideration for Small-State Citizens?

Inequalities in voting power are compatible with political equality if they satisfy principles of fair aggregation. The inequality must not be so great that it violates the sufficiency principle, by in effect disenfranchising those disfavored by the inequality. The inequality must not discriminate, for instance by reflecting or expressing degrading judgments of the disfavored citizens. And, if nontrivial, the inequality must be justified by the need to prevent the deliberative neglect of those favored by the inequality. So the Senate would be justified if, among the other criteria, its representational structure were necessary to protect the deliberative neglect of those favored by its inequalities—namely, the citizens of small states.[4]

I will grant, for purposes of the argument, that the inequalities involved in electing senators do not disenfranchise citizens from large states. This is possible only because there are relatively few citizens from small states, so it is at least plausible to argue that their votes do not dilute those of large-state citizens to the point of virtual worthlessness. (Similarly, it is at least plausible to argue that ordinary citizens in a large country would not be disenfranchised by granting just a few notables seventy votes, while granting the ordinary citizens just one. Granting seventy votes to half the country, however, would effectively disenfranchise the rest.) Some may resist this concession, in which case the objection to the current Senate system is straightforward. But for reasons of argumentative charity—and in deference to the views of most large-state citizens, who do not seem to see themselves as entirely disenfranchised when it comes to the Senate—I will set this point aside.

Is the disproportionate representation of small states in the Senate discriminatory in the sense of reflecting or expressing degrading judgments about large-state citizens? I think not. As a matter of fact, few large-state citizens seem to find the Senate's representational structure degrading. Political philosophers who consider the matter agree that there is nothing stigmatizing about the equal representation of states (though they rarely explain this conclusion).[5] While citizens' judgments may not be definitive of the presence of objectionable degradation, this quiescence is good evidence that the real social meaning of equal state representation in the Senate involves no invidious judgments about large-state citizens. One reason for this is that the disfavoring of large states is not "particular" in the sense of

---

4. A state is "small" for these purposes if its proportion of senators in the Senate is greater than its proportion of citizens in the US population (i.e., any state with a population less than one-fiftieth of the national population). If a state's proportion of senators is smaller than its proportion of the national population, it is "large." (By this measure, 17 states are large and 33 are small, according to the 2010 census, though several are near the border of large and small.) This is a rough measure of who benefits from the inequality, since some deviation from representation proportional to population is inevitable if senators are to represent constituencies exclusively within one state, state borders do not change, and the Senate does not grow very large (e.g., larger than the US House of Representatives).

5. Ronald Dworkin and Charles R. Beitz both suggest in passing that the Senate's disproportionate representation is not objectionably degrading, though neither pursues the issue in detail: Dworkin, *Sovereign Virtue*, 201; Beitz, *Political Equality*, 94.

targeting a fixed set of identifiable individuals for political opprobrium. At any given time, one could identify the individuals who reside in large states. But if migration between small and large states is high, if state citizenship is not a particularly salient part of people's identity, and if the judgments of small- and large-staters overlap sufficiently that disfavoring large states in the Senate does not appear to represent special antagonism to the judgments of large-staters, then we may have grounds for judging that the representational scheme is not objectionably particular. If there is something objectionable about this inequality, it most inheres not in the communication of inferiority through institutional inequalities, but rather in inequalities of consideration constituted or caused by the representative structure.

Inequalities in Senate representation are hardly trivial. A seventy-to-one ratio in voting power is enormous, as imaging that ratio in terms of actual votes suggests.[6] Even the difference in representation between moderately large and moderately small states is far from trivial. (West Virginians, for instance, have roughly four times the voting power of Virginians.)[7] The US Senate is one of the most unequally apportioned democratic legislative houses in the world.[8] Such considerable ratios constitute nontrivial inequalities in consideration in the aggregative system. They are also very likely to cause inequalities in deliberative consideration, granting small-state citizens more extensive hearings for their views at the expense of hearings for large-state citizens. It is true that this inequality is tempered by the bicameral system, with the House of Representatives distributing seats in a way that closely tracks state populations.[9] So there is less overall inequality in representation in the US Congress than there is in the Senate as a whole. Nevertheless, overall inequalities in total congressional representation remain considerable.[10] These inequalities

---

6. Given the important symbolic nature of the vote, a plural voting system with such a ratio might communicate a degrading meaning in a way that malapportionment at that ratio does not. So we must be careful in deploying our intuitions about one case in explaining the other. But the ratio itself has considerable pull on our intuitions.

7. The population of West Virginia in 2010 was approximately 1,853,000. The population of Virginia was approximately 8,001,000. Mackun and Wilson, "Population Distribution and Change."

8. Samuels and Snyder, "Value of a Vote," 662.

9. Samuels and Snyder find the US House of Representatives to be one of the least malapportioned legislative bodies in the world—that is, one of the closest to a standard according to which each member of a legislature represents the same number of constituents: ibid., 660–61.

10. Lynn A. Baker and Samuel H. Dinkin, using the Shapely-Shubik measure of "coalition-building power," find significant disproportions in power relative to population in the Congress as a whole. Baker and Dinkin, "Senate," 27.

are reinforced by the method for electing the president, which distributes Electoral College votes to states according to their number of congressional representatives.[11] Studies showing that equal state representation in the Senate has policy consequences favoring small states provide considerable evidence that these inequalities are meaningful and consequential in terms of the consideration granted to citizens from different states.[12] Differential treatment of different citizens is no direct proof of differential consideration; citizens with equal authority may well choose to favor some citizens in certain contexts. But the volume of evidence and the absence of obvious, general reasons for favorable treatment of small-state citizens provide some reason to think that these outcomes result from unequal power and the deliberative solicitude that goes along with it.

Differential consideration is not intrinsically objectionable. In chapter 6, I provided several reasons why some citizens might have claims to greater consideration than a simple principle of consideration proportional to numbers would require. Small-state citizens might have claims to greater voting power as a necessary means of preventing otherwise predictable deliberative neglect.[13] Perhaps, the argument goes, in a more majoritarian legislature, in which Senate seats were distributed proportionally to state populations, small-state citizens would often be denied their due consideration. This may have been one of the reasons supporting the Senate's apportionment at its founding. James Madison, an opponent of equal state representation, could hardly bring himself, when writing *Federalist* No. 62, to acknowledge any reason for the representative scheme, beyond the need to compromise with small states.[14] But a sympathetic rendering of small-state representatives' concerns in insisting on

---

11. Washington, DC, also has three Electoral College votes, despite having no congressional representation.

12. See, e.g., Lee and Oppenheimer, *Sizing Up the Senate*; Dahl, *How Democratic*, 46–54; Malhotra and Raso, "Racial Representation."

13. I am not aware of any reason to think that small-state citizens' claims are typically more urgent than those of large-state citizens, which was another reason I suggested in ch. 6 for greater scope of hearings.

14. "It is superfluous to try by the standards of theory, a part of the constitution which is allowed on all sides to be the result not of theory, but 'of a spirit of amity, and that mutual deference and concession which the peculiarity of our political situation rendered indispensable.'" Madison, "Federalist, No. 62," 416. Madison was from a large state (Virginia), and was writing most directly for an audience in a large state (New York), though Madison's opposition to equal state representation was vigorous and consistent enough that there is not much doubt about his sincerity on this point. Jeremy C. Pope and Shawn Treier argue that the equal-state-representation plan prevailed because northern concessions on counting slave populations for the purposes of representation caused North Carolina's

the "Connecticut Compromise" that established the equal representation of states in the Senate might well involve concern about the deliberative neglect of citizens in states like Rhode Island or Connecticut. (The other likely concern, protection of states' interests as states, I consider below.)

It is important not to confuse the chances that citizens of small states would not often get their way in a more proportional system from the risk of deliberative neglect. Populations that are small in the context of a nation of 300 million generally cannot expect to control policy outcomes. So the fact that, say, the 563,000 citizens of Wyoming might not have much decisive influence in a more proportional system is not itself a sign of deliberative neglect. One rough way of framing the question of deliberative neglect would be to ask whether the citizens of Wyoming would be any more subject to not getting their way (or, more precisely, not getting their due consideration in various forms) than any other similarly sized group of citizens—such as, say, the 595,000 citizens of the city of Milwaukee, Wisconsin.[15] The mere fact that the citizens of Wyoming might, like the citizens of Milwaukee in the current system, not regularly have their concerns granted special, explicit consideration in a more proportional national legislature does not itself ground a claim of deliberative neglect.

Do small-state citizens face risks of neglect warranting special consideration? There are good reasons to doubt. The social groups well represented by small-state officials are not ones we typically worry are vulnerable in ordinary egalitarian processes.[16] Evidence that small states reap distributional advantages (without any clear policy rationale, such as greater poverty in the states receiving more resources) from their disproportionate representation suggests that the voting inequality is not leading to equal treatment, but rather is leading to favorably unequal treatment. This, in turn, is (admittedly very rough) evidence that equal voting would be more likely to lead to equal treatment (reflecting equal consideration) rather than neglect.[17] One could dispute whether these distributional advantages had good rationales, or whether, even if they did not accord with any plausible principle of justice, this was evidence that large-state citizens

---

delegation, a pivotal vote, to support the Connecticut Compromise. Pope and Treier, "Reconsidering the Great Compromise."

15. For the Milwaukee 2010 census numbers, see "American Fact Finder."

16. Dahl, *How Democratic*, 52–54. Dahl made a similar argument 45 years earlier, in *Preface to Democratic Theory*.

17. Baker and Dinkin provide evidence of the disconnect between favoring small states in the distribution of resources and any poverty-based rationale, in "Senate," 39–42.

were being subjected to deliberative neglect (as opposed to egalitarian but low-quality decision making). But it is telling that such evidence as we have points toward the conclusion that small-state citizens are not especially vulnerable.[18] Defenders of the inequality must provide some reason to justify that inequality, and such reasons are hard to find.

If anything, the Senate has often served to exaggerate otherwise-existing inequalities in consideration—as it did by protecting southern slaveholder interests (relative to a more proportional system, which would have given greater influence to populous northern states) throughout the antebellum period.[19] Small states currently have lower concentrations of historically disadvantaged racial minorities than large states, so people of color are particularly disadvantaged by the Senate system.[20] If the Senate system were not so clearly protected by the Constitution, this system would likely be subject to legal challenges on the grounds that it amounts to racial vote dilution.[21] Even if we do not think that equal state representation in the Senate constitutes racial vote dilution, however, the fact that small-state citizens are, in aggregate, whiter than the United States as a whole raises further doubts that they are at special risk of deliberative neglect.

One might think that small-state citizens are vulnerable to the extent that they are disproportionately rural, in comparison to more urban large-state populations. A more proportional representative system, the argument might go, would in effect favor urban citizens, relegating rural citizens to irrelevance in voting coalitions, and thus neglect. There is a plausible case that citizens in rural areas are at risk of deliberative

---

18. Skeptics of reform tend to emphasize that the benefits to small-state citizens (and burdens on large-state citizens) are relatively small, rather than providing evidence that small-state citizens would be at risk of neglect if Senate seats were distributed more proportionally. See, e.g., Macedo, "Our Imperfect Democratic Constitution"; Mayhew, "Broken Branch," 366–67. Mayhew also notes that, contingently, the Senate's system does not advantage one political party (much) over another. Ibid., 365–66. But the characters of the parties themselves are significantly affected by the need to capture Senate seats in small states, thus presumably skewing the parties toward small-state concerns at the potential expense of large states.

19. As Dahl also points out: *How Democratic*, 52–54.

20. Malhotra and Raso, "Racial Representation." Cf. Macedo, who defends the Senate's malapportionment partly on the grounds that, on his view of the evidence, it appears not to reinforce any other objectionable hierarchy in American society—racial or class oppression, for instance. See "Our Imperfect Democratic Constitution," 611–18.

21. This dilution is unintentional (rooted as it is in state borders), so it would not violate the Fifteenth Amendment as construed in *City of Mobile v. Bolden*, 446 U.S. 55 (1980). But it could certainly face challenges under the Voting Rights Act, which encompasses voting procedures with discriminatory effects.

neglect.[22] They may not enjoy easy access to media, meaning it may be difficult for them to communicate their concerns (to each other or to non-rural citizens), and to gather information essential to their own judgment formation. They may have special concerns that are not shared by others (and so cannot rely on those others to demand consideration on their behalf). The truth of the matter obviously depends on the details. Wealthier people may not face these difficulties, no matter where they live. But rural citizens in general may have a colorable claim to special consideration even if they are otherwise not at risk due to poverty, racial discrimination, or other standard markers of social disadvantage.

The problem of this argument for purposes of defending the Senate is that Senate representation poorly tracks rural-urban divides. There are some small states that are not particularly rural, such as Rhode Island, Delaware, and Hawaii. If protection of rural citizens is the primary basis of claims for special representation in the Senate, these states are granted such representation at the expense of other states for no reason. For another, many rural communities are located within large states, such as California, New York, and Texas. A Senate with representation more proportional to population (which would likely require a larger Senate) would be more likely to represent those rural communities than does a system in which members of those communities must compete with millions of city dwellers in their states for their senator's attention. Even if citizens of very low density rural states, such as Montana, Alaska, and Wyoming, are entitled to some disproportionate consideration, this does not justify the Senate's representational structure. Equal state representation in the Senate is both a crude and an extreme method for granting deliberative solicitude to rural citizens. Absent any other reason to think that citizens of small states are at risk of deliberative neglect in a more proportional system, then, the Senate's inequalities cannot be defended as politically egalitarian.

II. Protecting State Autonomy?

I have so far assumed that the defense of equal state representation would be grounded in the claims of small-state citizens, in their role as members of a national democracy. Perhaps this is a mistake: perhaps the best defense of the Senate most directly refers to the claims not of small-state citizens, but of small states themselves. Ultimately, whatever claims states

---

22. The Supreme Court registered skepticism that this could justify malapportionment within states in *Gray v. Sanders*, 372 U.S. 368, 379 (1963).

may have are grounded in the claims of their individual citizens. But satisfying those foundational individual claims might require granting some status to states as collective entities. If that is true, then certain claims on national decision-making processes might make reference to states as collective entities, rather than making direct reference to the consideration or neglect of individual citizens. States within the United States may have some claim to political autonomy of a limited sort—some scope for organizing common life within the state according to the judgments of the state's citizens, relatively free of the authority of citizens from other states. Equal representation of states in the Senate may be justified, the argument goes, not as a means of directly protecting individuals in the national process, but as a means of protecting against national policies that would wrongly infringe state autonomy.[23]

This concern for state-autonomy protection was arguably present at the Constitutional Convention, as states that were more or less sovereign under the Articles of Confederation were concerned about maintaining autonomy (if not anything like full sovereignty) in the new constitutional system.[24] The claim that equal state representation in the Senate plays a special role in the so-called "political safeguards of federalism" has been recognized by the US Supreme Court.[25] I cannot here investigate the constitutional or moral grounds and extent of state autonomy, and I certainly do not assume that the Court's current doctrines regarding state autonomy are justified. But assuming that states have some legitimate interests in political autonomy, however limited, might this justify the Senate's representational structure?

I think not. First, it is not clear how equal state representation in the Senate protects autonomy. If representatives of states are interested in protecting state autonomy, there is no reason to think that this would be truer of small-state than large-state senators. So there is no reason to give disproportionate voting power to small-state senators. There may be reason to ensure that senators are elected from constituencies exclusively made up of citizens from one state, to guarantee at least one senator to

---

23. Misha Tseytlin perceptively notices the distinction between these two strands of argument, in "United States Senate."

24. Tseytlin denies that delegates to the convention were concerned about what he calls "sovereignty protection": ibid., 870. The evidence he marshals, however, is too vague to distinguish concerns about state autonomy from concerns about neglect of individual small-state citizens.

25. Garcia v. San Antonio Metropolitan Transit Authority, 469 U.S. 528 (1985). The classic academic statement is Wechsler, "Political Safeguards of Federalism."

each state, and perhaps even to require that senators are elected from at-large, statewide districts, to ensure that they feel responsible to the state as a whole. But absent some argument that large-state officials do not care about their states' autonomy, the autonomy-protection argument is no argument for special representation of small states.[26]

Perhaps the reason not to trust large-state senators to protect state autonomy is that their states are big enough that they can effectively control national policy, and so would be willing to sacrifice state autonomy for that national control (or whatever welfare benefits might come with greater national power). This may have been a plausible concern at the founding, both because the largest states made up a much larger proportion of the national population than the largest states do today, and because of general uncertainties about how the new constitutional system would operate.[27] Whatever might have been reasonable in 1787, however, individual large states today have no plausible expectation of dictating national policy to the extent that, if they were concerned about their political autonomy, national control could substitute for their own control of their state. So there is no reason to think that small states need protection against large-state senators eliminating state autonomy across the board.

Perhaps the risk is that large-state representatives would target small-state autonomy while respecting the autonomy of their own (large) states. This may attribute more plausible (if not charitable) motivations and capacities to large-state representatives than the concern about general autonomy stripping. So small states might have reason to want protection against large-state representatives using their power in national legislatures to target small-state autonomy.

The primary question facing this line of argument is whether protection against this kind of discriminatory depredation should come in the form of inequality in national decision-making processes. The Senate, of course, is involved in all national legislation, much of which has little or no bearing on state autonomy claims. Whatever autonomy claims states

---

26. Tseytlin, "United States Senate," 872–79, and Baker and Dinkin, "Senate," passim, each provide reasons grounded in the structure of the Senate to doubt that senators even from small states would prioritize state-autonomy protection.

27. According to the 1790 census, Pennsylvania, Virginia, and Massachusetts together had over 40% of the national population. In 2010, California, Texas, and New York made up only 26% of the national population. For the 1790 numbers, see *Return of the Whole Number of Persons*; for 2010, see Mackun and Wilson, "Population Distribution and Change." Madison, at the Constitutional Convention, explicitly denied that it was reasonable to fear a combination of Pennsylvania, Virginia, and Massachusetts, given their diversity of interests, in response to concerns raised by Luther Martin. Madison, "Notes on the Debates," entries for June 27–28, 1787.

have fall well short of claims to authority over anything that affects (or even substantially affects) the context of choice facing state governments. States as corporate entities do not have what, in chapter 2, I called second-order interests in how others' implicate or direct their wills.[28] Unlike individuals, states have at most only first-order autonomy interests—claims to decide certain matters for themselves. National policy that merely affects states does not trigger these first-order interests. This distinction between the interests of states and those of individuals is due to at least two factors. First, individuals, unlike states, are primary agents of moral concern, with minds and lives of their own, and so have a wider scope of autonomy claims. Second, satisfying individuals' claims to equal authority in national policy making (including claims derived from second-order autonomy interests) is generally inconsistent with granting claims of authority to states. Typically, such state authority would dilute the claims of the individuals. If states have claims to authority in national policy making, it is only on account of how state autonomy facilitates the claims of individuals—that is, if satisfying state authority claims did not dilute individual claims, but rather protected them.[29] In that sense, such state claims are derivative, rather than fundamental. So while some national policy making might implicate state autonomy concerns, and thus potentially trigger derivative state claims to authority, there is a wide scope of "national" issues that do not implicate state first-order autonomy interests, and thus do not trigger state authority claims at all.

Equal state representation in the Senate gives small-state representatives disproportionate authority over all federal legislation (as well as ratifying treaties and confirming executive and judicial officers).[30] So the autonomy-protection argument must explain why having that protection when it comes to matters that do trigger state autonomy concerns (e.g., national "commandeering" of state governments)[31] is worth the political

---

28. See ch. 2, § III.B.

29. Here I may depart from Niko Kolodny, "Rule over None II," 329–31. My argument is consistent with Koldony's claim that individuals might have interests that their groups, as groups, not be subordinated. (Such nonsubordination might involve or require autonomy of subnational corporate entities.) Kolodny's brief discussion of the US Senate suggests he thinks that such interests could justify what would otherwise be objectionable political inequalities. I doubt this is true, at least in cases where all citizens in the society under consideration have claims to equal political authority.

30. U.S. Const. art. II, § 2, cl. 2.

31. See, e.g., Printz v. United States, 512 U.S. 898 (1997); New York v. United States, 505 U.S. 144 (1992). I take no stand on the Court's commandeering jurisprudence, but if there are legitimate state autonomy claims, extreme forms of commandeering presumably do trigger them.

inequality involved in all matters before the Senate that do not trigger those concerns (say, regulation of interstate commerce, or funding for national defense). The proponent of the autonomy-protection defense of the Senate has a high argumentative burden, because the argument here is not, as in the case of supposed deliberative neglect of small-state citizens, that the representative inequality is in the service of true political equality in terms of appropriate consideration. Instead, the argument here is a defense of political inequality in the service of good substantive outcomes—that is, federal policy making that respects state autonomy. The autonomy-protection argument is thus compatible with my primary thesis, which is that the Senate violates the standards of political equality.

There are good reasons to doubt the autonomy-protection argument on its own terms, however—that is, as a claim that the Senate's representational scheme is justified despite its political inequality. There are, of course, risks that a legislature will produce bad or unjust outcomes of many different kinds. Violations of legitimate state autonomy claims are just one type of unjust outcome. When it comes to other risks, democratic societies find means of protection that do not rely on political inequality. One protection is an ethos according to which citizens and officials conscientiously strive to act justly and constitutionally. There are also various institutional means, including, in the United States, presidential veto on constitutionality grounds, and judicial protection of state autonomy.[32] Just as we ideally protect individual rights through egalitarian, democratic procedures, so, too, ought we protect state autonomy claims democratically. The idea that there should be inegalitarian "procedural safeguards of federalism" has it backward: instead of judicial deference in the light of equal state representation, a democratic system ought to have egalitarian legislatures with judicial protection, if the latter is necessary to protect against state autonomy infringements.[33] Whatever representational inequalities judicial review involves would only manifest in cases in which claimants brought challenges on the grounds of state autonomy, rather than, as now, in every matter before the Senate. Whatever the appropriate level of judicial enforcement, however, the state-autonomy argument on behalf of equal state representation is effectively an instrumentalist argument for a less democratic system, and should be doubted accordingly.

32. I discuss judicial review in ch. 11. If states do have autonomy claims, and these are at risk in an egalitarian federal legislature, then there might be good grounds for judicial protection of state autonomy according to the argument of that chapter.

33. This is compatible with accepting the point that there should be judicial deference with respect to state autonomy matters as long as the Senate exists in its current form.

This conclusion is supported by a notable tension in the state-autonomy argument. State autonomy itself depends on some argument that states and their citizens have special interests or identities that warrant some group autonomy at the subnational level.[34] The more states and their citizens have these distinct interests and identities, however, the more inequalities with respect to national matters become salient. If Montanans are really meaningfully distinct from New Yorkers in ways that justify separate autonomous subunits, each protected from federal encroachment, then New Yorkers have good reason to doubt that Montana's representatives to the national Congress will grant them due consideration, however conscientious the Montanans might be. That is, large-state citizens are increasingly at risk of neglect as large-state citizens, and the arguments for state autonomy suggest that disregarding this identity has considerable significance. (The arguments suggest that the inequalities involve relatively particular targeting, after all.) So the state-autonomy-protection argument reinforces the critique of the Senate as undemocratic, as it attempts to justify the Senate, all things considered.

III. What Follows? The Senate and the Electoral College

If the US Senate as currently constituted violates the requirements of political equality, what should US citizens do about it? In principle, the argument shows that the equal representation of states in the Senate should be eliminated. This does not mean that the Senate itself should be abolished. There are arguments for bicameralism that do not depend on the representation of states in the Senate. Madison's preferred justification in the *Federalist* involved both houses of the Congress representing the people and checking one another, a justification that, if sound, would survive a shift to a more proportional Senate.[35] Arguments like Madison's might support a claim that some forms of bicameralism better realize political equality, by giving incentives for members of each house to grant citizens consideration, the overall effect of which would be more egalitarian than a unicameral system. Or perhaps a Congress with a reformed Senate would be no better and no worse than a unicameral, egalitarian legislature on political-equality grounds, but preferable on other grounds, by tending to produce better outcomes. A reformed Senate could retain many distinctive

---

34. For skeptical discussion, see Rubin and Feeley, "Federalism." For a defense of federalism's potential to enhance democracy, see Stepan, "Federalism and Democracy."

35. E.g., Madison, "Federalist, No. 51," 350.

features of the upper house, including longer terms of office, staggered elections of the members, and perhaps election from at-large, statewide districts. More proportional representation would require a larger body, though it would not necessarily need to be as large as the House of Representatives, and so could retain whatever deliberative benefits attach to a smaller assembly.

In principle, then, a commitment to democracy requires reform of the Senate. In practice, though, the Constitution places enormously high barriers to such reform, prohibiting the elimination of any state's equal representation in the Senate without its consent. Wholesale reform of the Senate, then, would require the consent of every state that stood to lose power, as well as the standard (and demanding) requirements for amending the Constitution.[36] There may be other morally legitimate—and, on some unorthodox theories, even constitutional—means of effecting constitutional change, but all of these would require massive organizational efforts (and might introduce considerable constitutional instability).[37] Given this immense challenge, altering the Senate is likely not the best use of reformist efforts in the near term. This may be the truth in arguments of those who, like Stephen Macedo, consider the Senate to constitute "tolerable imperfection."[38] If "tolerable" means just or democratic, the arguments of this chapter show that the Senate is not tolerable. But if "tolerable" means "lower in priority than other injustices, such that we do not have adequate reason immediately to dedicate considerable resources toward changing," then the Senate probably is tolerable, so long as other priorities, organizational efforts for which compete with those needed to reform the Senate, persist.

The fact that Senate reform may have low priority given the limited extent of its injustice and the difficulty of change does not mean that the conclusion that the Senate violates the requirements of political equality is practically inert. First, reform in the longer term requires persuading citizens that the Senate's representational scheme is meaningfully

---

36. U.S. Const. art. V. An alternative, but still radical, route to reform would be for large states to break themselves up into smaller states, though this also raises a host of political and constitutional issues.

37. See, e.g., Amar, "Consent of the Governed." Bruce Ackerman's theory of constitutional change outside of Article V would be difficult to apply in this case, as it is hard to imagine irregular practices establishing a "constitutional moment" reforming the Senate, short of something close to massive disobedience (e.g., establishing popular "conventions" to replace the Senate). See Ackerman, *We the People*.

38. Macedo, "Our Imperfect Democratic Constitution," 618.

undemocratic. We have reasons to encourage others not to be too complacent about the inequalities embodied in their institutions, even if other injustices have greater claim on their attention and resources. Second, US citizens and officials have reasons to adopt a politically egalitarian ethos that counters some of the inequalities of the Senate. It may be hopeless to expect senators from small states to exhibit greater deference to large-state senators and their constituents, in order to compensate for their unfair voting advantages. Nevertheless, senators may have such obligations. To some extent these could be implemented through changes in the use of the filibuster (effectively, a practice requiring a three-fifths threshold for most legislation in the Senate) in ways that differentially favor large-state senators.[39] Moreover, whatever the practice of senators, many small-state citizens owe special consideration to large-state citizens (or, better, owe restraint in exercising their own unfair special consideration in the Senate) that they could manifest both in deliberation and voting.[40] It may be similarly naïve to expect enough small-state citizens to adopt such an ethos of restraint within the current constitutional order. But the present point is not that such an ethos is sufficient to establish a fairer system; it is just that the conclusion that the Senate is undemocratic does have immediate practical significance even if it does not require citizens to march in the streets for constitutional amendments.

A third, more structurally significant consequence of the critique of equal state representation in the Senate is that there is greater urgency to proposals to reform or abolish the Electoral College system for electing the president.[41] Because states are accorded Electoral College votes according to the number of representatives in the Congress, unfair representation in the Senate is echoed in the Electoral College. The critique of equal state representation in the Senate implies that this inequality of voting power in presidential elections is similarly undemocratic. The unfairness is moderated by the fact that the proportional representation in the House is also reflected in the Electoral College distribution, but the deviations from a proportional standard are considerable, and at the time of writing have been decisive in two of the last five elections (in 2000 and 2016). Just as there is no good reason grounded in deliberative neglect of small-state citizens

---

39. Eidelson, "Majoritarian Filibuster."

40. Some small-state citizens may be subject to deliberative neglect themselves (not necessarily having anything to do with their state of residence), in which case whether they have obligations of special consideration to others is complicated. Obligations of consideration probably require at least some minimal reciprocity.

41. U.S. Const. art. II, §1, cl. 2–3; U.S. Const. amend. XII.

for the Senate's representational scheme, there is no good reason to give small-state citizens disproportionate voting power in presidential elections. Similarly, there is no reason to think that this distribution inclines presidents to be more protective of state autonomy claims than a more egalitarian electoral system, nor that such autonomy claims would merit voting inequality with respect to the selection of an executive with broad powers.

Strictly speaking, this critique of the Electoral College's distribution of votes does not require abolishing the College itself. We could in principle separate the indirect representation function of the College—according to which citizens select electors, who in turn vote for the president—from the College's distribution of votes by state. In practice, however, the College's indirect representation function has been effectively abolished, with electors virtually all accepting the obligation to vote in the College for the presidential (and vice-presidential) candidates to whom they pledged before the election.[42] This is to the good, in my view, since a truly indirect election in which College electors had discretion to vote (as the founders originally intended) would unnecessarily and unfairly diminish the consideration granted to citizen voters in the aggregative and deliberative process for electing the president.[43] I set this issue aside, since there is little contemporary support for a more equitably arranged indirect vote for president. The relevant question is whether the current Electoral College system should be replaced by a national popular vote for the president. (An Electoral College system distributing electors to states according to their number of congressional representatives, but with a proportional Senate, would be a considerable improvement, but I see no reason to prefer that system to a national popular vote.) This need not require constitutional amendment, since states themselves, having the authority to appoint their electors as they choose, could choose to award them to (electors for) the winner of the national popular vote.[44] If enough states chose to do so, the Electoral College would always select the winner of the national popular vote.

The critique of equal state representation shows why we should prefer a national popular vote for the president to the current Electoral College

---

42. Some states require such fidelity as a matter of law, though these laws may not be constitutional. I believe that, in the system as it is, political equality requires electors to vote according to the popular vote in their state (though the details of how the vote translates into elector obligations may vary by state—for instance, in proportional or winner-take-all fashion). This is the best way to approximate democratic elections absent reform.

43. On the original intention in establishing the Electoral College system, see Hamilton, "Federalist, No. 68"; Amar, "Some Thoughts."

44. See, e.g., Amar, "Some Thoughts," 476–80.

system. While in principle voting inequalities such as those constituted by the Electoral College might be justifiable, in fact there is no claim that these inequalities are necessary to prevent the deliberative neglect of small-state citizens, whether in the upper house of the legislature or in presidential elections. There may be reasons, in a national-popular-vote system, to publicly (and disproportionately) fund presidential campaigning in remote areas, to prevent neglect of citizens in low-density areas.[45] But there is no reason to give citizens of such areas extra voting power. Moreover, a shift to a national popular vote might have collateral democratic benefits, encouraging campaigns to increase voter turnout in all parts of the country, where in the current system they can afford to neglect uncompetitive states, since their margins of victory or loss in those states have no effect on outcomes. The central reason to abolish the Electoral College, however, is its nakedly indefensible inequalities. The fact that these same inequalities are likely to persist in the legislature for the indefinite future makes it all the more urgent that large-state citizens are not also subject to neglect in the election of the national executive.

IV. Conclusion

Criticism of the Senate and the Electoral College is frequent among democratic theorists who turn their attention to the US Constitution. (Criticism of the Electoral College is more common in popular discourse, perhaps because it is a more esoteric and unusual system, and perhaps because it is more amenable to change.) Beyond adding my voice to this chorus of lament, I have tried to show that such criticisms do not depend on a simple majoritarian conception of democracy. The appropriate-consideration conception of political equality rejects the claim that such equality requires majority rule, and admits that some voting inequalities may be justified in order to prevent the deliberative neglect of citizens. Defenses of the Senate and the Electoral College often have the right form, in attempting to justify the relevant inequalities in terms of the special consideration due to citizens of small states. But these attempts at justification do not succeed; there is no special risk of neglect of small-state citizens that justifies the inequality. So rejection of the Senate's representational scheme does not require endorsement of majoritarianism. Meanwhile, the appropriate-consideration conception better directs us to the moral considerations at

---

45. Some such neglect occurs already in the current system; presidential candidates rarely make much time for citizens of Alaska, North Dakota, Vermont, and so on.

issue in evaluating the Senate and the Electoral College than does a simple condemnation in the name of majority rule. Defenders of the constitutional status quo are correct that simple majoritarianism does not present a compelling case for change. But this point is not sufficient to deny the democratic imperative for constitutional reform.

CHAPTER EIGHT

Proportional Representation

IN THIS CHAPTER I respond to the claim, common among political theorists who consider the matter, that political equality requires proportional legislative representation ("proportional representation," or "PR"). This issue involves fundamental questions about the proper relationship between citizens' votes and the makeup of the legislature, and therefore about the basic structure of electoral systems. Debates about proportional legislatures turn on what constitutes fair representation of groups of voters. Concern for the fair representation of groups need not require any special concern for groups as groups—for classes, races, economic sectors, political parties, or any other group, over and above the concern we owe to the individuals who make up the groups. As I argued in chapter 5, securing minimal consideration of individual citizens' judgments requires opportunities to form coalitions with others in order to secure hearings for the judgments they share in common. Representative legislatures by their nature involve coalition building in one way or another: legislators must form a coalition sufficient to pass legislation, and this grand coalition in turn is formed by many smaller coalitions that selected the representatives who formed the grand coalition. Legislative representation inevitably involves synthesizing the judgments of many different groups—some transient, coalescing only for the purpose of one legislative vote, others more stable. Different electoral rules provide different structures encouraging coalition building in different ways and at different stages in the collective decision-making process. Moreover, as a historical matter, legislative representation has often been a site for the exclusion and neglect of disfavored groups. If a theory of political equality is to guide choices and evaluations of electoral and legislative systems, then, it must include a view about the fair representation of groups in a democratic legislature.

PR has often been defended as uniquely fair: various democrats and constitutional reformers have suggested that political equality, or democratic values more generally, require PR.[1] One's view of PR also has logical precedence over other institutional design issues because, as we will see, proportional systems evade certain problems besetting traditional territorial-districting schemes. If political equality required PR, there would be little reason to take up these further problems, except as an exercise in ameliorating political injustices when major reform toward PR appears impossible.

In what follows I argue that PR is not a fundamental requirement of political equality. In section I, I explain some of the basic mechanics of PR systems, and discuss their virtues as described by defenders such as John Stuart Mill. In section II, I argue that the ability to elect a candidate of one's choice, in the sense that PR guarantees, does not constitute a necessary form of consideration for citizens. In section III, I argue that proportional representation of groups in the legislature does not necessarily guarantee appropriate consideration more reliably than single-member district (SMD) systems with plurality elections. In some circumstances, PR may better secure certain forms of consideration and practical consequence for citizens than would other legislative systems. But the suitability of different legislative schemes varies with historical and social context. In some circumstances, alternative systems may better secure consideration for group members without guaranteeing those members official presence in the legislature. Securing legislative presence often comes at the expense of voter authority over coalition formation in the legislature itself. There is no general reason to think this sacrifice is justified, either for particular groups or for the citizenry as a whole.

I. Defenses of Proportional Representation

There are many ways to implement a PR system. One system influential in the history of political thought is based on a single national constituency and single transferable voting. The English politician and lawyer Thomas Hare devised such a system in 1859, and John Stuart Mill defended Hare's system in his *Considerations*.[2] This system is only used in a few national

---

1. The classic statement of this view is by John Stuart Mill, in *Considerations on Representative Government*, ch. 7. See also Guinier, *Tyranny of the Majority*; Christiano, *Rule of the Many*, 207–42; Ward, "Contractarian Defence."

2. Hare, *Election of Representatives*; Mill, *Considerations on Representative Government*, 308–10.

jurisdictions today. PR is much more often manifest in "party-list" systems, in which each party wins seats in the legislature in proportion to the number of votes that party receives from the electorate.[3] I will focus on Hare's system, because it features several elements often praised by defenders of PR, and because of the considerable influence of Mill's defense. Much of the discussion will also be relevant for party-list PR systems.

Hare's system treats the citizenry as a whole as a single, national constituency or district. Votes are to be tallied across the nation as a whole, and any voter can vote for any candidate regardless of location or residency. There are no restrictions on ballot access: a voter may vote for anybody meeting the relevant qualifications for office. According to the single transferable voting scheme, voters list a number of candidates in preference order. Any candidate with enough first-place votes gains a seat in parliament. In the very likely event that all seats are not filled by candidates with sufficient first-place votes, surplus votes for elected candidates are "transferred" to citizens' next most preferred candidates; meanwhile, candidates with the lowest vote totals are also eliminated, and their votes transferred as well. Any candidate whose resulting total exceeds the threshold gains a seat. The process is repeated, transferring votes until all seats are filled.[4] This means that almost every individual successfully elects a representative.[5] Likewise, each representative has a constituency made up only of voters who voted for her (though not necessarily as their most preferred candidate). How does this result in any kind of proportionality? The idea is that any like-minded group—like-minded in the sense of supporting the same candidate or candidates—will successfully elect representatives in proportion to its numbers (so long as they are of the minimum size necessary to secure one seat). So, if Whigs make up forty percent of the national vote, the system will ensure that Whig candidates—that is, candidates supported by Whig voters—will make up very close to forty percent of the seats in the legislature. (Nothing in the Hare system requires formal party identification; proportionality could

---

3. See Farrell, *Electoral Systems*, chs. 4, 6.

4. This brief description leaves out important details regarding the counting and transfer algorithms. Mill's description is quite a good introduction to the basics; for more recent, detailed accounts, see Pukelsheim, *Proportional Representation*; Balinski and Young, *Fair Representation*.

5. Roughly speaking, this is true so long as at least one of the voter's preferred candidates garners enough votes to pass the threshold. In saying that the voter "elects" the representative, I mean that at least one of the voter's preferred candidates is elected into the legislature.

attach to informal social groups such as "laborers" as much as to parties, if that is the pattern according to which they coordinate.) The transfer system ensures that few votes are "wasted" either as surplus votes for candidates who have already crossed the victory threshold or as votes for candidates who have no chance of election.

Proponents typically emphasize two related features of the Hare system and its variants. First, under this system each individual succeeds in electing a representative of his choice, and consequently each representative has something of a unanimously supportive constituency. Second, the system guarantees the direct, visible representation of groups in the legislature according to their support in the population. This entails the proportional presence of minority groups in the legislature, in contrast to traditional territorial systems under which minorities might be underrepresented from the perspective of the proportionality standard.[6] Moreover, in the Hare system voters themselves decide, through their votes, which groups are salient in terms of meriting representation; there need be no *ex ante* determination by officials of which groups require legislative seats. (This is in contrast to party-list systems, in which questions may arise regarding which parties are on the ballot, and to quotas requiring the proportional representation of certain groups, such as racial minorities.) Groups need not even be consciously identified by voters or representatives, though in practice there is strong incentive for party members and other political entrepreneurs to encourage conscious group identification and voting according to that sense of identity. This proportional system also entails that a majority of legislators will virtually always represent a majority of the population in the sense that those legislators will collectively have received votes from a majority of voters. This second feature, then, suggests that PR guarantees majority rule and minority representation in the senses described. Let us consider the two features in turn.

II. Voter-Legislator Relationships

There is an obvious appeal to a guarantee that one will successfully elect a representative to the legislature. When one disapproves of "one's own" representative—the representative for the territorial district in which one lives, for example—one can easily feel alienated from that representative

---

6. I explained how plurality districts can produce disproportionate results in this sense in ch. 3.

and her work, and thereby feel inadequately represented. By contrast, when one has voted for a candidate who is elected to the legislature, one often feels as if one has a sympathetic, trusted voice in the assembly—someone who represents oneself in a substantive sense, and who can suitably serve as one's delegate or agent. Voters want their preferred candidates to win: that is primarily why they vote, after all.[7] A system that guarantees to virtually every voter that one of his or her preferred candidates will win a seat gives something desirable to every voter, and this seems to be a clear merit of the proportional system. Proponents of PR argue that this merit is a fundamental requirement of proper democratic representation: Mill claims that "real equality of representation is not obtained, unless any set of electors amounting to the average number of a constituency, wherever in the country they happen to reside, have the power of combining with one another to return a representative."[8] More recently, Lani Guinier has endorsed *"the equal opportunity to vote for a winning candidate* as a universal principle of political fairness."[9]

The conception of equal power or equal opportunity offered by PR systems is very specific. In one sense, voters in SMD systems with plurality-vote rules also have equal opportunity to elect candidates of their choice. That is, in principle, any of them can form a coalition with a plurality of the rest within their district to elect a candidate. When we abstract from the actual distribution of judgments, voters in such systems have equal chances of forming such coalitions, and in that sense have equal opportunity. (This is obviously a meaningful dimension of equality, ruling out as it does disenfranchisement, plural voting, and inequality in district size, though I argued in chapter 5 that strict equality in this dimension is not always necessary to satisfy principles of fair aggregation.) PR advocates insist on a further criterion; namely, that opportunities to elect, given the

---

7. Voters may have less instrumental, more "expressive," purposes in registering certain votes. Whatever we think of those purposes, the expressive meaning depends on the standard function of voting as endorsing a representative or policy outcome.

8. Mill, *Considerations on Representative Government*, 308. Mill's relationship to the ideal of political equality is complicated. His utilitarianism may suggest that his support for PR must be, at its foundation, consequentialist in a way that places little direct emphasis on political equality. But Mill's arguments for PR are consistently inflected with egalitarian language and appeals to fairness. These egalitarian moments in Mill's work may well be consistent with his consequentialism, but they suggest a deep egalitarianism in Mill's theory of value—that is, they suggest that Mill may have placed great weight on certain forms of equality in determining the relative value of different outcomes of action.

9. Guinier, *Tyranny of the Majority*, 122 (emphasis in original). Guinier interprets "equal opportunity" in the quoted phrase to require something like PR.

actual distribution of judgments, should not vary by one's location in the electoral system.

I do not believe that we should elevate the ability or opportunity to elect a representative to the legislature, in the sense just described, to the status of a basic requirement of political equality. In and of itself—setting aside for the moment the effects on the behavior of the legislature as a whole, and focusing on the successful election of a representative—the guarantee of casting a winning vote does not secure any meaningful component of consideration. First, successfully electing a representative is not necessary to satisfy the basic principles of fair aggregation I identified in chapter 5. Traditional territorial systems are categorically prohibited neither by the demand for basic, minimal consideration, such as that constituted by universal suffrage, freedoms of speech and coalition formation, individual demands for consideration in administrative and judicial procedure, and so on. Nor do SMD systems violate the antidegradation principle, because voting on equal terms in a losing effort is not by that fact indicative of a public judgment of one's inferiority.[10] The argument for PR, in terms of the appropriate-consideration conception, must be that it performs better than nonproportional, SMD systems in minimizing inequalities that cause or constitute deliberative neglect of voters who fail to elect candidates of their choice in proportion to their numbers. But while this may be true in certain contexts, it is not categorically true.

Casting a winning vote for a representative does not itself grant voters practical consequence in the legislature's deliberations on law and policy. If one's representative is ineffective or subject to severe deliberative neglect in the legislature and the public sphere at large, citizens may receive minimal consideration with respect to legislative outcomes. There is also the problem that voters may not be able to exercise authority over how representatives form coalitions, either to form a government or to pass legislation, a problem that would limit the consideration granted to citizens' judgments. The fact that they have cast a winning vote for a representative is limited consolation or compensation. Voters in SMD systems who voted for losing candidates also face these risks, of course. But this just

---

10. Charles Beitz makes a similar point in different terms in *Political Equality*, 133–34. Thomas Christiano complains that in making this argument Beitz emphasizes electoral equality at the expense of equality in the legislature, and more broadly in the decision-making process as a whole. Christiano, *Rule of the Many*, 232–33. But Christiano's complaint ignores Beitz's discussion of citizens' interests in "equitable treatment" and "deliberative responsibility," both of which lead Beitz to consider the effect of PR on legislative behavior. Beitz, *Political Equality*, 134–40.

shifts our focus to the performance of the legislature as a whole, and the wider deliberative process enabled or encouraged by the electoral system. I will discuss arguments on these grounds in the next section; for now, I emphasize that the guarantee of electing a candidate of one's choice is not a guarantee of these wider and more fundamental forms of consideration.

Representatives are not only responsible for deliberating about, and voting on, legislative proposals. They may provide valuable constituent services, overseeing administrative actions that bear on their constituents. With respect to these services, it may be valuable to have a representative in office for whom one has voted. In proportional systems, the identifiable relationship between representatives and individual constituents is attenuated, if not severed altogether. In the absence of territorial districts, representatives may not have identifiable constituents. The representative knows that she received enough votes to gain a seat, but does not know which voters provided the votes. This is true of the Hare system, in the absence of public, "open" ballots. It is also true, assuming private ballots, in party-list systems with national constituencies.[11] Mill advocates for open ballots; but if we support the modern consensus that votes should be private (primarily in order to limit intimidation and vote buying), then PR systems cannot easily claim to merit Mill's description of the system as one of "personal representation."[12] When representatives do not know who their constituents are, they have no particular responsibility (and, perhaps, little motivation) to provide targeted constituent services. By contrast, in SMD systems, representatives know (or can find out) that a citizen is a resident of their district, and in that sense a constituent.

We might wonder whether such personalized constituent services are really a creditable feature of a political process. We might wish that representatives oversee executive administration with the appropriate level of vigor, and with the common good in mind, without any special solicitude for particular citizens. To the extent that PR systems might limit personalized constituent service, in favor of a more national focus, this might be to the good. Of course, nothing prevents representatives in SMD systems from engaging in such public-spirited, impartial oversight. The reasons to prefer one or the other system in this regard depend on two factors. First,

---

11. Many PR systems do use smaller, multimember but subnational, districts, applying proportional voting rules to each. To this extent they preserve some connection between identifiable voters and representatives. This is a move away from "pure" PR to a more mixed system.

12. Mill, *Considerations on Representative Government*, ch. 10 (on the open ballot), 314 ("personal representation").

is impartial oversight best promoted by a system in which each representative has a relatively national orientation, or by a system in which each representative (all representatives together spanning the national jurisdiction) has a relatively particular orientation to an identifiable group of citizens? Second, apart from concerns about promoting good outcomes in administrative oversight, does relatively personalized orientation in such oversight grant to constituents a valuable form of consideration? On the first point, I do not see a reason to favor categorically the nationally oriented PR system, absent convincing research.[13] On the second point, there is some reason to think that citizen authority is better respected when citizens have opportunity to raise individual concerns about administrative process. This does not necessarily require identifiable representatives who "belong" to the citizen—the consideration could be guaranteed within the administrative procedure itself—but in some circumstances the opportunity for consideration through representative channels may be valuable.[14]

The result of these considerations is that we should not identify the equal opportunity to elect a candidate of one's choice, irrespective of one's location in an electoral system, as an essential constituent of political equality. Whether such opportunity is important depends on contextual factors, including the conduct of the legislature, the nature of administrative procedure, and the relationship between the legislature and the

---

13. It is not enough to establish that nationally oriented systems have better outcomes, by whatever metric. The question for our purposes is whether the process of decision making (including the decisions that emerge from administrative agencies, overseen appropriately by the legislature) accords appropriate consideration to each citizen. If the nationally oriented system produced more rational administration, in the sense of promoting good outcomes, at the expense of granting citizens due consideration in the relevant processes, this would count as a disadvantage in terms of political equality, not an advantage. For doubts about the quality of more locally oriented representation, see Pettit and Pettit, "Washington and Westminster Systems."

14. Party-list PR systems depersonalize representation in a way that may make it more difficult to sanction (through removal) individual representatives, because voters cannot vote directly to remove any individuals. Party-list systems may reduce the need for sanctioning of individuals: there is presumably less differentiation between individual representatives of the party, because the party presumably chooses its list with an eye toward loyalty to the party platform. (In this sense, PR systems have advantages in enabling "selection" of representatives who support a specified platform.) If this is supposed to be the defense against worries about the importance of electoral sanctioning, however, one wonders why there should be individual representatives at all, rather than legislative vote shares assigned to party leaders. (On this point see Pepall, *Against Reform*, 43–45.) If representation is at all individuated, there are reasons to value targeted electoral sanctioning as a means to promote proper consideration by representatives. On selection and sanctioning of representatives, see Mansbridge, "Rethinking Representation."

executive administration. This, I think, accords with the views of many PR proponents. While language about equality in representative selection is common, I am not sure that those proponents really mean to emphasize the intrinsic value of the guarantee of casting successful votes. Instead, the guarantee supposedly matters because of the consequences of the guarantee for the behavior of the legislature, and the resulting relationship between the citizens and the regime's laws and policies.[15] So it is to questions about the structure of the legislature that we should now turn.

III. Proportionality and Legislative Presence

PR is necessary, proponents say, because it alone secures for various groups of citizens a presence in the legislature, and the various forms of practical consequence for individual members of those groups that such presence supposedly entails. Mill presents such a claim, with special reference to the minority group about which he was most concerned, the "superior intellects and characters": though even in a proportionally representative legislature they "will necessarily be outnumbered, it makes a great difference whether or not they are heard."[16] Mill places great importance on the fact that these citizens are "heard" in the national legislature itself, through representatives that they selected, and not only on the hustings or in the more diffuse and informal public sphere. PR guarantees those special hearings for all groups of the requisite size, and so, the argument goes, it secures for them a morally essential form of consideration.

In evaluating this claim that proportional legislative presence constitutes or is necessary to promote essential forms of consideration, we should recall that we should reject what I called the "proportional-consideration" principle in chapter 6. This principle states that citizens' judgments should be granted a scope of consideration proportional to the number of citizens who support those judgments. I argued, first, that some very small minorities are underserved by the principle: they may be so small that proportional consideration would be trivial, and so proper consideration of their judgments requires superproportional consideration.[17] Second, there may be diminishing marginal returns to scope of consideration, so large groups—particularly supermajorities—require only an adequate level of consideration that falls short of what they would be granted

---

15. Christiano makes this point explicitly, in *Rule of the Many*, 233.
16. Mill, *Considerations on Representative Government*, 313.
17. See Kymlicka, *Multicultural Citizenship*, 149.

under proportionality. Third, because of the range of citizens' deliberative interests, including interests in individual judgment formation and proper deliberative synthesis at the regime level, appropriate consideration may require the consideration of a wider range of judgments than the proportionality principle requires.

The proportional-consideration principle does not itself imply that we should support PR systems; nor does the rejection of that principle imply that we should reject PR. It is an open question whether PR systems actually secure proportionality in the consideration granted to citizens that the more abstract principle requires. But the rejection of the proportional-consideration principle gives reason to favor nonproportional systems in some circumstances. Some nonproportional elements of an election system, such as smaller districts, the creation of "safe" districts for geographically concentrated groups, or the establishment of representative quotas, could protect small minorities.[18] (If minorities entitled to special consideration are geographically concentrated, the disproportionality possible in SMD systems may be a virtue.)[19] Very small minorities may require further protections in judicial and administrative procedure, if they are too small to elect a seat under any system that limits inequalities in voting power. These protections provide disproportionate protections for some citizens, though they are compatible with forms of PR in the legislature.

The argument for proportional legislative presence cannot rest on a general argument for proportional consideration. But it is nevertheless true that presence in the legislature secures for the present groups a certain kind of practical consequence. In any reasonable legislative system this would not count for nothing: not only would the representatives vote on the laws, and thereby potentially have some influence on the content of the laws up for a vote, but they would also be able to insist on some kinds of deliberative accountability, perhaps by making speeches on the floor of the assembly, or by formally presenting questions to opposition legislators and government officials. But while such practical consequence may not

---

18. Some broadly proportional systems adjust for these concerns—for instance, by establishing minimum guarantees of representation for certain groups, or by implementing so-called "degressive proportionality," which loosely means that larger groups get slightly less than proportional representation, and smaller groups get slightly more than proportional representation. Both features are present in elections for the European Parliament. Obviously these are moves away from pure proportionality. See Pukelsheim, *Proportional Representation*, 165–66.

19. In SMD systems, groups making up only a slight majority of one district's electorate can elect a representative. A group of this size would not typically be able to meet the threshold of votes for one seat in a proportional system.

be trivial, legislative presence is neither necessary nor alone sufficient for meaningful consideration, either in terms of deliberative accountability or in terms of influence over legislation.

Legislative presence is not sufficient for appropriate consideration because it is possible that the neglect of minority groups that supposedly infects traditional territorial systems would reproduce itself in the legislature of proportional systems. In PR systems, majorities pass legislation, and so some minorities must lose in the end, in the sense of not having their preferred proposals passed.[20] Presence in the legislature cannot change the fact that minorities are minorities, and thus prone to losing legislative votes. Nor can it guarantee that this aspect of what in chapter 3 I called the winnowing of judgments will occur in a fair and egalitarian manner. Indeed, if it is true that PR encourages tighter party discipline along with clear mandates for representatives supported by unanimous constituencies, then this may lead majority parties or coalitions to neglect minorities in opposition, precisely because providing meaningful consideration might lead to deviations from the party line or popular mandate.[21] Such neglect is also possible, of course, in SMD systems, particularly in contexts of high party polarization. But the closer connection between individual representatives and particular constituencies may enable greater actual or potential deviation from party platforms, and thus more scope for cross-party coalitions in the legislature. Merely increasing the possibility of such coalitions could cause greater deliberative consideration for different constituencies in the legislature.

Proponents of PR might respond that in practice legislative presence tends to militate against such deliberative neglect, by giving minorities a very visible public platform for advocacy as well as the benefits and resources of formal office. This is a plausible point. But whether the public platform and resources provided by legislative office guarantee meaningful consideration is a contingent matter, one that depends not only on other formal features of the collective decision-making process, but also

---

20. Indridi H. Indridason emphasizes the importance of majoritarianism in PR legislatures, a point he argues is often neglected in discussions of such systems, in "Proportional Representation."

21. This may be less of a problem in Hare systems without strong party organizations. In such systems (as Mill probably had in mind), voters would be primarily selecting individuals on their own merits, rather than on account of their party attachments. But in actual practice there are strong incentives for both parties and representatives to organize under party labels. Moreover, a system with minimal party identification poses its own problems, as I discuss below in the context of coalition formation.

on the structure of public communications, the political culture and the extent of a democratic ethos, and so on. (Ability to speak in the legislative chamber may not matter too much, as this may have limited direct effect—that is, effect independent of its effects on public opinion—on actual decision making. But this, too, is a contingent proposition.) Legislative presence is unlikely to be a disadvantage, of course; it is likely to involve some deliberative resources, and to command certain kinds of attention. But this does not establish that such deliberative gains cannot be provided in other ways in other systems.

One of the most attractive features of legislative presence for any group is that it provides an opportunity to form successful coalitions in the legislature. "Coalitions" here can refer either to coalitions that form a government, in a parliamentary system, or to more temporary coalitions that pass particular laws, in presidential or semipresidential systems in which the government is not exclusively accountable to the legislature (or, more rarely, parliamentary systems in which legislatures can propose and pass bills that lack government support without bringing down the government).[22] But this matter of coalition formation also raises one of the greatest difficulties with PR systems. Precisely because such systems facilitate the legislative presence of many smaller groups (relative to SMD systems), individual parties rarely win majorities of seats. Legislative and governing coalitions require the alliance of two or more parties. PR systems do not require parties to commit during the election to specific coalition partners.[23] In practice, pre-election coalitions between parties, in which the parties commit during the campaign to join together in a coalition after the election, commonly form but do not often win majorities alone.[24] This means voters have no simple means to communicate their judgments about which coalitions their preferred parties (or, in the Hare system, preferred representatives) should form.

---

22. Another important function of legislative coalitions is to maintain control of the legislative agenda. In the United States, for instance, this is done through election of the Speaker of the House and majority leader of the Senate, and the control of committee assignments. While in principle each house as a whole controls these matters, party membership in practice amounts to a commitment to vote in unison on these procedural control matters. As a result, cross-party majority coalitions on such matters are rare. This is very consequential for policy making. For a brief overview and useful citations, see Schepsle, "Dysfunctional Congress?" 375–77.

23. Given the variety of postelection contingencies, it might be difficult for a party that wanted to commit even to provide a complete description of its coalition-formation plans before the election (let alone to credibly commit to those plans).

24. See Golder, *Logic of Pre-electoral Coalition*, 1–10.

This lack of clear lines of citizen authority over representative coalition formation is a serious matter. Political equality involves equal citizen authority over what we do together, which requires authority over actual laws and policies. Legislation, in turn, depends on the actual majority coalitions that form in the legislature (whether these are necessary to form a government or not). Citizen authority over representative selection, then, does not amount to authority over laws and policies if citizens lack authority over how representatives join together in coalitions.[25]

Citizen authority over coalition formation need not amount to the right to issue binding mandates or instructions to representatives. Representatives need some discretion in order to satisfy the requirements of egalitarian deliberation, and to perform their role in the political division of labor. There are nevertheless reasons to believe that PR systems limit citizen authority over coalition formation much more than do SMD systems. First, representatives and parties in PR legislatures face complicated strategic situations when making choices about coalition formation after the election. It is not easy for citizens (or scholars) to predict how parties will respond to these situations. In particular, contrary to intuition (and some simple predictive models), we cannot assume that parties will only form coalitions with parties that are close neighbors on some ideological spectrum.[26] Small parties in particular may have disproportionate influence in these situations.[27] Second, voters cannot be sure that in making coalition decisions, parties are concerned only with advancing their policy aims. In parliamentary systems in which coalitions form governments, party elites making coalition decisions may also be influenced by the benefits of office holding. This introduces the prospect that parties may sacrifice some policy aims in order to join the government coalition, and this, in turn, further complicates the strategic situation.[28]

The point here is not that parties in PR systems are more venal or less high-minded than parties in SMD systems. The realistic expectation of strategic behavior (some of which may be motivated by conscientious pursuit of policy aims) makes it difficult for voters to predict coalition-formation decisions, and thereby makes it difficult for them to express their own relevant judgments through voting. A voter may believe the

---

25. The mere fact of electoral selection is inadequate to establish sufficient authority, as I argued in ch. 3, § II.B, and ch. 5, § I.C.

26. Indridason, "Proportional Representation."

27. Pepall, *Against Reform*, 36–40. Pepall's discussion is historically informed but somewhat anecdotal.

28. Baron et al., "Dynamic Theory."

Blues best represent his policy judgments, and hope for a Blue-Green coalition if the Blues do not win a majority, but prefers a Red-Green coalition to a Blue-White coalition. So the voter prefers the Blues if they win a majority or form coalitions with the Greens, but prefers the Greens if the Blues do not win a majority and are likely to form a coalition with the Whites. PR electoral systems make it difficult for the voter to register these important conditional judgments. This is particularly true when parties (or individual representatives) find it difficult to make credible commitments to coalition-formation decisions before the election.[29]

I emphasize that there is nothing intrinsically objectionable, or contrary to political equality, in strategic voting behavior. Nor is it wrong or defective for an electoral system to encourage or enable strategic voting. "Strategic" may even be a misleading label, used as it is in some contexts to denote action that takes other persons as obstacles or objects for use rather than as communicative partners.[30] In the context of voting (and coalition formation), the choice situation is defined in part by the existence of provisionally fixed judgments by others. Acting to advance the policies one considers best in that context is fully compatible with participating in a process that grants each citizen appropriate consideration, and so treats others as communicative partners over the course of that process. Part of respecting others' authority is precisely to accept at some point that they are entitled to have certain views, to give them weight, and thus to act as one sees fit (subject to various moral constraints) in the light of those fixed views.

The types of strategic choices a system tends to pose to its voters or officials may nevertheless constitute or cause unfairness. For instance, if voters must navigate especially complex strategic situations, or make strategic choices with little relevant information available, the system as a whole may be unfair. (If PR systems present unduly complex strategic situations to voters, for instance, this may amount to neglect of voters generally, or contribute to neglect specifically of voters with diminished opportunity to gather relevant information.) The objection we are currently considering, however, is not to unfairness in the presentation of strategic

---

29. On the significance of the inability to commit, see ibid., 723–24. Part of the reason official commitment is difficult is that voters often find it difficult to commit to electoral sanctioning of officials who renege on their commitments (because such sanctioning often runs contrary to voters' other policy aims). Voters may also be irrational and unpredictable when they do attempt to sanction. Achen and Bartels, *Democracy for Realists*, chs. 4–5.

30. See Habermas, *Theory of Communicative Action*.

choice itself, but rather the way opportunities for strategic choice for elites make it difficult for voters to exercise authority over laws and policies.

SMD systems do not enable voters to communicate conditional judgments directly about what representatives should do in various strategic situations any more than do PR systems. But the features of those systems that create disproportionality in party seats also create strong incentives for parties to encompass broad coalitions that can plausibly form legislative majorities or governments on their own. As a result, most candidates in general elections identify with such major parties. Such party identification amounts to a commitment on the part of the candidate to participate in the party's government coalition (in parliamentary systems) or to support generally the party's legislative coalition (in presidential systems). These commitments are not ironclad, but party discipline in these matters tends to be high, even if defections on votes for particular policies are common in presidential systems. As a result, voters have reliable pre-election information about the coalition-formation behavior of the candidates. Votes for the candidates, then, amount to authority over that behavior, and thus, to a greater extent than in PR systems, over the laws and policies themselves.

There is some evidence that ruling coalitions in PR systems tend to track the judgments of the median voter more reliably than coalitions (typically, parties that win a majority of legislative seats) in SMD systems.[31] One might suggest that this evidence alleviates concerns about unpredictable coalition-formation behavior. If, the argument goes, parties typically engage in strategic coalition formation in ways that end up tracking the judgments of a majority of voters, the possibility of odd, unpredictable coalition-formation decisions should not trouble us.[32] Moreover, if SMD systems produce less "congruence" between coalitions and voters, the argument continues, then their predictability in coalition formation comes at the expense of actually tracking voter policy judgments. At the extreme, this tracking failure results in rule by parties that failed to win

---

[31]. Powell, *Elections as Instruments*. In later work, Powell notes that SMD systems recently have shown greater "ideological congruence" in this sense than PR systems, but argues that this is an artifact of greater voter polarization in PR countries. Powell, "Representation in Context." (It is not clear whether PR systems tend to promote voter polarization. If they do, the effect of the system overall might be to undermine congruence.)

[32]. The congruence claim under consideration assumes that relevant political disagreement can be reduced to a single dimension, with voters' and parties' positions placed along a spectrum in that dimension. If that is true, then a coalition tracking the preference of the median voter on that spectrum would command the support of a majority of voters, at least relative to options at least one voter away from the median.

a majority (or even a plurality) of votes.[33] Thus, the argument concludes, there is little downside, and are some advantages, to the diverse forms of legislative presence enabled by PR systems.

These results showing greater congruence in the sense described do not, however, adequately respond to concerns about granting citizens consideration with respect to coalition formation. First, the argument depends on the claim that what matters in voter authority over legislatures can be adequately captured by measurement in a single ideological dimension. I do not question the considerable ingenuity and value of the relevant studies. But this is a very crude metric for what matters—that is, appropriate consideration of citizens' judgments throughout the political process. These judgments will not entirely reduce to a single dimension, because disagreements on one issue will not entirely predict disagreements on other issues. Strategic considerations in party (and coalition) formation will pressure representatives and voters to make decisions on packages of positions (roughly speaking, platforms). This will reduce the dimensions of choice in elections, and, as a result, the dimensions of policy judgment that voters can express through their votes.[34] But this does not mean that the resulting dimension of disagreement is the only one that matters for citizens. While their choices given the array of platforms on offer are certainly significant (that is why authority over coalition formation matters), the system's tendency to grant consideration along other dimensions also matters. Because responsiveness patterns along one dimension could coincide with many different responsiveness patterns along other dimensions, congruence in one dimension is insufficient to conclude confidently that PR systems are generally fairer than SMD systems.

Even if promoting congruence in the sense specified is a valuable feature of an electoral system, such congruence does not respond entirely

---

33. This is a common complaint against SMD systems. See, e.g., Shugart, "Jenkins Paradox," 144; Lijphart, "First-Past-the-Post"; Mill, *Considerations on Representative Government*, 304.

34. If voters generally do not form judgments independent of party leaders and related social elites—because, say, the voters take their cues from the elites—then the voters' judgments may well align more generally with the party platforms, and major political disagreement might be better represented by a single dimension. For evidence that many voters (in the United States) do defer to elites in this sense, see Achen and Bartels, *Democracy for Realists*. To the extent that voters exist whose judgments are not in such lockstep with party elites, however, congruence on one dimension would not guarantee appropriate consideration. Extreme deference to elites may also signal deliberative unfairness in other respects, and so may not be an ideal organizing principle for an electoral system (which is not to deny that the fact, if it is a fact, needs to be accounted for in shorter-term reform).

to citizens' claims to authority. Citizen authority requires that such congruence obtain because of, and in response to, citizen judgments—rather than, say, the fortuitous results of strategic choices by elites. It would not respect citizen authority to establish autocratic rule by someone who happened to be the median citizen, because the congruence in that system would not occur through the recognition of other citizens' authority. Similarly, if congruence in PR systems results from relatively unconstrained elite choice in ways that are not responsive to voters' judgments, that congruence does not amount to granting citizens' claims to consideration. To be clear, the mere presence of elite discretion in making strategic choices is not objectionable. If the system operates in ways that reliably shape strategic choices in ways that cause the regime as a whole to grant citizens' appropriate consideration, then that system is compatible with political equality. The problem arises if the system places few constraints on elite choice, however, in ways that make responsiveness to citizen authority less robust across elite preferences. In such circumstances, appropriate consideration is not guaranteed. As a result, in judging the significance of congruence in PR systems, we need to know whether that congruence is relatively robust across changes in elite preferences, and other factors that are independent of voters' judgments.

In general, SMD systems allow voters fewer opportunities for fine-grained choice in their selection of individual representatives, but grant them opportunities for clearer lines of authority over coalition formation. PR systems allow the opposite: greater range of meaningful choice as to individual representatives and parties, but less direct control over coalition formation. Proportional systems may be more desirable if it is appropriate for representatives to act as trustees or free agents, exercising their discretion in making choices about legislative or government coalition formation. Such systems probably do make free-agent models of representation more attractive, to the extent that the representatives' views in general may more closely reflect the views of voters than in SMD systems. Even granting this point, however, I believe, as I argued in chapter 5, that citizens are entitled to some authority over the deliberations and choices of elected representatives.[35] They are entitled to this authority even over representatives whom they generally like and admire. To the extent that PR systems of coalition formation escape that authority, they do not adequately respond to citizens' authority claims.

35. See also Eric Beerbohm's good arguments against trustee and free-agent conceptions of representation: *In Our Name*, ch. 8.

Voters in SMD systems also face challenges in communicating preferences about coalition formation. Though voters can identify prospective coalitions (associated with major parties) before an election, they have limited scope for shaping the nature of a coalition—that is, who makes up the party, and what constitutes the party platform (or, more minimally, the range of views that will be considered compatible with party affiliation). Integration of different groups into a coalition largely occurs within the major parties, both formally through primary elections and the forging of compromises between different wings of the parties, and more informally through public deliberations about the direction and character of the parties.[36] As Charles Beitz writes, "the real differences between [PR and SMD] systems involve the stage within the process of election and representation at which the positions are articulated and the framework within which divergent positions are compromised to form workable political coalitions."[37] At a minimum, we can say that which system better secures consideration in coalition formation varies by context, and depends on many fine-grained institutional and broader social factors. More positively, we can say that SMD systems allow more direct citizen control over coalition formation than do PR systems, and this provides them at least one advantage in responding to citizens' claims to consideration throughout the political process. Legislative presence in the sense enabled by PR systems make those claims harder to satisfy.

These considerations suggest some responses to the common criticism that SMD systems can empower a party with a majority of legislative seats despite not winning even a plurality of votes. First, total votes for parties are not always a perfect measure of underlying support. In SMD systems, for instance, the plurality-vote rules and district lines may cause some voters to decide not to vote, because they are confident that their preferred candidate will win (or lose) in their district.[38] Similarly, such voters might choose to vote for small-party candidates because the election of their preferred candidate (of the major-party candidates) is secure (or clearly out

---

36. See Levinson and Pildes, "Separation of Parties"; Rosenblum, *Side of the Angels*. On the ways legislative presence may trade off with other means of egalitarian integration within parties, see Karlan, "*Georgia v. Ashcroft*."

37. Beitz, *Political Equality*, 137.

38. There is some evidence that disproportionality in electoral systems depresses voter turnout: Banducci and Karp, "Electoral Systems." Banducci and Karp also find that coalition governments tend to depress turnout. PR systems more often produce coalition governments, but the overall effect of PR systems seems to be positive for turnout. The argument in the text shows, however, that some choices not to vote may not indicate diminished opportunity or lack of support for the political system.

of reach). In this context, one cannot infer from the fact that a party did not win a plurality of votes that it does not command plurality support.

The measurement problem aside, though, it is possible that SMD systems at times enable rule by parties that lack even plurality support among actual or potential voters. I agree that extreme forms of disproportionality, of which an outcome like this might sometimes be a species, is objectionable, as I have discussed in chapters 5 and 7. Even more modest disproportionality, which could cause "minority rule" in this sense when vote totals among major parties are close, might be objectionable if it resulted from, or caused, patterned deliberative neglect of certain groups (including large coalitions). (This suggests that SMD systems need to guard against various forms of gerrymandering, a point I will return to in section IV and in chapter 9.) That said, it is not clear to me that "minority rule" in this specific sense is intrinsically unfair. For it to be intrinsically unfair depends on a kind of amended equal-power conception of political equality, which I have rejected.[39] If voters from all coalitions are granted appropriate consideration in deliberation, and the electoral system satisfies all other requirements of fair aggregation, it is not easy to say why, exactly, rule by a coalition that won a majority of seats in otherwise fair elections despite not winning a majority of votes overall is unjust. I suspect that verdict depends on either something like a simple model of ideological congruence along a single dimension, or the fact that, in practice, the disproportionality in outcomes reflects more serious and systematic forms of neglect (for instance, through egregious partisan gerrymandering). The latter concern is serious, I think; I am less convinced that the former is of intrinsic significance.

Thomas Christiano presents a defense of a PR system that provides a different explanation for the importance of a certain kind of legislative presence. Christiano recommends a party-list system.[40] Christiano's argument primarily depends on his view that political equality requires a special division of labor between ordinary citizens and legislative representatives. Ordinary citizens, says Christiano, should determine the basic aims of the polity, while legislators should decide upon the best means to achieve those aims, including the best compromises between supporters

---

39. Strictly speaking, equal voting power is consistent with this "minority-rule" outcome (a fact that might give us pause in judging the result obviously unfair). But intuition of the intrinsic wrongness of this outcome depends on intuitions similar to those behind the equal-power view.

40. Christiano, *Rule of the Many*, 228–29.

of different aims.[41] Christiano argues that the party-list PR system would encourage responsible parties with representatives clearly accountable to the party platform, and would, because of proportional representation in the legislature and the anticipated fragmentation of parties, allow citizens a wide range of choice in their selection of aims.[42] Proportionality, according to Christiano, enables the representation of various citizen-chosen aims in the legislature, and helps fairly set the agenda for legislative deliberation. As a result, the system best secures the sovereignty over aims that he believes political equality requires.

Christiano's case for party-list PR is vulnerable to the extent that his theory of the fair division of political labor is vulnerable. I presented some objections to this division in chapter 4, section I. Aims and means cannot be clearly cordoned from each other in processes of practical reasoning: even if we can analytically distinguish means from aims, for instance, good deliberation often requires dialectical adjustment of means and aims in the light of how various aims and means relate.[43] This dialectical accommodation of means and aims is probably even more important when compromise is necessary between those who have different judgments as to aims, means, and the relationship between aims and means. If this is true, then Christiano's proposed division of labor may prove impossible to achieve, or, if possible, might promote poor collective deliberation to the extent that it prevents legislators from engaging in reasonable adjustment of aims and reasonable forms of compromise. (This is another version of the general problem of voters' authority over coalition-formation decisions.) Perhaps more fundamentally, however, this dialectical vision of practical reason calls into doubt the basis for the division of labor in the first place. If practical reasoning involves a complex dialectic between aims and means, respect for citizens' judgments should not be limited to respect for their judgments about the polity's aims. Instead, the decision-making system should be responsive to citizens' practical judgments more generally, including whatever constellation of aims and means the citizens consider salient and important. To the extent that party-list PR prevents that flexible responsiveness, it fails to respect citizens' jurisdiction.

If we do accept Christiano's proposed division of political labor, however, there is a strange interaction between the proportionality of representation and that division. Christiano argues that legislators should be

---

41. Ibid., 165–204.
42. Ibid., 215–31.
43. Richardson, *Democratic Autonomy*, 97–113.

delegates with respect to aims: that is, they should consider themselves bound by their party's aims (as ratified by their voters).[44] The result is a majoritarian legislative system. Majority coalitions or parties presumably lack any discretion to change their aims, and so are bound by Christiano's vision of political equality from giving much meaningful consideration to the judgments of aims rendered by minority parties and their constituents. Since judgments of aims are all that ordinary citizens are meant to render in this system, this means that the judgments of minority citizens are completely disregarded by the coalition that actually passes legislation. Consideration of those citizens' judgments is limited to granting them representatives in the legislature who, by hypothesis, are incapable of persuading other representatives of the validity of their aims. The representatives are admittedly permitted flexibility on questions of means, but it is hard to see why this should matter much to the minority citizens, given that the means in question are means to aims they do not endorse.[45] This hardly constitutes meaningful consideration of the minority citizens' judgments; on the contrary, it sounds like a mandate of deliberative neglect. The division of political labor has the consequence of rendering legislative presence relatively meaningless, except for the intrinsic reasons to value electing a candidate of one's choice, which I questioned in section II. That division of labor thus cannot save Christiano's case for PR.

IV. Conclusion

Neither the ability to elect a candidate of one's choice, nor proportionality in legislative presence, succeed in justifying the claim that political equality categorically requires PR. We cannot escape making more fine-grained judgments of legislative and electoral systems based on the institutional details of those systems and how they interact with other features of the regime and political society at large.[46] There are many relevant criteria, including the way the electoral system shapes constituent services and administrative oversight; respect for voter authority in coalition formation;

---

44. Christiano, *Rule of the Many*, 215–16.

45. I am also not sure there is any reason to think that this kind of consideration would be more reliably granted in the PR system as opposed to an SMD system. (This also encourages minorities to cloak their aims in the language of means, but perhaps we should not criticize Christiano's proposal on the grounds that some participants may engage in bad faith.)

46. To Mill's credit and Christiano's, this kind of holism is very much in evidence in their work.

the importance of legislative voice for minorities in the wider deliberative context; appropriate consideration of citizens' views, however widely those range; and fairness in opportunities for coalition building. Because there is a range of criteria with which to judge electoral systems, some of which tend to favor PR, and some of which tend to favor SMD systems, it may be that mixed systems, which combine elements of both systems, have promise.[47] The context in which electoral systems are embedded matters, so there is a limit to what philosophical argument about political equality alone can recommend. Such argument is valuable, however, if it can clarify what we should desire in electoral systems, and thus how to argue for particular institutions or practices in a given time and place.

While I believe the variety of criteria and their context dependence undermines categorical claims about the superiority of PR, it is also true that many of the virtues of SMD systems I have identified are contingent in a double sense. First, such systems, like all electoral systems, vary in their suitability to different contexts. Second, the virtues of SMD systems—even in contexts that are fitting—tend to require that the systems be implemented in certain ways, or at least that certain characteristic abuses be prevented. So, for example, protection of smaller-than-quota minorities (that is, minorities too small to elect a representative in a PR system) requires conscious attention to that protection in districting choices. Avoiding severe disproportionality and deliberative neglect requires protections against various forms of gerrymandering. The importance of citizen authority over coalition building within major parties requires agenda setting and candidate selection within political parties to satisfy relevant democratic criteria.[48] (Similar concerns may exist about party elites' agenda setting in PR systems, but there the lesser strategic imperative to vote for a given party renders this point less urgent.) So while SMD systems may manifest virtues that render them preferable to, or at least as desirable as, PR systems in some contexts, actually manifesting the virtues typically requires further egalitarian institutional choices beyond the macro-level choice of electoral system. While details matter in PR systems

---

47. Some of these systems may be vulnerable to particularly objectionable forms of strategic voting and manipulation, however. See Bochsler, "Quasi-Proportional Electoral System."

48. Achen and Bartels criticize efforts to "democratize" parties through, for instance, presidential primary elections: *Democracy for Realists*, 60–68. Without fully evaluating these criticisms, I note that the requirement that party agenda setting be compatible with citizen authority over coalition formation does not, without further argument, imply that elections are required for all party leadership positions.

as well, of course, it may be that SMD systems can vary more in their egalitarian characteristics owing to these finer-grained issues. That does not mean that political equality requires PR in all jurisdictions. But it does mean that nonproportional systems require various forms of institutional vigilance—one form of which, involving claims of racial vote dilution, we will discuss in the next chapter.

CHAPTER NINE

Racial Vote Dilution and Gerrymandering

THE PROBLEM OF RACIAL VOTE dilution is a problem that only arises in nonproportional systems, such as territorial-districting systems, as it involves questions about whether those groups that do not successfully elect a representative are thereby victims of political injustice. Vote dilution, as I understand it, occurs when territorial districts are designed in such a way as to deny proper representation to certain individuals or groups within given districts or throughout the jurisdiction subject to the districting scheme—usually by drawing district lines in such a way as to make it very unlikely that the disfavored groups will be able to elect a candidate of their choice. Exactly how this denies anyone proper representation, and whose votes are diluted, are central questions an account of vote dilution must address.

In the last chapter, I argued that the ability of any group above a certain threshold size to elect a candidate of its choice is not a universal requirement of political equality. This rejection of the categorical importance of legislative presence might seem to commit one to skepticism regarding the problem of vote dilution, since the aim of antidilution efforts is often to ensure that minority groups are able to elect candidates of their choice. In this chapter, however, I reject the skeptical position, and argue that racial vote dilution is indeed a serious political injustice. The appropriate-consideration conception of political equality best accounts for this injustice, and it has the virtue of doing so without committing its proponents to an inflexible demand for PR. Under some circumstances, certain districting schemes enable or promote deliberative neglect of identifiable racial minority groups. This neglect can manifest itself in various ways, violating different requirements of appropriate consideration. The demand for appropriate consideration, in turn, helps to identify cases of vote dilution, and to suggest remedies. These remedies may include attempts to secure legislative presence for minorities if that is the best way to secure appropriate consideration and due practical consequence; but, contrary to the worries of dilution skeptics, this need not involve any broader commitment to the proportional representation of fixed electoral groups. I discuss this issue of proportionality, unfairness, and district drawing further in a brief excursus on the problem of political gerrymandering.

I do not attempt to resolve the difficult doctrinal questions surrounding vote dilution claims in the United States. I do, however, explain and defend the claim that vote dilution constitutes unfair representation. This is a serious matter, as skeptics regularly question whether there is any coherent way to explain the injustice of vote dilution. (As we shall see, there is at the time of writing at least one such skeptic on the Supreme Court, and there have been several throughout its history.) Moreover, even without detailed doctrinal arguments, a firm theoretical grounding for claims that racial vote dilution is unjust provides reasons for action for legislators, officials, and ordinary citizens concerned to secure political equality.

I. Racial Vote Dilution: Doctrine and Skepticism

If one believes that political equality does not categorically prohibit traditional territorial systems, questions arise about whether political equality places any constraints on drawing territorial districts. In the United States, complaints about unfair district drawing have been common, as many of these issues have become matters for adjudication by federal courts. Important early cases in the 1960s challenged malapportionment—the existence of districts (each electing the same number of representatives) with vastly different population sizes.[1] Even after the Supreme Court established the "one person, one vote" rule requiring equal-population districts, activists, policy makers, and others raised complaints that some districting schemes were unfair. In recent decades complaints have included criticisms of "political gerrymandering," in which district lines are drawn either to advantage one political party, or to protect incumbent legislators more generally,[2] and accusations of racial discrimination in

---

1. Baker v. Carr, 369 U.S. 186 (1962); Reynolds v. Sims, 377 U.S. 533 (1964).

2. See, e.g., Vieth v. Jubilirer, 541 U.S. 267 (2004); Davis v. Bandemer, 478 U.S. 109 (1986); Gaffney v. Cummings, 412 U.S. 735 (1973). The Court did not reach the substance of a recent high-profile political gerrymandering case, resolving it on procedural grounds: Gill v. Whitford, 585 U.S. __, 138 S.Ct. 1916 (2018).

drawing district lines with supposedly inappropriate attention to the race of the citizens in different districts.[3] I discuss partisan gerrymandering in section V; for most of the chapter, I focus on related and regularly recurring complaints: claims of racial vote dilution. In a vote dilution claim, critics argue that a districting scheme, combined with the first-past-the-post elections ubiquitous in the United States, unfairly disadvantages minorities in a given district or in the districting scheme as a whole (usually a state). For historical and legal reasons, claims of vote dilution complain that districting schemes unfairly disadvantage racial minorities.

Historically, there is no doubt that invidious district drawing was one of many devices of election law white supremacists used to limit the political power of blacks as black suffrage increased toward the end of the Jim Crow era.[4] While such clear racism in districting has declined in recent decades, concerns remain that, whether because of subtler racism, struggles for partisan advantage, unintentional neglect, or an unwarranted majoritarianism, some districting schemes continue to deny racial minorities fair participation in collective decision-making processes. Claims of racial vote dilution regularly appear in the federal courts, and some still make their way to the Supreme Court.[5]

The US Supreme Court first upheld a claim of unfair vote dilution in the 1973 case *White v. Regester*,[6] and has recognized claims of vote dilution ever since.[7] In a case of vote dilution, the claim is that territorial district lines have been drawn in such a way as to unfairly disadvantage racial minorities, in violation of the Fifteenth Amendment,[8] or, more commonly, where there is no evidence of intentional racial discrimination, of the Voting Rights Act.[9] The immediate question such cases raise is how we can describe voters as unfairly disadvantaged when they are able to vote and when their vote weighs as much as any other vote, in the sense that districts are equal in population size. Intuitively, something seems

---

3. See, e.g., Shaw v. Reno, 509 U.S. 630 (1993).
4. See Issacharoff et al., *Law of Democracy*, 571–94.
5. E.g., Cooper v. Harris, 581 U.S. __, 137 S.Ct. 1455 (2017); Bartlett v. Strickland, 556 U.S. 1 (2009); League of United Latin American Citizens (LULAC) v. Perry, 548 U.S. 399 (2006); Georgia v. Ashcroft, 539 U.S. 416 (2003).
6. 412 U.S. 755 (1973).
7. E.g., *LULAC*; Thornburg v. Gingles, 478 U.S. 30 (1986).
8. U.S. Const. amend. XV. See City of Mobile v. Bolden, 446 U.S. 55 (1980) (holding that only intentional minority vote dilution violates the Fifteenth Amendment).
9. 42 U.S.C. § 1973 (2006) (prohibiting any "standard, practice, or procedure . . . which results in a denial or abridgement of the right of any citizen of the United States to vote on account of race or color").

wrong when, to take an extreme example, black voters make up forty percent of the voters of a state, but are arranged in districts in such a way that, even if they vote in rigid lockstep, they cannot elect any candidates of their choice to the state legislature. But is this intuition correct? And if so, how exactly should we describe this wrong?

The question is pressing, because, from the beginning, there have been skeptics on and off the Court about whether racial vote dilution really constitutes a wrong (and whether it constitutes a legal wrong cognizable by courts). Justice Harlan, in a case shortly preceding *White*, expressed skepticism regarding the Court's ability to explain the concept of vote dilution, and its ability to develop and enforce principles of fair electoral representation.[10] More recently, Justice Thomas, in an opinion joined by Justice Scalia, argued that the Courts should not recognize claims of vote dilution, instead regulating "only state enactments that limit citizens' access to the ballot."[11] Thomas argued that the vote dilution cases "have immersed the federal courts in a hopeless project of weighing questions of political theory—questions judges must confront to establish a benchmark concept of an 'undiluted' vote."[12] Thomas's view has, so far, only attracted one other justice, but his broadside against vote dilution doctrine presents a challenge that demands response.[13]

The challenge is particularly acute because the prevailing equal-power conception of political equality cannot recognize vote dilution as a problem at all.[14] Because vote dilution occurs in a context of (roughly) universal suffrage, equal district sizes, and majority or plurality elections, it occurs in a context of equal voting power that the equal-power account must ratify as fair. Justice Harlan made precisely this point, when he argued that the "principles of pure majoritarian democracy," which in his view inappropriately underpinned the reapportionment cases, were incompatible with any finding of vote dilution.[15] To the extent that we think

---

10. Whitcomb v. Chavis, 403 U.S. 124, 165, 167, 170 (1971) (separate opinion of Harlan, J.).
11. Holder v. Hall, 512 U.S. 874, 891, 893 (1994) (Thomas, J.) (concurring in the judgment).
12. Id., at 892.
13. See Guinier, "[E]racing Democracy."
14. "Equal-power-plus" views, which require equal voting power and some basic deliberative conditions like free speech rights, also cannot recognize vote dilution as a problem. Equal-influence views are unlikely to recognize the problem, though much depends on how the equal-influence requirement is meant to interact with principles of representation. If my arguments in this chapter are correct, some of the wrongs of racial vote dilution are not reducible to inequalities in (opportunity for) influence.
15. *Whitcomb*, 403 U.S. at 166 (Harlan, J.).

that vote dilution is at least potentially a problem, this is a serious strike against the equal-power view, since it cannot even acknowledge the issue.[16] Conversely, however, the fact that this account of political equality supports skeptics of vote dilution gives further intellectual credibility to the skeptical position, and reveals the need for a response.

The appropriate-consideration conception of political equality provides such a response. The core objection to vote dilution is that a given districting scheme, in a given social and institutional context, deprives minority voters of appropriate consideration. In what follows, I identify two ways in which districting schemes could constitute or cause the deliberative neglect of racial minorities, in ways that the ability to elect candidates of their choice could cure. These forms of neglect track different claims to consideration, suggesting that racial vote dilution includes a set of possible wrongs, not all of which are necessarily present at once.

II. Race-Based Deliberative Neglect

The most straightforward way a districting scheme might cause or constitute deliberative neglect of racial minorities is if it enables race-based failures of consideration that alternative districting schemes might limit or prevent. The most straightforward way in which such failures could manifest is through racial hostility and discrimination in democratic deliberation, voting, and representation. If, for instance, white citizens tend to ignore the judgments of black citizens, white-controlled media outlets do not report on black citizens' concerns or preferences, white voters refuse to vote for black candidates, or candidates elected by whites ignore the judgments of black constituents, then black citizens are denied appropriate consideration in one or more forms. The districting scheme presumably is not the root cause of such deliberative neglect. But if there existed an alternative districting scheme that secured for black voters with shared judgments the opportunity to elect some candidates of their choice, this alternative would be preferable on political-equality grounds. First, the protection of such opportunity in the context of deliberative neglect

---

16. This complaint may not apply to Jeremy Waldron, who restricts his argument for legislative supremacy to polities with "democratic institutions in reasonably good working order." Waldron, "Case against Judicial Review," 1361. The presence of minority vote dilution arguably implies that democratic institutions are *not* in good working order, and so Waldron's argument may not apply. Whether or not we see this as a weakness in Waldron's view, it suggests that, if racial vote dilution is a problem, then his view is not applicable in the current American context.

serves an important symbolic function in asserting black voters' entitlement to consideration (including in representation), and as such constitutes a valuable form of consideration. Second, in many cases such opportunities will promote various forms of consideration, in the form of more responsive representatives, and deliberative consideration in the context of new electoral incentives. When race-based deliberative neglect occurs, then, and is curable (if only to some extent) through districting efforts to improve minorities' opportunities to elect candidates of choice, failing to undertake those efforts constitutes racial vote dilution.

In the last paragraph I used the example of neglect due to racial hostility. Race-based deliberative neglect is a much broader concept, however, and need not involve animus toward racial minorities. Any pattern of deliberative neglect along racial lines can constitute racial vote dilution, whether grounded in hostility, benevolent but mistaken generalizations about racial groups, indifference, or negligence. In this respect my view is similar to that of Andrew Altman, who argues that vote dilution occurs when "minority-favored candidates are consistently defeated, and racial prejudice against the minority is a significant part of the reason for those defeats."[17] While Altman's "prejudice standard" may seem to come close to requiring racial hostility, his conception of "prejudice" is very broad. It "should be understood to include those feelings, values, and beliefs that involve, one way or another, the discounting of a person's interests on account of her race."[18] Altman's view is on target in emphasizing, in contrast to some courts and scholars, that race-based neglect of minority citizens in general can establish a claim of vote dilution, not merely racial discrimination against minority candidates.[19] And he is right to identify as objectionable a wide range of causes for that neglect.

The appropriate-consideration conception of political equality suggests some amendments to Altman's prejudice standard, however. First, because political equality is a matter of sharing authority equally, rather than acting in ways that weigh citizens' interests equally, the concern should not be the discounting of minority citizens' interests, but neglect of their judgments.[20] (In practice, the two forms of discounting will tend to travel together, and it may be difficult to distinguish evidence of one from evidence of the other.) Second, it is not necessary that the neglect cause minority-favored

17. Altman, "Race and Democracy," 186.
18. Ibid., 189.
19. Some scholars and courts have focused on discrimination against candidates. For discussion, see Elmendorf et al., "Racially Polarized Voting," 633–34.
20. See ch. 4, § I.

candidates to be consistently defeated. The neglect itself violates political equality. For there to be a claim that the districting scheme constitutes vote dilution, it must be the case that some alternative, typically one that would allow a neglected minority group to elect a candidate of its choice, would limit that neglect. But this could be true even when the status quo is not one in which neglect is causing minority candidates' defeat.[21]

Third, I believe Altman is wrong to require that a racialized pattern of deliberative neglect is only objectionable if it is "on account of race" in a narrow sense. I hold that all such racialized patterns of neglect are objectionable, and constitute racial vote dilution if there are districting alternatives that limit such neglect. Some patterns might not result from neglect on account of race, in the sense that race is the factor that most directly explains the neglect. For instance, simple ethnocentrism (attending more to those in one's "in-group" than to those in one's "out-group") may create racialized patterns of neglect when race happens to be a marker of relevant group membership, without race playing any deeper role in the explanation of the neglect.[22] Alternatively, a pattern of neglect might primarily derive from richer citizens' contempt for poorer citizens, in a way that might be genuinely robust across the races of poor people.[23] Such neglect is objectionable, whatever the patterns of its racial effects. If it happens that, in such a context, racial minority citizens are disproportionately poor, this would constitute a race-based pattern of neglect, even though the neglect would not be "on account of race" in a narrow sense. Of course, if "on account of race" is meant by Altman to include any reasons for neglect that result in racialized patterns, in parallel to "disparate impact" or "indirect" discrimination claims, then this aspect of my view is not an amendment of Altman's, but rather an elaboration of it.[24]

---

21. The defeat of the candidates might be overdetermined, though alternative districting arrangements might still limit the neglect. Or the neglect might primarily be a matter of denying claims to consideration in deliberation, which denial might be less likely under an alternative districting arrangement, given different strategic incentives for voters, candidates, and representatives.

22. In such cases, race presumably plays some causal role, as there would be some reason why race became the salient group marker. But in a sense the pattern of neglect would not be "on account of race," because, once the sense of group membership is formed, citizens might honestly say that they would respond similarly to "those people" (people in the out-group—people in "that neighborhood," say), whatever their race.

23. This is not to deny that rates of black poverty may in fact contribute to stigmatization of the poor generally in the United States, such that race might play a causal role in such scenarios.

24. The objectionable disparate impact here is not disproportionality in ability to elect candidates of choice. We are imagining cases of neglect that are objectionable independently

The reason that narrowly construed racial causes of neglect are not necessary to constitute race-based deliberative neglect is that such neglect is, by definition, objectionable as inconsistent with political equality. Such scenarios are not equivalent to innocent explanations for racially disproportionate results (the evaluation of which depends on one's views of disparate impact discrimination more generally); the scenarios we are imagining involve explanations for objectionable neglect that are not, in some fundamental sense, race-based, but which nevertheless manifest in racial patterns. This is an important corrective to some forms of vote dilution skepticism, which appear to infer from the (correct) proposition that it is not intrinsically objectionable not to be able to elect a candidate of one's choice, to the (sometimes correct) claim that racial patterns in being unable to elect a candidate of one's choice are unobjectionable, to the (incorrect) claim that objections to vote dilution are incoherent. That last inference is incorrect because some racial patterns in abilities to elect candidates of choice reflect or enable objectionable forms of deliberative neglect.

It is fair to question whether the racial pattern makes the neglect worse than unpatterned neglect, or neglect patterned in nonracial ways. In the context of histories of racial injustice, there are good reasons to be especially concerned about racial patterns of political inequality.[25] We may also have reason to infer, given those histories, that racialized patterns in political behavior are more likely to derive from neglect than from conscientious disagreement following appropriate consideration, in contrast to other patterns of political disagreement (such as those based on wealth, sector of employment, or neighborhood). And there are legal reasons in the United States to be especially concerned about racial neglect, given the Fifteenth Amendment and the Voting Rights Act. But this conception of racial vote dilution does not depend on any argument that racial patterns of neglect are intrinsically worse than other patterns.

Some strands of legal doctrine have tried to identify vote dilution not merely as the absence of electoral success, but as part of a broader pattern of neglect in the electoral and legislative process. The Court in *White v. Regester*, for instance, recognized that that vote dilution might imply that members of a racial minority "had less opportunity than did other residents . . . to participate in the political processes."[26] Lack of minority

---

of any patterns; what makes the patterns "on account of race" is that they manifest in racially patterned ways. I discuss disparate impact in candidate election in § IV.

25. M. Williams, *Voice, Trust, and Memory*.
26. 412 U.S. at 766.

legislative presence in the form of "legislators of their choice" is not intrinsically unfair, but may be objectionable in the broader context of deliberative neglect. This context of neglect is established with reference to what are known as the "Senate factors," after a set of criteria identified in the Senate Committee report attached to the 1982 amendments to the Voting Rights Act.[27] These factors, which include historical patterns of discrimination in election laws and in legislative policy, patterns of racial appeals in campaigns, and apparent nonresponsiveness of legislators to minority constituents, suggest that vote dilution is not about minority legislative presence per se, but the ways in which lack of presence reflects and enables broader failures of appropriate consideration throughout the collective decision-making process. Because the Senate factors focus on what I call race-based patterns of neglect that are "on account of race" in a narrow sense, they may be too restrictive. But they nevertheless show how the "totality of the circumstances" test for evaluating vote dilution claims points us to evidence of deliberative neglect.[28]

III. Fairness in Coalition Formation

The basis for racial vote dilution claims I have just surveyed depends on racial patterns in independently objectionable deliberative neglect, much of which might be identifiable within individual districts. But this is not the only basis for dilution claims. There are also ways in which the districting scheme itself can cause or constitute a failure of consideration in ways that are not reducible to violations of political equality entirely within individual districts. The scheme amounts to racial vote dilution when it creates racially patterned inequalities in voters' abilities to form broad coalitions in the electorate or legislature that provide a proper hearing for the voters' judgments.

---

27. See Thornburg v. Gingles, 478 U.S. 30, 44–45, 50–51 (1986); Issacharoff et al., *Law of Democracy*, 732–41; Altman, "Race and Democracy," 190–94. Nathaniel Persily provides a full list of the Senate factors, in "Promise and Pitfalls," 203: "(1) a history of official discrimination in voting; (2) racially polarized voting; (3) use of enhancing practices, such as at-large elections and majority vote requirements; (4) discrimination in candidate slating; (5) ongoing effects of discrimination in areas such as education, employment, and health; (6) racial appeals in campaigns: (7) lack of success of minority candidates; (8) significant lack of responsiveness of elected officials to the minority community; and (9) a tenuous policy justification for the challenged practice."

28. The Voting Rights Act § 2(b) establishes a "totality of the circumstances" test for violations of § 2 of the act.

I argued in the last chapter that citizens have claims to authority over how broad coalitions form in efforts to decide what we do together. Accordingly, political equality requires that voters have fair opportunities to participate in such coalitions. No citizen has a right to be in a coalition of any particular size or particular desirability, because other citizens are also free to form their own judgments and pursue their own coalitional strategies. But citizens nevertheless are entitled to an electoral system that does not shape the strategic situation for coalition formation in ways that predictably deny them appropriate consideration. How might an electoral system do that?

Consider a scenario in which some or all judgments of a group of voters are neglected, in violation of the obligations of others to grant them consideration in those others' deliberations. In some cases, this neglect could be the result of a lack of electoral incentive for any of those others to join in a coalition with the neglected group. That is, if there were any electoral incentive to join with the group—if accommodating the group members and their judgments increased the strength of the others in the electorate and, prospectively, the legislature—a coalition including the group would form, and, given the efforts of the coalition, its members' judgments would be granted due consideration in the process as a whole. In such a scenario, the existing electoral incentives, some of which are structured by the electoral system, are a but-for cause of the deliberative neglect. In that sense, voters in the neglected group have their opportunities for coalition formation unfairly restricted.

When electoral systems are functioning well, many voters will be a part of coalitions that fail to win elections, or fail to win enough to determine law and policy. This failure, when due to other citizens' disagreement after appropriate consideration, involves no objectionable inequality. In those cases, the system poses no barrier to coalition formation with any particular citizens. Citizens, moreover, have some incentive to join with any other group of citizens, in order to strengthen their coalition. It just happens that, for some citizens (whether considering individual districts or the jurisdiction or polity as a whole), too few others take up the opportunity to form a prospective coalition (presumably out of disagreement about what the coalition ought to do), and so it does not carry the electoral day.

Being unable to form a coalition to elect a candidate of one's choice in a district does not amount to a general lack of opportunity to join a coalition supporting one's judgments. In some cases, there are in principle enough voters, but the voters are spread out across districts too much to enable a given group of those voters to elect a candidate. Here, too, there is not necessarily any objectionable inequality of opportunity. Like-minded voters across districts may still form coalitions, succeeding in some districts and failing in others, with successful candidates securing consideration for all members of the coalition. While some members of the coalition may not be constituents of their coalition's representatives in a narrow sense, their judgments are nevertheless granted suitable hearings by "surrogate" representatives from other districts.[29] Individual coalition members in the electorate also may grant a kind of surrogate consideration to members in other districts, in part owing to their incentive to forge an effective coalition with voters in their own district who render judgments similar to those in other districts. Because surrogates have incentives to consider and advance the judgments of their constituents or fellow coalition members, they thereby have suitably strong incentives to consider and advance the judgments of sufficiently like-minded voters in other districts.

Problems arise, however, when the electoral system operates in ways that limit the formation of such district-spanning coalitions, and the well-functioning surrogate representation those typically involve, for reasons independent of political judgments following appropriate consideration. In such cases, coalitions and surrogates do not counter the deliberative neglect of certain groups, in part because of the strategic pressures imposed by the electoral system in a given context. Consider a group that is "submerged," in the sense that it is an electoral minority within its district. In many respects, the group wishes to form a broad coalition with the Whigs, sharing as it does judgments with many Whig voters in other districts. But the group also has some views on some issues that are not generally shared by other Whigs (or are shared but are considered much lower in urgency). The Whigs not in the submerged group would be willing to endorse the group's positions if having the group within their coalition advanced the Whigs' other goals. This might happen either because the group would increase the coalition's electoral strength, or because, upon granting due consideration of the group's judgments, either the Whigs or the group or both alter their judgments in ways that cause them to see their aims as linked. But because the group is submerged in its district, the Whigs have no such incentive. Thus, despite no judgment-based objections to joining with the submerged group, the Whigs have no particular interest in meaningfully including members of the group in their coalition. In such

---

29. See Mansbridge, "Clarifying the Concept," 627–28; "Should Blacks Represent Blacks," 642.

a case, the submerged group has no expectation of participating in a wide coalition, and enjoying the benefits of surrogate representation, and this results not from their unwillingness, nor from the unwillingness of (some) others, to "pull, haul, and trade to find common political ground," but from the strategic situation into which the electoral system places voters.[30]

What causes cases such as these to arise? First, there must be a submerged group with sufficient coherence to say of its members that they share judgments that are not being accorded appropriate consideration in the political process. Second, there must be differences between the judgments of group members and those of members of any potential coalition (that is, members who themselves are granted consideration within the coalition), such that the submerged-group members are not granted meaningful consideration through surrogate representation elsewhere in that coalition. Third, there must be the possibility of adequate coalition formation—in the sense of consideration of the group's judgments within a coalition and adequate efforts by the coalition to secure consideration of the group's judgments in the wider process—given different organization of the electoral system. This third condition is evidence that the existing lack of adequate coalition formation and surrogate representation is not due to principled refusal after appropriate consideration, but rather is a matter of deliberative neglect enabled by the low electoral significance of the submerged group.

Regarding the second condition, it is important to be clear about which differences between the submerged group and other potential coalition partners mark neglect. It is helpful to distinguish "fringe" members of a coalition from "irrelevant" members of a (potential) coalition. Fringe members of a coalition have extreme views relative to most of the coalition members, or the platform of the coalition as a whole, but they are given due consideration within the coalition, and prefer the coalition to other alternatives (at least among alternatives with reasonable prospects of electoral and legislative success). Fringe members have appropriate practical consequence on the coalition as a whole, but are too few or too extreme relative to other members to have their judgments closely reflected in the efforts of the coalition as a whole.[31] Irrelevant members (or,

---

30. Johnson v. De Grandy, 512 U.S. 997, 1020 (1994). The phrase is typically used to emphasize that members of racial minority groups should not take the protections of the Voting Rights Act to absolve them from obligations to engage in such political efforts.

31. Citizens with extreme views relative to others may be at risk of deliberative neglect. The point is that merely being on the fringe of a coalition does not constitute neglect, nor need it mark a particularly high risk of neglect.

more accurately, protomembers), by contrast, have little or no practical consequence on the coalition or its members—though, if the third condition is satisfied, they would have such consequences in a system in which they were more electorally relevant.[32]

The distinction between fringe and irrelevant members is important because one cannot infer simply from the fact that one is part of a small group of voters whose judgments are not clearly reflected in the platform of a wider coalition that one lacks adequate representation (surrogate or otherwise), and that one is thus subject to deliberative neglect. One may simply be a fringe member of a coalition, granted the full consideration to which one is entitled. If a group is submerged within one district, but is a fringe of a wider coalition (either in its own district or in the jurisdiction as a whole), then there is no neglect, and no claim sounding in political equality to a change in the electoral structure. Such claims only arise if the electoral structure causes a group to be irrelevant, and thereby neglected.

If significant political disagreement could be reduced to one's position along a one-dimensional spectrum, and voters' judgments had what social choice theorists call a "single-peaked" structure, according to which they prefer positions closer to their ideal point on the spectrum to positions farther away, there might generally be low risk of irrelevance. Citizens at the extreme ends of the spectrum might have good reason to expect reliable links with, and surrogate representation by, others on their side of the median citizen on the spectrum.[33] Any submerged group within one district (whether fringe or not in the jurisdiction as a whole) would get secure consideration, in part because of coalition efforts outside their district. This is less reliably true, however, in cases in which political disagreements operate across multiple dimensions. In such cases, a group that is submerged in its district in part or whole because of judgments along one dimension cannot be sure that group members will secure their consideration through coalitions in other districts, because those coalitions

---

32. It may be that, given the distribution of citizens' judgments, any possible districting scheme will produce some submerged groups irrelevant to any coalition. In such cases, the districting scheme ought to minimize this irrelevance, but remaining possibilities of neglect would need to be combated through other means.

33. Even here there may be neglect. And such neglect might ground a claim for changing the electoral structure to enable more extreme citizens to elect candidates of their choice, if that would cure the neglect. Nevertheless, in such cases, the electoral structure and the structure of preferences make it more likely that the divergence between extreme citizen views and coalition platforms is due to strategic considerations among an egalitarian coalition rather than to deliberative neglect.

may organize along other dimensions. Even if members of the submerged group share some of the judgments of a wider coalition when it comes to those other dimensions, with respect to the judgments along the dimension that is causing them to be submerged, their judgments are irrelevant to the coalition, and thus are at high risk of neglect.

The relevance of these considerations for racial vote dilution should be apparent. When members of racial minority groups with relatively cohesive judgments are submerged within a district, the question arises whether they are rendered irrelevant to wider coalitions in ways that subject them to neglect. We cannot assume that such submerged groups are adequately represented by a wider coalition spanning the jurisdiction, because we cannot assume that the group and its judgments along important dimensions are relevant to the coalition as a whole. This may be because the submerged group has judgments on racial justice issues that are irrelevant to the wider coalition in which they would otherwise be a part (because the coalition is primarily organized around economic issues, say). But this racially patterned neglect is objectionable whether or not the neglected judgments themselves involve explicit reference to race. What matters is that the submerged group is subject to neglect in part because of the way the structure of judgments in the population and the structure of the electoral system together render irrelevant its judgments along some dimension.

When opportunities for coalition building are limited in this sense, members of submerged groups can object that their vote is unfairly diluted. Notably, curing such dilution does not necessarily require the formation of districts in which members of the previously submerged groups themselves make up a majority ("majority-minority districts"). All that is necessary is that the new districting scheme render the previously submerged group electorally relevant in ways that secure appropriate consideration of its judgments. In cases of very high polarization in the judgments of members of different racial groups, cross-racial coalitions may be unlikely, and so participation in any wider coalition may require that members of the racial minority group be able to elect candidates of their choice on their own.[34] When some cross-racial coalitions are available in

34. This claim depends on the assumption that, once a legislator is elected by the group, the legislator will be treated as "relevant" by a wider legislative coalition. If that is not true—say, because racial polarization is so extreme that legislators representing whites will not form coalitions with legislators representing blacks—then there are effectively no coalition-formation opportunities for racial minorities. In this case there are reasons to be concerned about many forms of race-based deliberative neglect (and other forms of racial

the jurisdiction as a whole, however, enabling such coalition formation may only require districts that include sufficient members of the previously submerged group that they would have secure electoral relevance within a wider coalition.[35]

This claim of racial vote dilution on grounds of unfair restrictions on coalition formation does not require the conclusion that members of a racial minority group see their votes objectionably diluted whenever they cannot together elect candidates of their choice. Merely losing elections as an electoral minority is not evidence of political inequality. The trigger of this kind of vote dilution claim is that the electoral losses within one district (or a broader districting scheme) enable deliberative neglect in the political process as a whole. This neglect is not a matter of others' refusal to form alliances on principled grounds after due consideration of the group members' judgments, but involves failing to grant those judgments a proper place on the collective deliberative agenda, to pay them requisite attention, to grant them suitable deliberative weight, and so on. To the extent that these forms of neglect result from the structure of electoral incentives established by the districting scheme, they amount to vote dilution. When, by contrast, voters are in an electoral minority but have the opportunity to join coalitions that will meaningfully secure consideration of their judgments in the political process as a whole, their losses are consistent with political equality.

IV. Disparate Impact Discrimination and Political Justice

There may be one further ground for claims of racial vote dilution that does not depend on objectionable deliberative neglect. The argument is that when racial minorities cannot elect candidates of their choice roughly in proportion to their population, they are subject to disparate impact, or "indirect," discrimination. That is, the minority group disproportionately

---

injustice); there may be no special concern about the ways in which the districting scheme hinders coalition formation, however, since such coalitions are unavailing in such a polarized context. There may still be grounds for certain districting schemes, on the basis not of claims to coalition formation, but of the ability of minority-preferred candidates to provide important consideration, perhaps through constituent services.

35. Thus, in principle, minority voters' claims could be satisfied by so-called "coalition districts," in which they would not be a majority but would likely form an important part of a successful electoral coalition with voters of other races. See Georgia v. Ashcroft, 539 U.S. 416 (2003).

bears the burden of a formally race-neutral districting scheme that was implemented with no discriminatory intent. If such disparate impact on racial minority groups is unjustified, then the districting scheme would be objectionable.

As I argued in the last chapter, ability to elect a candidate of one's choice in the sense that the minority group lacks in the imagined scenario is not a necessary constituent of political equality. So a system that denies some members of a minority group that ability does not itself violate the requirements of political equality. But disparate impact claims do not require showing that the challenged conduct specifically deprives a citizen of something to which she is entitled. Someone objecting to a hiring exam that disproportionately selected against black applicants does not typically need to show that she in particular, nor black applicants generally, were entitled to the jobs at stake.[36] Similarly, one might argue, claims of disparate impact in the distribution of ability to elect candidates of choice need not rest on any claim of general individual or group entitlement to such ability.

But while a disparate impact claim does not require showing a direct denial of something to which one was entitled, there must be some entitlements of some kind being denied, in order for the putatively discriminatory policy or action to be wrong. One common theory of disparate impact discrimination holds that such norms advance the entitlements in distributive justice of the members of the groups protected by the norms. So, for instance, disparate impact protections in employment law promote distributive justice by effectively enlisting employers in ameliorating injustices that have manifested in socially patterned ways (burdening, for example, women and racial and religious minorities).[37] Another theory holds that the underlying entitlement is to not be subject to disparate treatment discrimination, and that protections against disparate impact discrimination are an important prophylactic against otherwise difficult to enforce antidiscrimination norms.[38] An application of disparate impact antidiscrimination norms to the vote dilution context thus may not require

36. According to most theories of disparate treatment, or "direct," discrimination, a successful claim of discrimination does not need to show that one was deprived of an entitlement, either. Someone fired (or not hired) because he was black does not need to show that he was as a general matter of law or justice entitled to the position. (The fact that the employer could have otherwise fired him at will, and so in that sense the employee had no entitlement to continued employment, does not defeat the discrimination claim.)

37. For two versions of this view, see Arneson, "Discrimination"; Gardner, "Liberals and Unlawful Discrimination."

38. See Anderson, *Imperative of Integration*, 144–48.

showing that the ability to elect candidates of choice is a requirement of political equality, but it does require some showing that such norms are necessary to protect some entitlements of protected groups.

I doubt this strategy for defending vote dilution claims can succeed, if, as I have framed them, they are meant to be independent of claims of race-based failures of consideration. If there are no such failures, there is no equivalent to the denial of distributive entitlements that disparate impact norms are supposed to protect against. Nor is there much need for a prophylactic rule, since there is no risk of underlying wrong to prevent. If, by contrast, there are real concerns about race-based neglect, I believe these are best captured by the approaches to vote dilution I have elaborated earlier in this chapter; there is no need for a general proscription against disproportionality in ability to elect candidates of choice.

There may be one indirect role for disparate impact antidiscrimination norms in the design of electoral systems. If there are general concerns about patterned distributive injustices (which are not derived from race-based deliberative neglect), and ease in electing candidates of choice helps prevent or ameliorate such injustices, there may be good reasons to design electoral systems so as to guarantee to vulnerable groups proportional ability to elect candidates of choice. These reasons are not reasons of political equality, since, by assumption, there would be no deliberative neglect in a system in which vulnerable groups did not enjoy this guarantee. But such a guarantee does not violate any requirement of political equality (assuming that the groups not vulnerable to distributive injustice would not be vulnerable to deliberative neglect if vulnerable groups were secure in their ability to elect candidates of choice). Citizens are permitted (perhaps required) to organize their political processes in ways that promote good outcomes, consistent with the requirements of political equality. Disparate impact antidiscrimination norms may direct us to one set of substantive concerns—possibly urgent concerns—that should guide electoral-system design. This may be of great practical significance to the legislatures, governors, commissions, and citizens who make districting choices. But that does not mean there is a disparate impact candidate-selection norm internal to political equality itself.

V. Partisan Gerrymandering: A Brief Excursus

The discussion of how districting schemes can cause or constitute racially patterned deliberative neglect sheds light on the related problem of partisan gerrymandering. Partisan gerrymandering, recall, involves drawing district lines in such a way as to advantage some party or parties at the expense of others. In the United States, though complaints about such gerrymandering are common, there is currently no federal judicial regulation of partisan district drawing, unless concerns about racial discrimination are involved.[39] Legal questions aside, whether partisan gerrymandering is wrong, and, if so, what explains the wrong, is a vexed question. As with racial vote dilution, this is in part because many equal-power views are indifferent between districting schemes (holding population size constant), and because objections to partisan gerrymandering may seem to require commitment to PR.

The appropriate-consideration conception shows why partisan gerrymandering is a political injustice, without requiring any commitment to pure majoritarianism or PR. As I suggested at the end of chapter 8, preventing gerrymandering and racial vote dilution may be necessary to render SMD systems adequate alternatives to PR. I argued there that political equality does not categorically require allocation of seats in the legislature to parties proportional to the votes they receive. However, great disproportionality is objectionable, while modest disproportionality may be objectionable if it reflects or causes deliberative neglect, including, of course, neglect of large coalitions. The objection to disproportionality, as explained in chapter 6, is that to some extent, judgments ought to be granted greater consideration by the regime as a whole if more citizens hold that judgment. This consideration should be manifest in the actions of representatives and the extent to which voters have authority over coalition formation, which is closely linked to the partisan composition of the legislature. The proportionality of consideration is only required to some extent because disproportionality may be required for minority protection, or because of diminishing claims to further consideration for supermajorities. Partisan gerrymanders that introduce great disproportionality in circumstances that are not required for either of these reasons objectionably neglect the citizens supporting disadvantaged parties.[40] Moreover, while

---

39. Cooper v. Harris, 581 U.S. __, 137 S.Ct. 1455 (2017). Recent efforts to get the Supreme Court to recognize a constitutional claim against partisan gerrymandering have temporarily stalled. See Gill v. Whitford, 585 U.S. __, 138 S.Ct. 1916 (2018). For background on the political issues, see McGrath et al., *Gerrymandering in America*.

40. When considering which "minorities" need protection, attention must be given to the legislature as a whole, and coalitions across the legislature's constituency. So, for instance, gerrymanders disproportionately favoring a minority within a state would not be justified for federal congressional districting unless that minority were at risk of neglect in the federal legislature.

some disproportionality introduced by SMD systems may be justified by the need to protect citizens' authority over representative-coalition formation (which is at risk in PR systems), that justification cannot support disproportionate districting schemes within an existing SMD system.

Partisan gerrymanders may be objectionable for reasons beyond legislative disproportionality per se. While partisan conflict is inevitable and unobjectionable, such conflict ought to respect obligations to grant consideration to political opponents, in both representation and deliberation. Deciding that others are wrong about some political matter after due consideration is consistent with political equality, while denying them that consideration is not. Partisanship itself is often praiseworthy, reflecting efforts to pursue justice. Partisan gerrymandering, however, may both reflect a disregard for the claims to consideration of disfavored voters, and may also encourage such disregard by candidates in protected districts.[41] Of course, it is difficult to disentangle evidence of partisan-based neglect from evidence of partisan disagreement. So this ground to object to gerrymanders may not often provide independent evidence for the wrongness of some districting scheme. But it does give us independent reason to be skeptical of disproportionate schemes.

Suspicion that such gerrymanders both reflect and cause deliberative neglect of partisan opponents is supported by the fact that the districting schemes generally have no particular advantage—in anything other than partisan terms—over alternatives. If they did have some such advantage, for instance in terms protecting racial minorities or an otherwise coalitionally irrelevant group in the sense introduced in section III, such schemes might be justified. But apart from those concerns, there is generally no reason to prefer one districting scheme over another, within fairly wide constraints (such as respecting "political subdivisions" such as cities or counties, whose residents may have common judgments not found elsewhere in a jurisdiction).[42] These reasons for general indifference between districting schemes are often used to protect gerrymanders, especially against judicial regulation, on the grounds that legislatures (or other line

---

41. The argument against partisan gerrymandering here does not depend the assumption that partisan gerrymandering has significant effects on policy outcomes, nor that "competitiveness" within individual districts (i.e., relative balance between supporters of major parties) ought to be maximized. But gerrymandering would be more objectionable if "safe" districts established by the district plan do in fact encourage neglect of citizens.

42. Nicholas O. Stephanopoulos and Eric M. McGhee, in an influential paper, also recommend allowing districters opportunity to defend disproportionate schemes on similar grounds, in "Partisan Gerrymandering," 837–38.

drawers) ought to be free to draw districts more or less as they please. But once objections to a particular scheme are identified, along the lines just suggested, the reasons for indifference show that there is no political inequality in demanding an alternative.

It is difficult to design clear standards for identifying when a districting scheme is disproportionate enough to render it objectionable. Any particular threshold is bound to be somewhat arbitrary, though this does not mean it is wrong to establish thresholds for practical purposes. Relevant factors include both the extent of disproportionality and how likely such disproportionality in favor of one party is likely to persist over the life of the districting scheme.[43] I believe it would be reasonable to consider any intentional districting for disproportionate partisan advantage to be prima facie evidence of inequality, as it suggests willingness to neglect voters and representatives of opposing parties, given that there is typically no good reason to support such gerrymanders. (Proponents of such a scheme should have opportunity to justify it on the grounds I suggested above that can support disproportionate schemes.) The objectionable nature of partisan motivation in district drawing may justify shifting responsibility for districting plans away from legislatures toward independent commissions that may be more insulated from partisan pressure and motivation.[44] Failing that, however, judicial regulation of legislative plans is warranted, as I discuss in section VI and in my discussion of judicial review in section IV of chapter 11.

VI. Implementation and Enforcement— and Skepticism Revisited

I have defended claims of racial vote dilution and partisan gerrymandering in abstract terms. Dilution occurs, I have said, when political processes involve race-based deliberative neglect, one important species of which involves unfairness in opportunities for coalition formation, and when the districting system enables or contributes to this neglect. Obviously, it is not easy to translate a general prohibition of such dilution into operational standards for designing districting or evaluating schemes. Exactly what evidence supports claims of deliberative neglect, as opposed to mere disagreement? How do we know that judgments are structured in ways that

---

43. See ibid., 889–90.
44. See Issacharoff, "Gerrymandering and Political Cartels"; Thompson, *Just Elections*, 173–79.

preclude coalition formation absent ability to elect candidates of choice? How much neglect is enough to trigger obligations to alter the districting scheme? How much cross-racial support is enough to render a particular district (or a jurisdiction as a whole) sufficient to enable fair coalition formation and adequate surrogate representation? Historical evidence is important, since it provides reasons to interpret contemporary evidence in the light of historical patterns of deliberative neglect of certain groups, including racial minorities. But interpreting this evidence requires judgment, and controversies about interpretations are inevitable.

Operational questions like these are important, especially in the United States, where most discussion of vote dilution occurs in the context of judicial enforcement of the Voting Rights Act (and, to a lesser extent, the Constitution). Courts (and the lawyers and legal scholars who mean to guide the courts) require some standards or rules with which to enforce prohibitions against racial vote dilution. Developing such standards or rules is not easy, and I have not attempted to do so here.[45] To lawyers familiar with live and long-standing controversies about just such matters of implementation and enforcement, this may be disappointing. But while I acknowledge that more work needs to be done in order to connect the appropriate-consideration conception of political equality to a program of legally protecting against racial vote dilution, the conclusions of this chapter have considerable practical significance. First, of course, as legal scholars well know, what rules and standards make sense depends on one's normative views about what racial vote dilution is, and why it is wrong. The aim of this chapter (and this book) is to provide defensible foundations for that legal enterprise. Second, the conception is not meant only, or even primarily, for courts. The objectionable features of racial vote dilution do not only provide reasons for courts to strike down dilutive districting schemes. They provide reasons for legislatures, executive officials, independent districting commissions, and ordinary citizens to support nondilutive schemes and to reject dilutive ones. In many cases, no precise rules or standards are necessary, because it is easy enough when drawing district lines to avoid anything close to racial vote dilution.[46] Because

---

45. On contemporary doctrinal challenges, see Elmendorf et al., "Racially Polarized Voting"; Persily, "Promise and Pitfalls."
46. It would be easier if the Court were more permissive in its so-called "racial gerrymandering" doctrine, as I believe it should be. See, e.g., Shaw v. Reno, 509 U.S. 630 (1993). Avoiding dilution is more difficult if districters are not permitted to draw lines intentionally to enable coalitions that prevent race-based neglect. There is no reason, in my view, that explicit consciousness of race in drawing district lines constitutes wrongful

avoiding racial vote dilution does not involve any institutional inequality—no plural votes, no extra-small districts, and so on—there is no competing threat that gives reason to avoid obviously nondilutive schemes.

In the judicial-enforcement context, there are some competing considerations. There are concerns about the proper role of the judiciary in policing the districting choices of elected state governments. One might object, as Justice Thomas does, that this account of the injustice of vote dilution demands of the courts that they immerse themselves in the "hopeless project" of developing a political theory of fair representation.[47] But to the extent that the Constitution or Congress has charged the courts with protecting against the abridgment of citizens' right to vote, the courts have no choice but to engage in such a project.[48] The courts are charged with developing the best-reasoned account of what constitutes such abridgment within the American legal context. The issue necessarily implicates questions of fair representation. Given their charge, the courts might as well operate according to the best theory on offer, consistent with other constraints on legal interpretation. If political equality requires preventing race-based deliberative neglect, then racial vote dilution is a serious political injustice, and one that warrants remedy by Congress and the courts.

It is important to emphasize how weak the objections to court action are. When a court requires that a jurisdiction replace a dilutive scheme with a nondilutive scheme, it does not require any inequality in voting power, access to the polls, or any other institutional entitlement that might trigger concerns about deliberative neglect. There is no legitimate concern about "reverse discrimination." By the lights of both the appropriate-consideration conception of political equality and the minimalist, equal-power conceptions apparently favored by vote dilution skeptics, the nondilutive schemes required by the courts are consistent with the demands of political equality. Judicial enforcement therefore is unlikely to infringe on any important interests, beyond those always involved when courts engage in judicial review of state laws and policies. If one is not skeptical of all judicial review, a role for courts in the enforcement of

---

discrimination, or political inequality, absent reasons to suspect that such consciousness reflects or promotes deliberative neglect. Jurisdiction-wide racial majorities are not typically vulnerable to deliberative neglect, particularly because views shared by supermajorities are often entitled only to subproportional consideration, for reasons explained in ch. 6, § III.B.

47. Holder v. Hall, 512 U.S. at 891, 892 (1994) (Thomas, J., concurring in the judgment).

48. Justice Stevens made just this point in his response to Justice Thomas. See id., at 957, 966 (separate opinion of Stevens, J.). See also Guinier, "[E]racing Democracy," 124.

norms against racial vote dilution is relatively easy to defend.[49] This is especially evident when we reconsider some common arguments for vote dilution skepticism.

Skeptics often argue that recognizing vote dilution as a harm requires giving special moral standing to groups—racial groups in particular—instead of, and possibly at the expense of, what they see as the proper concern for individual rights.[50] But a proper understanding of political equality reveals that it is at once individualistic in its moral foundations and capable of explaining harms that afflict groups. The claim to appropriate consideration belongs to each individual citizen, but, given the processes of aggregation and winnowing that are constitutive of democratic politics, neglect often threatens individuals differentially according to their membership in identifiable groups. Abstractly considered, deliberative neglect—lack of consideration—might threaten groups of any kind; in the United States, given its history, threats against racial minorities are especially salient, and citizens have rightly chosen to police them with special attention. Individual members of groups are unjustly deprived of consideration through the discounting of the political coalition through which they aimed to gain public consideration for their judgments.[51] Moreover, even if the injustice falls differentially on members of a group, or includes members of different groups, our evidence for such differentiated injustices will likely be limited; without such fine-grained evidence of varying consideration of individuals, evidence of the consideration of groups in the aggregate will often be a fair proxy for the scope of the underlying injustice to individuals.

A second, related concern of dilution skeptics is that claims of vote dilution require a contrasting conception of an "undiluted" vote, and that the inevitable standard must be the proportional representation of groups.[52] This is seen to be objectionable for a variety of reasons, from concerns that the drive for proportionality is based on disrespectful assumptions that

---

49. The most plausible grounds for objection in the US context are state-autonomy grounds—the claim that the Congress does not have the authority to regulate state election laws and procedures to the extent the Voting Rights Act does. This claim requires a very restrictive interpretation of § 2 of the Fifteenth Amendment, which gives the Congress the authority to enforce the amendment's antidiscrimination provision. I find such a restrictive interpretation unconvincing, but cannot press the case here.

50. See, e.g., *Holder*, 512 U.S. at 891, 903 (Thomas, J.); Epstein, "Tuskegee Modern," 875–76.

51. Cf. Heather Gerken's claim that the right to an undiluted vote is an "aggregate" right that belongs to individuals, the violation of which tends to occur simultaneously to members of groups. Gerken, "Understanding the Right."

52. See, e.g., *Holder*, 512 U.S. at 902–3.

members of racial groups think alike, to more general concerns that the courts ought not to force the choice of a particular, tendentious representational scheme.[53] The belief that recognizing vote dilution claims commits one to a proportionality standard is not entirely unfounded, as Guinier, for example, has called for certain PR schemes as remedies for some cases of vote dilution.[54] We need, however, no foundational commitment to PR in order to recognize claims of vote dilution. The basic commitment is to appropriate consideration—in particular, to the absence of race-based failures of consideration that could be cured by changes in a districting scheme. Just as there is no particular ethical status attributed to majority decision, there is no particular ethical status attributed to the proportional representation of groups in the legislature. As I argued in chapter 8, PR is not necessary to prevent deliberative neglect in general. Moreover, there is nothing in my analysis of racial vote dilution that requires PR. Proportionality is not the only, nor necessarily the best, path to representative fairness.

It is true that claims of vote dilution put a certain pressure on systems to move toward proportionality. This is because our evidence for vote dilution tends to be relatively coarse—for example, evidence about demographics and election results—and because the range of remedies is often thought to be limited (e.g., limited to demanding a certain number of "majority-minority" districts, in which a racial minority constitutes a majority in the district, out of a fixed number of total districts). If this pressure toward proportionality exists, though, it is not because those who recognize dilution claims are bent on imposing PR on the polity—it is simply because proportionality might sometimes make context-specific sense as a way to approximate appropriate consideration of all citizens. General objections to proportionality risk ignoring the merits of such context-sensitive claims, and, more importantly, the moral concern that lies at the root of vote dilution claims.

VII. Conclusion

When democratic procedures are working well, it is true that, as the Supreme Court puts it, "the power to influence the political process is not limited to winning elections," and that "an individual or group of

---

53. In territorial systems, since proportionality requires district drawers to develop districting schemes with an eye to some form of proportionality they consider significant, the proportionality is sometimes called "compulsory."

54. Guinier, [E]racing Democracy," 131–32; *Tyranny of the Majority*, 92, 118.

individuals who votes for a losing candidate is usually deemed to be adequately represented by the winning candidate."[55] These claims about the adequate representation of electoral losers depend, however, on reliable guarantees of appropriate consideration in deliberative processes, and fair opportunities for coalition formation across electoral districts. Race-based deliberative neglect undermines these guarantees and opportunities. It may sometimes be unobjectionable for a candidate to be sure of his victory despite the objections of an identifiable minority. This may be the case, for instance, in "safe" districts where citizens of one political party are an overwhelming majority. In such cases, we may have reason to believe that the representative's safety does not promote objectionable deliberative neglect—that the candidate does not so much neglect the minority opposition as consider and reject their views in a way consistent with the norms of appropriate consideration.[56] By contrast, in the case of racial vote dilution, representatives or other electors diminish the scope of minority voters' hearings in impermissible ways—not merely because of the lesser support for their judgments in the district. Claims of vote dilution precisely object that a given districting scheme enables or promotes deliberative neglect, by arranging voters in a way that they may be safely neglected: their judgments do not shape the common deliberative agenda, they are given little weight in deliberations, the regime and its officials do not make themselves deliberatively accountable to them, and so on. The possibility that electoral losers can have all their claims to appropriate consideration fully satisfied does show that proportional representation by race is not a universal requirement of political equality. We cannot make inferences about vote dilution simply by counting districts controlled by different racial groups. But the fact that districting schemes—and the ability to elect candidates of choice—can enable race-based deliberative neglect shows that racial vote dilution is a serious threat to political equality. Even in contexts of equal voting power and full access to the polls, good representation of electoral minorities cannot be taken for granted.

---

55. Davis v. Bandemer, 478 U.S. 109, 132 (1986).
56. As I argued in § V, however, partisan gerrymandering undermines our confidence about these cases.

CHAPTER TEN

Oligarchic Threats

WEALTH INEQUALITY in many societies is high and growing.[1] Considerable evidence shows that this inequality substantially affects democratic political processes, as wealthy citizens and corporations exert much greater influence on law and policy making than do poor or middle-class citizens.[2] Some scholars doubt whether we should label the United States a democracy, at least if "democracy" signifies a society in which citizens enjoy political equality.[3] These doubts present theoretical questions about what exactly political equality is, and whether great wealth inequality objectionably undermines political equality.

Normative theory has lagged behind empirical scholarship. Objections to wealth inequality on the grounds that it undermines democracy are common among liberal egalitarians and deliberative democrats.[4] But these objections are not always well developed, more or less taking as obvious the threat of wealth inequality to democracy.[5] Developed objections rely on the claim that political equality requires equal opportunity for political influence, which places constraints on the use of wealth in democratic deliberation, campaigning, and lobbying representatives. As I argued in chapter 6, however, this conception of political equality does not

---

1. Alvaredo et al., "Global Inequality Dynamics."
2. Gilens and Page, "Testing Theories"; Gilens, *Affluence and Influence*; Schlozman et al., *Unheavenly Chorus*; Bartels, *Unequal Democracy*.
3. Gilens and Page, "Testing Theories," 577; Bartels, *Unequal Democracy*, 287.
4. Rawls, *Theory of Justice*, § 36; J. Cohen, "Money"; Dworkin, *Sovereign Virtue*, chs. 4, 10; Habermas, *Between Facts and Norms*, ch. 9.
5. For criticism of Rawls, see Wall, "Rawls."

well capture citizens' claims to fair deliberation and representation, and mischaracterizes the appropriate remedies.[6]

These theoretical limitations are exaggerated by two problems. First, egalitarian theorists attend too little to the diverse mechanisms by which the rich can evade and undermine democratic norms. As a result, their principles of political equality fail to represent the range of democratic concerns. Second, such theorists (with the exception of Ronald Dworkin and Joshua Cohen) attend too little to the arguments of what I will call their *minimalist* opponents: those who believe that political equality requires only fair elections and unregulated deliberation.[7] Minimalists hold that equal votes guarantee equal citizen authority, and that freedom of speech ensures that all citizens have adequate opportunity to deliberate democratically as they see fit. If citizens do not exercise opportunities, or if they freely exercise them in ways that favor rich advocates, the argument goes, there is no unfairness. Proper understanding of the mechanisms of unequal influence, on this view, reveals them to be suitably democratic. An argument that wealth inequality threatens democracy must rebut minimalist arguments if it is to be persuasive. Theoretical neglect of these two problems has practical consequences, as defenders of the status quo can use plausible but mistaken conceptions of political equality to argue against reform.

The ideal of appropriate consideration makes clear that citizens not only have rights to participate in advocacy, but also have obligations to attend to the advocacy of others. The fact that citizens have entitlements and obligations in the role of advocate and that of listener highlights the centrality to a theory of political equality of a fair division of responsibility in ensuring that obligations are met and entitlements satisfied. A conception of fair responsibility plays a critical role in identifying oligarchic threats to political equality and justifying democratic responses. Both minimalist and equal-influence views ignore listeners' share of responsibility to secure advocates' consideration, and so fail to recognize serious forms of political unfairness.

In this chapter, I identify several oligarchic threats to political equality that arise in circumstances of great wealth inequality. The threats are diverse and not reducible to inequalities in opportunities for influence. I develop a conception of the fair division of responsibility among citizens

---

6. See also Pevnick, "Egalitarian Rationale."
7. Sullivan, "Against Campaign Finance Reform," and "Political Money"; Smith, *Unfree Speech*; Redish and Dawson, "Worse Than the Disease."

for ensuring appropriate consideration. I explain how this conception supports traditional democratic objections to poll taxes, and extend that logic to criticize onerous voting requirements. I apply the conception of fair responsibility to informal democratic deliberation, including electoral campaigning and practices of representation. This is the domain of much high-profile disagreement (especially in the United States) between reformists who believe we ought to legally limit the use of wealth in campaigns, and anti-reformists who object that such limits are unnecessary to secure democracy, and anyway violate principles of liberty. I argue that when there is great wealth inequality, decision-making systems often place unreasonable burdens on poorer citizens who seek to secure consideration. Thus democracies, even when they enjoy advanced communications technology, face certain deliberative scarcities—limits on the extent to which the polity can attend to, or consider, the judgments of its citizens. In such conditions, the special consideration of some—for instance, the rich—comes at the expense of the consideration of others—for instance, the poor. This fact explains what is wrong about a system that gives great consideration to the wealthy. It also supports rejecting the anti-reformist view that the disproportionate rule of the rich is an unavoidable consequence of political liberty.

I. Oligarchic Threats

Disenfranchisement of citizens who fail to meet some high threshold of personal wealth is definitive of oligarchy (the rule of the rich). Indirect institutional means of achieving the same political disregard for the poor are also incompatible with political equality. If poor citizens voted, but electoral systems discounted or diluted their votes, or they were systematically ignored in political deliberations, the regime would be politically unequal. There are a great many ways to be antidemocratic.

The problem of informal oligarchy is an urgent one for citizens of the United States. Political officials in the United States appear to respond much more to the views of wealthy citizens than they do to those of the poor.[8] In this section, I identify several threats that large wealth inequalities pose to political equality even in the context of formal equality in aggregative processes, such as exists, more or less, in many contemporary democracies. These oligarchic threats manifest as failures of consideration in deliberation, or in informal aggregative processes, such as in the

---

8. Gilens and Page, "Testing Theories," 565; Bartels, *Unequal Democracy*, 5.

relationship between citizens and representatives. Understanding these threats focuses our attention on the diverse ways wealth inequalities can undermine political equality, and points us to appropriate solutions.

The general problem is that great wealth inequalities may leave poorer citizens unable to secure reliable appropriate consideration. The concern is not that each citizen have equal opportunities for equal influence, nor equal resources for influence. Instead, the concern is that resource deficiencies make it difficult or impossible for poorer citizens to claim the authority to which they are entitled.

First, citizens require resources to be protected from others' manipulation—to have, in this sense, "autonomy protection." It may be difficult to distinguish clearly manipulative forms of communication and influence from benign forms (such as persuasion). The present argument only requires that there be some forms of communication and influence that are "manipulative," which in present context just means inconsistent with the deliberative entitlements of political equals. I do not think it is controversial that the set of manipulative communicative forms in that sense is not empty. (Consider deception, especially in cases in which exposing the deception is difficult.) Some deliberative practices and structures are not consistent with respect for other citizens as autonomous in the sense that they are entitled to form what are meaningfully their own judgments.[9] This conception of autonomy is political in that it does not require that citizens' internal constitutions be arranged in some way that meets philosophical standards of autonomy or self-rule. Instead, however the judgments are internally generated, a politically autonomous citizen is one whose judgments are hers in the sense that they are not improperly generated or controlled by others.[10] Both absolute poverty and great wealth inequality threaten this autonomy.

Autonomy protection is primarily a matter of access to education early in life, but it also requires reasonable access to information necessary to evaluate actual or possible attempts at manipulation. Access to information about relevant features of one's situation, and, in the context of elections, information about candidates and their claims, along with the skills necessary to interpret that information, is essential to citizens' judgment formation, another important deliberative interest of equal authorities.[11]

---

9. See ch. 6, § II.C.
10. See J. Cohen, "Deliberation and Democratic Legitimacy," especially 25–26.
11. Thus "false consciousness," false factual beliefs that one holds because of a lack of relevant information, or normative or evaluative beliefs that one would not hold but for the

Citizens require information about others' views to exercise opportunities for forming coalitions aimed at securing consideration for shared judgments. One cannot know what alliances and agreements are possible without some understanding of what other people think and value. Acquiring that knowledge takes resources.

Citizens also require resources for engaging in advocacy. They need time to engage in communication. Ensuring that one's views reach other citizens also requires adequate access to media or communication technologies. Citizens do not need the resources necessary for each to communicate directly with all; in conditions of scarcity (on which more below), this may be impossible. Appropriate consideration may often be achieved through the efforts of a coalition, formal or surrogate representatives, and so on.[12] But some resources are necessary to identify and communicate with others who may secure consideration for one's judgments.

If a society is so poor that all citizens lack the means to secure consideration, then there is equality of a kind, though not a democracy in a morally meaningful sense, because such a democracy requires equally sharing authority, not equally sharing inefficacy.[13] In any society not facing such extreme scarcity, failures of consideration that attend citizens without resources for meaningful autonomy protection, information gathering, and advocacy clearly violate political equality.

Other serious threats to political equality are more indirect. Rich citizens may be able to use their wealth to "capture" otherwise fairly elected representatives.[14] Apart from direct bribery, citizens can use wealth to hire lobbyists, advocates, and even media outlets aimed at setting representatives' deliberative agenda and shaping their information flow—for instance, giving them information, which may be presented in entirely public-spirited terms, about policy choices that favor the judgments of the wealthy citizen(s) funding the information sharing. These activities constitute capture if they lead the representative to neglect other citizens' judgments—for instance, by relying too heavily on information provided by the wealthy or their advocates. The problem is not the ability of the rich to fund advocacy per se; the problem is that the representatives are not adequately constrained—whether by other citizens, institutional arrangements, their own egalitarian ethos, or anything else—to grant

---

absence of relevant information, reflect political inequality if the false beliefs are held in part because of inadequate access to relevant information.

12. On surrogate representatives, see ch. 9, § III.
13. See ch. 2, § III.A; ch. 5, § I.
14. Guerrero, "Against Elections"; Pevnick, "Egalitarian Rationale."

appropriate consideration to all citizens and constituents. Great wealth inequality probably weakens those constraints; in any case, the use of wealth to advocate for one's own judgments in a context in which the egalitarian constraints are weak likely promotes deliberative neglect and undermines political equality.[15]

Another indirect oligarchic threat manifests in diffuse ways in the public culture. Great wealth inequalities enable the rich to shape that culture in ways that favor them. Citizens may have their attention drawn to the concerns or judgments of the wealthy at the expense of those of the nonwealthy. Valorization of the rich, perhaps stemming from common desires to emulate them or to enjoy their pleasures, may lead to various forms of political unfairness. If society develops a rhetorical ethos according to which certain mannerisms, forms of presentation and carriage, idioms, and so on, that are associated with the wealthy tend to be perceived (perhaps unwittingly) as markers of trustworthiness, intelligence, and good judgment, the wealthy and their advocates may be accorded greater deliberative weight than others, and achieve greater success in persuading others. When these differences are due to citizens' judgments (about the content of the messages, or about who is trustworthy or intelligent, and so on), there is no necessary inconsistency with political equality. Citizens' political authority includes entitlements to make such judgments—but only after due consideration. If citizens attend differentially to different claims or speakers in ways that do not track those citizens' own conscious judgments or evaluations, such differences constitute objectionable political inequalities.[16] Those not favored by the prevailing rhetorical norms or practices (typically, though not exclusively, the poor) are subject to deliberative neglect: other citizens fail to meet their obligations to grant those disfavored citizens proper consideration. This is true even if the norms or practices leading to unequal consideration were not created intentionally, and even if they are nondiscriminatory in the sense that, if poor citizens *did* act according to the favored norms (adopting the idiom and mannerisms of the rich, say), they would be granted the same consideration that the rich are typically awarded under those norms.[17] Even unintentional and nondiscriminatory norms and practices, if they cause deliberative neglect of some citizens, are incompatible with political equality. If

---

15. In terms of ch. 5, § I.C, these factors undermine the likelihood that representatives will engage in the required egalitarian synthesis of citizens' judgments.

16. See ch. 6, § II.

17. Expecting them so to act would be an unreasonable burden in many cases: see § II of this chapter.

great inequality increases the risk of cultures of neglect, it poses a threat to democracy.

Some of these failures of political equality are linked to inequalities in resources. If some people are too poor to have adequate resources for autonomy protection, great wealth inequalities amount to great inequalities in capacities for manipulation. While any manipulation is inconsistent with respecting another's equal status, greater inequalities in manipulation and manipulative capacity constitute greater, more objectionable, political inequalities. Similarly, inequalities in the resources necessary for exercising opportunities for coalition formation reliably lead to failures of consideration as successful coalitions crowd out the agendas of other potential coalitions.[18] Resource inequalities tend to cause representative capture and cultural skew.

Not all oligarchic threats are matters of resource inequality. Many vulnerabilities of poor and middling citizens trace to a lack of a satisfactory minimum in the resources and capacities necessary to secure appropriate consideration. If all citizens have adequate resources and capacities to resist manipulation, inequalities in resources that might be put to manipulative use are not particularly threatening. Great wealth inequalities may make the achievement of satisfactory minima difficult, and may make the achievements less secure once attained, if rich citizens are willing and able to use their resources to roll back those gains.[19] But wealth inequality is in principle more compatible with political equality the more that the necessary conditions for appropriate consideration for poorer citizens are secure.

Understanding the variety of oligarchic threats to political equality challenges prevailing conceptions of fairness in democratic deliberation. First, not all of these threats are reducible to inequalities in opportunities for political influence.[20] Second, the seriousness of these oligarchic threats is a challenge to minimalism. Minimalists must take the counterintuitive and largely unmotivated position that equal political authority is compatible with inequality in ignorance, in vulnerability to manipulation, and in command of the attention of others. But these are precisely inequalities in claims to authority—claims to create obligations for others to grant

---

18. This was very much a concern of anti-Federalist critics of the Constitution, who were worried that in large federal electoral districts, only the rich could form successful electoral coalitions, given the resources required to gather and spread relevant information: Holton, "Divide et Impera."

19. Winters and Page, "Oligarchy."

20. See ch. 6, §§ I and II.

consideration to one's views—or inequalities in the capacities necessary to exert meaningful authority.

Minimalists may retreat to the claim that, while claims to consideration are important constituents of political equality, poor and middling citizens bear the responsibility for any deficiencies in consideration. On this line of reasoning, skew or capture or manipulation reflect no political inequality, because failures of consideration are due to disadvantaged citizens' lack of exercise of political opportunity. This raises the essential question of how to allocate responsibility among citizens for satisfying the requirements of political equality.

II. The Fair Division of Deliberative Responsibility

Securing appropriate consideration involves responsibilities both for advocates and for listeners or readers—for both those endorsing certain judgments and those attending to others' judgments in the course of deciding what ought to be done together. Because these roles are connected—advocates aim to persuade listeners; listeners grant consideration to, and evaluate the claims of, advocates—the rights and responsibilities of citizens in one role depend on the rights and responsibilities of citizens in the other role. We thus require an account of a fair division of responsibility between citizens in securing the satisfaction of deliberative interests. We must determine, for instance, whether consideration is only due to those who vigorously exercise their formal political opportunities in ways that succeed in commanding attention, or whether prospective listeners have responsibilities to undertake positive efforts to grant consideration to others beyond whatever is necessary to preserve the formal opportunities.

Minimalists understand the importance of the responsibility question. They typically hold that listeners have no responsibility for granting consideration to any particular advocates. Nor do they believe that citizens in general are responsible for protecting one another's political autonomy or securing an unskewed context in which listeners can form judgments.[21] Formal opportunities for citizens to advocate and listen are adequate for political equality. Equal voting power, the argument goes, secures equal ultimate authority, while citizens are responsible for their own deliberative practices—gathering and interpreting information, forming judgments, deciding to advocate—regardless of who else funds advocacy or

---

21. Sullivan, "Against Campaign Finance Reform," 316; Smith, *Unfree Speech*, 86–88.

contributes to a cultural ethos.[22] This minimalist position rises or falls with its conception of fair division of responsibility, but reformists who reject the minimalist position do not adequately treat the issue.[23]

That citizens have some responsibility for securing the consideration of their own judgments is not controversial.[24] Because neither advocacy nor listening is costless, and because deliberative resources are limited, citizens must undertake some costs (in time, attention, and other resources) in order to secure consideration. What responsibility it is reasonable to assign to citizens depends on the costs to those citizens of that responsibility. I claim that political equality requires that citizens may claim appropriate consideration without experiencing unreasonable burdens. Let me explain.

First, a burden is unreasonable if it requires a citizen to sacrifice urgent interests. An interest is urgent if satisfaction of the interest is necessary for the exercise of authority in a social context. Such interests include interests in conditions physically necessary for the exercise of agency (and therefore authority), such as food, shelter, clothing, and basic health. They also include interests in conditions necessary for meaningful social interaction and participation in civil society, such as acquisition of language skills and relevant cultural knowledge, and the ability to appear in public with dignity and without shame, given conventional standards of decency.[25] Because the exercise of political authority is a social activity, capacities to function socially in a given context are prerequisites of that exercise. If a political system requires some citizens to sacrifice any of these interests as a condition of securing consideration, it fails to treat those citizens as political equals.

Second, a burden is unreasonable if it requires a citizen to default on justice-relevant obligations (or if it requires him to choose between such default and sacrificing urgent interests). Justice-relevant obligations are those a citizen must meet as a matter of social justice—that is, as mandated by that citizen's role in a fair scheme of social cooperation, as instituted in his society, or his role in producing such a fair scheme where it does not exist.[26] These do not include all moral obligations, as some obligations are not a matter of social justice. (If voting requires me to break my promise

---

22. Sullivan, "Political Money," 677; Smith, *Unfree Speech*, 35; Fried, "New First Amendment Jurisprudence," 250.
23. An exception is Ortiz, "Democratic Paradox."
24. J. Cohen, "Money," 296–97.
25. See Pettit, *On the People's Terms*, 87; Anderson, "Point of Equality."
26. See Rawls, *Theory of Justice*, § 2.

to have lunch with you, there is no violation of political equality, as that obligation, however real, is not a matter of social justice.) If justice requires that some citizens engage in productive labor, for instance, an assignment of responsibility is unfair if citizens who meet those requirements cannot, by virtue of meeting them, exercise political authority (or can only do so by sacrificing urgent interests).[27] Since society depends on caregivers (paid or unpaid), a decision-making process is unfair if it requires caregivers to choose between securing consideration, failing to satisfy their caregiving obligations, or sacrificing urgent interests. We are estopped from holding citizens responsible for failing to exercise political opportunities when society depends on those citizens engaging in labor or other activity that makes exercising the opportunities prohibitively difficult.

The prohibition on unreasonable burdens does not require that the state guarantee satisfaction of citizens' urgent interests or the easy discharge of their obligations. Other reasons of justice may obligate the state to take some of these responsibilities, but political equality only requires that exercising authority does not impose unreasonable burdens. The test permits procedures that disparately impact the poor, so long as no urgent interests or obligations are at stake. The fact that a procedure requires a greater sacrifice in well-being from the poor than from the rich (because the same economic costs of voting, say, burden the poor more, given decreasing marginal welfare gains from wealth) does not render the procedure oligarchic. If there are no unreasonable burdens, poorer citizens can be fairly held responsible for exercising their authority, and as such remain political equals. This is not an equal-resources requirement.

In many cases exercising advocacy is cheap. So unreasonable burdens may be easy to avoid. But these requirements are hardly toothless. They show that workers in precarious positions need protections so that when they exercise their right to vote, their livelihood is not at risk (say, from employers who resent the way a worker voted or who do not wish to grant time off to vote). The absolute cost it is reasonable to expect a citizen to bear to secure consideration varies by citizens' wealth.[28] Costs trivial to

---

27. The requirements need not be specific to those citizens—an obligation that they in particular must engage in vital sanitation work, say. It is enough that justice requires that *someone* perform the tasks, and that these citizens who happen to be the ones performing them, by virtue of performing them, must undertake substantial sacrifices in order to secure consideration.

28. It varies by other factors as well. Walking to a voting booth on election day may be very risky for someone with a compromised immune system, for instance, a fact which might entitle her to vote by mail, even if voting by mail involved high enough administrative

the rich can be prohibitive for the poor. A conception of responsibility must be cost relative, accommodating the claims of the poor.

One might wonder why only threats to urgent interests and justice-relevant obligations constitute unreasonable burdens. Why not object to any cost that prevents citizens from enjoying their full entitlements under the correct theory of distributive justice? One reason is methodological and practical. It is desirable for a public conception of political equality not to depend on controversial principles of justice. Democratic procedures ideally serve a practical function of reasonably managing disagreement about principles of justice.[29] Principles of political equality are substantive moral principles, so they cannot evade controversy. But they can better serve this disagreement-managing function of democracy if they limit their dependence on controversial, maximalist conceptions of justice. The unreasonable-burdens test does so by focusing on interests and social responsibilities on which virtually all theories of justice that support democracy would converge.[30]

The second reason to limit unreasonable burdens is that political equality is not reducible to other justice-related values. It is possible to enjoy political equality in the absence of full social justice. (Having to sacrifice a nonurgent interest to which one is entitled in order to secure consideration may be unjust, but does not prevent one from enjoying equal authority.)[31] The wrongs of political inequality are also distinct from other injustices. These wrongs involve different harms and can point to different remedies. Finally, what justice requires in the distribution of goods may itself depend on independent principles of political equality, at least if justice requires democracy. So we should not build into our conception of political equality the idea that any distributive injustice is antidemocratic. Hence it is preferable to have a conception of unreasonable burden that tracks citizens' claims to equal authority, rather than, say, equal consideration of all their interests.

The result is a conception of fair division of responsibility that acknowledges that poverty and economic inequality can threaten political inequality, without importing into democracy a maximal theory of justice.

---

costs that in general it would not be reasonable for able-but-sedentary citizens to expect others to bear those costs in order for the sedentary citizens to secure consideration.

29. Waldron, *Law and Disagreement*; Estlund, *Democratic Authority*, ch. 3.

30. Some (right-) libertarian conceptions of justice will not converge with other conceptions on these matters. I discuss these conceptions briefly in § IV.B.

31. There is an objectionable inequality if there is discrimination in who must sacrifice nonurgent interests in order to gain consideration, however. See ch. 5, § II.B.

It avoids a mistake many egalitarian democrats make, which is to assert that a commitment to democracy straightforwardly carries with it a commitment to substantial welfare guarantees.[32] Such arguments confuse economic and political equality, and limit the extent to which democracies may play pragmatic roles in managing disagreement about social justice. To illustrate: political equality does not require robust health-care guarantees to all citizens. It requires not guarantees of health per se, but rather guarantees that access to political consideration does not burden urgent interests. In some cases—say, fatal or mentally incapacitating illnesses—these guarantees may overlap. In other cases, however, the requirement of political equality is not health, but accommodations for the sick or disabled. Egalitarians should not be dismayed at this result. There are other grounds to defend welfare provision. Meanwhile, the resulting conception of democracy is more defensible, as its conception of citizen responsibility is more plausible and better tied to ideals of equal authority.

III. Access to Formal Participation

Contemporary democracies recognize something like the unreasonable-burden test in some cases. This is most apparent when it comes to formal participation rights, such as voting. Poll taxes—the requirement that citizens pay some fee in order to vote—are prohibited in the United States, for instance, by constitutional amendment.[33] Poll taxes require some citizens to bear unreasonable burdens in order to secure the consideration achieved by voting. There might be good reasons to fund elections through fees on users (i.e., voters), rather than from general public treasuries. But when such user-based funding schemes impose unreasonable costs on some citizens, they are incompatible with political equality. If any citizens are poor enough that the payment of some poll tax would threaten urgent interests or obligations, that tax is antidemocratic. Though in principle some poll taxes could be so cheap (or all citizens so wealthy) that the taxes impose no unreasonable burden, the general prohibition makes sense as a prophylactic rule and as a symbolic commitment to real, universal access to political authority.

The same logic applies to features of electoral administration that impose indirect costs on prospective voters. Restrictive voter registration

---

32. See, e.g., Habermas, *Between Facts and Norms*, 417–19; Forst, *Right to Justification*, 129; Brettschneider, *Democratic Rights*, ch. 6.

33. U.S. Const. amend. XXIV.

procedures or election-day identification requirements may cost poorer voters substantially if the formalities are not easy to satisfy cheaply. (The cost includes not just nominal fees, but also foregone wages if satisfying the formalities requires taking time off work, and costs of acquiring information about what is required.) Requiring in-person voting on a weekday imposes substantial costs on workers who cannot control their schedules and risk losing wages (or their jobs), especially if voting hours are restricted or it takes a long time to vote. Electoral systems can thus assign responsibility for securing consideration unfairly, implicitly imposing unreasonable costs on poorer citizens for the exercise of the franchise.

The problem of fair assignment of responsibility explains how what appears to be "self-disenfranchisement" may reflect objectionable inequality. Poorer citizens who are aware of the real and unequal costs of securing consideration may become (reasonably) alienated from a political society in which their efforts at judgment formation and advocacy are not accorded due consideration. Inequalities in costs of gaining information relevant to coalition formation may be enough to trigger such apathy, since disadvantaged voters would not be aware of opportunities to act together in ways that might be effective. In cases of reasonable alienation, poorer citizens may appear to be self-disenfranchising—that is, failing to exercise their political opportunities.[34] But this lack of effort is, by hypothesis, due to their reasonable expectations that they would not be granted due consideration without incurring unreasonable burdens. Patterns of political apathy that track reasonable alienation indicate political inequality, despite opportunities for influence.[35]

The unreasonable-burden test focuses our attention on the claims of the poor and vulnerable. The test also discounts the significance of some costs to the rich and secure. There is typically a sufficient level of consideration of some view (both at the level of individual listeners and of the regime as a whole) beyond which extra attention or deliberative weight matters little.[36] Costs to securing consideration beyond the ceiling of sufficiency do not merit much concern. It is no diminution of one's equal authority not to be able to create obligations for consideration beyond that ceiling of sufficiency. That does not mean it is wrong to continue advocacy efforts for one's position, of course. But it does mean that others have no

---

34. For the US case, see Bartels, *Unequal Democracy*, 275–82.

35. That perceptions of inequality may create reasonable alienation explains why critics of the role of wealth in electoral processes are right to express concern about "public confidence" in those processes: Hasen, *Plutocrats United*, 40.

36. See Dworkin, *Sovereign Virtue*, 381; ch. 6, § III.B.

further obligation to be solicitous of those efforts. Features of a decision-making process that impose costs on those efforts are not unfair.

Great wealth, and even great inequalities in wealth, may be compatible with political equality if the poorest citizens are wealthy enough that the political decision-making process does not impose unreasonable costs on them. That is, wealth inequalities may not amount to oligarchy if poor citizens have adequate resources with which to secure consideration. An "insulation strategy" insulating egalitarian political procedures from the effects of wealth inequality may be successful.[37] In such contexts, there may be good reasons to allow, or even encourage, greater deliberative "inputs" to political processes (e.g., greater provision of information and advocacy), however distributed, because, by assumption, this would not diminish the capacity of poorer citizens to secure consideration.[38] Democracy does not categorically require economic leveling. How much economic inequality is compatible with political equality depends on how well a society can secure consideration for the poorest when the poorest have far fewer resources than the wealthy.

IV. Informal Deliberation and the Case for Reform

These considerations justify important electoral reforms, notably the elimination of de facto poll taxes—features of election administration that impose unreasonable costs on poorer citizens. Some nevertheless deny that the ability of rich citizens to use their economic resources to shape political processes necessarily amounts to deliberative neglect of other, less wealthy citizens. Why can't the resources of the rich, the argument goes, contribute in benign or even salutary ways to deliberative processes? This idea is often behind "anti-reformist" arguments against campaign-finance restrictions in the United States.[39] These anti-reformist objections take two broad forms. First, anti-reformists argue that inequalities in resources cannot constitute political inequality so long as citizens enjoy equal voting rights and formal free speech guarantees. Second, they argue that restricting the use of wealth in political processes wrongly infringes citizens' liberty. I consider and reject each argument in turn.

---

37. The term "insulation strategy," comes from O'Neill, "Free (and Fair) Markets," 82. See also Rawls, *Theory of Justice*, § 36; Walzer, *Spheres of Justice*. For criticism of the strategy, see Thomas, *Republic of Equals*, ch. 4; Freeman, "Property-Owning Democracy," 16–17.

38. See ch. 6, § III.D.

39. See Sullivan, "Against Campaign Finance Reform," and "Political Money"; Smith, *Unfree Speech*; Redish and Dawson, "Worse Than the Disease."

IV.A. FORMAL OPPORTUNITY AND POLITICAL INEQUALITY

Wealth funds the acquisition and spread of information, and advocacy efforts, in ways that make it more likely for one's views about what to do to prevail. The wealthy may have far more resources at their disposal to provide such funding than do poorer citizens. Anti-reformists argue, however, that funding communication cannot undermine democratic deliberations. On the contrary, the argument continues, the speech that antioligarchic restrictions aim to inhibit may contribute to deliberations by providing more information, reaching a wider audience, stimulating discussion, or producing whatever other benefits free speech generally has for democratic deliberation.[40] According to this argument, efforts to bring resources to bear in the political sphere, so long as some basic fairness requirements like equal voting power and formal free speech rights are met, are consistent with political equality.

This important objection asserts that in democratic societies with basic free speech rights, there is no deliberative scarcity. "Deliberative scarcity" is a condition in which limits on deliberative resources such as speaking time, avenues for communication, listeners' time and attention, and so on, are substantial enough that the use of deliberative resources by some comes at the meaningful expense of the use of deliberative resources of others. To take a stylized and extreme example, imagine a hearing in which the decision maker (say, a judge) only grants the parties to a dispute a total of thirty minutes to advocate for their cause. The presence of deliberative scarcity in this stylized example need not prevent a fair hearing (presumably with equal division of time, absent special circumstances), but it does constrain the set of fair solutions.

The objection we are considering asserts that democratic political processes do not operate under conditions of deliberative scarcity. The classic anti-reformist idea that "more speech" is always consistent with political equality asserts that the use of extra deliberative resources by the rich does not come at the meaningful expense of the use of deliberative resources of others.[41] This claim counters equal-influence and equal-resource views of political equality. If the infusion of economic resources by rich citizens into political decision-making processes did not unduly skew processes of

---

40. Pevnick, "Egalitarian Rationale," 56–62.

41. Smith, *Unfree Speech*, 34, 80; Sullivan, "Political Money," 673; Redish and Dawson, "Worse Than the Disease," 1083–84.

judgment formation, nor undermine appropriate consideration of other, less well funded citizen advocacy, then there might not be any reason to object to that use of resources—even if it did grant rich citizens more influence than poorer citizens. Politics is, on this view, characterized by deliberative abundance.[42]

This claim that we enjoy sufficient deliberative abundance to render the considerable extra inputs of the rich benign does not imply that there are no oligarchic threats to political equality. Inadequate access to relevant information, lack of protection from manipulation, representative capture, and skewed political culture all could pose serious problems even when the advocacy of some came at no necessary expense to the advocacy of others. So the abundance objection does not establish that wealth inequality is safe for democracy. But it does support the claim that there is no inherent political inequality in great inequality of resources deployed for persuasion.

Deliberative abundance is conceivable; indeed, it serves as an ideal. While relative abundance may be a goal of policy (by making communication technology cheaper and more accessible, or by promoting certain kinds of civic education), whether we actually experience anything like abundance is a different matter. Scarcity is most apparent at the highest formal levels—such as national legislatures, administrative agencies, or courts—where there are clear limits on how much can be discussed or attended to in a given time period. The floor of the Senate is much closer to the thirty-minute hearing than is the public sphere at large. Similarly, individual representatives have only so much time during their terms to deliberate about policy, hear from constituents, and engage in constituent care. Time, attention, and staff resources spent attending closely to one lobbyist or donor limit how much will be spent on others.[43]

Pressing scarcity is less obvious in the wider public sphere, where economies of scale make it possible to widely distribute information and advocacy. Such abundance cannot obviate the scarcity present in important formal arenas, however. The fact that ordinary citizens might easily find a voice in the wider public sphere does not mean that it is easy to ensure that voice is represented in formal institutions. Moreover, scarcities exist

---

42. Fried, "New First Amendment Jurisprudence," 252.

43. Lobbyists often provide information—evidence and talking points in favor of a client's position—and thus, implicitly, resources to representatives: Hasen, "Lobbying." So representative attention is not entirely zero sum. But providing information cannot eliminate scarcities of time and attention, and further threats of neglect arise if representatives primarily receive well-organized information from a narrow class of constituents.

in the wider public sphere itself. Deliberative scarcity is not just a matter of how much time citizens have and how cheap information and communication are. Scarcity is also a function of the extent to which responsibilities are fairly divided, and the extent to which those responsibilities are actually, reliably met. If exercising even cheap communicative opportunities imposes unreasonable burdens on poor citizens, there is deliberative scarcity. Moreover, what constitutes scarcity (and unreasonable burden) depends on citizens' deliberative capacities. Lack of citizen capacities to resist manipulation creates artificial scarcities in citizen attention, and in the ability of citizens with limited resources to secure consideration.[44] Limited capacities for information gathering and interpretation make forming judgments and coalitions costlier, and so more likely to involve unreasonable burdens. Defects in institutional guarantees of consideration or in the wider democratic ethos may mean that listeners—especially officials—have more limited and skewed deliberative attention than is necessary, given material resources and technologies. We cannot infer from material abundance and cheap communication technology that the wider public sphere exhibits deliberative abundance. What may seem like cheap and accessible information (or opportunities for capacity development) may be unreasonably costly for poor citizens, given their poverty and the demands of their justice-relevant labor.

Anti-reformists may grant that greater consideration for the rich can have the consequence that other views receive less consideration. More television commercials in favor of a candidate may lead to diminished consideration for her less well funded competitors. But, the argument goes, there is nothing necessary about this consequence. Nothing about the presence of extra commercials requires anyone to engage in deliberative neglect of other candidates' efforts, or other citizens' judgments. In a free speech context, conscientious citizens can seek out and discover alternative candidates and views. Accordingly, the objection goes, advocacy of the various positions remains available to everyone, and there is

---

44. Whether the lack of capacity creates neglect depends on who is responsible for the lack. If some citizen were provided all resources and opportunities required to develop those capacities, her failure to develop the capacity would not license an objection to burdens that were due to her own inability (though she would still have objections against wrongful manipulation). I do not endorse a "starting-gate" conception of opportunity (Dworkin, *Sovereign Virtue*, 87), according to which others have *no* responsibility to aid capacity development after an initial provision of opportunity early in a citizen's life. This raises special complications involving responsibility in cases of those who squander fair opportunities. See Anderson, "Point of Equality," 319.

no deliberative scarcity. If there is any deliberative neglect, that is solely because of the failures of individual citizens or officials who fail to seek out available information.[45] This inattention of some, the argument concludes, is not the responsibility of wealthy advocates, nor should it be used to justify restrictions on politically engaged citizens.

This argument admits that in such a scenario there is deliberative neglect, and so political inequality. It posits that this inequality is the responsibility of those who unduly focus on well-resourced advocacy to the exclusion of other views. This implies that there are obligations to repair this inequality, though it is not clear who would bear the responsibility. Since some advocates are being wronged by the neglect, there may be a collective responsibility to indemnify those advocates through reform, if those who, on this view, are the neglectful citizens do not fulfill their primary obligations of repair. Thus this line of anti-reformist thought does not justify quietism about wealth inequality and democratic deliberation.

Leaving those implications aside, there is some truth to this line of thought. The advocacy of many different citizens is often "available" to anyone who chooses to seek it out, and thus amenable to consideration. It is a mistake, however, to infer from this fact that there is no deliberative scarcity. Whatever the literal availability of information about citizens and their judgments, there are relevant deliberative limits when it comes to citizens' role both as listeners to the claims of others and as political advocates—limits of time, attention, and other resources (including capacities to search for and sort information, and to hold representatives accountable for being captured). Securing consideration in deliberation may impose unreasonable burdens, particularly on citizens vulnerable to economic and other social disadvantages.

That seeking out politically relevant information can threaten urgent interests or justice-relevant obligations may seem exaggerated. But acquiring information necessary for adequate consideration is not simply a matter of changing channels or looking at a different online newspaper. Information about candidate platforms, the possibility of coalitions, performance of representatives, and so on, is not easy to find. (Readers of this book will not know all of this information.) The real cost of search time can be considerable for poorer citizens, especially if they have care responsibilities.

---

45. This line of thought has led Daniel Ortiz to worry that arguments for campaign-finance reform require the assumption that some (or many) citizens are "civic slackers": "Democratic Paradox," 903.

The cost of information acquisition also depends on one's capacities for searching and interpreting. If some citizens have been wrongly denied opportunities for relevant capacity development (through limited educational opportunity, say), the costs to them of acquiring information and otherwise gaining consideration will be higher, and it would be unfair to impose the responsibility for those extra costs on them. Other citizens bear responsibility for either assisting the disadvantaged citizens in developing the relevant capacities, or, and meanwhile, accommodating the citizens by taking positive efforts to provide an adequate deliberative context for their judgment formation, and to consider appropriately their judgments. The past unfairness changes what is a fair division of deliberative responsibility in the present.[46]

Given deliberative scarcity, the greater consideration that the rich use their economic resources to acquire in various forms really can, and does, come at the expense of consideration for less wealthy citizens. A serious democratic interest is sacrificed when the rich are given free rein to shape political deliberation. Greater consideration for the rich would not merely increase a certain kind of inequality, but otherwise take nothing from the poor. If that were all, anti-reformists might be right that reformers aim spitefully to "level down" political discourse, sacrificing the political liberty of the few for the specious equality of the many.[47] If deliberative scarcity prevails, however, the ability of the rich to translate economic into political power takes something—secure appropriate consideration—away from the poor. Structures of advocacy favoring the rich in ways that threaten the consideration of the poor are, morally speaking, implicit poll taxes.[48]

In the presence of scarcity, political institutions and practices involve deliberative triage—a focus on some judgments at the expense of others. What constitutes justified triage depends on principles of political fairness. In the context of great wealth inequality, poor citizens often have claims to priority in triage. Obligations to prevent imposing unreasonable

---

46. While this argument describes what fairness requires given previous injustice, the logic is not reparative: it is not about what is owed to these citizens in order to compensate for injustice. Instead, the argument establishes what accommodations are necessary to secure present fairness. This leaves open whether further reparative obligations obtain.

47. Sullivan, "Political Money," 667. This thought may have been behind the Supreme Court's famous declaration in *Buckley v. Valeo* that "the concept that the government may restrict the speech of some elements of our society in order to enhance the relative voice of others is wholly foreign to the First Amendment": 424 U.S. 1, 48–49 (1976).

48. The argument is thus not that unregulated funding promotes worse deliberation (cf. Beitz, *Political Equality*, 114, 202; Dworkin, *Sovereign Virtue*, 364–65), but that deliberation is unfair, in that it fails to respect the authority of disadvantaged citizens.

burdens on the exercise of political authority, and to accommodate those wrongly denied capacity-development opportunities, give those citizens claims to priority in deliberative attention and resources. Efforts to grant those citizens consideration take precedence over the extra inputs of rich citizens who already can fund a great deal of advocacy and information gathering.[49]

IV.B. POLITICAL LIBERTIES

A second important anti-reformist argument is that, even if the extra inputs of the rich do create political inequality, restricting such inputs would wrongly infringe citizens' political liberty. In the United States, this is often framed as the claim that such restrictions violate the First Amendment's free speech guarantee.[50] I do not engage the legal argument here, but I reject the moral argument: in conditions of scarcity, restricting the funding of advocacy by the rich in order to secure appropriate consideration for the poor does not restrict political liberty in any important sense. While it may limit liberty in some more general sense, such limits are ubiquitous and can promote freedom overall.

One feature of political liberties—part of what defines them as *political*—is that they involve rights to exert authority. This is clearly true of the right to vote: it is a right to exert a certain authority that others must respect (by recognizing the results of an election or referendum). Citizens' claims to authority extend beyond the simple right to vote. We have diverse claims to consideration throughout collective decision-making processes. That is, we have political liberties to engage in efforts (such as advocacy) that trigger claims to consideration. When we engage in such efforts, we impose obligations on others—not to engage in the action we advocate for, but to deliberate about action in a certain way. Accordingly, the political liberties are not liberty rights, but claim rights; they are not merely permissions to engage in some action, but also impose positive duties (of consideration) on others.[51] A conception of political equality specifies what a democratic political liberty is a liberty *to*.

---

49. In principle, there could be a society of great wealth inequality in which rich elites were at special risk of deliberative neglect (given cultural and political dominance by the working class, say, as feared by J. S. Mill). In practice, such threats to the rich have not materialized.

50. U.S. Const. amend. I: "Congress shall make no law . . . abridging the freedom of speech."

51. See Wenar, "Nature of Rights."

Realizing everyone's political liberty in common therefore does not merely require that nobody be forcibly prevented from engaging in certain actions. It also requires ensuring that relevant authority claims are satisfied. This is, again, clear enough in voting: the relevant political liberty is not satisfied by allowing everyone to cast a vote, with no regard for how the votes will be counted or how the count will bear on the relevant outcomes. (We could hardly call that "voting.") The same is true of advocacy: realizing everyone's political liberty requires not just allowing anyone to say anything, but requires efforts to ensure that everyone is granted appropriate consideration. In contexts of deliberative scarcity, this may require regulation (as elections do). Such regulation may limit a certain citizen's inputs—such as funding of advocacy—but this does not infringe that citizen's political liberty, because the liberty only involves a claim to appropriate consideration. So long as the citizen whose input is restricted still has secure access to consideration, there is no infringement—and the restriction may be necessary to secure the consideration, and thus the political liberty, of others. In the same way, it is no restriction on a rich citizen's political liberty that the law prevents others from counting his vote more than once, or prevents him from buying others' votes.

One might object that we do not have obligations to ensure everyone's realization of their political liberties. Perhaps, instead, there are "side constraints" that forbid any restriction of political liberty.[52] When the state engages in such restriction—for instance, by limiting funding for advocacy—it violates the side constraint, a violation that cannot be justified by the goal of enabling others' enjoyment of liberty.[53]

This argument cannot succeed if the underlying liberty is not the entitlement to engage in some action (engaging in speech, or putting a ballot in a box), but rather the entitlement to some share of authority (others granting consideration to one's speech or one's vote). Private actions can violate this liberty. These actions need not be intentional (like voter intimidation or election fraud); they may be unintentional, and even excusable (like funding advocacy that in concert with other such funding has the unintended effect of denying appropriate consideration to others). On standard views, even unintentional violations of a liberty justify defensive measures by others, including third parties, such as the state.[54] If the

---

52. On side constraints, see Nozick, *Anarchy, State, and Utopia*, 29.
53. Smith, *Unfree Speech*, 76; Fried, "New First Amendment Jurisprudence," 234.
54. There may be pragmatic worries about empowering a state to make regulatory judgments. But there is no categorical objection on liberty grounds to such regulatory

underlying analysis of political liberty is correct, state regulations securing political equality justifiably protect such liberties from private infringement. They violate no side constraint.[55]

An anti-reformist might concede the point about political liberty, but claim that my argument keeps the normative focus too narrow. Perhaps restrictions on speech in the service of political equality do not violate political liberty, so understood. Nevertheless, the response goes, they do objectionably restrict freedom of speech in a broader sense.

In what sense do restrictions on the funding of political advocacy restrict freedom of speech? The restrictions would not stop rich citizens from speaking or writing in ways that do not use funds in excess of required limits. The answer, according to anti-reformists, is that resources are necessary to engage in meaningful, effective communication. Restrictions on the use of resources for communication effectively restrict communication, and thus, the argument goes, wrongly restrict freedom of speech.[56]

Effective political communication does require resources. One can only engage in advocacy if one has spare time and opportunities to gather relevant information, all of which require material resources. But this does not mean that any restriction on the use of resources for speech violates freedom of speech. Consider, in what follows, a restriction on the use of more than $100,000 in funding for electoral advocacy within a two-year period. The number is arbitrary; I just picked a number far larger than the vast majority of citizens in contemporary democracies are currently able to spend, whatever the intensity of their political judgments. Arguing that this restriction unjustly infringes rich citizens' freedom of speech has doubtful implications, which I consider sufficient to reject the claim.

Laws restrict citizens' use of resources for speech all the time. This happens when governments take citizens' resources, as through taxation. Anti-reformists about campaign finance usually do not mean to reject

---

policies. Moreover, pragmatic evaluation must incorporate concerns about political equality that the political liberties protect.

55. The First Amendment's categorical insistence that Congress pass "no law" infringing freedom of speech may seem to support a more radically anti-statist side-constraint view. If our interpretation of the First Amendment should turn on the role of free speech in a democracy, however, "free speech" in the political context should be defined as speech that does not infringe the political liberties of others. I acknowledge that this is a big interpretive "if," however. See Mill, *On Liberty*, ch. 2; Meiklejohn, *Free Speech*; Habermas, *Between Facts and Norms*, especially ch. 8; Post, *Citizens Divided*; Brettschneider, *When the State Speaks*.

56. Pevnick, "Egalitarian Rationale"; Sullivan, "Against Campaign Finance Reform," 315–17; Smith, *Unfree Speech*, ch. 6.

wholesale the government's right to tax. They must explain, then, why it is permissible for the state to prevent citizens' use of resources for any purpose (including speech) through tax policy, but not permissible to prevent citizens' use of resources for speech in particular. If the specific restriction on use for speech prevented meaningful advocacy—prevented citizens from securing appropriate consideration—then it would be objectionable. (So too would a confiscatory tax that rendered advocacy impossible.) But for any given level of resources left to a citizen, it is hard to see why a targeted restriction involves any more infringement of speech rights than any taking of resources.

One might think that there is something suspicious about a policy targeting the use of resources for political speech in particular, as opposed to taking resources that could be used for any purpose. One reason might be that there is no legitimate purpose served by such restrictions. But if my arguments are correct, the important purpose of political equality is served by restrictions in some circumstances.[57] Another reason for the distinction is that it is simply wrong for the government to target speech. But I do not see what the argument could be for this claim. We are not considering policies that engage in "viewpoint discrimination," targeting speech of a particular content, nor policies that directly prohibit speech. The anti-reformist argument under consideration is about the importance of resources for meaningful free speech. The tailoring of the restriction on resources does not bear on that argument. The distinction between taxes and campaign-finance restrictions for purposes of that argument cannot be sustained.[58]

There is another way in which we standardly restrict citizens' use of resources for speech. This is by maintaining a society in which some people have fewer resources available to fund speech than they would like. Just as the rich citizen is unable to use resources for advocacy beyond the $100,000 threshold, the poor citizen is unable to use more than $25, say, for such advocacy, given her limited means, urgent interests, and justice-relevant obligations. If the one resource limit constitutes a restriction on the freedom of speech, why doesn't the other?

---

57. Thus this book provides philosophical support for Hasen's legal argument in *Plutocrats United* that political equality should be considered a compelling state interest that justifies some campaign-finance regulation under the First Amendment.

58. There might be concerns about the ease of abuse of a targeted restriction on the use of resources for speech. In response, we could say the same for tax policy—but we do not take this risk to render unjustified the government's taxing power. In any case, this prophylactic concern about targeted restrictions does not establish that such restrictions are in principle wrong.

The likely answer is that, according to the anti-reformist, restrictions on the rich involve interfering in the exercise of speech freedoms, whereas failing to grant resources to the poor merely involves failing to promote the exercise of speech freedoms. The anti-reformist insists on prohibitions on interference, and takes no position on promotion. This, again, is a side-constraints interpretation of the freedom. For all this argument establishes, we may have obligations to promote the exercise of free speech by poor citizens, whether through subsidizing campaign donations in particular or redistributing wealth more generally, so this argument does not suffice to defend the status quo. But we cannot, according to the argument, promote the free speech of the poor by interfering with the free speech of the rich.

This argument fails to recognize that the limited resources of the poor are precisely maintained by actual and threatened interference. When the government protects your property by enforcing your rights against trespass and theft and so on, it prevents me from taking your resources in order to fund political advocacy. It threatens interference if I attempt such taking, and typically will interfere with such attempts. I am not saying it is wrong for the state to protect certain property rights and entitlements—even against politically engaged Robin Hoods. The point is just that, if free speech rights are violated any time the state engages in interference to restrict resource use for speech, then protection of property rights and other distributive entitlements constitute violations of free speech.[59] Any conception of free speech that has this implication is misguided.

Anti-reformists may object that the difference between restrictions on the rich citizen's use of his resources to fund speech and the restrictions on the poor citizen's ability to steal resources from others to fund speech turns is that in the former case, the citizen is being prevented from using her own property, whereas in the latter case, the citizen is being prevented from using someone else's property. This way of defining speech freedoms faces serious problems. First, consider the claim that one has the right to use all and only one's conventionally defined property to fund speech. Since some conventional property regimes are unjust, this implies that unjust (but legal) deprivations of resources never violate speech rights. This is false, and conflicts with the key anti-reformist premise that wrongly taking resources does violate speech rights. Moreover, campaign-finance regulations partly determine conventional property rights (by defining

---

59. This argument owes much to G. Cohen, *Self-Ownership*, ch. 2. See also Sunstein, *Partial Constitution*, 204–9.

what one may legally do with one's wealth), so such regulations could not violate speech rights on this account.

Second, consider the more likely view that one has the right to use all and only the resources to which one is justly entitled to fund speech.[60] This ties objections to campaign-finance regulations to the justice of the status quo: if the status quo distribution is unjust, then those who have less than they are justly entitled to have free speech claims, while those who have more than they are justly entitled to have no complaint against campaign-finance regulations. So this version only supports partial and precarious objections to campaign-finance schemes in the current world.[61]

Many anti-reformists probably believe that current distributions of wealth are just or nearly enough just that campaign-finance regulations would, by this argument, violate the rights of most people affected. The reason the argument reaches this conclusion, however, has little to do with free speech. By defining the scope of speech rights in terms of one's resource entitlements, this argument prioritizes property-rights protection and distributive justice over any values having to do with speech or (non-economic) liberty. This is not a position grounded in any serious valorization of speech or civil liberty. The view is antidemocratic, and relatively unfriendly to a robust culture of free speech, in demoting those values below protection for property entitlements, which are defined independently of what is necessary to protect democratic or free speech values.

Refuting this libertarian or classical-liberal theory of justice is well beyond the scope of this book. The argument shows that anti-reformism depends on such a theory of justice, rather than on a coherent theory of free speech or civil liberty. It shows that such a theory of justice is oligarchic in its devaluation of political equality.[62] Absent such an oligarchic theory, the (correct) anti-reformist premise that resources are necessary for democratic speech supports reform. One's free speech rights are not violated by limits on resource use for political advocacy, so long as one may use enough resources to secure appropriate consideration in an egalitarian decision-making process, as well as other interests or claims protected by speech freedoms. What those other interests or claims might be requires a full theory of free speech, which I cannot provide here. But there is no reason to think their protection requires unlimited resource use. Thinking

---

60. Dworkin, *Sovereign Virtue*, 202.
61. Ibid., 364.
62. Some libertarians might happily acknowledge this: Nozick, *Anarchy, State, and Utopia*, ch. 9.

it does would lead to the uncomfortable proposition that virtually nobody enjoys free speech. While we should doubt that free speech values are fully enjoyed by those who have very few resources, there is little in the history of free speech theory or jurisprudence to suggest that its benefits only apply to the extremely wealthy. Restrictions on the unlimited use of resources for speech, then, do not constitute violations of free speech even if they do involve interference in choice.

V. Conclusion

Great wealth inequality poses a variety of threats to political equality. These are not reducible to a concern about equal influence, equal resources, or equal deliberative inputs such as quantity of communication. Instead, we must acknowledge that democracy involves citizen authority and obligation throughout processes of deliberation and representation. We must share on equal terms responsibility for meeting those obligations. The critique of oligarchy thus improves our understanding of democracy. It also suggests directions for future empirical research on inequality, focusing on the extent to which different oligarchic mechanisms manifest, and the extent and sources of deliberative scarcities.

One essential defense against oligarchy involves devoting resources and protection to those most disadvantaged by wealth inequality. This "lifting-the-floor" strategy is not simply a matter of enabling poorer citizens to fund more advocacy or increasing their deliberative inputs. Political equality requires opportunities for developing capacities for resisting manipulation and autonomously forming political judgments, and for gathering and sharing relevant information. It requires critique of cultural features that tend to make citizens unwittingly responsive to the claims of the rich, and unduly dismissive of the claims of the poor. Citizens and the media must develop a politically egalitarian ethos, according to which they strive to become aware of, and publicize, the judgments of the poor. A democratic society must pursue institutional measures for securing the appropriate authority of poorer citizens over representatives and officials. A vigilant, empowered electorate is presumably necessary to secure this authority, but it may not be sufficient. Making representative relationships with lobbyists and donors transparent may help, as might institutions specifically charged with gathering and publicizing the concerns of poorer citizens.[63]

---

63. See McCormick, *Machiavellian Democracy*, ch. 7.

If measures to directly secure consideration for the poor are inadequate on their own, and deliberative scarcity remains, then restrictions on the deliberative inputs of the rich are justified. These "lowered ceilings" must not be so low as to preclude meaningful consideration for advocates. If this requirement is met, the political liberties and free speech rights of the rich would be respected at least as well as the liberties and rights of the poor are respected in unrestricted systems in which some citizens are too poor to fund advocacy they support.

Though political equality requires efforts to improve the capacities and increase the influence of the poor, and perhaps to restrict the inputs of the very rich, the aim is not strict equality. In the context of adequate capacities and secure consideration for all citizens, inequalities in inputs may be justified, and even desirable. The more an institutional structure and democratic ethos guarantees consideration for all citizens suitable for political equals, the less concern there need be for inequalities in influence and inputs. In such a democracy, citizen autonomy and the reliable satisfaction of listener obligations would prevent the inequalities in inputs and even influence from translating into deliberative neglect of those with fewer inputs or less influence. But this security of consideration in the context of input inequality cannot be assumed. On the contrary, it is an ideal the achievement of which requires vigilant defense against oligarchy.

CHAPTER ELEVEN

Judicial Review

MOST OF THIS BOOK has proceeded under the assumption that citizens elect, and exercise authority over, officials, who in turn make laws and policy decisions. In some countries, however, special courts have the constitutional authority to strike down legislation or executive action on the grounds that the law or action violates some fundamental or constitutional law. These courts are always, to my knowledge, staffed by unelected judges (though often the judges are appointed by elected officials).[1] This raises the question whether such judicial review is compatible with political equality. I will assume in this chapter that "judicial review" involves not only the ability of a court to strike down legislation and executive action, but also the inability of the legislature to overturn the judicial decision through ordinary legislative processes. That is, I assume that, if judicial decisions can be overturned through political (that is, nonjudicial) means, this requires greater consensus than is required for ordinary legislation—whether that must take the form of a constitutional amendment, or a supermajority in the legislature. Milder forms of judicial review, according to which court rulings could be overturned by ordinary legislative majorities, raise fewer democratic concerns.[2] Here I explain the legitimate democratic concerns about judicial review, survey some defenses of judicial review I believe are insufficiently egalitarian, and argue that there are conditions under which the stronger form of judicial review would be compatible with political

---

1. In some US states, justices on the highest court are elected. I am not aware of any judicial elections for national supreme courts, however.
2. On weaker forms of judicial review, see Waldron, "Case against Judicial Review," 1355–59. On the variety of constitutional court arrangements in European states, see Scheppele, "Guardians of the Constitution."

equality, though such conditions probably require considerable reform of judicial review as currently practiced.

I. Interpretation, Authority, and Democracy

Justifying judicial review is challenging because at first blush it can seem, as Alexander Bickel put it, like a "deviant institution in the American democracy."[3] Of course, in its authorization of unelected officials, judicial review is not so deviant, as we regularly authorize administrators and independent commissioners to make important political decisions. Some theorists have developed innovative views explaining how constitutionalism might serve to enable, rather than constrain, the rule of citizens—for instance, by establishing regular processes through which citizens participate in decision making.[4] I do not disagree, but it is difficult to establish that *judicial review* in particular (as opposed to constitutionalism generally) is necessary to enable democratic processes. Moreover, much judicial review involves substantive engagement with the content of statutes—whether they deny citizens equal protection or establish cruel punishments, for example—in a way that cannot be described as enabling citizen authority in any direct way. So the power of unelected judges to strike down legislation calls for some justification, since granting such power over legislation to unelected officials appears to conflict with basic democratic intuitions.

One might deny the relevance of these intuitions in the following way. When judges strike down legislation, they are only applying law that prohibits certain legislation. This law, let us assume, has democratic credentials—say, it stems from a democratically authorized constitution, or a parliamentary law passed by a supermajority. In applying the law, the judges therefore only carry out the democratic process by which citizens exercise authority on equal terms. For citizens to determine what we do together, the norms and policies collectively decided upon must have some bearing on what is actually done, and applying a law is one way of ensuring that bearing. So the judges play a constitutive role in a democratic process. Moreover, because they are merely applying law, the argument continues, they do not themselves engage in independent decision making about what citizens ought to do together; they merely facilitate

---

3. Bickel, *Least Dangerous Branch*, 18; see Waldron, "Case against Judicial Review"; Bellamy, *Political Constitutionalism*; Waldron, *Law and Disagreement*.

4. See, e.g., Holmes, *Passions and Constraint*.

the authority of the lawmakers—in this case, the citizens acting on equal terms. Because they exercise no independent authority, it does not matter that they are selected by appointment, rather than by a politically egalitarian method. This is an egalitarian version of Alexander Hamilton's defense of judicial review in *Federalist* No. 78, on the grounds that "the courts were designed to be an intermediate body between the people and the legislature, in order, among other things, to keep the latter within the limits assigned to their authority."[5]

There are two problems with this defense. The first is that, as we have defined the practice, judicial review establishes greater-than-ordinary requirements for legislation reversing the judicial decision. If the ordinary requirements typically satisfy the standards of political equality, imposing more difficult requirements may constitute an objectionable inequality. The second is that even if judges reviewing legislation are engaged in the interpretation of law, it does not follow that they do not independently play a role in determining what citizens do together. And so we do have reason to be concerned about whether their playing that role is consistent with political equality. I will elaborate on each problem in turn.

Greater-than-ordinary requirements for legislation that would otherwise run afoul of the judiciary are a problem if those greater requirements violate standards of political equality. (This problem is usually discussed in terms of supermajority requirements for constitutional amendments or otherwise overturning the judiciary, given the tradition of identifying ordinary legislative processes as majoritarian. This identification is contentious, as I will discuss in section IV. Because I do not believe political equality generally requires strictly majoritarian legislative processes, I use the more general language of "greater-than-ordinary" or "stricter" requirements.) The present point is that these greater requirements may violate political equality by making it too difficult to pass certain legislation.[6] In terms of the appropriate-consideration conception, the requirements would constitute or cause deliberative neglect of those citizens who favored the blocked legislation, which would have legal force but for judicial review.

Niko Kolodny argues that supermajority rules do not require any special democratic justification.[7] While such rules favor status quo laws or policies over proposed changes, he argues that this inequality between

---

5. Hamilton, "Federalist, No. 78," 525. I discuss views closer to Hamilton's own version in § III.

6. Christiano, *Constitution of Equality*, 258–59; Brettschneider, *Democratic Rights*, 138.

7. Kolodny, "Rule over None II," 323–25.

positions does not amount to inequality among citizens. The supermajority rule does not grant more power or influence to any citizens; any citizen can contribute equally to maintaining the status quo or to a change, even if the latter requires a larger coalition. Generalizing the point, if Kolodny is right, the greater-than-ordinary legislative requirements established by judicial review would be consistent with political equality despite favoring the status quo more than do ordinary procedures.

Kolodny is right to argue that stricter requirements are impersonal in a way that renders them less objectionable than more targeted political inequalities, such as plural-voting schemes.[8] Such rules nevertheless involve diminished responsiveness to citizen authority. If citizens support some law or policy, as determined by processes satisfying principles of fair aggregation and deliberation, respect for their authority requires implementing that law or policy. It is true, as Kolodny says, that refusing to implement the favored law or policy does not allow the minority to rule. (The minority cannot determine policy; it can only block certain policy). Nevertheless, denying authority to the judgments of citizens in the coalition determined successful by the fair process constitutes failure to grant those citizens due consideration.[9] So the type of neutrality that stricter standards embody is not sufficient to constitute political equality, even if we have no special democratic concern about the decision making of judges themselves.

The second problem with the egalitarian-Hamiltonian defense sketched above, however, is that there are grounds for democratic concern about judicial decision making. It is a mistake to think that judges merely apply existing law in ways that do not independently determine what citizens do together. There are reasonable disputes about how much discretion the law permits in various cases. There is, moreover, considerable debate about whether, in exercising such discretion, judges are making law (as positivists believe), or are permissibly enforcing as law some putative principles of morality (as antipositivist or "natural law" theorists believe). But that judges inevitably enjoy some discretion is a matter of agreement between many positivist and natural law

---

8. On objections to targeting and "particular" inequalities, see ch. 5, § II.B.

9. This disagreement with Kolodny derives from my view that political equality requires respect for citizen authority (which, in Kolodny's language, requires "equal positive influence"). This view rules out systems in which nobody has any authority ("equal but zero influence"), and involves more skepticism about the role of impersonal factors, such as laws passed by people long dead, that limit the authority of people living. See ch. 2, § III.A; ch. 5, § I.

theorists.[10] This discretion is often greater when judicial review of legislation is at issue, since the constitutional laws involved are often written in general, sweeping terms, and so do not narrowly constrain judicial decision making. As a result, judicial decisions play a significant role in determining what citizens do together, so those decisions implicate citizens' authority claims. This is all the more true in cases of judicial review, as judicial discretion in such cases involves not only discretion in implementing democratic law but possibly discretion in negating democratic law.[11]

The fact that legal interpretation implicates citizen authority does not mean that political equality requires direct citizen oversight over judicial decisions. Implementing democratic norms and policies, which requires interpretation, is part of respecting equal citizen authority. There is no categorical requirement that the interpretation itself involve a particular distribution of political power, any more than political equality requires direct-democratic legislation.[12] Moreover, if legal interpretation is an appropriate way to determine certain matters, such authority could be exerted either over the interpretations themselves, or over the proper principles of interpretation.[13] Recognizing citizen authority over judicial decision making is thus compatible with taking seriously the proposition that legality involves interpretation, as opposed to a new round of unfettered discretion in decision making. The point is simply that citizens are entitled to equal authority in the process that includes lawmaking and interpretation.

These considerations show that, contrary to the egalitarian-Hamiltonian position, judicial review does raise democratic concerns. In the next two sections, I discuss some attempts to respond to those concerns in ways that I believe understate the significance of political equality.

II. Instrumentalism

One straightforward way to justify judicial review is to argue that, either in general or in some particular context, a regime with judicial review

---

10. See Dworkin, "Model of Rules I"; Shapiro, *Legality*, chs. 8–9.
11. Leiter, "Constitutional Law."
12. Ch. 3, § II.A.
13. This parallels my argument in ch. 5, § I, that we should respect citizens' authority at different levels of generality. This leads us to consider which institutional schemes might solicit better, clearer, and more relevant exercises of authority. Mariah Zeisberg provides an excellent discussion of these issues as they apply to democratic control of constitutional interpretation, in "Should We Elect."

produces better outcomes than a regime without judicial review. These instrumental justifications—particularly those emphasizing judicial review's role in protecting individual liberties—are common and influential.[14] It is worth distinguishing two kinds of good outcomes judicial review might be said to promote. Some goods directly bear on the political egalitarianism of political procedures—the protection of political speech, say, or the regulation of elections—call these "democratic consequences" of judicial review. Contrast these with outcomes the goodness of which does not directly involve political egalitarianism—the prevention of racial discrimination in the distribution of goods, say, or the prevention of unjust forms of punishment—call these "nondemocratic consequences." (I do not mean "undemocratic"; I mean "not involving political equality.") One might claim that judicial review is justified on the grounds that its promotion of democratic consequences outweighs any constitutive political inequality involved in the practice of judicial review itself. Because citizens are entitled to enjoy political equality over time, there may be cases in which political inequalities at one time are effectively compensated for by greater equality over time.[15] So this form of justification may be consistent with principles of political equality. As described, however, it addresses a nonideal condition, since it accepts that judicial review is constitutively undemocratic, if democratic enough in its consequences to justify that episodic inequality.[16]

Instrumental arguments stressing nondemocratic arguments are a different matter, because they aim to justify judicial review without reference to constitutive or causal connections to political equality. Instead, they argue that judicial review promotes good outcomes in some nondemocratic dimension. Some theorists emphasize the possibility that judicial review will promote the equal treatment of citizens, or values like autonomy that the theorists believe also underpin political equality.[17] But these outcomes are "nondemocratic" in my sense, in that they do not bear directly on the egalitarianism of political processes.

---

14. See, e.g., Fallon, "Core of an Uneasy Case"; Doherty and Pevnick, "Good Procedural Objections."

15. Ch. 3, especially § III.

16. Waldron emphasizes the nonideal nature of justification on grounds of democratic consequences (he calls cases in which such justifications apply "non-core cases"): "Case against Judicial Review," 1359–60.

17. Beitz, *Political Equality*; Dworkin, *Freedom's Law*; Christiano, *Constitution of Equality*, 278–80; Brettschneider, *Democratic Rights*, ch. 7. These authors vary in their confidence that these egalitarian consequences might actually justify judicial review.

Instrumental arguments depend on questionable and difficult-to-prove empirical claims, though this is probably inevitable, since any sensible view of institutional design must include some role for evaluating the consequences of different choices.[18] The more serious problem is that they aggravate the charge of judicial review's antidemocratic character. The explicit posture of these views is that systems including judicial review are superior to more democratic arrangements because judges make better decisions than ordinary citizens and their chosen representatives. I argued in part I of this book that instrumentalism about political regimes is unjustified—even in the pursuit of egalitarian outcomes—and so it cannot justify judicial review, except perhaps in exceptional circumstances.[19]

III. Popular Hamiltonianism

A second important type of defense of judicial review aims to preserve its democratic credentials. This defense pursues Hamilton's line of thought that judicial review, while sometimes thwarting elected representatives, might nevertheless implement the rule of the people. In rejecting the simple rendering of Hamilton's idea in section I, I emphasized doubts about whether judicial review of legislation enacted by elected representatives was consistent with democratic ideals. The more sophisticated Hamiltonian strategy now under consideration begins with the recognition that democracy is not primarily concerned with the rule of elected legislatures, but rather with the rule of the people as a whole. If one could show that the judicial enforcement of popularly enacted constitutional rules against elected legislatures enabled or constituted rule of the people, the thought goes, then judicial review might be vindicated as democratic.

Something like this popular (that is, "people"-based) Hamiltonian strategy is present in the sophisticated and ingenious constitutional theories of Jed Rubenfeld and Bruce Ackerman.[20] I will not be able to do justice to these authors' arguments in this short discussion. Instead, I will register some doubts about the general strategy. The common problem is that, in de-emphasizing political equality as a principle regulating decision-making processes, the Hamiltonian approach gives us little

---

18. On the evaluation of judicial review's outcomes, see Harel and Kahana, "Easy Core Case," 8–10.

19. Ch. 2; see also Wilson, "Against Instrumentalism about Democracy"; Waldron, "Case against Judicial Review," 1353.

20. Rubenfeld, *Freedom and Time*; Ackerman, *We the People*.

reason to promote or respect the "rule of the people" as the authors variously conceive of it.

Rubenfeld believes that a people secures its freedom and rule by making and holding itself to commitments over time.[21] These commitments take the form of democratically written constitutional laws, which bind the people to certain principles and institutions, whatever the people's present preference at any given time.[22] Legislative supremacy precludes freedom because that, says Rubenfeld, amounts to government by present will of the people rather than rule by commitment.[23] Hence the need for a judiciary to enforce the observance of democratically enacted constitutional commitments.

Let us accept for the moment that commitment requires a separation of the willing actor and the interpreting actor.[24] It is still not clear why the legislature is not capable assuming the mantle of constitutional interpreter. The legislature is not the people, and it does not straightforwardly represent the people's will, present or otherwise. (In my view, it should engage in egalitarian synthesis of citizens' judgments, but this is hardly brute mirroring of aggregate will.)[25] Legislation is a process that unfolds over time, and one that could be principled and committed.[26] There is space for the legislature to "displac[e] will in favor of commitment," and thereby to enable the people to achieve self-government.[27]

The preceding argument shows that Rubenfeld's theory cannot establish that judicial review (or constitutionalism) is necessary for democracy. But this is no deep flaw, as there may be many institutional manifestations of democracy. A more serious problem is that Rubenfeld cannot provide us with reasons to prefer one institutional scheme to another, because virtually every scheme opens up space for commitment over time, and thus could potentially be a vehicle for popular self-government by Rubenfeld's lights. Democracy then becomes detached from any concrete institutional requirements, and might license arrangements we would conventionally describe as highly undemocratic. Rubenfeld requires what we would

---

21. Rubenfeld, *Freedom and Time*, 143–44.
22. Ibid., 167–68.
23. Ibid., 172–73.
24. I am not sure this is true, as the possibility of commitments by individual persons shows.
25. Ch. 5, § I.C.
26. Rubenfeld elsewhere recognizes the temporal extension of legislative processes, as he skillfully argues that identifying and representing the preferences of a single moment is impossible: *Freedom and Time*, 74–88.
27. Ibid., 107.

recognize as conventionally democratic forms in the creation or revision of commitments—that is, at the level of constitutional design and amendment.[28] (It is not clear what criteria we use to judge an act of constitution writing "democratic," nor why those criteria do not apply to political institutions more generally.) But popular self-government does not require anything conventionally democratic—even in the form of elections—at the level of ordinary politics and legislation. Rubenfeld's view is thus reminiscent of Hobbes's: in Rubenfeld's work, as in *Leviathan*, popular control of politics exhausts itself in the initial stage of state making—of commitment making or "authorization"—and need not manifest in any concrete way in the course of day-to-day rule. Like Hobbes, Rubenfeld seems committed to the view that the people rule whether the actual government is democratic, aristocratic, or monarchical. Rubenfeld's is a sophisticated "fair-authorization" view, which, I have argued, fails to respond to the requirements of political equality.[29]

Bruce Ackerman's theory of "constitutional dualism" centers on a distinction between "normal politics," which involves the rule of officials, and "constitutional politics," which manifests the rule of the people. Ackerman motivates concern for the rule of the people by setting high standards for what counts as truly popular activity, in terms of breadth and temporal extent of participation, quality of deliberation, and extent of popular agreement.[30] Such activity establishes constitutional law. He stresses that the ordinary operation of representative institutions does not meet these standards. Ackerman's defense of judicial review is rooted in skepticism of the legislature, and indeed of all representative political institutions.[31] This is not to say that the Supreme Court, say, exercising powers of judicial review accurately represents the people.[32] The usual ("normal") function of political institutions is not to authentically express popular will, but rather to get on with governing as best as possible in a way loosely connected through elections to the interests of citizens, while various "preservationist" aspects of the constitutional scheme (most notably, the Supreme Court) work to ensure that the few past political decisions that did legitimately claim the authority of the people continue to command respect.[33]

28. Ibid., 163–68.
29. Ch. 3, § II.B.
30. Ackerman, *We the People*, 272–88.
31. Ibid., 181.
32. Ibid., 184.
33. Ibid., 60.

Ackerman believes we owe special deference to those acts that do legitimately claim popular authority, even if they represent past political authority.[34] The difficult question is why we should defer to these past decisions, given that they are past. (As "constitutional moments" are rare, most past decisions are, for most citizens at most times, long past.) That is, we are left with the same problems that face the simple Hamiltonian view that I identified in section I: how judicial discretion establishing greater-than-ordinary standards for legislation can be consistent with political equality. The fact that judges aim to enforce laws that once clearly met high democratic standards—perhaps even high egalitarian standards—does not address that question about how to manifest and sustain political equality in the present and future.

These Hamiltonian approaches help to describe the value in having higher or constitutional laws, and help explain how the interpretation and enforcement of law over time can itself be essential to democratic government. But these efforts cannot justify judicial review as the mechanism of interpretation and enforcement, because they do not include principles of institutional choice that extend beyond constitutional moments, and apply more generally to all collective decision making. The Hamiltonian approach may complement a theory of political equality in addressing certain questions of constitutional theory, but it cannot replace scrutiny of judicial review according to the standards of political equality.

IV. Judicial Review and Appropriate Consideration

Is judicial review compatible with political equality? In addressing the "counter-majoritarian" version of this question, discussions often exhibit the following standard dialectic. In response to complaints about the judiciary's failure to meet certain democratic standards (e.g., majoritarianism), commenters note that legislative representation also fails to meet those standards. This may be because of bicameralism, legislative procedure, the structure of electoral systems, party organization, the nature of common deliberation, or other factors. An even-handed skepticism of representative institutions, commenters conclude, elevates the case for judicial review.[35]

---

34. Ibid., 263–64.
35. Watkins and Lemieux, "Compared to What?"; Doherty and Pevnick, "Good Procedural Objections"; Lever, "Democracy and Judicial Review"; Kyritsis, "Representation and Waldron's Objection"; Eisgruber, *Constitutional Self-Government*; Ackerman, *We the People*.

I believe this dialectic frames the inquiry properly. The proper question is whether a regime that includes judicial review better satisfies democratic standards than one that does not, taking into account the limitations of both. The most sustained and sophisticated attempts to answer this question, however, give too short shrift to political equality—as opposed to other ideals such as impartiality in decision making, quality of deliberation, and extent of participation—in their evaluation.[36] In what follows, I outline some conditions under which a regime including judicial review could better secure political equality than a regime without such review.

The counter-majoritarianism of judicial review is not itself an objection to the practice, as political equality does not require equal power distribution or simple majoritarianism, direct or legislative.[37] Instead, political equality requires institutions that secure the appropriate consideration of all citizens' judgments over the course of political decision-making processes. That said, I argued in section I that establishing greater-than-ordinary requirements for certain legislation fails to respect citizen authority if ordinary requirements for legislation partly constitute egalitarian procedures. So a nonmajoritarian version of the concern about judicial review persists.

Here I follow a politically egalitarian version of the standard dialectic. Some aggregative procedures—such as greater-than-ordinary legislative requirements—that would otherwise be objectionable can be justified if they are necessary to prevent deliberative neglect.[38] Judicial review would be justified if it were necessary to prevent deliberative neglect in ordinary processes. Because supermajority rules are less of an affront to political equality than, say, unequal voting weights—because, as Kolodny argues, there are no particular citizens targeted by such rules—the argumentative burden for proponents of judicial review is lighter than for proponents of unequal voting.

There are a number of familiar reasons that judicial review might protect against deliberative neglect. First, judicial enforcement of certain rules might encourage elected officials to consider constituents' judgments in a fairer way than they would absent judicial enforcement. This claim, relying on a version of John Hart Ely's "representation-reinforcing" function of judicial review, becomes especially plausible once we abandon the idea that fair representation simply involves respecting the will of the

---

36. Watkins and Lemieux, "Compared to What?"; Eisgruber, *Constitutional Self-Government*, 84.

37. Part II, especially chs. 3 and 5.

38. Ch. 5, § II.A.

majority.³⁹ If fair representation involves egalitarian synthesis of citizens' judgments—including, to some extent, the judgments of electoral losers—there may be scope for judicial intervention to encourage representatives to alter their behavior accordingly. This argument does not require any belief that judges are better at making well-reasoned decisions about fair representation than ordinary citizens or elected officials. Instead, judicial review might serve to improve egalitarian representation because courts are given specific constitutional charges to do so, and an institutional position that can influence other officials and representatives.⁴⁰ Judges are fallible, and it is possible that judicial review could establish perverse incentives for unfair representation. But a well-designed system could improve the egalitarian quality of representation and deliberation.

A second line of reasoning suggests why political equality might require judges not only to police representational processes directly, but also to enforce broad substantive principles. In given contexts, we may reliably predict that certain claims will regularly get short shrift from elected officials—that is, judgments of certain content will likely be denied appropriate consideration. This might result from features of the other parts of the representative system, which may establish incentives to ignore or devalue judgments of certain kinds.⁴¹ Delegating the enforcement of certain rules to the judiciary might restore the balance by securing a fair hearing for citizens with judgments of certain content. Judges might be more receptive to such judgments, and the prospect of judicial enforcement might encourage officials to consider judgments that they might otherwise tend to ignore.⁴² Substantive constitutional provisions therefore might be justified by the procedural ideal of guaranteeing citizens appropriate consideration.

One might object that this argument smuggles back into the justification of judicial review the instrumentalist arguments I set aside earlier. Arguments about the predictable devaluation of judgments of certain content may appear to be arguments that elected officials will get decisions

---

39. Ely, *Democracy and Distrust*, 87. The phrase suggests that Ely was concerned with fair, equal representation generally, which he explicitly denies is equivalent to actual representation of majority preferences. See ibid., 82. If this is right, then Bruce Ackerman is wrong to characterize Ely as a "monistic democrat"—that is, one who believes that "democracy requires the grant of plenary lawmaking authority to the winners of the last general election": Ackerman, *We the People*, 8–9.

40. Lever, "Democracy and Judicial Review," 807; Eisgruber, *Constitutional Self-Government*, 60.

41. See ch. 6, § III.B.

42. See, e.g., Black, *New Birth of Freedom*, 125; Perry, *Constitution*, 102.

wrong, and that judges will get them right. My argument, however, does not depend on any claim that judicial review leads to better outcomes; it only depends on the claim that judicial review fosters in the system as a whole appropriate consideration for all citizens' judgments. It may be important to consider a certain range of views more than legislatures are prone to do, even if we do not guarantee that such views ultimately prevail in collective decision-making processes. Encouraging detailed judicial consideration of certain kinds of claims gives claimants a more expansive public hearing for their views than they might otherwise get. Substantive views would be differentially treated not because of the specific content of the views, but because of some general feature of the claim—for instance, its ostensible urgency, or its proneness to deliberative neglect in the context of the other parts of the representative system.[43] This may lead to the claimants achieving their preferred outcome, either in court or through the public dialogue that follows a judicial loss. It may not have such an effect—but this would not imply that the institutional exercise was futile, as the consideration itself may have been required by political equality.

While in principle substantive judicial protections can protect against deliberative neglect, they still raise concerns about political equality. Even if judges are appointed by elected officials, citizen authority over the judges is attenuated and indirect. Moreover, in exercising authority, judges—skilled lawyers who often come from privileged backgrounds, and who often spend much of their adult lives in relatively elite circles—may not be particularly likely to be representative of citizens in general, nor particularly aware of the concerns and judgments of disadvantaged citizens. So, even when acting in good conscience, the exercise of their discretion may be skewed in ways that neglect some citizens.

Judicial review may nevertheless be justified. There must be reason to think that such review really does better secure appropriate consideration than do alternative arrangements that do not involve judicial review. This requires well-tailored substantive constitutional provisions that ensure special consideration for those vulnerable to deliberative neglect, without granting authority to judges beyond that needed for such security. Such narrow grants of judicial authority also have the virtue of limiting judges' discretion, and thus more closely approximating an impersonal supermajority rule. Institutional checks—including limited judicial terms, more democratic participation in judicial confirmation, and the possibility of easier (if not fully majoritarian) overturning of judicial decisions—can lead judges to

---

43. See ch. 6, §§ III.B–C.

use what discretion they have in ways that grant consideration to citizens' views.[44] These checks may also limit concerns about the general oligarchic temperament of judges, though judicial selection should also explicitly take such representative concerns into account. Finally, judicial doctrine and interpretive method could develop in ways that incorporate these concerns about judicial authority. This does not mean that judges should generally defer to elected officials; the justification for judicial review, if there is one, is precisely that full deference to such officials may cause or constitute deliberative neglect of some citizens. Instead, it means that judges should interpret substantive constitutional provisions with an eye to securing consideration for those who are vulnerable to neglect, when the claims of such citizens are at issue, and to exercising deference when they are not.[45] Of course, even with such methods in hand, judges would have the authority to determine in any given case whether deference was warranted or not. Delegation of such authority is justified if there is good reason to believe that judges, in the proper institutional context, can be better trusted to make those judgments than a system in which such delegation was absent. If this is true, we need not think of judicial review as a democratic loss that is sometimes counterbalanced by the democratic gains that come from good constitutional decisions.[46] Instead, judicial review could serve as a constituent part of a genuinely politically egalitarian regime managing the inevitable risks of deliberative scarcity in a particular historical context.

V. Conclusion

The arguments for judicial review I have sketched in the previous section do not settle anything. Judicial review is justified, if it is, because it preserves the fairness of deliberative and representative processes, because

---

44. In the United States, because the Senate, but not the House, plays a role in federal judicial appointments, the inequalities in the Senate I criticized in ch. 7 aggravate concerns about inequalities in judicial review. One way to foster more democratic judicial review would be to reform the Senate or to include the House in appointments. Like most other reforms, this would require constitutional amendment. On more and better political involvement in judicial selection, see Zeisberg, "Should We Elect"; Leiter, "Constitutional Law."

45. This interpretive mandate assumes that such methods are consistent with the law the judges are charged to enforce. Many influential views of legal interpretation turn in part on judgments about the appropriate role of a judiciary in a democracy (or in a given regime's particular constitutional order). To the extent the regime is or should be committed to political equality, a politically egalitarian orientation would be consistent with these interpretive approaches.

46. This is the view of Christiano and Brettschneider.

constitutional provisions and interpretive doctrine shape and constrain judicial behavior, because judges have certain incentives or skills that lead them to approach decisions in distinctive ways, because courts exhibit special solicitude for those whom electoral processes often neglect, and so on. Whether these conditions are met or not in particular circumstances is a matter for empirical evaluation. The appropriate-consideration account of political equality pursues the insights of the standard dialectic—the need to compare critically the judiciary and other democratic institutions—and provides the standards for that comparison. This account incorporates the insights of process theories while still explaining the value of judicial enforcement of substantive constitutional provisions. The approach incorporates instrumentalist intuitions about the virtues of judicial review in a way that does not devalue democratic processes of decision making. This discussion shows at least the potential for a justification of judicial review compatible with genuine democracy. This does not amount to a defense of existing practices of judicial review, however. The egalitarian concerns about such review are serious, and responding to those concerns would, in many countries, likely require considerable reform of the content of constitutional laws, processes of judicial selection, and methods of constitutional interpretation. Here as elsewhere, the appropriate-consideration conception provides tentative support for existing institutions in broad strokes, but requires considerable revision of political practice if societies are rightly to claim the status of democracy.

Conclusion

DEMOCRACY AND EQUALITY are intimately linked. We cannot understand or properly respond to one ideal without the other. Democracy's value stems in significant part from the way it manifests and sustains citizens' equal status. Social equality requires democratic institutions and practices, because part of what it is for people to relate as equals is to share authority over what they do together. The design of democratic institutions—and our conduct of democratic practices—should be guided by this egalitarian ideal of sharing authority as civic friends. We ought to orient our efforts to establish and maintain equal relations with the democratic constituents of equality in view. We treat people as equals in part by sharing with them authority over how we treat one another. There is risk in granting authority to others. But a society of equals is a great reward.

Sharing authority equally is not the same as equalizing power or influence over what is done. When citizens mutually respect one another's authority, they allow others to shape their own deliberations and actions in certain ways. They thereby limit the operation of certain forms of power, and constrain inequalities of power. So it is true that democracy in its fullest realization denies great imbalances of power. But I have argued that it does not consist in equality of power. Equal power can be consistent with forms of discrimination, neglect, and subordination, while unequal power can—if authority is shared on equal terms—be consistent with social and political equality. This latter point may seem spurious in a world characterized by substantial, harmful inequalities of power. But diagnosing the problem at its root as one of unequal authority has immediate implication, in this world of grossly unequal power, as a guide to how best respond to those inequalities and their attendant injustices.

The idea of sharing authority can appear confusing or absurd when we think of authority only as the power to obligate others to do what one says.

In our ordinary lives, however, we grant one another much more nuanced and diverse forms of authority than this. That is, we grant one another consideration. In many of our best relationships, we manage to do this on equal terms. Responding appropriately to others' claims of consideration often requires great sensitivity, understanding, and appreciation of what makes our relationships valuable. Developing that sensitivity, understanding, and appreciation in the context of relations with other citizens is not easy, but the task is possible and entirely coherent. Improving our theories and practices of democracy and equality requires it.

The ideal of equally sharing diverse forms of authority illuminates the complexity of equality in democratic deliberation and representation. Democratic deliberation requires proper protections of citizens, and widespread dispositions to grant consideration to one another in the course of individual decision making. It also requires, in large societies, institutions and structures of communication that integrate distributed deliberative practices in a way that preserves equal authority.[1] Representation plays a central role in that integrative process. That role shapes what it means to be a good democratic representative. Representative institutions and practices must be responsive to ideals of fair aggregation and to the demands of fair deliberation. These ideals are connected, in together constituting an ideal of equally shared authority, sustained over time.

The democratic ideal is therefore internally diverse. It responds to concerns about, among other things, autonomy in judgment formation and communication, the conditions of access to authority, formal power, opportunities to coordinate with others, and discrimination in the conduct of collective decision making. This tracks the diversity and plurality of social equality itself, with its attention to fairness, respect, fraternity and sorority, and so on. This plurality need not be overwhelming or incoherent. I have tried to show that both the democratic ideal and the egalitarian ideal of which it is a part form coherent unities with great appeal that can provide us moral and political guidance.

One may still wonder after all this just how important it is to organize collective decision making in an egalitarian way. While I believe the arguments provided in part I reveal urgent reasons to satisfy the requirements of political equality, it is true that in politics there are many urgent reasons, often pointing in different directions. I will conclude by offering some reasons to think that the conflict between justice and political

---

1. I discuss the problem of "deliberative integration" (though with little focus on equality as a regulating ideal) in Wilson, "Deliberation."

equality is nevertheless not so stark. Political equality itself, moreover, may be a kind of impetus for the development of a more just society.

It is easy to think that political equality conflicts with justice when one understands political equality simply as equality of power or influence. What reason do we have to think that a collection of individuals struggling to overcome one another's resistance to the prevalence of their own views will produce just outcomes? Such arguments as we have in favor of the wisdom of democratic decisions trade less, I suspect, on the equal division of power than on other features of politically egalitarian decision making that tend to accompany roughly equal divisions of power. These features are very much like the commitments to the practical consequence of each citizen in deliberation and aggregation that are required by the appropriate-consideration conception of political equality. Appropriate consideration requires a range of salutary deliberative practices on the part of a regime, including granting hearings to a wide range of views, and structuring a fair synthesis of diverse judgments. From the perspective of political equality, these practices are generally justified not by their efficacy in producing good collective decisions, but by the respect the practices show to citizens whose judgments they consider. But it would not be surprising if these respectful practices also proved relatively effective in producing just decisions. At a minimum, fair practices will tend to eliminate failures due to deliberative neglect and unwarranted exclusions. More maximally, there may be reason to believe that certain fair deliberative practices, including the satisfaction of citizens' various deliberative interests, constitute good epistemic procedures as well.[2] The claim is admittedly speculative; but it seems much more plausible to think that appropriate consideration of each constitutes good epistemic practices than does ratifying the results of a fair power struggle. This would give us reason to think that politically egalitarian societies are likely to produce just outcomes, whatever those outcomes are, because those societies feature reliably adequate epistemic practices of collective decision making.

A second reason to believe that political equality may not compete with justice as much as simple thought experiments involving unjust majorities imply depends on the proposition that justice itself is, in broad strokes at least, relatively egalitarian. This is a controversial matter. But if it is true, as I suspect it is, then there is good reason to think that political equality itself is a requirement of justice, and moreover that the demands

---

2. This is a common theme of Habermas, *Between Facts and Norms*. For suggestive passages see, e.g., 127, 151, 170, 486. See also Nelson, *On Justifying Democracy*.

of political equality and the demands of egalitarian justice will overlap considerably. Relatively egalitarian justice will require political equality because such a conception of justice will have to place great weight on egalitarian relations of the kind constituted and promoted by democratic political systems. We can conceive of nondemocratic political systems that produce egalitarian results, such as an egalitarian distribution of resources. But such systems could not sustain egalitarian social relations, and the equal status of citizens, when hierarchy is visibly built into their public constitutions. So while it remains true that politically egalitarian systems might produce decisions that violate the requirements of egalitarian justice, so too would it violate the requirements of justice to impose a nondemocratic system in order to produce better results. Justice itself, to the extent that it requires the equal status of citizens, ensures its own broad compatibility with political equality.

The requirements of political equality may also lead us to a more just society—and not only for the tautological reason that justice includes political equality. Political equality requires reliable guarantees of consideration for each citizen's judgment. In its fullest form, this consideration requires, in institutions and practices, a great deal of empathy and deliberative charity. It requires a commitment to recognizing the urgent claims of others. It requires a society where citizens are all capable of claiming the hearings they are due, and all others are willing to grant them. The motivations, dispositions, habits, and institutions necessary to satisfy these requirements are also likely to support stable, just policies and institutions. Those motivations, dispositions, habits, and institutions may indeed go a long way toward constituting a just society. Good democrats make good neighbors.

These reflections do not suffice to establish the compatibility of justice and political equality, either conceptually or in terms of practical likelihood. Some of these ideas reveal just how ambitious the maximal ideal of political equality is: rather than a humble way station far removed from the remote goal of justice, it may be quite close to justice, and so similarly remote from us. But this should not be too daunting. The democratic gains of the last few centuries have been remarkable, even if these advances have sometimes proved uncertain and reversible. Perhaps we can make similarly great strides in the future. If the realization of political equality remains far from complete today, this is because, for all of its historical associations with mediocrity, democratic society is extraordinary.

BIBLIOGRAPHY

Achen, Christopher H., and Larry M. Bartels. *Democracy for Realists: Why Elections Do Not Produce Responsive Government.* Princeton, NJ: Princeton University Press, 2016.

Ackerman, Bruce. *We the People.* Vol. 1, *Foundations.* Cambridge, MA: Belknap, 1991.

Allen, Danielle. *Talking to Strangers: Anxieties of Citizenship since Brown v. Board of Education.* Chicago: University of Chicago Press, 2004.

Altman, Andrew. "Race and Democracy: The Controversy over Racial Vote Dilution." *Philosophy & Public Affairs* 27 (1998): 175–201.

Alvaredo, Facundo, Lucas Chancel, Thomas Piketty, Emmanuel Saez, and Gabriel Zucman. "Global Inequality Dynamics: New Findings from WID.world." *American Economic Review* 107 (2017): 404–9.

Amar, Akhil Reed. "The Consent of the Governed: Constitutional Amendment outside Article V." *Columbia Law Review* 94 (1994): 457–508.

———. "Some Thoughts on the Electoral College: Past, Present, and Future." *Ohio Northern University Law Review* 33 (2007): 467–80.

"American Fact Finder." US Census Bureau, n.d. (data from 2010 Demographic Profile), accessed April 5, 2019, https://factfinder.census.gov/faces/nav/jsf/pages/community_facts.xhtml.

Anderson, Elizabeth. "Democracy: Instrumental vs. Non-instrumental Value." In *Contemporary Debates in Political Philosophy*, edited by Thomas Christiano and John Christman, 213–27. Malden, MA: Wiley-Blackwell, 2009.

———. *The Imperative of Integration.* Princeton, NJ: Princeton University Press, 2010.

———. *Value in Ethics and Economics.* Cambridge, MA: Harvard University Press, 1993.

———. "What Is the Point of Equality?" *Ethics* 109 (1999): 287–337.

Applbaum, Arthur Isak. "Legitimacy without the Duty to Obey." *Philosophy & Public Affairs* 38 (2010): 215–39.

Aristotle. *Nichomachean Ethics.* Translated by Martin Ostwald. Upper Saddle River, NJ: Prentice Hall, 1999.

———. *The Politics.* Translated by Carnes Lord. Chicago: University of Chicago Press, 1984.

Arneson, Richard J. "Democracy Is Not Intrinsically Just." In *Justice and Democracy: Essays for Brian Barry*, 40–58. Cambridge, UK: Cambridge University Press, 2004.

———. "Democratic Equality and Relating as Equals." *Canadian Journal of Philosophy* 36 (2010): 25–52.

———. "Discrimination, Disparate Impact, and Theories of Justice." In *Philosophical Foundations of Discrimination Law*, edited by Deborah Hellman and Sophia Moreau, 87–111. Oxford: Oxford University Press, 2013.

Baker, Lynn A., and Samuel H. Dinkin. "The Senate: An Institution Whose Time Has Gone?" *Journal of Law & Politics* 13 (1997): 21–103.

Balinski, Michel L., and H. Peyton Young. *Fair Representation: Meeting the Ideal of One Man, One Vote*. Washington, DC: Brookings Institute, 2001.

Banducci, Susan A., and Jeffrey A. Karp. "Electoral Systems, Efficacy, and Turnout." In *The Comparative Study of Electoral Systems*, edited by Hans-Dieter Klingemann, 109–34. Oxford: Oxford University Press, 2009.

Baron, David P., Daniel Diermeier, and Pohan Fong. "A Dynamic Theory of Parliamentary Democracy." *Economic Theory* 49 (2012): 703–38.

Barry, Brian. "Is Democracy Special?" In *Democracy, Power and Justice: Essays in Political Theory*, 24–60. Oxford: Clarendon, 1989.

Bartels, Larry. *Unequal Democracy: The Political Economy of the New Gilded Age*. Princeton, NJ: Princeton University Press, 2008.

Beerbohm, Eric. *In Our Name: The Ethics of Democracy*. Princeton, NJ: Princeton University Press, 2012.

Beitz, Charles R. *Political Equality*. Princeton, NJ: Princeton University Press, 1989.

Bellamy, Richard. *Political Constitutionalism: A Republican Defence of the Constitutionality of Democracy*. Cambridge, UK: Cambridge University Press, 2007.

Bickel, Alexander. *The Least Dangerous Branch*, 2nd ed. New Haven, CT: Yale University Press, 1986.

Bird, Colin. "Status, Identity, and Respect." *Political Theory* 32 (2004): 207–32.

Black, Charles. *A New Birth of Freedom: Human Rights, Named and Unnamed*. New York: Grosset, 1997.

Bochsler, Daniel. "A Quasi-Proportional Electoral System 'Only for Honest Men'? The Hidden Potential for Manipulating Mixed Compensatory Electoral Systems." *International Political Science Review* 33 (2012): 401–20.

Brennan, Jason. *Against Democracy*. Princeton, NJ: Princeton University Press, 2016.

Brettschneider, Corey. *Democratic Rights: The Substance of Self-Government*. Princeton, NJ: Princeton University Press, 2007.

———. *When the State Speaks, What Should It Say? How Democracies Can Protect Expression and Promote Equality*. Princeton, NJ: Princeton University Press, 2012.

Brighouse, Harry. "Egalitarianism and Equal Availability of Political Influence." *Journal of Political Philosophy* 4 (1996): 118–41.

———. "Political Equality and the Funding of Political Speech." *Social Theory and Practice* 21 (1995): 473–500.

———. "Political Equality in Justice as Fairness." *Philosophical Studies* 86 (1997): 155–84.

Buss, Sarah. "Appearing Respectful: The Moral Significance of Manners." *Ethics* 109 (1999): 795–826.

Christiano, Thomas. *The Constitution of Equality: Democratic Authority and Its Limits*. Oxford: Oxford University Press, 2008.

———. *The Rule of the Many: Fundamental Issues in Democratic Theory*. Boulder, CO: Westview, 1996.

Cohen, G. A. "On the Currency of Egalitarian Justice." *Ethics* 99 (1989): 906–44.

———. *Self-Ownership, Freedom, and Equality*. Cambridge, UK: Cambridge University Press, 1995.

———. *Why Not Socialism?* Princeton, NJ: Princeton University Press, 2009.
Cohen, Joshua. "Deliberation and Democratic Legitimacy." In *The Good Polity: Normative Analysis of the State*, edited by Alan Hamlin and Philip Pettit, 17–34. Oxford: Blackwell, 1989.
———. "For a Democratic Society." In *The Cambridge Companion to Rawls*, edited by Samuel Freeman, 86–138. Cambridge, UK: Cambridge University Press, 2003.
———. "Money, Politics, and Political Equality." In *Philosophy, Politics, Democracy: Selected Essays*, 268–302. Cambridge, MA: Harvard University Press, 2009.
Cooke, Jacob, ed. *The Federalist*. Middletown, CT: Wesleyan University Press, 1961.
Cooper, John. "Aristotle on the Forms of Friendship." *Review of Metaphysics* 30 (1977): 619–48.
Cox, Adam. "The Temporal Dimension of Voting Rights." *Virginia Law Review* 93 (2007): 361–413.
Dahl, Robert A. *How Democratic Is the American Constitution?* New Haven, CT: Yale University Press, 2001.
———. *A Preface to Democratic Theory*. Expanded ed. Chicago: University of Chicago Press, 2006.
Daniels, Norman. "Equal Liberty and Unequal Worth of Liberty." In *Reading Rawls*, edited by Daniels, 253–81. New York: Basic Books, 1975.
Darwall, Stephen. *The Second-Person Standpoint: Morality, Respect, and Accountability*. Cambridge, MA: Harvard University Press, 2006.
Doherty, Kathleen, and Ryan Pevnick. "Are There Good Procedural Objections to Judicial Review?" *Journal of Politics* 76 (2013): 86–97.
Dworkin, Ronald. *Freedom's Law*. Cambridge, MA: Harvard University Press, 1996.
———. *Law's Empire*. Cambridge, MA: Harvard University Press, 1986.
———. "The Model of Rules I." In *Taking Rights Seriously*, 14–45. Cambridge, MA: Harvard University Press, 1977.
———. *Sovereign Virtue: The Theory and Practice of Equality*. Cambridge, MA: Harvard University Press, 2000.
Ebels-Duggan, Kyla. "Against Beneficence: A Normative Account of Love." *Ethics* 119 (2008): 142–70.
Eidelson, Benjamin. "The Majoritarian Filibuster." *Yale Law Journal* 122 (2013): 980–1023.
Eisgruber, Christopher L. *Constitutional Self-Government*. Cambridge, MA: Harvard University Press, 2001.
Elmendorf, Christopher S., Kevin M. Quinn, and Marisa A. Abrajano. "Racially Polarized Voting." *University of Chicago Law Review* 83 (2016): 587–692.
Ely, John Hart. *Democracy and Distrust*. Cambridge, MA: Harvard University Press, 1980.
Epstein, Richard A. "Tuskegee Modern, or Group Rights Under the Constitution." *Kentucky Law Journal* 80 (1992): 869–86.
Estlund, David. *Democratic Authority: A Philosophical Framework*. Princeton, NJ: Princeton University Press, 2008.
———. "Political Quality." *Social Philosophy and Policy* 17 (2000): 127–60.
Fallon, Richard H., Jr. "The Core of an Uneasy Case *for* Judicial Review." *Harvard Law Review* 121 (2008): 1693–1736.

Farrell, David M. *Electoral Systems: A Comparative Introduction*. 2nd ed. Basingstoke: Palgrave Macmillan, 2011.
Fiss, Owen. "Groups and the Equal Protection Clause." *Philosophy & Public Affairs* 5 (1976): 107–77.
Forst, Rainer. *The Right to Justification: Elements of a Constructivist Theory of Justice*. New York: Columbia University Press, 2012.
Frankfurt, Harry. "Equality as a Moral Ideal." *Ethics* 98 (1987): 21–43.
Freeman, Samuel. "Property-Owning Democracy and the Difference Principle." *Analyse & Kritik* 35 (2013): 9–36.
Fricker, Miranda. *Epistemic Injustice: Power and the Ethics of Knowing*. Oxford: Oxford University Press, 2007.
Fried, Charles. "The New First Amendment Jurisprudence: A Threat to Liberty." *University of Chicago Law Review* 59 (1992): 225–53.
Gardner, John. "Liberals and Unlawful Discrimination." *Oxford Journal of Legal Studies* 9 (1989): 1–22.
Gerken, Heather K. "Understanding the Right to an Undiluted Vote." *Harvard Law Review* 114 (2001): 1665–1743.
Gilens, Martin. *Affluence and Influence: Economic Inequality and Political Power in America*. New York: Russell Sage and Princeton University Press, 2012.
Gilens, Martin, and Benjamin I. Page. "Testing Theories of American Politics: Elites, Interest Groups, and Average Citizens." *Perspectives on Politics* 12 (2014): 564–81.
Golder, Sona N. *The Logic of Pre-electoral Coalition Formation*. Columbus, OH: Ohio State University Press, 2006.
Goodin, Robert, and Christian List. "Special Majorities Rationalized." *British Journal of Political Science* 36 (2006): 213–41.
Guerrero, Alexander A. "Against Elections: The Lottocratic Alternative." *Philosophy & Public Affairs* 42 (2014): 135–78.
———. "The Paradox of Voting and the Ethics of Political Representation." *Philosophy & Public Affairs* 38 (2010): 272–306.
Guinier, Lani. "[E]racing Democracy: The Voting Rights Cases." *Harvard Law Review* 108 (1994): 109–37.
———. *The Tyranny of the Majority: Fundamental Fairness in Representative Democracy*. New York: Free Press, 1994.
Habermas, Jürgen. *Between Facts and Norms: Contributions to a Discourse Theory of Law and Democracy*. Translated by William Rehg. Cambridge, MA: MIT Press, 1996.
———. "Discourse Ethics: Notes on a Program of Philosophical Justification." In *Moral Consciousness and Communicative Action*, translated by Christian Lenhardt and Shierry Weber Nicholsen, 43–115. Cambridge, MA: MIT Press, 1990.
———. *The Theory of Communicative Action*. Vol. 2, *Lifeworld and System: A Critique of Functionalist Reason*. Translated by Thomas McCarthy. Boston, MA: Beacon, 1985.
Hamilton, Alexander. "The Federalist, No. 68." In Cooke, *Federalist*.
———. "The Federalist, No. 78." In Cooke, *Federalist*.
Hare, Thomas. *A Treatise on the Election of Representatives, Parliamentary and Municipal*. New and rev. ed. London: Longman, Green, and Roberts, 1861.

Harel, Alon, and Tsvi Kahana. "The Easy Core Case for Judicial Review." *Journal of Legal Analysis* 2 (Winter 2010): 1–30.

Hasen, Richard L. "Lobbying, Rent Seeking, and the Constitution." *Stanford Law Review* 64 (2012): 191–253.

———. *Plutocrats United: Campaign Money, the Supreme Court, and the Distortion of American Elections*. New Haven, CT: Yale University Press, 2016.

Hausman, Daniel M., and Matt Sensat Waldren. "Egalitarianism Reconsidered." *Journal of Moral Philosophy* 8 (2011): 567–86.

Hellman, Deborah. *When Is Discrimination Wrong?* Cambridge, MA: Harvard University Press, 2008.

Hellman, Deborah, and Sophia Moreau, eds. *Philosophical Foundations of Discrimination Law*. Oxford: Oxford University Press, 2014.

Hinton, Timothy. "Must Egalitarians Choose between Fairness and Respect?" *Philosophy & Public Affairs* 30 (2001): 72–87.

Hobbes, Thomas. *Leviathan*. Edited by Edwin Curley. Indianapolis: Hackett, 1994.

Holmes, Stephen. *Passions and Constraint: On the Theory of Liberal Democracy*. Chicago: University of Chicago Press, 1995.

Holton, Woody. "'Divide et Impera': *Federalist 10* in a Wider Sphere." *William and Mary Quarterly* 62 (2005): 175–212.

Indridason, Indridi H. "Proportional Representation, Majoritarian Legislatures, and Coalitional Voting." *American Journal of Political Science* 55 (2011): 955–71.

Issacharoff, Samuel. "Gerrymandering and Political Cartels." *Harvard Law Review* 116 (2002): 593–684.

Issacharoff, Samuel, Pamela S. Karlan, and Richard H. Pildes. *The Law of Democracy: Legal Structure of the Political Process*. Rev. 2nd ed. New York: Foundation, 2002.

Julius, A. J. *Reconstruction*. Princeton, NJ: Princeton University Press, forthcoming.

Karlan, Pamela S. "*Georgia v. Ashcroft* and the Retrogression of Retrogression." *Election Law Journal* 3 (2004): 21–36.

Karpowitz, Christopher F., and Tali Mendelberg. *The Silent Sex: Gender, Deliberation, and Institutions*. Princeton, NJ: Princeton University Press, 2014.

Keyssar, Alexander. *The Right to Vote: The Contested History of Democracy in the United States*. New York: Basic Books, 2009.

Knight, Jack, and James Johnson. "What Sort of Equality Does Deliberative Democracy Require?" In *Deliberative Democracy: Essays on Reason and Politics*, edited by James Bohman and William Rehg, 279–319. Cambridge, MA: MIT Press, 1997.

Kolodny, Niko. "Rule over None II: Social Equality and the Justification of Democracy." *Philosophy & Public Affairs* 42 (2014): 287–336.

Kymlicka, Will. "Left-Liberalism Revisited." In *The Egalitarian Conscience: Essays in Honour of G.A. Cohen*, edited by Christine Sypnowich, 9–33. Oxford: Oxford University Press, 2006.

———. *Multicultural Citizenship: A Liberal Theory of Minority Rights*. Oxford: Clarendon, 1995.

Kyritsis, Dimitrios. "Representation and Waldron's Objection to Judicial Review." *Oxford Journal of Legal Studies* 26 (2006): 733–51.

Lee, Frances E., and Bruce I. Oppenheimer. *Sizing Up the Senate: The Unequal Consequences of Equal Representation*. Chicago: University of Chicago Press, 1999.

Leiter, Brian. "Constitutional Law, Moral Judgment, and the Supreme Court as Super-Legislature." *Hastings Law Journal* 66 (2015): 1601–16.

Lever, Annabelle. "Democracy and Judicial Review: Are They Really Incompatible?" *Perspectives on Politics* 7 (2009): 805–22.

Levinson, Daryl J., and Richard H. Pildes. "Separation of Parties, Not Powers." *Harvard Law Review* 119 (2006): 2311–86.

Lijphart, Arend. "First-Past-the-Post, PR, Michael Pinto-Duschinsky, and the Empirical Evidence." *Representation* 36 (1999): 133–36.

Locke, John. *The Second Treatise of Government*. In *Two Treatises of Government*, edited by Peter Laslett. Cambridge, UK: Cambridge University Press, 1988.

Macedo, Stephen. "Our Imperfect Democratic Constitution: The Critics Examined." *Boston University Law Review* 89 (2009): 609–28.

Mackun, Paul, and Steven Wilson. "Population Distribution and Change: 2000–2010." US Census Bureau, 2011, accessed April 5, 2019, http://www.census.gov/prod/cen2010/briefs/c2010br-01.pdf.

Madison, James. "The Federalist, No. 39." In Cooke, *Federalist*.

———. "The Federalist, No. 51." In Cooke, *Federalist*.

———. "The Federalist, No. 58." In Cooke, *Federalist*.

———. "The Federalist, No. 62." In Cooke, *Federalist*.

———. "Notes on the Debates in the Federal Convention." Avalon Project, Yale Law School, Lillian Goldman Law Library, n.d., accessed April 5, 2019. http://avalon.law.yale.edu/subject_menus/debcont.asp.

Malhotra, Neil, and Connor Raso. "Racial Representation and U.S. Senate Apportionment." *Social Science Quarterly* 88 (2007): 1038–48.

Manin, Bernard. *The Principles of Representative Government*. Cambridge, UK: Cambridge University Press, 1997.

Mansbridge, Jane. "Clarifying the Concept of Representation." *American Political Science Review* 105 (2011): 621–30.

———. "Rethinking Representation." *American Political Science Review* 97 (2003): 515–28.

———. "Should Blacks Represent Blacks and Women Represent Women? A Contingent 'Yes.'" *Journal of Politics* 61 (1999): 628–57.

May, Kenneth O. "A Set of Independent Necessary and Sufficient Conditions for Simple Majority Decision." *Econometrica* 20 (1952): 680–84.

Mayhew, David R. "Is Congress 'the Broken Branch'?" *Boston University Law Review* 89 (2009): 357–69.

McConnell, Michael W. "The Redistricting Cases: Original Mistakes and Current Consequences." *Harvard Journal of Law and Policy* 24 (2000): 103–17.

McCormick, John. *Machiavellian Democracy*. Cambridge, UK: Cambridge University Press, 2011.

McGrath, Anthony J., Charles Anthony Smith, Michael Latner, and Alex Keena. *Gerrymandering in America: The House of Representatives, the Supreme Court, and the Future of Popular Sovereignty*. Cambridge, UK: Cambridge University Press, 2016.

McKerlie, Dennis. "Dimensions of Equality." *Utilitas* 13 (2001): 263–88.
———. "Equality and Time." *Ethics* 99 (1989): 475–91.
Meiklejohn, Alexander. *Free Speech and Its Relation to Self-Government*. New York: Harper, 1948.
Mendelberg, Tali, and John Oleske. "Race and Public Deliberation." *Political Communication* 17 (2000): 169–91.
Mill, John Stuart. *Considerations on Representative Government*. In *On Liberty and Other Essays*, 203–467. First published 1861.
———. *On Liberty*. In *On Liberty and Other Essays*, 1–128. First published 1859.
———. *On Liberty and Other Essays*, edited by John Gray. Oxford: Oxford University Press, 1998.
———. *The Subjection of Women*. In *On Liberty and Other Essays*, 469–582. First published 1869.
Miller, David. "Equality and Justice." *Ratio* 10 (1997): 222–37.
Moreau, Sophia. "What Is Discrimination?" *Philosophy & Public Affairs* 38 (2010): 143–79.
Mueller, Dennis C. *Public Choice III*. Cambridge, UK: Cambridge University Press, 2003.
Nagel, Thomas. "Equality." In *Mortal Questions*, 106–27. Cambridge, UK: Cambridge University Press, 1979.
Nelson, William N. *On Justifying Democracy*. Boston, MA: Routledge, 1980.
Nietzsche, Friedrich. *On the Genealogy of Morality*. Translated by Maudemarie Clark and Alan J. Swensen. Indianapolis: Hackett, 1998.
Norman, Richard. "The Social Basis of Equality." *Ratio* 10 (1997): 238–52.
Nozick, Robert. *Anarchy, State, and Utopia*. New York: Basic Books, 1974.
Ober, Josiah. "Democracy's Dignity." *American Political Science Review* 106 (2012): 827–46.
O'Neill, Martin. "Constructing a Contractualist Egalitarianism: Equality after Scanlon." *Journal of Moral Philosophy* 10 (2013): 429–61.
———. "Free (and Fair) Markets without Capitalism." In *Property-Owning Democracy: Rawls and Beyond*, edited by Martin O'Neill and Thad Williamson, 75–100. Malden, MA: Wiley-Blackwell, 2012.
———. "What Should Egalitarians Believe?" *Philosophy & Public Affairs* 36 (2008): 119–56.
Ortiz, Daniel R. "The Democratic Paradox of Campaign Finance Reform." *Stanford Law Review* 50 (1998): 893–914.
Parfit, Derek. "Equality or Priority?" In *The Ideal of Equality*, edited by Matthew Clayton and Andrew Williams, 81–125. Basingstoke: Palgrave MacMillan, 2000.
———. *On What Matters*. Vol. 1. Oxford: Oxford University Press, 2011.
Pepall, John. *Against Reform*. Toronto: University of Toronto Press, 2010.
Perry, Michael J. *The Constitution, the Courts, and Human Rights: An Inquiry into the Legitimacy of Constitutional Policy Making by the Judiciary*. New Haven, CT: Yale University Press, 1982.
Persily, Nathaniel. "The Promise and Pitfalls of the New Voting Rights Act." *Yale Law Journal* 117 (2007): 174–254.
Pettit, Philip. *On the People's Terms: A Republican Theory and Model of Democracy*. Cambridge, UK: Cambridge University Press, 2012.

———. *Republicanism: A Theory of Freedom and Government*. Oxford: Oxford University Press, 1997.

———. "Responsibility Incorporated." *Ethics* 117 (2007): 171–201.

———. *The Robust Demands of the Good*. Oxford: Oxford University Press, 2015.

Pettit, Philip, and Rory Pettit. "The Washington and Westminster Systems." Appendix to Philip Pettit, "Varieties of Public Representation," in *Political Representation*, edited by Ian Shapiro, Susan C. Stokes, Elisabeth Jean Wood, and Alexander S. Kirshner, 82–87. Cambridge, UK: Cambridge University Press, 2010.

Pevnick, Ryan. "Does the Egalitarian Rationale for Campaign Finance Reform Succeed?" *Philosophy & Public Affairs* 44 (2016): 46–76.

Pitkin, Hanna Fenichel. *The Concept of Representation*. Berkeley, CA: University of California Press, 1967.

Plato. *The Republic of Plato*. Translated by Allan Bloom. New York, 1968.

Pope, Jeremy C., and Shawn Treier. "Reconsidering the Great Compromise at the Federal Convention of 1787: Deliberation and Agenda Effects on the Senate and Slavery." *American Journal of Political Science* 55 (2011): 289–306.

Post, Robert. *Citizens Divided: Campaign Finance Reform and the Constitution*. Cambridge, MA: Harvard University Press, 2014.

Powell, G. Bingham. *Elections as Instruments of Democracy: Majoritarian and Proportional Visions*. New Haven, CT: Yale University Press, 2000.

———. "Representation in Context: Election Laws and Ideological Congruence between Citizens and Governments." *Perspectives on Politics* 11 (2013): 9–21.

Pukelsheim, Friedrich. *Proportional Representation: Apportionment Methods and Their Applications*. Cham, Switzerland: Springer, 2010.

Rawls, John. *Justice as Fairness: A Restatement*. Cambridge, MA: Belknap, 1999.

———. *The Law of Peoples*. Cambridge, MA: Harvard University Press, 1999.

———. *Political Liberalism*. Expanded ed. New York: Columbia University Press, 2005.

———. *A Theory of Justice*. Rev. ed. Cambridge, MA: Belknap, 1999.

Raz, Joseph. *The Authority of Law: Essays on Law and Morality*. New York: Oxford University Press, 1979.

———. *The Morality of Freedom*. Oxford: Oxford University Press, 1986.

Redish, Martin H., and Elana Nightingale Dawson. "Worse Than the Disease: The Anti-Corruption Principle, Free Expression, and the Democratic Process." *William & Mary Bill of Rights Journal* 20 (2012): 1053–84.

Return of the Whole Number of Persons within the Several Districts of the United States, According to "An Act Providing for the Enumeration of the Inhabitants of the United States;" Passed March the First, One Thousand Seven Hundred and Ninety-One. US Census Bureau facsimile of repr. ed. London: J. Phillips, 1793, accessed April 5, 2019, https://www2.census.gov/prod2/decennial/documents/1790a.pdf.

Richardson, Henry. *Democratic Autonomy*. Oxford: Oxford University Press, 2002.

Risse, Mathias. "Arguing for Majority Rule." *Journal of Political Philosophy* 12 (2004): 41–64.

Rosenblum, Nancy L. *On the Side of the Angels: An Appreciation of Parties and Partisanship*. Princeton, NJ: Princeton University Press, 2010.

Rousseau, Jean-Jacques. *Of the Social Contract*. In *The Social Contract and Other Later Political Writings*, translated by Victor Gourevitch, 39–152. Cambridge, UK: Cambridge University Press, 1997.

Rubenfeld, Jed. *Freedom and Time*. New Haven, CT: Yale University Press, 2001.
Rubin, Edward L., and Malcolm Feeley. "Federalism: Some Notes on a National Neurosis." *UCLA Law Review* 41 (1993): 903–52.
Samuels, David, and Richard Snyder. "The Value of a Vote: Malapportionment in Comparative Perspective." *British Journal of Political Science* 31 (2001): 651–71.
Sanders, Lynn M. "Against Deliberation." *Political Theory* 25 (1997): 347–76.
Scanlon, T. M. *What We Owe to Each Other*. Cambridge, MA: Harvard University Press, 1998.
———. *Why Does Inequality Matter?* Oxford: Oxford University Press, 2018.
Scheffler, Samuel. "Choice, Circumstance, and the Value of Equality." *Politics, Philosophy & Economics* 4 (2005): 5–28.
———. "The Practice of Equality." In *Social Equality: On What It Means to Be Equals*, edited by Carina Fourie, Fabian Schuppert, and Ivo Wallimann-Helmer, 21–44. Oxford: Oxford University Press, 2015.
———. "What Is Egalitarianism?" *Philosophy & Public Affairs* 31 (2003): 5–39.
Schemmel, Christian. "Distributive and Relational Equality." *Politics, Philosophy & Economics* 11 (2011): 123–48.
———. "Luck Egalitarianism as Democratic Reciprocity? A Response to Tan." *Journal of Philosophy* 109 (2012): 435–38.
Scheppele, Kim Lane. "Guardians of the Constitution: Constitutional Court Presidents and the Struggle for the Rule of Law in Post-Soviet Europe." *University of Pennsylvania Law Review* 154 (2006): 1757–851.
Schepsle, Kenneth. "Dysfunctional Congress?" *Boston University Law Review* 89 (2009): 371–86.
Schlozman, Kay Lehman, Sidney Verba, and Henry E. Brady. *The Unheavenly Chorus: Unequal Political Voice and the Broken Promise of American Democracy*. Princeton, NJ: Princeton University Press, 2012.
Sen, Amartya. "On the Status of Equality." *Political Theory* 24 (1996): 394–400.
Shapiro, Scott J. *Legality*. Cambridge, MA: Belknap, 2011.
Shiffrin, Seana Valentine. "Egalitarianism, Choice-Sensitivity, and Accommodation." In *Reason and Value: Themes from the Moral Philosophy of Joseph Raz*, edited by R. Jay Wallace, Philip Pettit, Samuel Scheffler, and Michael Smith, 270–302. Oxford: Oxford University Press, 2004.
Shugart, Matthew Soberg. "The Jenkins Paradox: A Complex System, yet Only a Timid Step towards PR." *Representation* 36 (1999): 143–47.
Siegel, Reva. "Equality Talk: Antisubordination and Anticlassification Values in Constitutional Struggles over *Brown*." *Harvard Law Review* 117 (2004): 1470–1547.
———. "She the People: The Nineteenth Amendment, Sex Equality, Federalism, and the Family." *Harvard Law Review* 115 (2002): 947–1046.
Singer, Peter. *Democracy and Disobedience*. Oxford: Clarendon, 1973.
Smith, Bradley A. *Unfree Speech: The Folly of Campaign Finance Reform*. Princeton, NJ: Princeton University Press, 2001.
Stepan, Alfred. "Federalism and Democracy: Beyond the U.S. Model." *Journal of Democracy* 10 (1999): 19–32.
Stephanopoulos, Nicholas O., and Eric M. McGhee. "Partisan Gerrymandering and the Efficiency Gap." *University of Chicago Law Review* 82 (2015): 831–900.
Still, Jonathan. "Political Equality and Election Systems." *Ethics* 91 (1981): 375–94.

Stone, Peter. "The Logic of Random Selection." *Political Theory* 37 (2009): 375-97.
Sullivan, Kathleen M. "Against Campaign Finance Reform." *Utah Law Review* (1998): 311-29.
———. "Political Money and Freedom of Speech." *University of California, Davis Law Review* 30 (1997): 663-90.
Sunstein, Cass R. *The Partial Constitution*. Cambridge, MA: Harvard University Press, 1993.
Tawney, R. H. *Equality*. 5th ed. London: Allen and Unwin, 1964.
Thomas, Alan. *Republic of Equals: Predistribution and Property-Owning Democracy*. Oxford: Oxford University Press, 2016.
Thompson, Dennis F. *Just Elections: Creating a Fair Electoral Process in the United States*. Chicago: University of Chicago Press, 2004.
Tocqueville, Alexis de. *Democracy in America*. Edited by J. P. Mayer. Translated by George Lawrence. New York: Harper Perennial, 1988.
Tseytlin, Misha. "The United States Senate and the Problem of Equal State Suffrage." *Georgetown Law Journal* 94 (2006): 859-88.
Tuck, Richard. *Free Riding*. Cambridge, MA: Harvard University Press, 2008.
Viehoff, Daniel. "Democratic Equality and Political Authority." *Philosophy & Public Affairs* 42 (2014): 337-75.
Waldron, Jeremy. "The Core of the Case against Judicial Review." *Yale Law Journal* 115 (2006): 1346-406.
———. *The Dignity of Legislation*. Cambridge, UK: Cambridge University Press, 1999.
———. *Dignity, Rank, and Rights*. Oxford: Oxford University Press, 2015.
———. *Law and Disagreement*. Oxford: Oxford University Press, 1999.
Wall, Steven. "Rawls and the Status of Political Liberty." *Pacific Philosophical Quarterly* 87 (2006): 245-70.
Walzer, Michael. *Spheres of Justice: A Defense of Pluralism and Equality*. New York: Basic Books, 1983.
Ward, Hugh. "A Contractarian Defence of Ideal Proportional Representation." *Journal of Political Philosophy* 3 (1995): 86-109.
Watkins, David, and Scott Lemieux. "Compared to What? Judicial Review and Other Veto Points in Contemporary Democratic Theory." *Perspectives on Politics* 13 (2015): 312-26.
Wechsler, Herbert. "The Political Safeguards of Federalism: The Role of the States in the Composition and Selection of the National Government." *Columbia Law Review* 54 (1954): 543-60.
Wenar, Leif. "The Nature of Rights." *Philosophy & Public Affairs* 33 (2005): 223-52.
Williams, Bernard. "The Idea of Equality." In *In the Beginning Was the Deed: Realism and Moralism in Political Argument*, 97-114. Princeton, NJ: Princeton University Press, 2005.
Williams, Melissa S. "The Uneasy Alliance of Group Representation and Deliberative Democracy." In *Citizenship in Diverse Societies*, edited by Will Kymlicka and Wayne Norman, 124-52. Oxford: Oxford University Press, 2000.
———. *Voice, Trust, and Memory: Marginalized Groups and the Failings of Liberal Representation*. Princeton, NJ: Princeton University Press, 2000.

Wilson, James Lindley. "Against Instrumentalism about Democracy." Unpublished manuscript. Last modified October 19, 2018.
———. "An Autonomy-Based Argument for Democracy." Unpublished manuscript. Last modified March 31, 2019.
———. "Deliberation, Democracy, and the Rule of Reason in Aristotle's *Politics*." *American Political Science Review* 105 (2011): 259–74.
Winters, Jeffrey A., and Benjamin I. Page. "Oligarchy in the United States?" *Perspectives on Politics* 7 (2009): 731–51.
Wolff, Jonathan. "Fairness, Respect, and the Egalitarian Ethos." *Philosophy & Public Affairs* 27 (1998): 97–122.
Wolin, Sheldon S. "Democracy: Electoral and Athenian." *PS: Political Science and Politics* 26 (1993): 475–77.
Wood, Gordon S. *The Creation of the American Republic, 1776–1787*. 2nd ed. Chapel Hill, NC: University of North Carolina Press, 1998.
Young, Iris Marion. "Activist Challenges to Deliberative Democracy." *Political Theory* 29 (2001): 670–90.
———. *Justice and the Politics of Difference*. Princeton, NJ: Princeton University Press, 1990.
Zeisberg, Mariah. "Should We Elect the U.S. Supreme Court?" *Perspectives on Politics* 7 (2009): 785–803.

INDEX

absolute monarchs, benevolent rule by, 123n
Achen, Christopher H., 214n48
Ackerman, Bruce, 188n37, 274, 276–77, 279n39
Administrative Procedure Act, 121n7
aggregation, fair. *See* fair aggregation, principles of
aggregation of citizen judgments, 8; deliberation and (*see* deliberation); fair-aggregation rules for democratic, 88–89; formal and informal, 116–17 (*see also* deliberation; elections/electoral systems; representation; voting); individual entitlements in the process of, 119–22; inequalities in political procedures (*see* political procedures); as a winnowing down process, 80, 86–87, 113, 117
Altman, Andrew, 221–22
Anderson, Elizabeth, 27n19
antidegradation principle/requirement, 8, 136, 138–39, 198
Applbaum, Arthur, 106n19
appraisal respect, 20n5, 69
appropriate consideration, 7–8, 96–97, 141–42; aggregative processes, egalitarian constraints on, 117 (*see also* sufficiency principle); Altman's prejudice standard and, 221–22; authority, as a form of, 105–10; benevolent rule of an absolute monarch and, 123n; of citizens' judgments, 119–22; deliberation and, 144–45 (*see also* deliberation); elections as a means to secure, 124–25; fair deliberation as, 157–69 (*see also* deliberation, fair); institutional means of securing and, gap between, 133; judicial review and, 277–81; legislative presence as insufficient for, 203; obligations of representatives and, 129–32; partisan gerrymandering and, 233–35; political degradation and, 138, 140–41; political equality as, 6, 110–14; racial vote dilution, accounting for, 216–17, 220 (*see also* racial vote dilution); sufficient, demand for (*see* sufficiency principle); unequal voting in the Senate and Electoral College, applied to, 191–92; virtual representation, possibility of, 125–28; voting not required by, 123–24; wealth inequality and, 244 (*see also* wealth inequality); women's suffrage and, 127–28
Aristotle, 21, 33n32, 54, 63n16
Arneson, Richard, 39n41
assembly, freedom of, 120–22
authority: absence of as insufficient for friendship, 59; appropriate consideration as a form of, 105–10; of citizens, political equality and, 97–105; command, 106–9, 111–14; conception of, claims to consideration and, 6, 96–97; decision-making discretion and, 104–5; equal sharing of among friends, 56–60; of expectations and of persons, distinction between, 98–100; level of generality of claims to, 100–104; political obligations and, 97–98; practical consequence as a form of, 106–10 (*see also* practical consequence); sharing, 283–84; unequal, resentment of, 63–64; voting as an alienation of, 130–32
authorization, fair. *See* fair authorization
autonomy: "first-order" and "second-order," distinction between, 69, 185; political inequality and the denial of citizen, 69–70; protection of state in the Senate, 182–87
autonomy protection, 244

Baker, Lynn A., 178n10, 180n17, 184n26
Banducci, Susan A., 210n38
Barry, Brian, 89n28
Bartels, Larry M., 214n48
Beerbohm, Eric, 101, 103n13, 129n22, 132n29

[299]

Beitz, Charles, 100n6, 111n26, 163n46, 177n5, 198n10, 210
Bickel, Alexander, 84n19, 269
Bird, Colin, 20, 119n4
Brettschneider, Corey, 120n5
Brighouse, Harry, 146–50, 152–53, 166n57
Brown v. Board of Education, 140n43
Buckley v. Valeo, 259n47

causal relationships: homology between cause and effect, 54
Christiano, Thomas: Beitz argument, complaint about, 198n10; citizen judgments limited to aims, not means, 100–101; equality and hierarchy, potential coexistence of, 133n32; majority rule, view of, 78n10; party-list proportional representation, defense of, 211–13; on proportionality, 163; publicity of political equality, requirement for, 105n17
citizens: aggregation of judgments (*see* aggregation of citizen judgments; fair aggregation, principles of); appropriate consideration of views of (*see* appropriate consideration); authority as obligating, 97–98; authority of based on judgments rather than interests, 99–100; basic political freedoms for, 119–20; coalition formation, authority over, 204–9; degradation of, antidiscrimination requirements regarding, 136–41; deliberative responsibility among, fair division of, 248–53; democratic, 24; division of labor between representatives and, 101, 211–13; entitlements of consistent with political equality (*see* sufficiency principle); equality of status for, 23–25, 49, 119 (*see also* status); exclusions from in a democracy, 24–25; expectations constituting equality of status for, 27; individual entitlements required for minimal consideration of judgments, 119–22; judicial decisions and, 272; jurisdiction of, 49; level of generality of judgments that are authoritative, 100–104; moral obligation and authority of, 104–5; obligations of representatives to, 129–32; political equality, denial of, 67–72; practical consequence and the authority of (*see* practical consequence); selection for office by lot or rotation, 90–91, 113, 123; self-respect of, 61–62, 70–71
civic friendship, 60
coalitions: control of the legislative agenda by, 204n22; formation of, 204–10, 225–29; "fringe" and "irrelevant" members of, distinction between, 227–28; racial vote dilution and formation of, 224–30; of the rich, concerns regarding, 247
Cohen, G. A., 170
Cohen, Joshua, 242
collective decision-making: aggregation of citizen judgments in (*see* aggregation of citizen judgments); appropriate consideration in (*see* appropriate consideration); over time, requirements of, 75–76, 79–80 (*see also* time); reasons to pursue and support, 72 (*see also* political equality); requirements of political equality and, 50, 118 (*see also* sufficiency principle); as supportive of other forms of equality, 54
complete lives approach to equality, 90–92
consideration, appropriate. *See* appropriate consideration
Constitution, United States: First Amendment, 121n7, 260, 262n55; Fourteenth Amendment, Equal Protection Clause, 133n33; Fifteenth Amendment, 218, 223, 238n49; Nineteenth Amendment, 128
constitutional dualism, 276–77
counsel, 107, 109–10
culture: deliberative neglect of the poor and, 246; racial inequality and, 169

Dahl, Robert, 76–77
Darwall, Stephen, 20, 69
de facto persuasiveness, 153–54, 156–57, 167
deliberation: as aggregative, 117; command authority and, 112; de facto persuasiveness in, 153–54, 156–57; democratic, requirements of, 87–89; equality of influence position and (*see* equality of influence/equal opportunity for influence/equal-influence

views); fair division of responsibility for, 248–53; freedom of speech and, 120; informal process of aggregation, as part of, 116–17; oligarchic threats as failures of consideration in, 243–44; political equality and, 143–44; power in, 158; as a process that occurs over time, 79–80; requirements of, 162, 244–45; urgency principle in, 162

deliberation, fair, 170–71; as appropriate consideration, 157–69; citizens' interests with respect to, 145; deliberative oligarchy, concerns regarding, 168–69; distribution of power and, 89, 158; equal consideration of views and, 163–65; fair aggregation and, 88; fair hearing from others, claim to, 159; justified inequalities in, 165–67; plurality of interests, consideration and, 158–60; proportional consideration and, 160–64; as remedy for equal-influence views, 144

deliberative abundance/scarcity, 255–59

deliberative neglect, 134–36, 151, 163; deliberative scarcity and, 257–58; gerrymanders and, 234; judicial review and, 278–80; legislative presence and, 203; race-based, 220–24, 229, 235–36, 236–37n46, 238, 240; rich elites at risk of, 260n49; unequal voting in the Senate and, 176–77, 180–82, 186, 189n40

deliberative triage, 165, 259

democracy: allegiance to, 1; challenges to the egalitarian tradition of, 22, 26–27, 56; direct, 80–83, 119, 127; disagreement over the structural design of, 1–2; distributive justice and, 166; egalitarian tradition of, 21–22; as equal power, 76–79 (*see also* equal-distribution/power approach); in its aspirational sense, 48; judicial review and (*see* judicial review); nonalien rule as a requirement of, 19; political equality and, 2–4, 18–26, 283 (*see also* political equality; status); reasons to support, 19–20; representative vs. direct, 82–83; as rule of the people, 18–19; social egalitarianism and, 26–27 (*see also* social equality); social equality and, 17–18, 54–55

Dickens, Charles, 33
Dinkin, Samuel H., 178n10, 180n17, 184n26
direct democracy, 80–83, 119, 127
discrimination: disparate impact, 230–32; political antidiscrimination requirements, 136–41
distribution of goods: basic moral concerns and, 23; democratic egalitarianism and, 26; equal distribution of power (*see* equal-distribution/power approach); equality of conditions and, 22; leveling down to obtain equal, 118–19; over time, complete-lives approach to, 90–92; over time, simultaneous segments approach to, 92–94; stoic egalitarian objection to focus on relational values and, 43–45
districts/districting: drawing of, court cases addressing, 217–19; gerrymandering (*see* gerrymandering); indifference between schemes of, 234–35; racial vote dilution (*see* racial vote dilution); single-member district systems (*see* single-member district systems); size of and malapportionment concerns, 125, 135
Dworkin, Ronald, 145, 147–48, 163n46, 177n5, 242

egalitarianism: equality of status and, 23–26; "merely basic" and "substantive," contrast of, 30–31; social and democracy, 26–27 (*see also* social equality); as a social ideal (*see* social equality)
elections/electoral systems: campaign finance reform, 254, 258n45, 262–65; coalitions and (*see* coalitions); consideration secured by, 124–25; gerrymandering (*see* gerrymandering); mixed systems, promise of, 214; national popular vote for president, argument for, 190–91; political equality and, 123–24; proportional representation (*see* proportional representation); single-member district systems (*see* single-member district systems). *See also* districts/districting; voting
Electoral College: abolishment of, 190–91; appropriate-consideration conception applied to, 191–92; inequality in voting

Electoral College (*continued*)
  power involved in, 85n21, 175–76, 179, 189–90; reform of, proposal for, 190
Eliot, George, 1
Ely, John Hart, 137, 278–79
equal-distribution/power approach, 7, 75–76; aggregative processes, firm constraints on, 117; arguments for, 76–79; direct democracy required/rejection of representation by, 80–83, 119; fair authorization to accommodate representation in, 83–87; fair deliberation and, 87–89; representation and deliberation over time and, 79–80; temporal challenges for, 89–94; undue permissiveness and undue rigor, combining, 142; vote dilution, non-recognition of, 219–20
equality: complete-lives approach to, 90–92; global principles of, 39–41, 46; justifications of, 38–39; political (*see* political equality); of power, 59n12; simultaneous segments approach to, 92–94; social (*see* social equality); vices of, 45–46. *See also* inequality
equality of influence/equal opportunity for influence/equal-influence views, 8, 145–47, 170; arguments against, 147–57; citizens with pregiven preferences, assumption of, 158; compounded inequalities over time, problem of, 93n39; content of views, problem of, 148–51, 169; deliberative oligarchy problem and, 168–69; different types of influence, problems of, 151–55; effort levels, problem of, 147–48; equality in deliberation, errors regarding, 144; equal-resources views and, 155–57; racial vote dilution and, 219n14
equality of opportunity, 144, 146–47, 155, 226
equal-power-plus views: racial vote dilution and, 219n14
equal-resources view, 155–57
Estlund, David, 97n1, 100, 119n3, 131n27, 166–67
exclusionary reasons, 107–9

fair aggregation, principles of, 88, 116, 176, 197–98, 211, 271, 284

fair authorization: egalitarianism of representation under, 85–87; in the equal-distribution/power approach, 83–84; power inequalities and, 84; Rubenfeld's view of popular rule as, 276
fair deliberation. *See* deliberation, fair
fair responsibility, 242–43
false consciousness, 244–45n11
Federalist Papers, The, 84n19, 179, 187, 270
freedoms, political, 119–22, 260–66
Fricker, Miranda, 153n24
friends/friendship: political equality and, 56–60; social equality and, 33–35; unequal authority among, 63–64

Gerken, Heather, 238n51
gerrymandering, 9–10, 133–34; complaints against, 217–18; need to guard against in single-member districts, 211; objectionable nature of, 232–35; racial vote dilution (*see* racial vote dilution)
groups: proportional representation and, 196, 201–4; representation of, 122, 193
Guinier, Lani, 160n41, 197, 239

Habermas, Jürgen, 120n5, 164
Hamilton, Alexander, 270, 274
Hare, Thomas, 194–96
Harlan, John Marshall, 140
Harlan, John Marshall, II, 219
Hasen, Richard L., 263n57
hierarchical relationships: claims for and objections to, 64–67; friendships and, 33–34n33; reasons to preserve, 66n22; renouncing claims of, 33; restrictions on speech and assembly supporting, 120; social equality and, 29; vices of, 41
Hobbes, Thomas, 18–19, 107, 109, 112, 276

Indridason, Indridi H., 203n20
inequality: arguments for justified, 176–77; authorized by a fair process, 84 (*see also* fair authorization); coexistence of political equality and, 3; deliberation and, 143 (*see also* deliberation); in fair deliberation, 165–67; objectionable features of political (vices of oligarchy), 37, 67–72; objectionable features of social (vices of inequality), 37–41; in political procedures (*see* political procedures);

of voting power, 124–25; wealth (*see* wealth inequality). *See also* equality

influence: conditional, 146; different types of, 152–53; inequalities of compatible with political equality, 167; limits on due to others' judgments and not reducible to others' judgments, distinction between, 150n17; manipulative, 152–56, 244; political, definition of, 145; wealth inequality and, 255–56 (*see also* wealth inequality). *See also* equality of influence/equal opportunity for influence/equal-influence views

information: access to, 244–45; cost of acquiring, 258–59

institutions and practices: design of, democracy vs. oligarchy and, 64; design of, outcomes and, 2; political equality and, 5; political procedures (*see* political procedures); requirements of political equality and, 50

instrumentalism: judicial review and, 272–74, 279–80; political regimes and, 62–64

insulation strategy, 166, 254

judicial review, 10, 268–69, 281–82; appropriate consideration and justification of, 277–81; counter-majoritarianism of, 78n10, 277–78; democratic concerns raised by, 271–72; institutional checks on, 280–81; instrumentalism as defense of, 272–74, 279–80; justification of, 269–70; popular Hamiltonianism as defense of, 274–77; supermajority rules and, 270–71

justice: political equality and, 46–47, 284–86; social equality and theories of, 29–30, 46

justice-relevant obligations, 249–50

Karp, Jeffrey A., 210n38

Kolodny, Niko: absence of authority as sufficient for equal relations, 59; asymmetry in the objections of inferiors and superiors noted by, 66n21; equal-but-low power/authority as consistent with political equality, 119n4; equal-influence requirements, commitment to, 159nn36–37; equal-resources position of, 155–57; influence, distinction in types of, 155; political inequalities in the Senate, justification for, 185n29; principal-agent model of representation, egalitarian features of, 101n10; reform of hierarchical societies, existence of reasons to avoid, 66n22; on supermajority rules, 270–71, 278; synthesizing of different egalitarian ideals, suggestion of, 36n36

leveling down, 102, 118–19

libertarian/libertarianism: conceptions of justice, 251n30; friendship, 59; merely basic egalitarianism of, 31

Locke, John, 49, 61, 131n28

lot, citizens selected for office by, 90, 113, 123

Macedo, Stephen, 181n20, 188

Madison, James, 19, 82–83n17, 179, 187

majority rule, 78–79, 270

Manin, Bernard, 81n14

marriage, patriarchal, 57–58

Martin, Luther, 184n27

Mayhew, David R., 181n18

McConnell, Michael W., 125n15

McCormick, John, 24n15

McGhee, Eric M., 234n42

McKerlie, Dennis, 92, 94n

Mill, John Stuart: democracy and social equality, belief regarding the relationship of, 54; egalitarianism and arguments for proportional representation, 197n8; open ballots, advocacy for, 199; plural voting, promotion of, 76, 125n14, 175; political inequality and disrespect, on the relationship of, 68; proportional representation, promotion of, 194–95, 197

minimalists, 242, 247–49

minority rule, fairness of, 211

Moreau, Sophia, 137n

Nietzsche, Friedrich, 31

oligarchic threats, 242–48

oligarchy: democratic rejection of, claims to equal status for citizens and, 21; informal, 243; instrumental argument for, 62–64; intrinsic argument for, 62, 64–67; justifications for, 62–63;

oligarchy (*continued*)
  rejection of, rejecting distinctions in political status between citizens and, 19–20; status and, 24; vices of, 37, 67–72. *See also* wealth inequality
O'Neill, Martin, 24, 44
Ortiz, Daniel, 258n45

Parfit, Derek, 25–26, 118
partisan gerrymandering. *See* gerrymandering
Persily, Nathaniel, 224n27
Pettit, Philip, 42n
Pevnick, Ryan, 159n36
philosophy, question of impact of, 11–14
Pitkin, Hannah, 86
Plato, 54, 62–63
Plessy v. Ferguson, 140
political antidiscrimination requirements, 136–41
political equality: appropriate consideration as, 110–14 (*see also* appropriate consideration); arguments favoring oligarchy over, 62–67 (*see also* oligarchy); authority as the subject matter of, 97–105; central claims about, 5–6; challenges to, 22, 26–27, 56; citizen self-respect and, 61–62; core democratic aspiration of, 18–26; deliberative triage required by, 165; democracy and, 2–4, 283 (*see also* democracy); democratic citizen status under, 24 (*see also* citizens); direct democracy and, 82–83; economic inequalities compatible with, 165–67; entitlements consistent with (*see* sufficiency principle); as equality of political power among citizens (*see* equal-distribution/power approach); equality of poverty and leveling down problems, 102, 118–19; equal treatment distinguished from, 100; friendship and, 56–60; good outcomes and, potential tension between, 4; instrumental value of, 50–55; intrinsic value of, 55–72; justice and, relationship of, 251, 284–86; meaning of for citizens, 28, 49; minimalist position regarding, 242, 247–49; overview of the argument regarding, 7–11; political inequality vs., 67–72; in a political process that occurs over time, 89–95 (*see also* time); principles for judging violations of, 134–41; proportional representation and, 193–94 (*see also* proportional representation); social equality and, relationship of, 17–18, 22–23, 27–28, 51–52; social equality as causally promoted by, 51–55; social equality as partially constituted by, 51–52, 55; theories of justice and, 46–47; theory of, 11–14, 19–21, 49–50, 94–95; wealth inequality and, 254, 266–67 (*see also* wealth inequality)
political liberties, anti-reformist argument based on, 260–66
political procedures: antidiscrimination requirements for, 136–41; deliberative (*see* deliberation); deliberative neglect and institutional inequalities, 134–36; denials of political equality in, 133–34; voting (*see* voting)
poll taxes, 252, 254, 259
Pope, Jeremy C., 179–80n14
Post, Robert, 120n5
Powell, G. Bingham, 207n31
power: equal distribution of (*see* equal-distribution/power approach)
PR. *See* proportional representation
practical consequence: command authority vs., 112–13; as a form of authority, 106–10
prejudice standard, 221
proportional-consideration view/proportionality principle, 160–64, 201–2
proportional representation (PR), 193–94, 213–15; coalition formation and, 204–10; defenses of, 194–96; group representation not a commitment to, 122; legislative presence and, 201–13; national- vs. locally-oriented systems and, 200n13; partisan gerrymandering, as solution to, 233; party-list systems of, 200n14, 211–13; vote dilution, as solution to, 239; voter-legislator relationships under, 196–201

race: cultural norms and achievement of equal influence, problem of, 169;

Plessy v. Ferguson and, 140; the Tuskegee gerrymander, 133–34; "whites-only" political primaries, 134

racial vote dilution, 9, 135, 216–17, 240; court cases addressing, 218–19, 223; disparate impact discrimination and, 230–32; doctrine of, 217–19; fairness in coalition formation and, 224–30; implementation and enforcement against, 235–38; as race-based deliberative neglect, 220–24, 229, 236–37n46; skeptics regarding, 219–20, 223, 238–39; unequal voting in the Senate as, 181; "vote dilution," meaning of, 216

Rawls, John: on the difficulties of distinguishing between "particular" and "general" rules or policies, 141n46; economic inequality, concerns regarding, 165–66; on equality in an egalitarian society, 23; global ideal of equality, stability of, 40; on majority rule, 78n10; public accessibility of society's commitment to justice, requirement for, 105n17; reflective equilibrium, 103n13; self-respect, social relations and, 61n13

Raz, Joseph, 107

reciprocal courtesy, 32, 60

recognition respect, 20, 69

reflective equilibrium, 103n13

representation: of Americans in the Westminster parliament, 126; "captured" representatives, problem of, 245–46; command authority and selection of representatives, potential parallel of, 113n28; delegate-trustee distinction, alternative to, 132; direct democracy vs., 82–83; discretion of representatives, exercise of, 87; division of labor between citizens and representatives, 101; of electoral losers, 239–40; equally sized districts for, 77–78; fair-authorization view and, 85–87; of groups, 122; ideal of, 132; inequality in voting power inherent in, 80; obligations of representatives, 129–32; proportional (*see* proportional representation); rejection of in equal-distribution/power approach, 80–83; scarcities faced by representatives, 256; surrogate, 226–27; unequal in the Senate (*see* Senate, United States); universal actual (direct democracy), 126–27; virtual, 125–28; winnowing down citizen judgments, process of, 86–87, 113. *See also* voting

respect: egalitarian and nonegalitarian, 29; political exclusion as disrespectful, 68–69; self-respect of citizens, 61–62, 70–71

responsibility, fair. *See* fair responsibility

Reynolds v. Sims, 76n1

Richardson, Henry, 103n15

Risse, Mathias, 79n12

rotation of office, 90–91

Rousseau, Jean-Jacques, 21, 54, 82n16, 140–41

Rubenfeld, Jed, 79n13, 274–76

Samuels, David, 178n9

Sanders, Lynn M., 168n62

Scalia, Antonin, 219

Senate, United States: appropriate-consideration conception applied to, 191–92; federal judicial appointments, role in, 281n44; inequalities of power involved in, 85n21; institutional structure of, 175; protection of state autonomy, argument for, 182–87; reform of, 187–89; special consideration for small-state citizens, argument for, 176–82; unequal representation in, 175–76, 178–79; unfair representation in the Electoral College and, 189

Senate factors, 224

simultaneous segments approach to equality, 92–94

Singer, Peter, 89n28

single-member district (SMD) systems: antidegradation principle, nonviolation of, 198; coalition formation in, 205, 207–10; disproportionality in, 202, 210–11, 234; gerrymandering, need to guard against, 211 (*see also* gerrymandering); neglect of minorities and minority parties as a possibility in, 203, 229; proportional representation systems, contrasted with, 214–15; voter-legislator relationships in, 197–99

SMD. *See* single-member district systems
Snyder, Richard, 178n9
social choice theory, 77, 228
social contract theory, 50
social equality: abstract egalitarian ideals and, 36–37; basic vs. substantive egalitarianism and, 30–31; behavioral norms for face-to-face relationships, 31–36; combining positive and negative strategies in arguing for, 41–42; democracy and, connection between, 17–18; equality of status, argument for, 23–24; framework of, 28–30; global principles of, 39–41, 46; hierarchical relationships and, 29; political equality and, relationship of, 17–18, 22–23, 27–28, 51–52; political equality as causally promoting, 51–55; political equality as partially constituting, 51–52, 51–55; special forms of precedence in relations among equals, 33n31; stoic egalitarian objection to, 42–45; theories of justice and, 29–30, 46; vices of inequality and, 38–41; vision of, 27–37
Socrates, 12
speech: directed, protections for, 121; freedom of, 120–21, 260–66
"starting-gate" conception of opportunity, 257n
status: advantages of using a concept of, 25–26; definition of, 20–21; descriptive and aspirational, distinction between, 21; equal, distributive inequalities and, 44; equal citizen (*see* citizens; political equality); hierarchical relationships and, 65 (*see also* hierarchical relationships); objections to using a concept of, 24–26; political equality and, 21, 49 (*see also* political equality); renouncing claims of superior, 33; self-respect and, relationship of, 61–62; in social interaction, 21 (*see also* social equality)
Stephanopoulos, Nicholas O., 234n42
Stevens, John Paul, 237n48
Still, Jonathan, 77n6
stoic equality objection, 42–45, 140n44
sufficiency principle, 117–19; degrading rules and procedures and, 138; deliberate neglect and, 135; elections and representation as requirement of, 123–28; individual entitlements as requirement of, 119–22; leveling down objection and, 118–19; obligations of representatives as requirement of, 129–32
suffrage: universal or near-universal, 3, 76, 124, 125n14, 128, 198; women's, 126–28, 138–39
supermajority rules, 270–71

Tawney, R. H., 170–71
Thomas, Clarence, 219, 237
time: citizens' equal status over, securing, 95; complete-lives approach to equal distribution over, 90–92; equal authority over, appropriate consideration and, 111; as a factor in collective decision-making, 75–76, 79–80; political equality and, 5–6; simultaneous segments approach to equal distribution over, 92–94; temporal challenges for the equal-distribution/power approach, 89–94
Tocqueville, Alexis de, 21–22, 32, 35, 54, 60–62
Treier, Shawn, 179–80n14
Tseytlin, Misha, 183nn23–24, 184n26
Tuck, Richard, 113
Tuskegee gerrymander, 133–34

unreasonable burdens: imposition of, 257–58; prohibition against, 249–54
urgency principle, 162
utilitarianism, merely basic egalitarianism of, 30–31

value complementarity, 41–42
vices of equality, 45–46
vices of hierarchy, 41
vices of inequality, 37–41
vices of oligarchy, 37, 67–72
Viehoff, Daniel, 36n36, 59, 119n4
virtual representation, 125–28
vote dilution: racial (*see* racial vote dilution); skepticism regarding, 219–20, 223, 238–39
voting: alienation of authority through, 130–32; appropriate consideration, not required by, 123–24; distribution

of voting power, 124–25; equal power in, 76–79 (*see also* equal-distribution/power approach); mandates delivered by, 124n; plural, 125, 175; political liberties and, 260–61; poll taxes, wealth inequality and, 252; regime accountability, as basis for, 123; restrictive registration for, 252–53; strategic, 206–7; turnout, electoral systems and, 210n38; unequal in the Electoral College (*see* Electoral College); unequal in the Senate (*see* Senate, United States); universal or near-universal suffrage, 3, 76, 124, 125n14, 128, 198. *See also* elections/electoral systems; representation

Voting Rights Act, 218, 223–24, 227n30, 236, 238n49

Waldron, Jeremy: citizen actions, objection to assumption about, 161n43; democratic consequences, justification on grounds of, 273n16; legislative supremacy, support for, 84n19; majority rule, arguments in favor of, 79n12, 89n28, 112; racial vote dilution, inapplicability of argument to, 220n; voting as the cause of outcomes, argument for, 113–14

wealth inequality, 10, 241–43, 266–67; access to formal participation and, 252–54; deliberative scarcity, lack of as argument against reform, 255–60; insulation strategy separating political procedures from, 166, 254; oligarchic threats and, 243–48; political liberties as argument against reform, 260–66; reform, arguments against, 254–66; unreasonable burdens and, 250–51, 253–54, 257

welfare provision, 252

White v. Regester, 218, 223

Williams, Melissa S., 153n24

A NOTE ON THE TYPE

THIS BOOK has been composed in Miller, a Scotch Roman typeface designed by Matthew Carter and first released by Font Bureau in 1997. It resembles Monticello, the typeface developed for The Papers of Thomas Jefferson in the 1940s by C. H. Griffith and P. J. Conkwright and reinterpreted in digital form by Carter in 2003.

Pleasant Jefferson ("P. J.") Conkwright (1905–1986) was Typographer at Princeton University Press from 1939 to 1970. He was an acclaimed book designer and AIGA Medalist.

The ornament used throughout this book was designed by Pierre Simon Fournier (1712–1768) and was a favorite of Conkwright's, used in his design of the *Princeton University Library Chronicle*.